THE CAMBRIDGE COMPANION TO

THE HELLENISTIC WORLD

This Companion volume offers fifteen original essays on the Hellenistic world and is intended to complement and supplement general histories of the period from Alexander the Great to Kleopatra VII of Egypt. Each chapter treats a different aspect of the Hellenistic world – religion, philosophy, family, economy, material culture, and military campaigns, among other topics. The essays address key questions about this period: To what extent were Alexander's conquests responsible for the creation of this new "Hellenistic age"? What is the essence of this world and how does it differ from its Classical predecessor? What continuities and discontinuities can be identified? Collectively, the essays provide an in-depth view of a complex world. The volume also provides the most recent bibliography on the topics along with recommendations for further reading.

Glenn R. Bugh is associate professor of ancient and Byzantine history at Virginia Polytechnic Institute and State University in Blacksburg, Virginia. A recipient of fellowships from the American School of Classical Studies in Athens, the Center for Hellenic Studies in Washington, DC, and the Institute for Advanced Study in Princeton. NJ, he recently served as Whitehead Visiting Professor at the American School of Classical Studies. He is the author of *The Horsemen of Athens*.

THE CAMBRIDGE COMPANION TO

THE HELLENISTIC WORLD

Edited by

GLENN R. BUGH

Virginia Polytechnic Institute and State University

CAMBRIDGE
UNIVERSITY PRESS

CAMBRIDGE UNIVERSITY PRESS
Cambridge, New York, Melbourne, Madrid, Cape Town, Singapore, São Paulo

Cambridge University Press
40 West 20th Street, New York, NY 10011-4211, USA

www.cambridge.org
Information on this title: www.cambridge.org/9780521828796

First published 2006

Printed in the United States of America

A catalog record for this publication is available from the British Library.

Library of Congress Cataloging in Publication Data

The Cambridge companion to the Hellenistic world / edited by Glenn R. Bugh.
p.   cm.
Includes bibliographical references and index.
ISBN-13: 978-0-521-82879-6 (hardback)
ISBN-10: 0-521-82879-1 (hardback)
1. Mediterranean Region – History – To 476.   2. Greece – History –
Macedonian Hegemony, 323–281 B.C.   3. Greece – History – 281–146 B.C.
4. Hellenism.   I. Bugh, Glenn Richard, 1948–   II. Title.
DE86.C35   2006
938′.08 – dc22   2005028730

ISBN-13   978-0-521-82879-6 hardback
ISBN-10   0-521-82879-1 hardback

ISBN-13   978-0-521-53570-0 paperback
ISBN-10   0-521-53570-0 paperback

Contents

‰

Contents

ILLUSTRATIONS

❧

Contributors

⌾

WINTHROP LINDSAY ADAMS is Professor of History at the University of Utah. His publications include "The Successors to Alexander," in *The Greek World in the Fourth Century*, edited by L. A. Tritle (Routledge, 1997), and *Alexander the Great: Legacy of a Conqueror* in the *Library of World Biography* series, edited by P. N. Stearns (New York, 2004), as well as a number of articles on ancient Macedonia.

A. B. BOSWORTH is Professor of Classics and Ancient History at the University of Western Australia. Among his many publications are *The Legacy of Alexander: Politics, Warfare, and Propaganda under the Successors* (Oxford, 2002); *Conquest and Empire: The Reign of Alexander the Great* (Cambridge, 1988); *A Historical Commentary on Arrian's History of Alexander*, 2 vols (Oxford, 1980, 1995); and *Alexander and the East: The Tragedy of Triumph* (Oxford, 1996; hardback reprint, 2001).

GLENN R. BUGH is Associate Professor of Ancient History at Virginia Polytechnic Institute and State University. His publications include *The Horsemen of Athens* (Princeton, 1988) and articles on Athens in the Hellenistic period, Polybios in the *Alexiad* of the Byzantine princess Anna Comnena, and the Greek mercenary cavalry in early sixteenth-century Venice. He has given papers at international conferences on the survival of democratic institutions in Hellenistic Athens, Menander and mercenaries, and the use of lasers in the study of inscriptions. He is under contract with Cambridge University Press for a book on fourth-century B.C. Athens.

JOHN K. DAVIES, FBA, is Emeritus Professor of Ancient History and Classical Archaeology at the University of Liverpool. He is the author of numerous articles, essays, and books, including the *Athenian Propertied Families* (Oxford, 1971, 2nd edn. in preparation), *Democracy and Classical Greece* (Stanford, 1978, 2nd edn., 1993), and *Cambridge Ancient History*,

2nd edn., VII.1, chapt. 8 (1984), and co-editor of *Hellenistic Economies* (Routledge, 2001). His work has focused largely on the economic, social, cultural, and administrative history of classical and Hellenistic Greece.

ERICH S. GRUEN is the Gladys Rehard Wood Professor of History and Classics at the University of California at Berkeley. His research deals with the political and cultural history of Rome, Hellenistic societies, and the Jews in the Greco-Roman world. His numerous publications include *The Hellenistic World and the Coming of Rome* (Berkeley, 1984), *Heritage and Hellenism: The Reinvention of Jewish Tradition* (Berkeley, 1998), and *Diaspora: Jews Amidst Greeks and Romans* (Cambridge, MA, 2002).

MOGENS H. HANSEN is Professor of Classics and Director of the Copenhagen Polis Centre at the University of Copenhagen. He is the author and editor of numerous articles and books on Greek political systems and the Greek polis from the archaic through the Hellenistic period, including *The Ancient Greek City-State* (Copenhagen, 1993); *Polis and City-State: An Ancient Concept and Its Modern Equivalent* (Copenhagen, 1998); *The Athenian Democracy in the Age of Demosthenes*, 2nd edn. (London, 1999), and (co-edited with T. H. Nielsen) *An Inventory of Archaic and Classical Poleis* (Oxford, 2004).

GEORGIA IRBY-MASSIE is Assistant Professor of Classics at the College of William and Mary. She is the author of works on ancient religion, Roman epigraphy, and ancient science, including (co-edited with P. T. Keyser) *Greek Science of the Hellenistic Era: A Source Book* (Routledge, 2002) and *Biographical Encyclopedia of Ancient Natural Scientists* (under contract, Routledge).

PAUL T. KEYSER is an independent scholar, IBM's Watson Research Center, Hawthorne, New York, and holds two PhD degrees, one in physics, the other in classics. He is the author of works on gravitational physics and numerous articles on ancient science, including (co-edited with G. Irby-Massie) *Greek Science of the Hellenistic Era: A Source Book* (Routledge, 2002) and *Biographical Encyclopedia of Ancient Natural Scientists* (under contract, Routledge).

NITA KREVANS is Associate Professor of Classics at the University of Minnesota. She has published articles on Hellenistic and Latin poetry, including "Dido, Hypsipyle and the Bedclothes," in *Hermathena* (2003) and "Callimachus and the Pedestrian Muse," in *Hellenistica Groningana* 7 (2004). Her forthcoming book, *The Poet as Editor: The Poetic Collection from Callimachus to Ovid*, is being published by Princeton.

JON D. MIKALSON is William R. Kenan Jr. Professor of Classics at the University of Virginia. He is the author of numerous books on ancient Greek religion, including *Honor Thy Gods: Popular Religion in Greek Tragedy* (Chapel Hill, NC, 1991), *Religion in Hellenistic Athens* (Berkeley, 1998), *Herodotus and Religion in the Persian Wars* (Chapel Hill, NC, 2003), and *Ancient Greek Religion* (Blackwell, 2005).

GRAHAM J. OLIVER is Lecturer in Ancient Greek Culture at the University of Liverpool. His publications include articles on the economy of Athens in the Hellenistic period and several co-edited books, including *Hellenistic Economies* (Routledge, 2001). His monograph, *War, Food, and Politics in Early Hellenistic Athens* is being published by Oxford (2006). His new edition of state laws and decrees of Athens, 321–301 B.C., will appear as a fascicle in the third edition of *Inscriptiones Graecae*, Vol. 2.

SUSAN I. ROTROFF is Jarvis Thurston and Mona Van Duyn Professor in the Humanities at Washington University, St. Louis, Missouri. Her primary interests are in the topography of ancient Athens and in Hellenistic material culture, particularly pottery. Her most recent books include *Hellenistic Pottery: Athenian and Imported Wheelmade Table Ware and Related Material, Athenian Agora* (Princeton, 1997); *The Hellenistic Pottery from Sardis* (Cambridge, MA, 2003), co-edited with A. Oliver, Jr.; and *Hellenistic Pottery: The Plain Wares, Athenian Agora* (Princeton, 2005).

ALEXANDER SENS is Associate Professor of Classics at Georgetown University. He is the author of numerous articles and monographs on Hellenistic literature, including *Theocritus: Dioscuri (Idyll 22): Introduction, Text, and Commentary: Hypomnemata* 114 (Göttingen, 1997) and *Archestratos of Gela: Text, Translation, and Commentary* (with S. D. Olson; Oxford, 2000).

ROBERT W. SHARPLES is Professor of Classics at University College London. He is the author of articles and books on Hellenistic philosophy, including *Stoics, Epicureans, Sceptics: An Introduction to Hellenistic Philosophy* (Routledge, 1996); *Theophrastus of Eresus: Sources for His Life,*

Writings, Thought and Influence, Commentary vols. 3.1, *Sources on Physics* (Leiden, 1998) and 5, *Sources on Biology* (Leiden, 1995); and *Alexander of Aphrodisias: Supplement to On the Soul* (Duckworth, 2004).

D. GRAHAM J. SHIPLEY, FSA, is Professor of Ancient History at the University of Leicester and Fellow of the Society of Antiquaries of London. He is the author of numerous articles and books on the Hellenistic period, including *A History of Samos 800–188 BC* (Oxford, 1987) and *The Greek World after Alexander 323–30 BC* (Routledge, 2000), and co-author of *The Laconia Survey*, I–II (London, 1996–2002, British School of Athens).

ANDREW STEWART is Professor of Ancient Mediterranean Art and Archaeology at the University of California at Berkeley. He is the author of numerous articles, field reports, and books on Hellenistic art and architecture, including *Attika: Studies in Athenian Sculpture of the Hellenistic Age* (London, 1979); *Greek Sculpture: An Exploration* (New Haven, CT, 1990); *Faces of Power: Alexander's Image and Hellenistic Politics* (Berkeley, 1993); *Art, Desire, and the Body in Ancient Greece* (Cambridge, 1996); and *Attalos, Athens, and the Akropolis: The Pergamene "Little Barbarians" and Their Roman and Renaissance Legacy* (Cambridge, 2005).

DOROTHY J. THOMPSON is a Fellow of Girton College and Isaac Newton Trust Lecturer in the Faculty of Classics at Cambridge University. She is the author of numerous articles and books on the social and economic aspects of Greco-Roman Egypt, including *Memphis Under the Ptolemies* (Princeton, 1988). Her two-volume work (co-authored with W. Clarysse), *Counting the People of Hellenistic Egypt*, is being published by Cambridge (2006).

PREFACE

Almost four years ago, I accepted the invitation to edit this volume in the "Companion" series of Cambridge University Press. The opportunity to publish a book on the Hellenistic world was too tempting to refuse. I started out my graduate career with every intention of following in the footsteps of W. W. Tarn, but along the way, I was drawn to other projects, some only distantly related to the Greek world. But I never forgot my first calling and made a special point of including the rich Hellenistic material in my book on the *Horsemen of Athens* (1988). In truth, I have never strayed too far from Hellenistic Athens, as my publications and papers attest, and still intend one day to write a monograph on Athens in the second century B.C. My nearly thirty-year-long association with the American School of Classical Studies at Athens, from graduate Fellow to visiting professor, has inspired and nurtured much of this interest. The warmth and hospitality of the American School and the support of its director, S. V. Tracy, a dedicated Hellenist, and his staff have been greatly appreciated. Thanks go also to Greg Nagy, director of the Center for Hellenic Studies in Washington, DC, who kindly granted me access to the center's splendid library (along with a guest room in the Stoa) on several research trips.

No book, especially not an edited one, can be written without the assistance of friends and colleagues. I single out a few by name: Linda Fountaine, my former department executive assistant who produced the initial merging of the chapter bibliographies and provided general administrative support; Tom Henderson, a doctoral student at Florida State University and the Lucy Shoe Meritt Fellow at the American School of Classical Studies in Athens for 2004–2005, who spent many hours tidying up the general bibliography and crafting a draft of the timeline; Maria Liston, the American School Wiener Lab Visiting Research Professor for 2004–2005, who tracked down a number of bibliographical references; John Boyer, former student and instructor in the Geography Department at Virginia Tech, who produced the maps; and

Gail Marney, graduate student at Virginia Tech, who assisted with the index.

Finally, I wish to express my appreciation to Beatrice Rehl, editor of Cambridge University Press, who offered both sympathy and encouragement all along the way. As for my contributors, it has been an honor to have collaborated with such a distinguished group on this book, and I cannot thank them enough for their understanding during the dark days of submission delays. Inevitably there is some duplication of discussion between chapters, but I felt it essential to let each author's voice sound through, e.g., both Shipley and Stewart discuss town planning, and Sharples and Krevans and Sens overlap on philosophers and literary figures. Special thanks go to Graham Shipley for interrupting his busy schedule to read over parts of the proofs and catching many errors that escaped my eye. Needless to say, I bear sole responsibility for any errors yet remaining.

And for my wife, Suzanne, who thought that I had taken up permanent residence at my office, beatification for her patience is a lock.

Glenn R. Bugh
Athens and Blacksburg, June 2005

Abbreviations

Abbreviations for ancient authors and their works can be found in *OCD*[3] or in H. G. Liddell and R. Scott, eds. *A Greek-English Lexicon*, 9th edn., with revised supplement. Oxford, 1996. What follows is a list of abbreviations for journals and special epigraphical or papyrological collections. Of particular relevance to Chapter 5, papyri are abbreviated according the system described in J. F. Oates et al., *Checklist of Editions of Greek, Latin, Demotic and Coptic Papyri, Ostraca and Tablets*, BASP Supplement 9, 5th edn. (Oakville, CT, 2001).

AC	*L'Antiquité classique*
AJA	*American Journal of Archaeology*
AJP	*American Journal of Philology*
AncSoc	*Ancient Society*
AncW	*Ancient World*
BAR	British Archaeological Reports
BASP	*Bulletin of the American Society of Papyrologists*
BCH	*Bulletin de correspondance hellénique*
BICS	*Bulletin of the Institute of Classical Studies*
BJHS	*British Journal for the History of Science*
BSA	*Annual of the British School at Athens*
C&M	*Classica et Mediaevalia*
CA	*Classical Antiquity*
CAH	*Cambridge Ancient History*
CJ	*Classical Journal*
CQ	*Classical Quarterly*
CR	*Classical Review*
CRAI	*Comptes rendus de L'Académie des Inscriptions et de Belles-Lettres*
EA	*Epigraphica Anatolica*
EK	L. Edelstein & I. G. Kidd. *Posidonius I. The Fragments*, Cambridge, 1972, 1989

FGrH	F. Jacoby, *Die Fragmente der griechischen Historiker*, Berlin, 1923–58
G&R	*Greece and Rome*
GGA	*Göttingischer Gelehrte Anzeigen*
HSCP	*Harvard Studies in Classical Philology*
ICS	*Illinois Classical Studies*
*I.Fay.*I	E. Bernand, *Recueil des inscriptions grecques du Fayoum.* Tome I. *La "méris" d'Hérakleidès.* Leiden, 1975
I. Délos	*Inscriptions de Délos.* Paris, 1926–72
IPArk	G. Thür & H. Taeuber, *Prozessrechtliche Inschriften der griechischen Poleis: Arkadien.* SBWien 607 (1994)
IG	*Inscriptiones Graecae.* Berlin, 1873–
ISE	L. Moretti, *Iscrizioni storiche ellenistiche*, 2 vols. Florence, 1967–76
JAOS	*Journal of The American Oriental Society*
JHS	*Journal of Hellenic Studies*
JRS	*Journal of Roman Studies*
LIMC	*Lexicon Iconographicum Mythologiae Classicae* (1981–)
Milet I.3	A. Rehm & G. Kawerau, *Das Delphinion in Milet.* Berlin, 1914
ML	R. Meiggs & D. Lewis, ed., *A Selection of Greek Historical Inscriptions to the End of the Fifth Century B.C.* Oxford, 1969
NC	*Numismatic Chronicle*
OCD[3]	S. Hornblower & A. Spawforth, eds. *The Oxford Classical Dictionary*, 3rd ed. Oxford & New York, 1996
OGIS	W. Dittenberger, *Orientis Graecae Inscriptiones Selectae*, 2 vols. Leipzig, 1903–1905
PDIA	*Proceedings of the Danish Institute at Athens*
RC	C. B. Welles, *Royal Correspondence in the Hellenistic Period.* New Haven, CT, 1934
REG	*Revue des études grecques*
RhM	*Rheinisches Museum für Philologie*
RO	P. J. Rhodes & R. Osborne, eds. *Greek Historical Inscriptions 404–323 BC.* Oxford, 2003
SCO	*Studi classici et orientali*
SEG	*Supplementum epigraphicum Graecum.* Leiden, 1923–
SH	H. Lloyd-Jones & P. Parsons, ed. *Supplementum Hellenisticum.* Berlin, 1983
Staatsverträge II	H. Bengtson, ed., *Die Staatsverträge des Altertums* II. Munich & Berlin, 1962

Syll.[3]	W. Dittenberger, *Sylloge inscriptionum Graecarum.* 3rd edn. (and revised), 4 vols. Leipzig, 1915–24
TAPA	*Transactions of the American Philological Association*
Tod, *GHI*	M. N. Tod, *Greek Historical Inscriptions*, vol. II, Oxford, 1948
UPZ	U. Wilcken, *Urkunden der Ptolemäerzeit.* Berlin and Leipzig, 1927–1957
ZPE	*Zeitschrift für Papyrologie und Epigraphik*

HELLENISTIC TIMELINE

≈

323 B.C.	Death of Alexander the Great (13 June); organization of succession; Ptolemy becomes satrap of Egypt; outbreak of Lamian War
322	Battle of Krannon: Antipatros defeats southern Greeks
321	Triparadeisos Conference: Antipatros declared regent
319	Death of Antipatros, Polyperchon declared regent
317–307	Demetrios of Phaleron governs Athens
316	Kassandros ousts Polyperchon; executes Olympias
316–289	Agathokles' rule in Syracuse
315	Antigonos founds League of Islanders; Antigonos' proclamation at Tyre: declares freedom for Greeks; Ptolemy proclaims freedom of Greek cities
312	Battle of Gaza: Ptolemy and Seleukos defeat Demetrios, son of Antigonos
312–11	Seleukos in Babylon; beginning of Seleukid dynasty; temporary peace among the Successors
307	Demetrios, son of Antigonos, takes Athens, deposes Demetrios of Phaleron (finds refuge in Ptolemaic Egypt)
307–304	Kassandros besieges Athens
306	Battle of Salamis (Cyprus): Antigonos and Demetrios defeat Ptolemy and declare themselves kings; Pyrrhos becomes king of Epiros
305–304	Demetrios I Poliorketes fails to take Rhodes; Ptolemy, Lysimachos, Seleukos, and Kassandros declare themselves kings
304	Demetrios Poliorketes raises siege of Athens
302	Antigonos I and Demetrios Poliorketes revive League of Corinthos; Philetairos becomes Lysimachos' governor at Pergamon
301	Battle of Ipsos: Kassandros, Seleukos, and Lysimachos defeat Antigonos I and Demetrios Poliorketes; death of Antigonos

I; division of Alexander's empire into three Successor kingdoms secure

300–295	Lachares' tyranny in Athens
297	Kingdom of Pontos founded
295	Macedonian garrison installed in Athens
290	Aitolian League takes control of Delphi
287	Athens revolts from Demetrios Poliorketes
286	Demetrios Poliorketes captured by Seleukos; death in captivity (283)
281	Battle of Korupedion: Seleukos I defeats and kills Lysimachos; assassination of Seleukos; Philetairos becomes dynast of Pergamon
280–275	Pyrrhic Wars in Italy and Sicily
280	Refoundation of Achaian League
277	Antigonos II Gonatas defeats Gauls, becomes king of Macedonia and establishes Antigonid Dynasty
275	Pyrrhos is defeated by the Romans and evacuates Italy
275–215	Rule of Hieron II of Syracuse; ally of Rome
274–271	First Syrian War
272	Pyrrhos invades Laconia, killed in Argos
267–263	Chremonidean War
263	Antigonos Gonatas captures Athens
261–253	Second Syrian War
255	Cappadocia breaks away from Seleukid kingdom
251	Aratos frees Sikyon and joins Achaian League
250	Bactria breaks away from Seleukid kingdom; Parthians seize eastern satrapies
246–241	Third Syrian War
245	Establishment of the Parthian kingdom; Aratos becomes general of Achaian League; Antigonos Gonatas takes Corinth
243	Aratos captures Corinth
241	Attalos I declares himself king of Pergamon
229	First Illyrian War: Rome takes action against Queen Teuta to end her piratical activity in Adriatic; Athens freed from Macedonian control
222	Battle of Sellasia: Achaian League and Antigonos III defeat Kleomenes and Spartans
220–217	Social War
219–217	Fourth Syrian War
219	Second Illyrian War: Romans defeat Demetrios of Pharos

218	Hannibal invades Italy
217	Battle of Raphia: Ptolemy IV defeats Antiochos III and gains Coele-Syria
216–205	First Macedonian War
215	Philip V makes treaty with Hannibal
213–211	Roman siege of Syracuse; Archimedes killed
212	Rome makes treaty with Aitolians against Philip V
212–205	Campaigns of Antiochos III "the Great": temporarily regains eastern satrapies
205	Peace of Phoinike
202–201	Philip V campaigns in the Aegean
202–200	Fifth Syrian War
200–197	Second Macedonian War
200	Battle of Panion: Antiochos III defeats the Egyptian forces and regains Coele-Syria
197	Battle of Kynoskephalai: Roman legions under Flamininus defeat Philip V
196	Flamininus declares the restoration of Greek freedom at the Isthmian Games
192	Aitolians attack Sparta, assassinate Nabis; Philopoimen defeats Sparta and enrolls her in Achaian League
191–188	Rome's Syrian War against Antiochos III
189	Battle of Magnesia: Coalition of Rome, Pergamon, and Rhodes defeat the forces of Antiochos III
188	Peace of Apamea: Antiochos forced to abandon all land north of Tauros
187–183	Eumenes II's war against Bithynia
183–179	Eumenes II's war against Pontos
172–168	Third Macedonian War
168	Battle of Pydna: Romans defeat Perseus and dissolve the Antigonid dynasty
169–168	Sixth Syrian War
167–160	Revolt of the Maccabees
156–154	Attalos' war with Prusias of Bithynia
149	Attalos II and Nikomedes depose Prusias of Bithynia
148	Macedon becomes a Roman province
146	Revolt of Achaians; Mummius sacks Corinth – end of Achaian League; Scipio sacks Carthage in Third Punic War
142	Rome recognizes independence of Jerusalem
134	Antiochos VII retakes Jerusalem
133	Attalos III bequeaths the Pergamene kingdom to Rome

129	Death of Antiochos VII; Asia becomes a Roman province; Judea regains independence
129–126	M. 'Aquillius organizes the province of Asia
113	Mithridates VI Eupator of Pontos seizes power
88–85	First Mithridatic War
88	Mithridates organizes massacre of 80,000 Romans in Asia; Athens sides with Mithridates
86	Sulla sacks Athens
83–81	Second Mithridatic War
74	Nikomedes of Bithynia bequeaths his kingdom to Rome; Rome annexes Cyrenaica as a province
73–69	Third Mithridatic War
66–63	Fourth Mithridatic War
64	Syria becomes a Roman province; Seleukid kingdom ends
63	Suicide of Mithridates; Pompey captures Jerusalem
48	Battle of Pharsalos: Caesar defeats Pompey; Pompey assassinated in Egypt
44	Assassination of Julius Caesar
42	Battle of Philippi: Antony and Octavian defeat Brutus and Cassius
31	Battle of Actium: Octavian and Agrippa defeat Antony and Kleopatra
30	Suicide of Antony and Kleopatra; Octavian dissolves the Ptolemaic kingdom

HELLENISTIC MAPS

ℰℴ

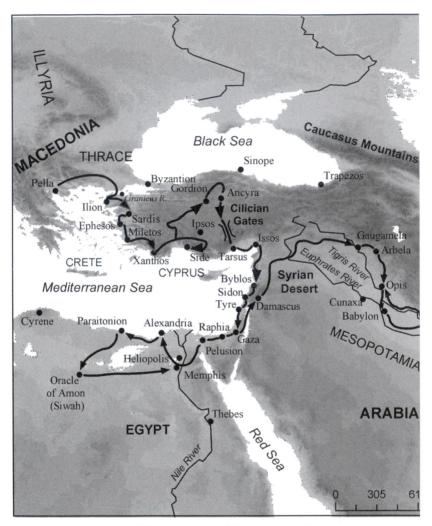

MAP 1. The campaigns of Alexander the Great.

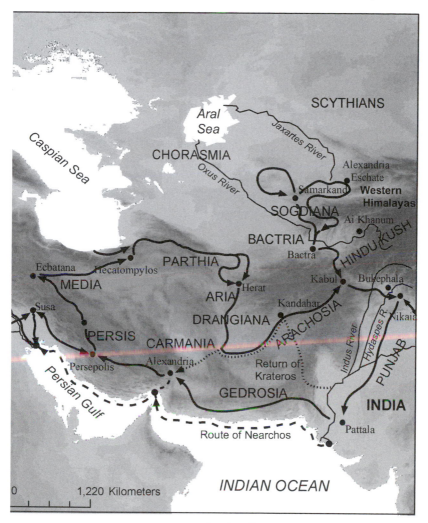

MAP I (continued).

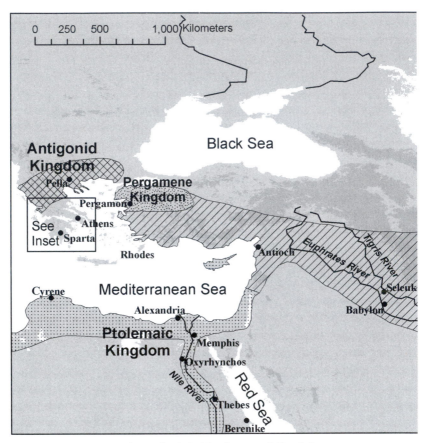

MAP 2. The Hellenistic kingdoms and Greek leagues.

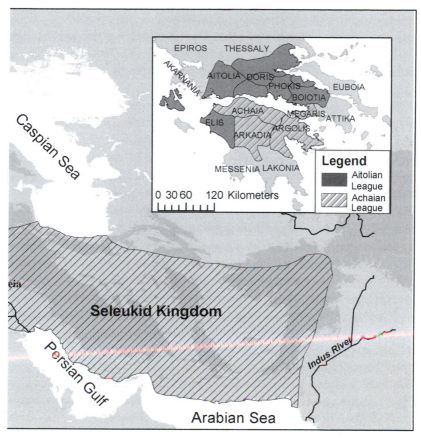

MAP 2 (*continued*).

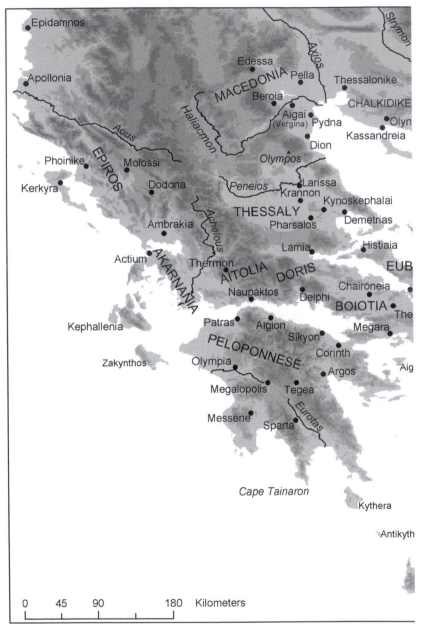

MAP 3. Greece.

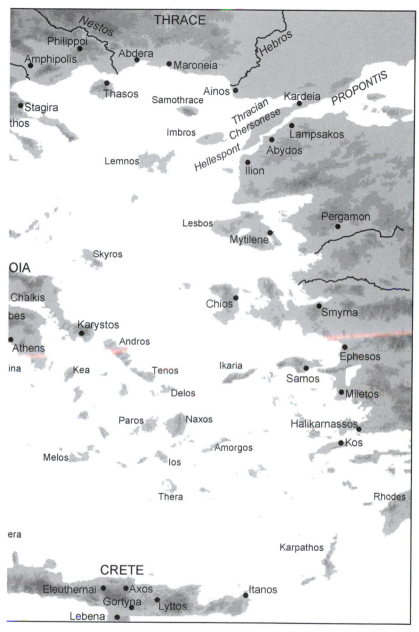

THRACE

Nestos

Philippoi

Amphipolis

Abdera

Maroneia

Hebros

Thasos

Samothrace

Ainos

PROPONTIS

Stagira

thos

Kardeia

Thracian Chersonese

Imbros

Hellespont

Lampsakos

Abydos

Ilion

Lemnos

Lesbos

Pergamon

Mytilene

Skyros

OIA

Chalkis

bes

Chios

Smyrna

Karystos

Andros

Athens

Kea

Ikaria

Ephesos

ina

Tenos

Samos

Delos

Miletos

Paros

Naxos

Halikarnassos

Melos

Amorgos

Kos

Ios

Thera

Rhodes

era

Karpathos

CRETE

Eleuthernai

Axos

Gortyna

Lyttos

Itanos

Lebena

MAP 3 (*continued*).

INTRODUCTION

Glenn R. Bugh

⌘

I n 1836, the German scholar J. G. Droysen coined a new term in his three-volume history of the period from the time of Alexander the Great to the coming of Christianity, *Geschichte des Hellenismus*. Because the German word *Hellenismus* cannot be translated into English as "Hellenism" (which has a different meaning), it has become customary to apply its adjectival form "Hellenistic" to this period. For Droysen, *Hellenismus* signified a fusion of Greek and Eastern cultures that supplied the fertile soil from which Christianity emerged. It was a grand and formative period leading to a revolutionary universal religion. However, over the intervening 170 years or so, Droysen's positivist outlook did not win over many academics, who continued to view the Classical period of the fifth and fourth centuries as the "golden age" of Greek achievement. Much of the literature produced after Alexander the Great (d. 323) was dismissed as derivative, decadent, and quite frankly, inferior. The scholars of the great Library of Hellenistic Alexandria must accept some blame for this. They are credited with compiling canonical lists of the "greats" in various literary genres, all of whom lived in the Archaic or Classical periods, and these "best" works were more likely to be copied (and thus survive) and to form the basis of the educational curriculum in antiquity and beyond. Who could presume to compete with the masters? A quick glance at Green (1990) attests the enduring power of this negative legacy.

According to one school of thought, it was inevitable that the Romans would conquer the intemperate and feckless Hellenistic Greeks on the battlefield, even as they co-opted and transmitted the legacy of their illustrious *Classical* past to Western civilization and the world. The Roman poet Horace said it succinctly, *Graecia capta ferum victorem cepit* ("captured Greece captured its fierce conqueror"). The denigration of the Hellenistic achievement could be discounted as hyperbolic and old-fashioned, but scholarly books on Greece continue to be published with little or no serious discussion of the Hellenistic period and with no shame attached to rounding out surveys of Greek history with the battle of Chaironeia in 338 or the death of Alexander in 323, as if Greek history had ended and the nearly 1,500 documented *poleis* (see Hansen & Nielsen, 2004) sprinkled throughout the Mediterranean, Black Sea, and Asia had mysteriously vanished.

In addition, trying to determine what constituted the appropriate chronological parameters of the Hellenistic world was, and still is, problematic. In an influential book by M. Cary, *A History of the Greek World 323–146 B.C.*, 2nd edn. (London, 1951), it is clear that the creation of the province of Macedonia and the destruction of Corinth in the Achaian War marked the natural political and military end of the Hellenistic period, and what followed belonged more properly to the history of the Roman Republic. Even the learned and balanced synthesis by F. W. Walbank, *The Hellenistic World*, rev. edn. (Cambridge, MA, 1992) – which I used profitably for years as the main text for my own undergraduate course, "Alexander the Great and the Hellenistic World" – concludes with a brief chapter, "The Coming of Rome," which does not carry the story beyond the mid-second century B.C. Most scholars today, receptive to political and military precision, are inclined to end the story of the Hellenistic world with the death of Kleopatra VII of Egypt in 30 B.C., the last in the royal line of Macedonian Ptolemaic kings and the last ruler of Alexander's successor kingdoms. The transformation of Egypt into a Roman province by Octavian (Augustus) therefore marked the end of a long process of conquest and annexation that began in the late third century with the Illyrian and Macedonian wars.

For this volume, I, too, have adopted the traditional bookends of Alexander the Great and Kleopatra, the beginning and end of a 300-year period of Macedonian rule. But it is a choice of convenience and custom. The many and diverse aspects covered in the following chapters cannot all be inserted into a timeline, any more than thinking that the Greeks woke up on June 11, 323 B.C., with the e-news of Alexander's death and pulled out their "New Era" calendars or that the Greeks living across thousands of miles of Alexander's mighty empire thought that their world had come to a close with the passing of a colorful and gifted queen in distant Egypt. History does not happen this way, and part of the task of this collection of essays has been to identify and explain what was new and different about the Hellenistic world and what was more properly a continuation of ideas, customs, institutions, and so forth, already evident in the Classical period. To understand change, we are obliged to cast our glance back over the whole period and, after examining all the evidence available to us, try to pinpoint the moment when it is first observed and follow its consequences over time. A great battle can serve as a signpost for change if its results lead to a more permanent rearrangement of political and military power, but this will not be adequate to explain new literary, economic, artistic, religious, or philosophical ideas or even a new ceramic shape. In the end, why do we insist on using the term Hellenistic, "Greek-like," rather than, for example, "late classical" or even "post-classical"? Do the conquests of Alexander and the world created by them justify the adoption of a new periodic term? The answer must inevitably be both "yes" and "no."

One reason that has discouraged Classicists from studying the Hellenistic period seriously is the daunting array of eastern languages necessary to decipher the primary documents. The world created by Alexander's conquests encompassed, after all, millions of non-Greek-speaking peoples from Egypt to India. It seems so heterogeneous, so vast and diffuse, compared with the relative simplicity and accessibility of the world of Archaic and Classical Greek city-states. Most western Classicists are trained to read Greek and Latin, along with German, French, and often Italian and modern Greek, but feel uncomfortable, if not totally lost, in the rich archives of the ancient Near East. I count myself among them. It is very difficult for a single scholar to know all the languages spoken and written in the Hellenistic world, and even the most intrepid has to turn to the kindness of collaborators.

Even the study of the "Greek" part of the Hellenistic world is not without its obstacles. The Archaic and Classical periods can be reconstructed through the narratives of the "great" historians, Herodotos, Thucydides, and Xenophon, and through the speeches and dialogues of the orators and philosophers of the fourth century B.C., but the Hellenistic world has no comparable historian or orator to tell its story, no contemporary voice to articulate its importance, with the exception of Polybios of Megalopolis in the second century B.C. (see Chapter 6 and the many works of F. W. Walbank in the bibliography). But Polybios' histories (264–146 B.C.) are not preserved in full, and his thematic goal was to explain the rise of the Roman Empire from 220 to 167 B.C. (Second Punic War to the fall of the Antigonid dynasty), not to provide a narrative history of the Hellenistic world. We can recover some of his history from the Roman historian Livy, but his adaptation will never be equal to the original. Not only would we dearly love to have all of Polybios' history, but also that of the Stoic philosopher and polymath, Poseidonios of Apameia (Syria), who continued Polybios' narrative down to 88 B.C. Almost nothing of Poseidonios' universal history has survived. So, it is not that there weren't contemporary historians of the Hellenistic world, it is the sad fact that most of their works have perished. In the first century, Diodorus of Sicily composed a universal history from the mythological past to 60 B.C. that included the Hellenistic period. He borrowed extensive passages from fourth-century and Hellenistic historians, like Ephoros of Kyme, Hieronymos of Kardia, Timaios of Tauromenion (on Sicily), Polybios, and Poseidonios of Apameia, but our text of Diodorus breaks off after the battle of Ipsos in 301 B.C. We are perhaps more fortunate with Alexander the Great because the second-century-A.D. biographer Plutarch of Chaironeia and the historian Arrian of Nikomedia [for commentary, see Bosworth, (1980b) and (1995)] preserved important contemporary but now-lost sources, for example, Ptolemy I Soter, the founder of the Ptolemaic dynasty, and Nearchos, Alexander's admiral.

If we do not have direct access to a contemporary narrative, how can we know anything about the Hellenistic world? To be sure, there are hundreds of fragments of Hellenistic historians preserved as citations in later sources – these texts are available in F. Jacoby's monumental *Die Fragmente der griechischen Historiker* (Berlin, 1923–1958); a new edition and commentary of Parts I, II, and III, *Brill's New Jacoby*, is being prepared under the editorship of Ian Worthington, assisted by a team of over ninety scholars in sixteen countries – but these give us only disconnected snapshots. A viable alternative has been to turn to subdisciplines within the broad field of ancient history, and here is where an exciting new world continues to unfold before our eyes. The advent of scientific archaeology in the late nineteenth century has not only added to a greater assemblage of artistic and architectural artifacts from the Hellenistic period (see Chapter 8), but has also generated a huge supply of pottery from excavations throughout the Greek world. This body of evidence has allowed scholars to refine or establish a more secure Hellenistic chronology and given us a more fulsome sense of material culture (see Chapter 7).

Archaeology has also led to an exponential increase in the numbers of inscriptions (epigraphy) that give us immediate and direct access to the Hellenistic landscape, that allows us to step into the minds of kings [see Welles (1934)] and citizens of the Greek *poleis* at a precise moment in time. It is not an exaggeration to claim that a history of Hellenistic Athens could not have been written save for the bounty of inscriptions coming from excavations – see Habicht (1997a), and the same could be said for Delphi and Delos. In addition to the great corpus of Greek inscriptions, *Inscriptiones Graecae* (Berlin, 1873–) – a new edition is in press for fourth-century Attic inscriptions – there are helpful select collections, like W. Dittenberger, *Orientis Graeci Inscriptiones Selectae*, 2 vols. (Leipzig, 1903–1905) and his *Sylloge Inscriptionum Graecarum*, 3rd edn., 4 vols. (Leipzig, 1915–1924); L. Moretti, *Iscrizioni storiche ellenistiche*, 2 vols. (Firenze, 1967–1976); and P. J. Rhodes & R. Osborne, *Greek Historical Inscriptions 404–323 BC* (Oxford, 2003). New inscriptions can be found in *Supplementum Epigraphicum Graecum* (*SEG*), 1923–. To make sense of these inscriptions, one can turn to B. H. McLean, *An Introduction to Greek Epigraphy of the Hellenistic and Roman Periods from Alexander the Great to the Reign of Constantine (323 B.C–A.D. 337)* (Ann Arbor, MI, 2002).

Equally important is the study of coins (numismatics); for example, what can the iconography of Alexander on his coins tell us about his claims of divinity or, for that matter, his Successors?; what prompted the Seleukids to put an elephant on their coins, and what would we know about the Greeks in Bactria and India during the third to the first centuries B.C. without the stunning coinage of their rulers and excavations at Ai Khanum in Afghanistan (see Holt, 1999)? No less spectacular has been the recovery of papyri from Egypt (papyrology) that has given us, to name but a few notable examples, the *Athenaion Politeia* attributed to Aristotle (the only Greek city-state constitution preserved of the hundreds he wrote); a complete play (*Dyskolos*) and substantial portions of six others by the New Comedy poet Menander of Athens; and recently, a third-century B.C. papyrus roll containing 100 epigrams of Poseidippos of Pella, a relatively unknown but important Hellenistic poet (see Gutzwiller, 2005 and Chapter 9). But papyri also provide priceless information on the mundane daily lives of the Greeks, Macedonians, and Egyptians during the Ptolemaic period; see, for example, A. S. Hunt, C. C. Edgar, and D. L. Page, *Select Papyri*, 4 vols. (Loeb Classical Library, Cambridge, MA, 1950) and the work of Dorothy. J. Thompson in Chapter 5. One can write a social and economic history of Ptolemaic Egypt in ways not possible for the other Hellenistic kingdoms. There are hundreds of papyrus rolls that still await conservation and decipherment in museum archives throughout the world, and laser technology has revolutionized our ability to read texts no longer visible to the unaided eye.

Understanding the Hellenistic world requires persistence and patience, but the problems are not insurmountable (collections of primary documents and all of the principal authors are available in English; see following discussion), and the dividends are well worth the time invested. This view is confirmed by the increase of interest in the Hellenistic world in the last twenty-five years or so. It can no longer be called a neglected or discredited field, certainly not among the increasing numbers of scholars who have taken up the cause of that Edinburgh savant, W. W. Tarn (and G. T. Griffith, *Hellenistic Civilisation*, 3rd edn., London, 1952). There have been numerous international conferences since the 1990s on various aspects of the Hellenistic world, for example, economy (Liverpool), pottery (Greece), sculpture and architecture (Athens), Macedonians in Athens (Athens); military and civic institutions of Greek cities of Anatolia (Lyon); and multiauthored anthologies of papers and essays have appeared in rapid succession, as in Cartledge et al. (1997), Ogden (2002), and Erskine (2003).

This volume continues in this robust tradition. As the title implies, *Cambridge Companion to the Hellenistic World*, it is intended to be a "companion," to complement and supplement general histories of the period (see the Bibliographical Note at the end of the Introduction). Each chapter can stand alone and treats a specific area of interest, for example, economy, philosophy, art and architecture, religion, and so forth, and directs the reader to the latest and most useful publications on the subject. In my initial invitation, I challenged the contributors to think "outside of the box" and not to let convention or precedent dictate the form or content of their chapters. This has led to some intriguing approaches. Each chapter invariably reflects the interests, idiosyncrasies, and specialization "comfort zone" of the contributor, but the creative process insists on such intellectual freedom. In the final analysis, the goal was to add to the growing body of knowledge of the Hellenistic world and to communicate it to an audience that thirsts for more substance than a Hollywood movie on Alexander the Great.

A note on style. There are at least three models available to Classicists: letter-for-letter transliteration, Latinizing, and some form of Anglicizing. In the spelling of Greek names and places, I have chosen to adhere as closely to the original Greek as possible (in the German classical tradition), for example, employing "os" and "on" endings instead of the Latin "us" and "um" (thus, Antigonos, not Antigonus), and "ai" instead of "ae" (Achaian, not Achaean), and "k" instead of "c" (Poliorketes, not Poliorcetes), but dogmatic uniformity leaves us with some very strange-looking and unsightly words. So, like all other Classicists, I have chosen to compromise on certain famous names, preferring to retain Philip, not Philippos; Alexander, not Alexandros; Ptolemy, not Ptolemaios; Epicurus, not Epikouros; Corinth, not Korinthos; Cyprus, not Kupros; and so forth. As long as there is no confusion as to the identity of the individual or the place, I am content with my aesthetic choices.

BIBLIOGRAPHICAL NOTE

The bibliography on Alexander the Great is too vast to list here and is ever expanding. It is sufficient (and efficient) to refer the reader to the learned article (with earlier literature) by A. B. Bosworth in the third edition of the *Oxford Classical Dictionary* (see following), s.v. Alexander III (pp. 57–9) and to Chapter 1 of this volume.

For a quick read on the Hellenistic world, see S. M. Burstein, *The Hellenistic Period in World History* (American Historical Association, Washington, DC, 1996). Walbank, *The Hellenistic World* (1992; see earlier mention) is an admirable little book by the foremost authority on Polybios, but the most in-depth single volume on the period is now G. Shipley, *The Greek World after Alexander 323–30 BC* (London & New York, 2000). Peter Green, *Alexander to Actium: The Historical Evolution of the Hellenistic Age* (1990) is a breathtaking monument to the author's erudition. F. Chamoux, *Hellenistic Civilization*, translated from French by M. Roussel (London, 2003), is a worthy replacement for Tarn's classic work of the same title (see previous mention). Standard for the field is the multivolume, multiauthored *Cambridge Ancient History*; the relevant volumes are VI, 2nd edn. (1994); VII.1, 2nd edn. (1984); VII.1, 2nd edn. (1984: Plates to Vol. VII.1); VII.2, 2nd edn. (1990); VIII, 2nd edn. (1989); and IX, 2nd edn. (1994). For the best one-volume dictionary in English on the ancient world, see S. Hornblower and A. Spawforth, *The Oxford Classical Dictionary* (*OCD*), 3rd edn. (Oxford, 1996). For geographical reference, the standard work is now R. J. A. Talbert, ed. (with many collaborators), *Barrington Atlas of the Greek and Roman World* (Princeton & Oxford, 2000).

Two of the most learned works on the Hellenistic period are in French, Préaux (1978) and Will (1979–1982), the latter dealing primarily with political history, the former with culture and society. The magisterial three-volume work by M. I. Rostovetzeff, *The Social and Economic History of the Hellenistic World* (Oxford, 1953) still holds its own, even as J. K. Davies and colleagues in Liverpool critique and refine his ideas through the venue of international conferences (see Archibald et al., 2001).

There are a number of useful collections of documents in translation that cover the Hellenistic period: Austin (1981, a new edition is in preparation); Bagnall and Derow (2nd edn., 2004); Burstein (1985); and Sherk (1984). Bagnall and Derow are particularly strong on the papyrus documents of Egypt. All of them include a large selection of Hellenistic inscriptions. English translations of the major authors can be found in the Loeb Classical Library, with facing Greek or Latin text (Cambridge, MA) and in the paperback Penguin Classics series, which is a popular choice for college-level courses.

1: ALEXANDER THE GREAT AND THE CREATION OF THE HELLENISTIC AGE

A. B. Bosworth

❧

"The name of Alexander marks the end of one age of the world, the beginning of another." This lapidary and much-quoted apophthegm is the starting point of Johann Gustav Droysen's revised *Geschichte des Hellenismus*. It appeared in 1877, when Droysen was in his seventieth year, at the peak of his powers and reputation, and the republication was a tribute to the notoriety that his work had achieved at the time of Germany's unification. His vision of the Macedonia of Philip and Alexander was not intended as a political manifesto for the present, but it was eagerly seized upon as foreshadowing what could be achieved by the German states united under the leadership of the Prussian monarchy.[1] An autocratic regime, based on enlightened cultural and political principles, had first conquered and then civilized the world, and the process might be repeated in the modern era. Under those circumstances, it was easy to accept the picture of Alexander as the inaugurator of a new age, and Droysen's conceptual model, despite some protests, has been almost universally accepted. Alexander, consciously or unconsciously, created a new world informed by Greek culture and absolute monarchy, which lasted until the dominance of Rome as a world power, and Droysen termed the process "Hellenismus." This was not entirely novel, for the term had been in vogue as a label for the Greek *koine* as spoken and written by non-Greeks in the eastern Mediterranean after Alexander,[2] but Droysen extended it from a merely philological concept to encapsulate what he saw as the essence of a whole epoch.

Droysen's view of Alexander took shape early in his life. In 1833, at the tender age of 25,[3] he published his *Geschichte Alexanders des Grossen*. This is a highly rhetorical portrait, which explicitly presents Alexander as an Aristotelian superman, a prime example of living law.[4] But Alexander is not autonomous. He is an instrument of history and of God himself. His conquests inculturate the barbarian east, but at the same time, they hasten the degeneration of the native inspiration of the Greek world. A levelling process takes place, a fusion ("Verschmelzung") of east and west encouraged by the overarching monarchy of Alexander and his Successors. The crucial aspect of the fusion was religious syncretism, the tendency to see all divinities as related manifestations of a single godhead.[5] It was a process that created a predisposition to monotheism, but at the same time there was a universal loneliness and desperation, a yearning for a redeemer. Hence, the spread of Christianity was the result of the general levelling that Alexander had inaugurated. He was a tool in the hands of a personified history, pursuing predetermined ends beyond his comprehension. In this model, Rome is an irrelevancy, except insofar as the Romans absorbed Greek culture and promoted its international dissemination. The culmination of the process is not Augustus and the end of the Ptolemaic regime but the ministry of Jesus.

This general vision is strongly influenced by Hegelian idealism and reflects Droysen's student years in Berlin, but he remained true to it in his old age and retained the key passages in the second edition. In particular, he did not tone down the denigratory references to the eastern peoples under Persian domination[6] and continued to represent Athens' history in the fourth century as progressive degeneration. Neither view is acceptable in current thinking, nor would many scholars accept the religious determinism that underlies Droysen's model. Yet, Alexander remains entrenched as the inaugurator of a new age. One might query the utility of the blanket label. It encourages a dangerous disregard of political and cultural continuity, and underestimates the reaction against Alexander after his death.

Reaction there certainly was. That can be seen in the sphere that Alexander made most his own: military conquest. Alexander's reign witnessed a practically unlimited series of campaigns, which saw the annexation of the Persian Empire as it existed at his accession and then the conquest of the old Persian satrapies in the Indus valley. He planned to advance east to the Ganges plain and the outer ocean, but was frustrated by his men who wished to enjoy the benefits of conquest rather than fight endlessly in the monsoon rains. On his return to the west, he turned his energies to expansion to the south and west, preparing a naval expedition against the spice lands of Arabia and constructing a vast arsenal on the Cilician coast in anticipation of a major offensive

in the west against Carthage and perhaps Southern Italy.[7] The extent
and indeed the historicity of these last plans are in dispute, but there
can be no doubt that Alexander was credited with an unlimited urge
for conquest. Arrian expresses the opinion that he would never have
ceased campaigning, competing with himself if there were no rivals left
to surpass,[8] and that was the impression Alexander's marshals attempted
to propagate. Immediately after his death, the regent Perdikkas produced and had read memoranda that proposed enormous expenses for
conquest in the western Mediterranean, including a military road across
North Africa to the Straits of Gibraltar. The troops who were apprised
of the project were impressed by its ambition but not by its practical-
ity and voted to quash it.[9] Marshals and men were in agreement, and
nothing more was heard of world conquest.

The empire was expanded, but not outwards. In 322, Perdikkas
fought a campaign against the Cappadocian dynast Ariarathes, but it
was a tidying exercise. Ariarathes had been a vassal of the Persian
King, sending forces to Ochos' invasion of Egypt, and in 333, he had
been spared invasion by Alexander.[10] He became de facto independent
and refused to accept Macedonian sovereignty; and in what Alexander
must have seen as exacerbated rebellion, he had sent a contingent to
Gaugamela.[11] Perdikkas's campaign, then, was not an extension of the
empire; it was containment of insurrection, and the punishment meted
out to Ariarathes (mutilation and impalement) was that suffered by
rebels against the Persian throne. This was consolidation, not expansion. Indeed, what we find in the years after Alexander is a certain
contraction, best illustrated in Seleukos' treaty with the Mauryan king
Chandragupta. The occupation of the Indus lands was proving unsus-
tainable even under Alexander, and there was pressure on the provinces
adjacent to the Hindu Kush as early as 316.[12] Ten years later, after a
show of force, Seleukos conceded the eastern satrapies of his kingdom to
Chandragupta in return for 500 war elephants.[13] The transaction would
be unthinkable under Alexander or any of his Persian predecessors, but
Seleukos was under threat from his fellow dynast Antigonos and was
prepared to sacrifice territory for military advantage. Somewhat earlier,
Antigonos himself had sanctioned an attack on the Nabataean Arabs,
which the contemporary historian Hieronymos denounced indirectly,[14]
and Alexander's own aggression against the Saka tribes north of the Syr
Darya was represented as pointless waste by the Alexandrian historian
Kleitarchos.[15] The same pattern of thought recurs in Plutarch's story
of the debunking of Pyrrhos's aspirations by the Epicurean philosopher and diplomat, Kineas, whose message is that one can enjoy all

the advantages of conquest by remaining at peace.[16] From this perspective, external conquests were extravagant indulgences, and Alexander's example was to be avoided.

The Successors did not, of course, renounce war. Military operations were constant, but they took place within the context of a contracting and fragmenting empire, as regional dynasts contended for preeminence. Two factors came into play: first, the murderous struggle for supremacy that had plagued the Macedonian aristocracy for the duration of the Argead monarchy and, second, the system of provincial government that Alexander inherited from the Achaemenids. It had created a network of satraps, local despots who could exploit the military and financial resources of their territories.[17] There was little, if any, central supervision, and Alexander was forced to impress his regal authority on satraps who had proved unreliable. On two occasions, after the rebellion in the central satrapies instigated by Bessos (330–327) and on his return from the Indus lands (325–324), he extensively purged his Iranian governors and replaced them by relatively low-ranking Macedonians. That was a marked change from the early years of the campaign, when the satraps he appointed tended to be Macedonians of the highest distinction, like the royal Bodyguard Balakros, who was married to a daughter of the regent Antipatros,[18] or Antigonos himself, who came from the nobility of the capital.[19] Part of the motivation was political, to detach men who had been prominent in his father's reign, so that he could impress his own will on the remaining army commanders. That was a continuing process. By the end of 330, he had disposed of Parmenion, his father's senior general, after securing the condemnation of his son Philotas for alleged complicity in a court conspiracy.[20] Two years later, he personally drove a spear into his senior cavalry commander, Kleitos, after Kleitos had drunkenly criticized the increasingly absolutist tendencies of the monarchy.[21]

A highly significant episode occurred in late 325 when Alexander purged the European military commanders in Media. They were accused of exploitation and misgovernment, no doubt with some justification, and Alexander allegedly claimed that they had acted on the assumption that he would never return from India.[22] At the same time, there was a nationalistic insurrection in Media, led by a pretender who had assumed the upright tiara, the exclusive headdress of the Kings of Persia. The leaders of the rebellion were captured and brought before Alexander.[23] However, the success is accredited, not to the European commanders of the holding army, but to the Iranian satrap of Media, who was unwilling to see a competitor usurp power. His European colleagues seem to have taken no action, and it is possible that they had no objection to an oriental rival to Alexander. If that were widely believed, it is hardly surprising that Alexander had them tried and executed. The senior commander was Kleandros, brother of the great marshal Koinos, who had represented the cause of the common soldier against Alexander's imperialist ambitions in India. Kleandros was also connected with the administrator of the central treasuries, Alexander's boyhood friend Harpalos. Both originated in the once independent principality of Elimiotis in the south west of Macedonia,[24] and together they dominated the military and financial administration of the Iranian heartland. There must have been a fair degree of collaboration, and it was prudent of Harpalos to take flight back to the Greek mainland once he heard of Kleandros's execution.[25] From Alexander's viewpoint, it appeared that his commanders were in league with native insurgents and harbored ambitions of creating an independent regime. He removed the immediate threat and ensured that any further satrapal appointees were men of relatively humble pedigree. The crushing of dissent at court was paralleled by denial of the resources for revolt in the satrapies.

Once Alexander was dead, the situation changed radically. The first act of the drama was near civil war, with Macedonian infantry and cavalry playing off against each other and the Macedonian marshals intriguing for supremacy. It was only with the utmost difficulty that Perdikkas achieved the regency, and he did so against the forthright opposition of Ptolemy and others.[26] He could only keep his hold on the kings and the army if he surrounded himself with men personally loyal to himself, like his brother Alketas and his brother-in-law Attalos, or Aristonous, who had given him valuable support at his accession to the regency.[27] Other marshals he assigned to the satrapies by a skillfully manipulated process of sortition. Ptolemy received Egypt, a world in itself, conveniently isolated from the central capitals of the empire. In contrast, Lysimachos and Leonnatos had the satrapies on either side of the Hellespont, where they would be in constant friction. In effect, Perdikkas was reversing the trend of Alexander's last years, which was to minimize the risk of disorder in the satrapies and consequently to consolidate the absolute power that he had acquired. Perdikkas' aim was to set his rivals at each others' throats, sacrificing regional stability in the search for a personal predominance that he never acquired.

The process continued two years later, when the new regent Antipatros made a secondary distribution in the name of the kings and then, in 319, returned to Macedonia with the kings, who were never again to set foot in Asia.[28] This marked the real beginning of the new age.

Alexander had exercised sovereign power over the whole of his empire and did all he could to reduce the local power of the satraps. Thanks to Antipatros, central control gradually disappeared. The satraps were formidable men who had either received their satrapies from Alexander or saw them as their proper reward for their part in the conquest of the Persian empire. It was impossible to control them from Macedonia, and they would not easily accept the authority of the guardian of the kings, especially if (like Antipatros and his son Kassandros) they had not participated in the war of conquest. Satrapies accordingly became dynastic holdings, as Seleukos was to inform Antigonos when he demanded to audit the accounts of his administration: "he was not obliged to undergo scrutiny with regard to the country which the Macedonians had given him because of the services they had received from him in Alexander's lifetime."[29] The name of Alexander was used to justify a power base independent of the monarchy, a situation that he would have regarded as anathema. Universal kingship based on conquest of an ever-expanding empire was replaced by regional ambition that fed on and diminished the territories he had acquired.

For Droysen, the real beginning of the new age was the famous episode at the Babylonian city of Opis when Alexander crushed the unrest in his army and turned towards his Iranian troops. He could dispense with the tool that had brought him world conquest and could rely on an ecumenical army that had replaced any regional affiliation with loyalty to himself.[30] Now the world literally revolved around his absolute monarchy. There is a good deal of truth in this picture. In particular, Droysen laid proper stress on the levying of the *Epigonoi*. These were Iranian adolescents who had been conscripted in the eastern satrapies and trained in Macedonian weaponry and discipline. By early 324, the first contingent, said to have been around 30,000 strong, appeared in Susa and joined Alexander's military establishment, giving an impressive display of parade ground discipline.[31] They were intended to supplement the native Macedonian troops, who had thwarted his ambitions in India and in extremity could be used against them, as Alexander spectacularly did at Opis.[32] However, for Droysen, the Macedonians had lost many of their national characteristics and had become impregnated by the culture of the peoples they had conquered, and the assimilation foreshadowed a more general fusion, which was to be the basis of the Hellenistic state.

This takes things much too far. Alexander certainly used the new Iranian recruits to intimidate his Macedonians, and for a few tense days, he threatened to replace them *in toto,* giving the distinctive Macedonian unit nomenclature to the Iranians. This was traditional Argead policy, to use military titles for political purposes, and was reminiscent of the extension of the once elite terms of "Companion" and "Foot Companion," to the entire body of cavalry and infantry.[33] Alexander was doing the same on a much greater scale. However, once the Macedonians had given way and accepted the mass demobilization, there is little further reference in the sources to the Iranian troops. The *Epigonoi* stayed with Alexander, but they are not explicitly mentioned. Instead, a few days before his death, we hear of a mixed phalanx, in which Macedonians, paid at special rates, formed the front and rear, while Persian light infantry, armed with bows and javelins, filled out the twelve inner ranks.[34] It was intended for use against disciplined heavy infantry, the barrage of missiles from the Persians creating breaks in the enemy line, which the Macedonians could open out with their eighteen-foot *sarisai*. It is interesting that Macedonians were used as the front line troops and not the *Epigonoi,* who were more closely related to the Persian light armed in language and culture. The privileged soldiers, paid at premium rates, were Macedonians, and it looks as though the troops that Alexander retained at Opis were treated as elite. Rightly so. Alexander's veterans had an expertise honed by years of continuous campaigning, which the *Epigonoi* for all their flashy drill could not match. The Macedonians scoffed at them as "war-dancers," and they were to prove their point at the Battle of Paraitakene (late 317), when the 3,000 Silver Shields (the survivors of Alexander's foot guard) routed the mass of mercenaries and Macedonian-trained Asiatics with minimal casualties.[35]

The *Epigonoi* enjoyed only a brief prominence. They were quickly absorbed into a broader mass of Macedonian trained infantry, with Alexander's veterans taking a preeminent position as the men who had conquered the world under Alexander. The same applies to the Persian aristocracy. At Opis, they had been pivotal in bringing Alexander's men to heel, when the king presented them with military commands and created a select group of "Kinsmen" who were given the privilege of the royal kiss.[36] At the banquet of reconciliation, he made a solemn prayer for Macedonians and Persians to enjoy concord and partnership in the empire,[37] but there is little evidence of partnership. After the disturbances while he was away in India, Alexander replaced most of his Iranian satraps with Greeks or Macedonians. Those who were retained in office were the handful who had shown outstanding loyalty and had put down rebellion (Phrataphernes and Atropates) and his father-in-law Oxyartes, who held sway in the remote Kabul valley.[38]

The famous mass marriage at Susa fits well into this context. It was celebrated in the spring of 324, after Alexander concluded his march from the Indus to Mesopotamia. In scenes of unprecedented splendor, Alexander married two princesses of the Achaemenid royalty, and around ninety of his Companions took brides from the Iranian nobility.[39] This could be viewed as a continuation of traditional Argead policy, which saw marriage as a means of consolidation. Philip himself had notoriously married for war, taking two Thessalian brides after he had acquired control over Larisa and Pherai: There were also Illyrian and Getic wives, not to mention Alexander's own mother Olympias, who came from the royalty of neighboring Molossia.[40] Alexander himself was little more Macedonian than the children he planned to engender with his Persian wives. The rationale was the same as Philip's, to create pockets of loyalty within the conquered territory, and hopefully the offspring of his mixed marriages would be as acceptable to the families of both parents as he himself (and still more his sister, Kleopatra) was in Molossia. There was perhaps another factor at work. The Argead house had allied itself with the Persian nobility in the distant past, when the sister of Alexander the Philhellene had been given to the son of the Persian commander in Thrace after Macedonia became a vassal state.[41] Now the roles were reversed. The scale of the Susa weddings was something extraordinary, but its rationale goes back to previous Macedonian history and Macedonian diplomatic procedure. It was not a revolutionary experiment in cultural fusion. Nor was it a model that his Successors followed. The Macedonian bridegrooms were not (as many have thought) reluctant to marry Persian ladies,[42] but the dynasties that succeeded Alexander tended to exchange brides among themselves. There was no conscious attempt to intermarry with the native aristocracy, even in the house of Seleukos, whose heir was the son of his Iranian bride Apame.

There is a similar pattern with Alexander's city foundations. This is the area in which he is thought to have been most revolutionary, and his fame as a city founder is only second to his fame as a general. One of Plutarch's most fervid and inspirational passages (*Mor.* 328e) rhapsodizes over the civilizing effect of the new settlements: "by establishing more than seventy cities among barbarian races and sowing Asia with Hellenic governance Alexander overcame their uncivilized and bestial way of life. . . . Those who avoided Alexander were less fortunate than those who were conquered by him; for the latter had no one to put an end to the misery of their existence, while the others were compelled by their conqueror to enjoy happiness." This was a passage that underpinned Droysen's concept of the Hellenistic world. The inculturation of Greek values was a necessary condition for the blending of east and west to fulfill the divine purpose, and Droysen took over Plutarch's panegyric almost verbatim.[43] But there is little trace of a cultural mission in the source tradition for the actual foundations. Most of the attested Alexandrias were in the east of the empire. They were envisaged as military foundations, as is explicit in the foundation of Alexandria Eschate (Chodzhent) on the south bank of the river Iaxartes. The area appeared to have the resources capable of supporting an expanding city and was well placed for a possible invasion of the lands of the nomad Saka peoples and also to repel a nomad incursion.[44] It is the military aspect that is stressed, to the exclusion of any economic, let alone cultural, motives. The intention was to have a garrison population of Greek mercenaries, superannuated Macedonians, and perhaps friendly natives, who would be supported by an agrarian population already established in the area. That can be seen in the one excavated foundation, the site of Ai Khanum on the Oxus River. There, the surrounding plain had been cultivated for centuries and had an elaborate network of irrigation canals when the westerners arrived.[45] There is no trace of urban settlement, and it must be the case that a new foundation was imposed on a comparatively rich agricultural system that could generate the surplus required by the superimposed military population.[46]

It is not surprising that Alexander's plans to found Alexandria Eschate led to a local revolt that rapidly spread through the vast territory north of the Hindu Kush. His foundation was not seen as a cultural benefaction but as a sinister parasite, exploiting the local agricultural resources and depressing the lifestyle of the agrarian population, which now had to provide for many thousand more mouths. And these cities were very populous. According to Diodorus,[47] the Alexandria which was founded by the Hindu Kush (Begram?) accommodated 3,000 Greeks and Macedonians and 7,000 natives. Presumably, the natives were the existing population who had to support a very substantial garrison population, which was expanded two years later by an additional influx of military settlers. The expansion was a natural result of the revolt that had broken out at the time that Alexandria Eschate was established and had taken two years (329–327) to suppress. The reprisals involved considerable dislocation of the natives, who were allocated to garrison foundations, sometimes at a considerable distance from their original domicile. The grim pattern continued as Alexander moved through Bajaur and Swat, putting down local resistance as he went. The cities were a means of containing rebellion in the future, and they were inevitably seen as garrison centers. Nothing could be further from a policy of cultural diffusion. The settlers were seen as aliens and viewed themselves as aliens, as was demonstrated after Alexander's death, when more than 20,000 of the Greeks in the upper satrapies made common cause and attempted to return to the Aegean.[48] Their motive was allegedly "longing for Greek culture and mode of life,"[49] and the conditions under which they lived were profoundly non-Greek. They were reluctant settlers, kept in place by fear of the living Alexander. That fear was reinforced by Alexander's marshals at Babylon, who sent a large expeditionary force to block their passage back to Greece. After a pitched battle, the settlers were worsted and agreed to return to their settlements – only to be massacred by the Macedonians who disregarded the sworn pact. Nothing could make it clearer that the settlements were to be permanent garrison establishments and service there was a life sentence.

The parallel for Alexander's eastern foundations was provided by Philip himself. After several campaigns in Thrace, he established a number of cities, the most famous being Philippopolis (Plovdiv), which he established with a population of 2,000 immigrant settlers.[50] They were later thrown open to destitute Athenians after Antipatros deprived them of their citizen rights at the end of the Lamian War.[51] Like Alexander's settlers, they were reluctant colonists, implanted "to put a curb on the Thracians' boldness" (Diod. 16.71.2). There was no conscious attempt to Hellenize the Thracians, and by all accounts, Philip's colonists would have been very incongruous cultural apostles (Philippopolis was facetiously nicknamed Poneropolis, "Crook City").[52] Similarly, the populations of Alexander's cities will have been originally very rough and ready. However, once the settlers saw themselves as fixtures, they gradually introduced the amenities of civilized life and used the income from the land to install the theatres and gymnasia, which were the infrastructure of Hellenic culture. By the early third century, the inhabitants of remote Ai Khanum were visited by the leading peripatetic philosopher Klearchos of Soloi, who brought with him an authorized copy of Delphic maxims, some of which were inscribed in the precinct of Kineas, the Thessalian officer who had supervised the original foundation and was posthumously honored as a hero.[53] The peripatetic influence was further – and most remarkably – displayed in the remnants of a speculative treatise on metaphysics, which was scraped off the treasury floor by archaeologists (and so preserved in mirror image).[54] Hellenic culture had indeed penetrated, but it was the culture of the immigrants, which they recreated in Bactria after they were denied return to their actual homelands. There is no indication that it percolated to the indigenous agrarian population. The children of Persia, Susiana and Gedrosia did not, as Plutarch claimed, learn to recite the tragedies of Euripides and Sophocles. Instead, in Babylon at least, the Hellenic and Babylonian communities remained separate; one had its social and cultural center in the Greek theatre, the other in the great sacral complex of Esagila.[55]

At the heart of Droysen's concept of Alexander, the inaugurator of the new age is his vision of the god king. Absolute monarchy was the basis of Alexander's regime, and it was underpinned by promotion of his godhead. This was a purely political process. The worship of the ruler, which Alexander explicitly requested from the cities of Greece, was designed to inculcate a universal veneration for monarchy, and in an age where there was little deep-seated religious conviction, it provided a focus for displays of loyalty to the ruling dynasty and, more importantly, a foundation for the universal monotheism that was to come with Christianity.[56] The religious determinism, again, shapes the historical vision, and it is difficult to accept Droysen's conviction that the absolute monarchy of Alexander was a brand new development. Once again, Philip is at the background. There is little doubt that he presented himself as something superhuman. Comparatively early in his reign, he had acquired the city of Krenides, with its access to the prodigiously productive mines of Mt. Pangaion, and renamed it after himself.[57] It was now Philippoi, the plural form deliberately reminiscent of the great divine foundations of Athens and Thebes. The implication was clear. By the end of his reign, Philip was more explicit. A few days before his death, he is alleged to have displayed his own image along with the twelve Olympians and did so before an audience of envoys and well-wishers from the entire Greek world (Diod. 16.92.5). Shortly before that, he had begun the building of the celebrated Philippeion at the entrance to the sacred area of Olympia, a circular construction that accommodated statues of gold and ivory (the traditional materials for cult images).[58] What exactly he envisaged is uncertain, for the building was completed after his death, but the three male images were of himself, his father Amyntas III, and his son Alexander.[59] This was clearly what Alexander wished to be on display: three generations of quasi-divine rulers, culminating in himself.[60]

Alexander had an example in his father to follow. He was clearly predisposed to think himself divine, however incongruous it may appear to modern scholars prone to project their own skeptical rationalism on Macedonian monarchs. Alexander could trace his lineage back to Herakles through his father and to Achilles and even Priam through the Molossian royal house to which his mother belonged; and he was to celebrate the connection at the site of Troy when he set foot on Asian soil.[61] His mother had, it seems, given him reason to believe that his natural father was Zeus rather than Philip. It was an attractive suggestion, recalling the dual paternity of his ancestor Herakles,[62] and the visit to the sanctuary of Zeus Ammon in the Libyan Desert confirmed his belief. His first historian, Kallisthenes, depicted him on the eve of Gaugamela praying to the gods for victory on the grounds of his divine sonship, and his father duly complied. Divine sonship was enhanced by achievement. Alexander's military successes were unparalleled, and he could be viewed as an Aristotelian superman, so far above the rest of humanity that he could be regarded as a being of a different sort.[63] The rivalry with Herakles and later Dionysos became an obsessive game as Alexander's court flatterers found evidence of their presence as far afield as Uzbekistan, Nuristan, and the Indus valley, and in every case, Alexander matched or bettered them. It was a natural step to suggest that he was of the same essence as his divine models and would be translated to another sphere once his mortal existence was terminated.

His marshals too could be seen as more than human. His favorite Hephaistion was given heroic honors, the traditional reward of city founders (Hephaistion had been active in such foundations in the northwest), and his worship was sanctioned by the oracle at Siwah and actively promoted empirewide. The most spectacular celebration of the new hero was in Egypt, where the governor Kleomenes established a shrine and had Hephaistion's name embedded in commercial contracts, but evidence of the cult has been found as far afield as Macedonia,[64] and in Athens, the orator Hypereides (*Epitaphios* 21) was to claim that it was forced on a reluctant population. Alexander considered his own cult should be equally ecumenical, and it was suggested that it would be proper to establish it. Even in Athens, there was a debate about the introduction of cult honors.[65] Its chief proponent, the orator Demades (F 12 de Falco) claimed that the decree was framed by war, using the spear of Alexander, and there is a late tradition that its content was to worship Alexander as the thirteenth Olympian.[66] The parallel with Philip could not be clearer. The king was literally added to the pantheon.

The contrast with his Successors is striking. What in Alexander was passionate belief in his divinity became a matter of polite diplomatic interchange, as when the little city of Skepsis voted Antigonos a precinct, altar, and cult statue in recognition of his defense of Greek liberty.[67] It was recognition of the immense power of the ruler, not unlike the votes for Alexander in Athens and elsewhere. But there is no parallel to Alexander's self-conscious promotion of his own divinity, the inspiration for Apelles' famous portrait of him with the thunderbolt of Zeus,[68] which he himself imitated in the great victory coins that he had struck after his Indian campaigns (once again there is nothing in later iconography to compare). There is a faint echo in Seleukos' claim to double paternity, as the son of Apollo,[69] but Seleukos, it seems, never attempted to emulate the achievements of the gods. In that Alexander was unique.

His uniqueness was underscored by his posthumous reputation. From the moment of Alexander's death, his marshals attempted to recreate themselves in his image. His Bodyguard Leonnatos imitated his characteristic hairstyle and took over the trappings of monarchy: Nesaean horses (the perquisite of the Persian kings) and a cavalry guard of Companions.[70] The attributes of Persian and Macedonian royalty were blended, but the scale was almost absurdly different. Leonnatos was the satrap elect of Hellespontine Phrygia, appointed by his previous colleague Perdikkas. His authority was confined to a comparatively small territory in northwest Asia Minor; yet, he assumed the airs and trappings of a universal monarch. The ambition was clear, but the resources were lacking.

Nowhere is the contrast clearer than in Macedonia itself. By the time of Chaironeia, the kingdom was a superpower, enjoying a supply of trained manpower and an economic strength that was unrivalled in the Greek world. The situation had changed for the worse during Alexander's reign. When the Lamian War broke out in 323, Antipatros, viceroy in Macedonia, was embarrassed by the lack of available troops and promptly suffered the first battle defeat an army from Macedonia had experienced since Philip's setback at the hands of the Phokian condottiere Onomarchos long ago in 353.[71] The situation was exacerbated when further troops left Macedonia during the war against Perdikkas. Antipatros' deputy, Polyperchon, was so denuded of resources that he was unable to prevent the Aitolians from annexing most of the Thessalian cities.[72] Further disruption occurred in 319, when Polyperchon and Antipatros' son Kassandros came into conflict over the control of the kings and the government of Macedonia. The upshot was that the political situation regressed to what it had been in the early part of the fourth century B.C. The conflicting dynasts used the Greek cities of the south for military and political purposes, fomenting constitutional change and promoting friendly political factions, exactly as had happened after the King's Peace, when the Spartans encouraged oligarchic regimes that would be dependent on them to stay in power, while Athens espoused the cause of Greek liberty and autonomy. The same process took place under Macedonia, except that the protagonists on both sides were Macedonians. Oligarchy was Antipatros' preferred method of government, as it was for his son, who supported the regime of Demetrios of Phaleron in Athens, and democracy (in name at least) was necessarily the political system espoused by Polyperchon and later by Demetrios Poliorketes.[73] The background was one of continuous military activity, with Macedonian led armies (predominantly of mercenaries) attempting to outmaneuver each other for the military control of southern Greece. The complicated situation was even more precarious when the dynasts east of the Balkans impinged on Greek politics. For a brief spell in 312, two nephews of Antigonos, Telesphoros and Polemaios, originally commissioned to protect the freedom of the Greeks, had turned against each other and were fighting a campaign in the Peloponnese; at the same time, Polyperchon himself was active in a little enclave his son had created around Corinth, and all were theoretically at war with Kassandros.

This fragmentation contrasted totally with the situation at the end of Alexander's reign, when as ruler of Asia he received a plethora of embassies from almost all the western world and dictated his will to them. There were dissenters, notably the Athenians, who were threatened with the loss of the island of Samos, where as much as a third of their population may have been domiciled,[74] but even Athens stopped short of military resistance and resorted to flattery, conceding Alexander divine honors. The reason was simple: the overwhelming force that Alexander could command. No one subsequently was to dispose of such vast resources. Antigonos came close in 316, after he disposed of Eumenes and commanded a united army comprising 50,000 infantry and 12,000 cavalry, but he immediately embarked on a costly war against the other dynasts and was never able to deploy his army as a whole. There were always other contenders for supremacy, and the unique coercive force that Alexander could apply at the end of his reign was never matched. His Successors were absolute kings in the areas they could control, but there were always checks in the shape of other aspirants. In contrast, Alexander had been the great collector. He had under his direct or indirect control most of the armed forces of the Macedonian and Persian regimes, and the accumulated reserves of the Persian Empire were his to dispose of. The combination of ships, men, and money was irresistible during his lifetime, but was dispersed by his death. His career, it can be argued, was a continuous acquisition of power, with the resources of Macedonia enlarged by the vast reserves of bullion and manpower afforded by the Persian Empire. That was the foundation of an absolute monarchy that had practically no limits. But it was a monarchy based on external conquest and existed largely for conquest. It created a stage on which rival dynasts could compete for a supremacy none of them could achieve, and the military basis of it, the combination of Macedonian, Asiatic, and mercenary forces, was dispersed between the contenders. Alexander remained a symbol of invincibility and world empire, but in practice, he had little concrete effect on the regimes that succeeded him. If there was a new age, it began in 319, when Antipatros returned to Macedonia with the two kings, one an infant, the other mentally incompetent, and in effect separated the Argead kingship from Alexander's conquests in Asia.

BIBLIOGRAPHICAL NOTE

Droysen's initial work on Alexander was published by G. Finke (Berlin, 1833), entitled *Geschichte Alexanders des Grossen*. It was reprinted, with an Introduction by Helmut Berve in 1931 (Alfred Kröner Verlag, Leipzig). The expanded second edition appeared as the first volume of Droysen's *Geschichte des Hellenismus* (Gotha 1877–8), and was reprinted in 1952 (shorn of many of the footnotes) under the editorship of Erich Bayer. There is now a new edition, under the auspices of the Alpha Bank, which contains Droysen's footnotes, expanded by bibliographical references compiled (originally in Greek) by Renos, Herkos, and Stantes Apostolides. The German text, edited by Armin Hohlweg, was published in 2004 by ars nova (Neuried).[75] Droysen's concept of Hellenismus has been fully discussed, with exhaustive bibliography, by Reinhold Bichler (Bichler 1983). For details of the initial reception of his Alexander history, see also Bosworth (2003a) 187–95.

There is a neverending output of monographs on Alexander. For general surveys see, *exempli gratia*, Wilcken (1967); Bosworth (1988a); Hammond (1989); Green (1991). Those who wish to delve deeper should consult the standard editions of the primary sources: P. A. Brunt's two-volume Loeb text of Arrian (1967–83), J. C. Yardley and W. Heckel's Penguin Classics edition of Curtius Rufus (Harmondsworth, 1984), C. B. Welles's Loeb edition of Diodorus Siculus, Book XVII (1963), and Yardley and Heckel's translation and commentary on Justin XI–XII (Oxford, 1994). The fragments of the non-extant historians have been amassed by Jacoby, *FGrH* 117–153, accessible, in translation, in Robinson (1953). They have been discussed by Pearson (1960). For brief overviews of the source tradition, see Bosworth (2000) and Baynham (2003). There have been numerous collections of essays with a direct bearing on the themes of this chapter. See in particular Griffith (1966); Bosworth & Baynham (2000); and Roisman (2003). Bosworth (2002) deals in detail with the history and source tradition of the period after Alexander.

NOTES

1 See the remarks of his son Gustav [Droysen (1910)111], bitterly contrasting the chequered initial reception of the work with its three reprints after Prussia's victories over her "old enemy."

2 For a detailed discussion of the evolution of the concept, see Bichler (1983) 33–54, discounting the influence of Herder, which had been advocated by (among others) Momigliano (1955).

3 Which, coincidentally, was the age at which Robin Lane Fox published his *Alexander the Great* (1973), a work of an avowed atheist to set against that of a deeply devout Lutheran!

4 The crucial passage (Arist. *Pol.* 3.1284ª:10–1, 13–4) appears on the frontispiece, and the first pages define Alexander as one of the elect of history, a passage of fervid rhetoric that was deleted in the second edition.

5 This is expounded in the first edition [Droysen (1931) 486–7], insisting that the Hellenistic centuries were the period of godlessness and an increasingly strident cry for a redeemer. The passage is reshaped more elegantly, but with essentially the same content in the second edition [Droysen (1952) 444–5].

6 See, for instance, the naive paraphrase of Plutarch's celebrated encomium (*Moralia* 328c) of Alexander the universal civilizer [Droysen (1931) 485], expanded in Droysen (1952) 443. The predominant task of "Hellenismus" was to shatter the fetters of superstition among the eastern peoples, "in short, to emancipate them for life in history." The wording is essentially the same in both editions.

7 On the source tradition, see Högemann (1985) with Buraselis (1988); Bosworth (1988b) 187–202.

8 Arr. 7.1.4, a verdict of the Alexander historian Aristoboulos, which Arrian repeats in his own name (Strab. 16.1.11 (741) = FGrH 139 F 56; so Arr. 7.19.6).

9 Diod. 18.4.2–6; Badian (1967); Heckel (1992) 151–3; Bosworth (2002) 58–63.

10 Diod. 31.19.3–4; 18.16.1–2. Cf. Hieronymos. FGrH 154 F 2–3 with Hornblower (1981) 239–45. On Alexander's attitude to past vassals of Persia who failed to acknowledge his sovereignty, see Bosworth (1996) 133–65.

11 Arr. 3.8.5 with Bosworth (1980b) 291–2; Curt. 4.12.12.

12 Bosworth (1996) 118–20; (2002) 164–6.

13 Strab. 15.2.9 (724); Plut. *Alex.* 62.4; Just. 15.4.12, 21; App. *Syriaca* 55.282. See Schober (1981) 156–93.

14 Diod. 19.97.3–6. Cf. Hornblower (1981) 47–9, 144–50; Bosworth (2002) 187–209.

15 This comes through the medium of the Roman author Curtius Rufus (7.8.11–30). Cf. Baynham (1998) 87–9; Bosworth (2002) 195–6; Ballasteros-Pastor (2003).

16 Plut. *Pyrrhos* 14.4–14, on which see Lévêque (1957) 288–92.

17 On the satrapal system, see Briant (2002), esp. 697–728, and for a brief discussion of Alexander's arrangements, Bosworth (1988a) 229–45.

18 Arr. 2.11.10; on Balakros's background, see Heckel (1987), Badian (1988), Bosworth (1994).

19 Billows (1990) 17, 399–400; contra Heckel (1992) 50–1.

20 This is a hugely controversial episode: cf. Badian (1960); (2000) 64–9; Heckel (1977); Bosworth (1988a) 101–4. But whatever view one takes of Philotas's guilt, there is no doubt that his removal resulted in a major restructure of Alexander's high command.

21 The details are variously transmitted, but the objection to despotism is a common element (Arr. 4.8.4; Plut. *Alex.* 51.2; Curt. 8.1.33–4).

22 Curt. 10.1.7; cf. Arr. 7.4.2–3. Allegations of misgovernment in Arr. 6.27.4; Curt. 10.1.2–4. For detail, see Badian (1961) 19–25.

23 Arr. 6.29.3. On this and other local insurrections see Badian (2000) 89–95.

24 For the evidence, see Heckel (1992) 58, 213.

25 On this much-vexed issue, see Badian (1961); Jaschinski (1981); Bosworth (1988a) 149–50, 215–20; Habicht (1997a); Blackwell (1999).

26 For full discussion with bibliography, see Bosworth (2002) 29–63.

27 All three played significant roles and held independent commands under Perdikkas during the First Coalition War. For details, see Heckel (1992) 150–1, 172–4, 181–2, 275–6.

28 On the background, see Billows (1990) 69–73; Bosworth (2002) 14–9.

29 Diod. 19.55.3 with Bosworth (2002) 212–3. Compare Arr. *Succ.* F 1.36: the Indian kings Taxiles and Porus were retained in office at Triparadeisos "because it was not easy to displace them, commissioned as they were with their realms at the hands of Alexander" (cf. Diod. 18.39.6; 19.48.2).

30 "Das Werkzeug, mit dem das Werk der neuen Zeit geschaffen war, von der mächtigen Hand des Meisters zerbrochen wurde": Droysen (1931) 458, repeated verbatim in the second edition [Droysen (1952) 418].

31 Arr. 7.6.1. 8.2; Plut. *Alex.* 71.1; Diod. 17.108.1–2. For the training and later history of these troops see Hammond (1990).

32 Arr. 7.11.1–3. Diod. 17.108.3 explicitly terms the *Epigonoi* a "counter-formation"; cf. Briant (1982) 32–9; Bosworth (1980a) 17.

33 See, for instance, Milns (1976) 89–96; Hammond and Griffith (1979) 705–13; Errington (1990) 243–4.

34 Arr. 7.23.3–4, 24.1 = Aristoboulos, *FGrH* 139 F 58. For discussion, see Bosworth (2002) 79–80.

35 On "war dancers," see Plut. *Alex.* 71.3. For the encounter at Paraitakene, see Diod. 19.28.1, 29.3, 30.5–6 with Bosworth (2002) 134, 138–9, 151–5.

36 Arr. 7.11.1, 7; cf. Briant (2002) 309–10, 780–3.

37 Arr. 7.11.8–9, a passage that was crucial to Sir William Tarn's hypothesis that Alexander envisaged a universal brotherhood of man [Tarn (1948) ii 440–9]. For a more realistic interpretation, see Badian (1958) 428–32.

38 On Atropates's services see previous mention. Phrataphernes also arrested a usurper [Curt. 10.1.39; cf. Badian (2000) 91–2]. On the disappearance of Iranian satraps, see Bosworth (1988a) 240–1; Brosius (2003) 190–3.

39 Arr. 7.4.4–7; Ath. 12.538b–39a (from the eye-witness, Chares of Mytilene: *FGrH* 125 F 4); Plut. *Alex.* 70.2, *Mor.* 338c; Diod. 17.107.6. On the detail, see Brosius (1996) 77–9; Ogden (1999) 43–8.

40 The prime text is a fragment of the Peripatetic philosopher Satyros (quoted by Athenaios 557b–e), on which, see Tronson (1984); Ogden (1999) 17–26; Carney (2000) 52–81.

41 Hdt. 5.21.2, 8.136.1; Just. 7.3.7–9. On the political context, see Badian (1994b) 108–16.

42 According to Arrian (7.6.2), the marriages were not to the taste of "some" of the bridegrooms, but they were clearly in the minority. The only bride known to have been divorced (Amastris, the daughter of Darius's brother and wife of Krateros), fully consented to the arrangement, which transferred her to the bed of Dionysios, the ruler of Pontic Herakleia [Memnon, *FGrH* 434 F 1 (4.4)].

43 Droysen (1931) 485, (1952) 442, both passages rather unhappy elaborations of Plut. *Mor.* 328c.

44 Arr. 4.1.3–4, on which, see Bosworth (1995) 15–7; Fraser (1996) 151–3, noting that Alexandria Eschate is the only eastern foundation of Alexander to appear in a documentary record of the third century B.C. These cities did not make an impact as cultural centers.

45 Gardin (1980).

46 On this, Just. 12.5.12 is explicit for Alexandria Eschate, and Curt. 7.6.27 agrees. Arrian 4.4.1 describes the native population as "volunteers." On the tradition, see Briant (1982) 244–8; Bosworth (1995) 26–7.

47 17.83.2; cf. Curt. 7.3.23. The city was expanded in 327 with another influx of locals and discharged mercenaries, and the community was placed under the direct rule of one of the Companions [Arr. 4.22.5; cf. Bosworth (1995) 143].

48 Diod. 18.4.8, 7.1–9. See also Sachs and Hunger (1988) 211. For discussion, see Schober (1981) 32–7; Holt (1988) 87–92; Bosworth (2002) 61–2. There had been an earlier, premature attempt to return in 325, after a false report that he had died in India (Diod. 17.99.5–6; Curt. 9.7.1, 11).

49 Diod. 18.7.1. Compare 17.99.5: "they had long resented their settlement among the barbarians."

50 Details in Theopompus, *FGrH* 115 F 110. Cf. Hammond & Griffith (1979) 557, 673.

51 Habicht (1997a) 44–5; Poddighe (2002) 66–73.

52 The twin foundation of Kabyle was back under Thracian rule before 300 B.C. [Calder (1996)].

53 Robert (1968); Fraser (1996) 155–6.

54 Bernard (1978) 456–60, suggesting an early third-century date. There is an accessible photograph in Green (1990) 334.

55 The relevant documents are conveniently assembled by van der Spek (2001).

56 Droysen (1931) 461–2: essentially the same, with the rhetoric modified, in Droysen (1952) 423–4.

57 For the historical context, see Hammond and Griffith (1979) 358–61, acknowledging that the name is unprecedented, but declining to hazard a guess at what it was advertising.

58 See Lapatin (2001), esp. 115–9.

59 Paus. 5.20.9–10. According to another, corrupt passage of Pausanias (5.17.4) Olympias and a Eurydike were also honored with chryselephantine statues, but were transferred to the nearby temple of Hera. The date and circumstances of the removal are uncertain, but it seems as though some Argead ladies were invested with the attributes of divinity.

60 There is a rather dubious tradition that Amyntas received a cult at Pydna during his lifetime, and its sanctuary, the Amynteion, was still in existence early in Philip's reign [Habicht (1970) 11–3; contra Badian (1981) 39–40].

61 Arr. 1.11.8, 12.1; Plut. *Alex.* 15.8–9. See Bosworth (1988a) 38–9. Some skepticism in Badian (2002) 37–8.

62 Thanks to Herodotus (6.69), a similar story was in vogue about the Spartan king Demaratos. For the tradition (which goes back at least to Eratosthenes) that Olympias encouraged the rumor, see Plut. *Alex.* 2.5–3.4 with Hamilton's commentary [Hamilton (1968) 4–7]; Fredricksmeyer (2003) 271–4.

63 I have presented this interpretation at length elsewhere: see Bosworth (1996) 88–132.

64 Arr. 7.23.7–8 (Kleomenes). On the cult in Macedon, see Voutiras (1990).

65 Hyp. *Dem.* 31–2 with Whitehead (2000) 370, 455–60; Din.1.94 with Worthington (1992); Ath. 6.251b.

66 Ael. *VH* 5.12. He is also said to have proposed the same decree for Philip (F 81 de Falco).

67 *OGIS* 6 [translated by Austin (1981) 59–60]. Cf. Habicht (1970) 42–44.

68 Plin. *NH* 35,92; Plut. *Alex.* 4.3; cf. Stewart (1993a) 193–7. On the coins, see Bosworth (1996) 6–8; Lane Fox (1996).

69 Just. 15.4.2–10; App. *Syr.* 56.284–5; Habicht (1970) 85–6; Ogden (1999) 118–9.

70 Arr. *Succ.* F 12 (Roos). Krateros is also attested to have dressed exactly like Alexander, omitting only the diadem; his troops (in 322) treated him openly as a king [Arr. *Succ.* F 19 (Roos)].

71 Bosworth (2002) 75–9 contra Badian (1994a) 267; Billows (1995) 193.

72 Diod. 18.38.5–6; cf. Bosworth (2002) 82.

73 On the background see Habicht (1997a) 44–81.

74 Habicht (1996). For the political situation see Bosworth (1988a) 220–28; Worthington (1994b); Blackwell (1999) 121–4.

75 I acquired this work too late to use in my footnotes, which I would have done in preference to Bayer.

2: THE HELLENISTIC KINGDOMS

Winthrop Lindsay Adams

⟨℘⟩

INTRODUCTION

The emergence of the major states in the Hellenistic World was the result of a complicated series of events, a mixture of various traditions, and the existence of some very forceful personalities. All of these combined to make Hellenistic kingship, as well as the kingdoms themselves, unique. The most influential personality, even in death, was that of Alexander the Great, and he left his mark on all the kingdoms. But the strength of the personalities among the Successors (Diadochoi) was equally distinct. A generation and a half of almost-constant civil war among the Macedonian Successors to Alexander provided the context in which these kingdoms were formed. Finally, in each kingdom, the traditions of the native peoples and their natural resources made a mark on that development as well. Many of the aspects of Hellenistic kingship were passed on to the Romans, along with the religious and cultural heritage of the Hellenistic World, to be adapted and find its culmination in Roman imperial culture.

THE AFTERMATH OF ALEXANDER'S DEATH

When Alexander the Great died in Babylon in June 323 B.C.,[1] he left behind more questions than he had resolved. Worse, he had failed to provide for any succession. Over the previous year, half of the twenty provincial governors (satraps) had either already been executed for treason and malfeasance or were awaiting that fate, which hamstrung the normal machinery of government. The leading figures of the last decade were all gone, dead from the strains and conditions of the campaigns themselves or executed in the intrigues of court politics. Parmenion,

Philotas, Nikanor, Kleitos, Koinos, and Hephaistion were all dead. Only Antipatros remained as regent in Macedonia and general for Europe, but even in this case, the general Krateros was returning to Macedonia at the head of 10,000 veterans with orders to relieve him. The office of Chiliarch (essentially the "Prime Minister") had been officially vacant since Hephaistion's death the year before, though Perdikkas was carrying out the functions of the office.

For all intents and purposes, there was no government. No permanent structure for the empire had been created. Alexander's approach had been to tinker with the existing Persian institutions: Civil functions in each satrapy had been split off from the military ones, with the latter always in the hands of a Greek or Macedonian commander. All financial affairs had been placed in a central office, but its head, Harpalos, had fled after massive embezzlement and was now a fugitive. No one had replaced him, except Alexander himself.

The most pressing problem, however, was a successor. One of Alexander's wives, Roxane, was pregnant, which presented the possibility of a direct male heir. The only other dynastic choice was Alexander's half brother, Arrhidaios, who was reputedly mentally or emotionally incompetent.[2] Beyond these choices, there were a host of potential usurpers. It was, in fact, this last group that initiated the Wars of the Diadochoi, and saw to the end of the Argead Dynasty. And it was from among this same group that the dynasties of the three major Hellenistic Kingdoms emerged.

The council of officers that gathered at Babylon within a few days of Alexander's death consisted of the second rank of commanders. The most experienced generals weren't there at all: Antipatros and Krateros. It did not possess any clear authority to make arrangements. Perdikkas claimed that Alexander had given him his signet ring, but there had been no witnesses. Among those present were all but one of the men who would be the major figures of the next generation and who made themselves kings in the coming years: Kassandros, Seleukos, Lysimachos, and Ptolemy. The remaining future king, Antigonos the One-Eyed (Monophthalmos), was on duty as a general in Asia Minor.

Ptolemy suggested that the council itself should govern the empire, exercising royal authority without a king, and await the outcome of Roxane's pregnancy before making any other decision regarding the succession. It was a popular position, but Perdikkas wanted executive control for himself. Given the fact that the rule of an empire by committee is a formula for disaster, it is hardly surprising that they compromised and chose both proposals. Perdikkas was confirmed as

Chiliarch, and they decided to wait on the formal succession. Almost without knowing it, they had begun to change the nature of kingship and taken the first steps to institutionalize it. But, as will happen continually over the next forty years, events ran ahead of them.

While the officers talked, the men of the Macedonian Phalanx acted. They proclaimed Arrhidaios to be king, as the only surviving son of Philip II. They stormed the palace where the council was meeting and forced them to accept another compromise. Arrhidaios, now called Philip III, was recognized as king, but provision was made for a joint kingship should Roxane bear a son, naming Perdikkas and Leonnatos as the child's potential guardians. Indeed, Roxane did bear a son a few months later, named for his father: Alexander IV. Perdikkas was confirmed as Chiliarch and shortly after had Meleager, the leader of the Phalanx and Philip III's guardian, killed. The council then, under the authority of Philip III Arrhidaios, appointed new satraps and army commanders. Unity appeared to be restored.

But it was only appearance. Perdikkas had already begun consolidating his power, seeing to it that all the potential rivals at court were given satrapies and commands away from the center. Antipatros and Krateros were jointly named generals for Europe, which took care of the two senior commanders. Antipatros later offered to solidify the position among the leading figures with marriage alliances.[3] Antigonos the One-Eyed was reconfirmed as satrap of Greater Phrygia and thus was kept out of the picture. Leonnatos was given Hellespontine Phrygia, and Alexander's Greek secretary, Eumenes of Kardia, Cappadocia. Two more court favorites and potential rivals then were gone. Ptolemy chose Egypt as his satrapy, one presumes after a good deal of thought, and removed himself. Seleukos, the former commander of the Hypaspists, was promoted to command the Companion Cavalry; Kassandros (the son of Antipatros) took Seleukos' place at the head of the Hypaspists (where Perdikkas could watch them both as his own subordinates).[4]

THE WARS OF THE DIADOCHOI

What emerged over the next few months was a struggle for the control of Alexander's empire by trying to control the two kings. As neither king was able to rule in his own right (because of incompetence on the one hand, and infancy on the other), they became the symbols of power for other factions. Alexander's mother, Olympias, offered a marriage alliance to Perdikkas in 322, namely the hand of Alexander's sister Kleopatra.[5] The price for that marriage was dropping the alliance with Antipatros, Olympias' archrival. The possibility of being a royal uncle and regent, which could mean a path to kingship itself, was too much for Perdikkas to let go. Further, Ptolemy entered the picture at this point by hijacking Alexander's funeral cortege on its way back to Macedonia, diverting it to Egypt. Two factions emerged at this point: Perdikkas and his party, which had control of the kings, and a group of commanders, who either feared Perdikkas' ambitions or had ambitions of their own, or both.

Antipatros and Krateros led one army of the coalition from Macedonia into Asia Minor to attack Perdikkas from the north. Perdikkas detailed Eumenes of Kardia to slow them up in Asia Minor while he took care of Ptolemy in the south. Eumenes managed to kill Krateros in personal combat, but Antipatros and the rest of army brushed past him. In the meantime, Perdikkas repeatedly failed to force the Nile line against Ptolemy in Egypt. The result was that his own officers killed Perdikkas, and the army deserted to Ptolemy.

In 321, at Triparadeisos in Syria, Alexander's Grand Army met for what would be the last time. Antipatros was named by it as regent for the kings, whom he took back to Macedonia. Antigonos was to command a field army to crush Eumenes. The other satrapal appointments were reconfirmed. But within two years, Antipatros was dead of natural causes, and the struggle for control of the kings (and the empire) was renewed. Philip III Arrhidaios and his wife were killed in 317 by Olympias, who was executed the next year as Antipatros' son, Kassandros, solidified his power in Macedonia.[6] At the same time (316) in Asia, Antigonos the One-Eyed engineered the betrayal of Eumenes of Kardia and proclaimed himself to be the "Lord of Asia," though not yet daring to call himself "king."

The generals and satraps continued to rule in the name of Alexander IV, who was now under the control of Kassandros. Though Antigonos' ambitions were clear, he still used Alexander IV and the legitimacy of the Argead House as pretext for a new war. Just as the other satraps had joined against Perdikkas, a new coalition of Kassandros in Macedonia, Ptolemy in Egypt, Lysimachos in Thrace, and Seleukos in Babylon now allied against Antigonos. The major players, however, were becoming fewer in number.

Another war raged inconclusively down to 311. At that point, a general peace was negotiated. This left Antigonos in control of Asia and the others in their original territories. Only Seleukos was excluded from the treaty altogether. It is very likely that as part of the settlement Kassandros was to eliminate Alexander IV before he came of age to rule. Indeed, by 309, Alexander IV was dead, killed in secret but buried in public by Kassandros at Aigai (probably in Tomb III in the Great Tumulus at Vergina).[7] But for now, all the major figures maintained the fiction that they ruled in Alexander IV's name.

PERSONAL KINGSHIP AND THE EMERGENCE OF THE KINGDOMS

Individual skirmishing between the rival generals occurred over the next five years. In the course of these struggles, the son of Antigonos the One-Eyed, Demetrios (who was later given the nickname of "Poliorketes" or "Sacker of Cities"), managed to liberate Athens from Kassandros and his puppet, Demetrios of Phaleron. For this, both he and his father were recognized as "Savior Gods," and two new tribes were established in their honor at Athens. Then, Demetrios, in command of the Antigonid fleet, defeated Ptolemy in a naval engagement off Cyprus in 306 (see also Chapter 13 in this volume). This was the occasion for Antigonos to have himself and Demetrios both formally proclaimed as "kings" by his army. It was also the signal to the rest of the dynasts to end the fiction of ruling in the name of the Argead House. Ptolemy, Seleukos, Lysimachos, and eventually Kassandros all followed suit. The Antigonids had done so through the mechanism of their army, visibly connecting to the previous Macedonian custom.

There is considerable disagreement as to whether the custom could be characterized as truly electing the kings or simply proclaiming the acceptance of the succession. In this case, it was done at the instigation of Antigonos and was clearly not part of a dynastic succession. Rather, it was meant to establish a new dynasty. At the very least it amounted to a public acknowledgment of his kingship, regardless of what it drew from old practice. It is very likely, as a result, that the others used the same mechanism and for the same reasons. There had been a clear break with the Argead dynasty, and this was a step toward establishing legitimacy in the eyes of their Macedonian followers. It was another step toward the institutionalizing of the monarchy.

It also signaled a new round of wars. Antigonos and Demetrios tried to invade Egypt to displace Ptolemy in late 306 and failed miserably. At this point, Demetrios then besieged the city of Rhodes over the course of the next year and failed again. Demetrios got his nickname as the "Sacker of Cities" as an ironic result of this failure (see Chapter 13 in this volume for discussion). In 304, the Antigonids decided to try their luck against Kassandros in Greece, with considerably more success. Demetrios broke the siege of Athens by Kassandros and restored the Hellenic League (to bring the Greek *poleis* in on the Antigonid side). By late 302, Demetrios was poised for the invasion of Macedonia itself.

At this point, Kassandros took the initiative to restore the old coalition. If Antigonos gained control of Asia and Macedonia, he would pose too great a power for the others to survive. They made common cause, and the decisive battle was fought at Ipsos in the spring of 301. Lysimachos and Seleukos, commanding the allied army, defeated and killed Antigonos, while Demetrios retreated to the port cities in the Aegean still held by the Antigonids and to the command of the great Antigonid fleet.

This did not end the maneuvering. The victors soon fell out among themselves, as Demetrios must have hoped. Kassandros died of consumption over the winter of 298/7 and his son, Philip IV, followed him within the year, dead from the same cause. The remaining two sons fell out over the exercise of royal authority, which opened the way for Demetrios. In 294, he invaded Macedonia, killed one of Kassandros' sons, and drove the other out. Following precedent, Demetrios had his army proclaim him "king" of Macedonia. The dynasty of Kassandros was extinguished in short order. While this was going on, the other kings were solidifying their positions. Ptolemy was well established in Egypt, and likewise Lysimachos in Thrace. Indeed, the two entered into a marriage alliance, with Lysimachos marrying a daughter of Ptolemy.[8] Seleukos had begun as the least secure of the dynasts, but by this time, he had control of most of the old area of the Persian Empire and begun a bitter rivalry with Ptolemy.

Demetrios had hoped to use Macedonia as the springboard to rebuild Alexander's empire. After all, Alexander had done so. As it turned out, just as Alexander's adoption of the rituals and attitudes of eastern kingship had alienated many of his Macedonians, so too did Demetrios' imitation of those same practices have a like effect on the Macedonian homeland. Further, Demetrios' open ambitions made him a target for both Lysimachos and Pyrrhos of Epiros. And the latter had a legitimate claim on Macedonia, related by blood to Alexander and the Argead House. By 287, the Macedonians were fed up and withdrew their support from Demetrios, forcing him to flee the kingdom. Lysimachos and Pyrrhos divided Macedonia up between them. It was the low point in Macedonia's fortunes.

Demetrios left his young son, Antigonos Gonatas, to control what was left of the Antigonid forces in Greece proper, while he himself took command of the fleet and left to try his hand in Asia Minor. But in the maneuvering against Lysimachos, Demetrios' luck finally ran out. He fell back to the south and was captured by Seleukos in 286. Demetrios spent the remaining three years of his life in captivity. For all intents and purposes, the struggle was down to three dynasts: Lysimachos of Thrace, Ptolemy of Egypt, and Seleukos of Asia. No one gave much thought to Antigonos Gonatas. But none of them had forgotten about Alexander the Great or the ambitions that had created his empire in the first place.

Lysimachos now made his bid for ultimate power, the key to which would be the control of Macedonia. He had pushed Pyrrhos out of Macedonia and Thessaly by 285. Equally, he expanded his control in Thrace all the way to the Danube. But at this point, Lysimachos' position was weakened by a dynastic struggle within his family, which led him to order the death of his own son, Agathokles, in late 283 or early 282. Agathokles had been popular, but more importantly, his widow appealed to Seleukos for aid in 282.[9]

With clear signs of weakness and disintegration evident in Lysimachos' kingdom, Seleukos saw this as his opportunity to bid for control of Alexander the Great's empire. The two armies met at Korupedion in Asia Minor in the late spring or early summer of 281. Seleukos defeated Lysimachos, who was killed in the course of the struggle. By the end of summer, Seleukos crossed to Europe claiming control of Macedonia and Thrace as well as Asia. Everything but Ptolemy's Egypt was now his, and Seleukos seemed on the verge of reuniting the empire. But at this very point, Seleukos' chief aide, Ptolemy Keraunos (the dispossessed son of Ptolemy I of Egypt), assassinated him.

The possibility of reuniting Alexander's empire faded to a dream, and the army eventually proclaimed Ptolemy Keraunos as king of Macedonia, in what was now a well-established if too often practiced procedure. It was short lived. Ptolemy himself was killed in a Celtic invasion of Macedonia in 279. Within two years (277), the Macedonians proclaimed Antigonos Gonatas as king, in the absence of any other possible candidate.[10] Antigonos managed to make it stick, and campaigning over the next seven years established the Antigonids as the new dynasty of Macedonia, one that would last for the rest of Macedonia's independence.

What has been a long tale covering the chaos that followed Alexander's death is nevertheless a necessary one to understand what now emerged. At the end of it, there were three royal houses left of all the potential leaders that had begun the struggle: the Ptolemies in Egypt, the Antigonids in Macedonia, and Seleukos' son, Antiochos I, who had been ruling in his father's absence as joint monarch and now carried on the Seleukid tradition in Asia. But the dream of Alexander's empire and the ambitions of these royal houses remained.

The idea of empire was an underlying principle and desire in each of the major kingdoms. The starting point for each kingdom had been the same. The trappings of monarchy and Macedonian kingship in each would be the same, though each would also react in different ways to the conditions of the lands and peoples they ruled. Each kingdom would have its own advantages and disadvantages in the struggles that followed over the next four generations, but the dreams of Alexander and his empire always lurked behind them. One can now talk meaningfully of the formations of these kingdoms, which controlled the Hellenistic world.

ANTIGONID MACEDONIA

Macedonia claimed the direct inheritance of the traditions of Philip and Alexander's kingdom. The major divisions and shape of the kingdom remained the same as they had been under Philip II, and for that matter, under Kassandros. Antigonos II Gonatas was not only the son of Demetrios Poliorketes; his mother had been Kassandros' sister Phila, which added to his legitimacy among the Macedonians. To a large extent, he adopted the policies of Kassandros, which had been in turn based on those of Philip II. The major goal was to protect the kingdom itself.

To the north and west, this meant a strong defense against the Illyrians and now the Celts as well. To the south, it meant at least the passive control of Greece and to the east the maintenance of the frontier in Thrace. These had been the traditional external problems of Macedonia throughout the fifth and fourth centuries. Added to these was a wary defense against the ambitions of the other Hellenistic monarchies, who sought to get at Macedonia primarily through Greece or Thrace. These areas were not so much threats in their own right as pawns for others. This was a legacy of the Wars of Succession.

Internally, Antigonos Gonatas had a number of advantages. He had a reasonably homogeneous population in comparison to the other Hellenistic monarchies, internal lines of communication, and an existing infrastructure of roads, fortresses, and resources on which to build. But the Macedonian population had been reduced dramatically. Antigonos could not stop the flow of settlers leaving for the new city foundations in the other Hellenistic kingdoms. The very nature of these Macedonians made them valuable commodities in the Hellenistic East. Alexander had left some 7,600 men behind with Antipatros at the beginning of the campaigns in 334, while he himself took with him in the initial expedition, or received as reinforcements later on, some 60,000 more Macedonians. Based on the usual ratio of the military muster representing about 10 percent of the overall population, the number of Macedonians altogether must have been around 700,000. Under the Antigonids, the full Macedonian levy dropped to around 25,000 men (15,000 in the phalanx itself, plus others including mercenaries). That meant that at least two thirds of the population must have emigrated. Those that were left were arguably the best troops in the Hellenistic World, man for man, but they were fewer in number. It did relieve one traditional problem for the Macedonian monarchy: There was little or no sign of the internal dissent that had plagued the kingdom in the fifth and early fourth centuries.

Equally, that it was Macedonia itself must have affected the nature of the monarchy. The Macedonians had already demonstrated to Antigonos' father that there were things which they would not condone and had thrown Demetrios Poliorketes out. That example must have been ever before Antigonos Gonatas. He, too, had been proclaimed "king" by the Macedonian army in 277. As with the Argead kings, the Antigonids of Macedonia were expected to lead the army personally, and all of them did so, as opposed to the Ptolemaic record in this area. There is a longstanding debate over the nature of the Macedonian kingship, one group of scholars holding that it was always a constitutional monarchy and another that it was always an autocracy. Oddly, neither side seems to allow for development. But insofar as there is written evidence for the constitutional position, it largely comes from Antigonid Macedonia.[11] A popular monarch might occasionally get away with murder, literally, but clearly there were Macedonian sensibilities to which, to a large extent, Antigonos Gonatas and his successors paid attention. Nor was there ever any sign in Antigonid Macedonia of the "ruler cult" that emerged in the other Hellenistic kingdoms, despite the examples not only of Philip and Alexander, but Antigonos the One-Eyed and Demetrios Poliorketes.[12]

In Antigonos' case, he was both a popular monarch and one who enjoyed a long reign of nearly forty years. Despite all the odds, Antigonos Gonatas died a natural death in 239, which went even further toward firmly establishing his dynasty. That popularity was based on the success of Antigonos' policies and the defense of the realm. In terms of the traditional problems, Antigonos continued the construction of border fortresses (*stratopeda*) against the Illyrians and the Celts along the western mountainous approaches to upper Macedonia. To fill in for troop shortages, Antigonos tended to stock these posts with Cretan and Arkadian mercenaries. The result was that Macedonia, especially to the west, became an onionskin of defensive layers and almost unassailable, even to the Romans in the second century. The north, with the access down the great river valleys of the Axios (Vardar) and the Strymon (Struma), was more of a problem and would remain so even for the Romans in the first century.[13]

To the south, and the control of Greece, Antigonos also took great care. For most of his early reign, there were Macedonian garrisons and pro-Macedonian tyrants throughout Greece, even in Athens. The rise of the Aitolian League and the Achaian League greatly cut into this, but Antigonos' goal was not so much domination as it was to use Greece as a buffer to keep out his Ptolemaic and Seleukid rivals. To do that, he maintained three great fortresses at key points, called by the Greeks the "Three Fetters." The first of these was the city and great Antigonid naval base at Demetrias, located at the head of the Gulf of Magnesia, founded by and named for his father. Demetrias insured that Antigonos Gonatas and his successors could transport troops quickly to Greece as needed, rather than maintaining large forces there or fighting their way each time along the land route through Thermopylai. The second "Fetter" was the fortress city of Chalkis on the island of Euboia, which lay near the Euripos channel. Here, the island was only 45 yards from mainland Greece. Further, it was this that permitted the Macedonians to bypass the traditional choke point at Thermopylai, which was usually controlled by the Aitolians. This guaranteed the passage into Central Greece. Finally, there was the great fortress at Acrocorinth, the sugarloaf mountain just on the outskirts of the city of Corinth at the Isthmus. This secured entry into the Peloponnesos. Thus, Antigonos Gonatas could move armies virtually anywhere in Greece with relative security and ease.

Acrocorinth periodically was lost to the Macedonians, especially after Aratos of Sikyon rose to power in the Achaian League. But by one means or another, the Antigonids always managed to regain control of it. And with Acrocorinth came the shipyards at Corinth, which the Antigonids used to maintain and rebuild their fleet. On two occasions, at Kos around 254 and at Andros around 246, Antigonos Gonatas led the Macedonian fleet to victory over the Ptolemies. Those victories would have been impossible without the control of Corinth's shipyards. Philip V would use them to the same advantage at the end of the third century.

To pay for all of this, Antigonos Gonatas turned to commercial development. The mineral resources, timber, and trade produced roughly the same income as they had under Philip II. This was not inconsiderable, but the problem was that the Ptolemaic and Seleukid resources were so vast. Nevertheless, Pella became a commercial center as well as the capital. The famous Macedonian mosaics at Pella came from the rich residential district by the Loudias River, not the government buildings, and were the byproduct of that trade. At the head of the Thermaic Gulf, the city of Thessalonike (named by Kassandros for his wife) grew even faster. It sat both on the old royal road that ran from east to west and on the Axios River route north into the upper Balkans. Two other cities grew and prospered as well. Amphipolis, which lay on the lower reaches of the Strymon, enjoyed the same advantages as Thessalonike, but added timber and gold from Mount Pangaion to the mix. And Kassandreia (on the old site of Potidaia on the Pallene promontory) was refounded by Kassandros and named for him. It dealt with the rich agricultural products of the Chalkidic peninsula and the Anthemos. In particular, it was noted for its Mendean wine, which was aggressively marketed from Kassandros' time on (even using cups especially designed by the sculptor Lysippos).

If its resources were considerably less than the Seleukids and Ptolemies, Antigonid Macedonia nevertheless had enough for its needs. The fortresses to secure the kingdom were built and maintained. There was enough for Antigonid fleets, which enjoyed success at very key points throughout its history. Though there were occasional barbarian incursions into upper Macedonia, they were few and always countered vigorously by the monarchy. Macedonia under the Antigonids was secure, reasonably prosperous, and genuinely independent. It maintained its potential in the game for Alexander's empire. More importantly, as the reign of Philip V demonstrates, the Antigonids still had the ambitions and the personal ability to reconstruct Alexander's empire.

PTOLEMAIC EGYPT

Ptolemy I Soter[14] had chosen Egypt at the very outset and deliberately. It had a number of clear advantages. First, it was readily defensible, as

Ptolemy proved against Perdikkas in 322 and then later Antigonos the One-Eyed in 306. Indeed, the Nile line has only been forced a dozen times in history. So Egypt provided a strategic location for Ptolemy and his successors against external forces. Secondly, it was equally secure internally. Egypt was the classic land of despotism. It consists, in traditional Egyptian terms, of the Two Lands: the Nile Delta on the one hand, and the Nile Valley on the other. From Memphis at the southern end of the Delta to Elephantine and the First Cataract, it was a 750-mile-long valley, never wider than 15 miles at any point. It was also clearly delineated, as it was possible to stand literally with one foot on arable soil and one on complete desert. With a garrison at Memphis and another at Elephantine, the populace of the Nile Valley was trapped, for there was nowhere else to go but desert, the same deserts that protected Egypt from outside invasion. Finally, all land was "king's land," and Egypt could be and indeed was run as a state monopoly producing surpluses in grain and luxury goods.

Ptolemy, and for that matter the Seleukids, had one problem that Antigonid Macedonia did not: large native populations. In this case, it was one that was itself homogeneous and had thousands of years of culture and tradition binding it together. From the beginning, Ptolemy rejected Alexander's approach to fusion. There was no native elite anyway that could correspond to the Persians in Asia. Thus, Ptolemy chose to maintain two distinct identities: He was a Macedonian king to his Greeks and Pharaoh to his Egyptians, at least after 306. There had been two Greek cities, both in the Delta, when Ptolemy came to Egypt as satrap: the old Panhellenic trading colony at Naukratis and Alexandria, which became his capital. He also founded a city about halfway up the Nile Valley, just north of Abydos, which was named for him: Ptolemais. These cities each had a large Greek population brought in by Ptolemy and the usual trappings of Greek civic government and institutions. There was also a considerable settlement of Greeks around the Fayoum, the lake district west of the lower Nile Valley, and Memphis. Here, they were established as cleruchs (military colonists) and settled on good land to provide the basis for the Ptolemaic phalanx.

The rest of Egypt was kept divided into the forty-two districts (called *hsaput* in Egyptian and *nomos* in Greek), which had been traditional for over 3,000 years. Here, some seven to ten million native Egyptians lived the same life they had always led. They worshipped the traditional gods, and the Ptolemies endeavored to keep up the old religion and the old ways.[15] The images of the Ptolemies were executed in traditional Egyptian style on the monuments and buildings. Indeed, one could not tell them apart from the images of the previous native dynasties. The inscriptions were written in traditional hieroglyphics, in demotic (a cursive script based on hieroglyphics) and Greek. The title used by the Ptolemies was the ancient formula: "King of the Two Lands." Each Ptolemy bore the traditional five names of Pharaoh in the cartouche, only one of which was his actual call name and the rest were connected to the old gods and religious formulas. In short, to the average native, they were still ruled by their own kings. Even this was to Ptolemy's advantage, as by tradition, all land was Pharaoh's, all wealth was Pharaoh's, and all life was Pharaoh's. An Egyptian priest, Manetho, wrote a history of the dynasties of Egypt in Greek for Ptolemy, placing him as the founder of the Thirtieth Dynasty and thus incorporating them into the Egyptian fabric. But it will not be until the last of that Dynasty that anyone one of them, in this case Kleopatra VII, bothered to learn Egyptian.

Each *nomos* was administered by a Greek governor or *strategos*. In each district, there was a small population of cleruchs as well, set up like local squires, to provide security and help with the administration of the district. Altogether, this amounted to a thin veneer of Greco-Macedonians set over a very large population of natives. Normally, nothing disturbed the lives of the natives aside from the traditional taxes they had always paid. They were not used in administration or the armed services. Occasionally, in national emergencies, the Ptolemies did arm and train these natives to fill out the phalanx, as Ptolemy IV would do at the end of the third century. This was usually followed by a period of native unrest and rebellion, but not a permanent condition.

The economic resources of Egypt were vast. The state monopoly on grain made Egypt the main grain exporter in the Mediterranean, even through the Roman period when Egypt became the personal possession of Augustus and his successors. The spread of Greek culture throughout the Hellenistic East, the desire for those populations to maintain their Greek heritage in humane letters, and the growth of bureaucracies to govern these areas also increased the need for paper. Egyptian papyrus provided the main source for this and another major export crop. Finally, trade down the Nile for luxury items, such as ivory, ebony, gold and jewels from Africa, and incense coming up the Red Sea from Yemen, filled out the economic picture.

It all provided a fabulous income. Even more important, the security of the kingdom and its geographic advantages meant that there was very little overhead necessary to maintain the government. The

Seleukids had a far larger economy and income, but they also had to protect a larger area both externally from barbarians and internally from bandits and rebels, as well as the upkeep of a massive infrastructure. This meant that the Ptolemaic revenues provided a disposable income far greater than any of the other kingdoms. The estimates of the royal treasury in the time of Ptolemy II Philadelphos range up to 800,000 talents. If the security of Egypt was its first great advantage, its wealth gave the Ptolemies its edge in the rivalries among the Hellenistic kingdoms. It made possible a brilliant court life.

Alexandria was the jewel in the crown of that court (Figure 13). It lay on the westernmost mouth of the Nile, across Lake Mareotis. The old Egyptian city of Rhakotis had been refounded by Alexander the Great and named for him. It eventually grew to a city of 300,000 people under the Ptolemies. Lake Mareotis protected the site from the hottest of the Egyptian weather, giving it a Mediterranean climate. The city was divided into five districts. The Alpha and Beta districts made up the royal compound, which comprised a third of the city. The old Egyptian city of Rhakotis became the Gamma district, the native quarter. The Ptolemies encouraged a large Jewish migration to Alexandria, and Jews were used both in the administration and as crack mercenaries.[16] This Jewish population occupied its own area in the city, the Delta district. Finally, the Greek population settled into the swank suburban region of Eleusis (the Epsilon district).

The Ptolemies lavished their wealth on Alexandria. A great trade harbor was established behind the protective island of Pharos, on which sat the giant lighthouse that was one of the wonders of the ancient world. That harbor was the conduit for Egyptian trade and another source of royal revenue. The royal compound held palaces, its own harbor, docks, warehouses, barracks, and temples. Among the temples was the Sema, which housed the Sarcophagus of Alexander. It was the hijacking of Alexander's funeral cortege that had prompted the first War of the Successors. Ptolemy made the temple for Alexander's body, which also served as a talisman for his kingdom. Also, he established in the compound the Museum, a library and school of the Muses to rival Athens as a cultural center. Ptolemy and his heirs used culture as a diplomatic weapon, and it was his deliberate intent to make Alexandria the cultural center of the Hellenistic world. The Library grew to over a million works, including the original manuscripts of Aeschylus, Sophocles, Euripides, and Aristophanes. To a large extent, the survival of the ancient Greek literary heritage is the result of the Museum and the Ptolemies' efforts.

The central bureaucracy that ran the kingdom did so from Alexandria. There was a prime minister, or "*Dioiketes*," who supervised the various departments. It was staffed largely by Greek and Jewish scribes. There were few Egyptians involved at any level, except in the Egyptian priesthoods. The city administration had, at least initially, all the trappings of Greek government: a self-governing *boule* or council (which seems to disappear after Ptolemy I Soter); elected magistrates (who became appointed ones after Ptolemy I); a gymnasiarchal system for educating the Greek youth; and an ephebic corps to train them for the army.

At Alexandria, the Ptolemies strove to maintain their *persona* as Macedonian kings. Ptolemy, whichever Ptolemy, wore the traditional garb: the *kerausia* (or felt cap), the *chlamys* (or Macedonian military cloak), and the *stephanos* (or fillet crown). There were royal pages (*basilikoi paides*), royal huntsmen (*kynagidoi*), Companions (*Hetairoi*), and Foot Companions (*Pezetairoi*). There was no substance to the form, however. The institutions were empty symbols, for there was no assembly, and after Ptolemy I (over the next ten generations) only one Ptolemy ever again commanded his own troops in the field.

Nevertheless, those forces were considerable. The Ptolemies had relatively small but efficient armies of up to 30,000 men. About 15,000 were drawn from the Greco-Macedonian population of Egypt, and the remainder of the army was made up of mercenaries paid for by the Egyptian trade. The primary Ptolemaic arm was the navy, again made possible by its fabulous wealth. The Ptolemaic fleet at its height amounted to 1,200 vessels of all types. The Ptolemies went in for larger fleet vessels: septiremes (over twice the size of the traditional trireme) and decaremes, most of which were also cataphracts (or decked over to carry catapults and various armament). They even experimented with ships that had manpower ratios of twenty, thirty, and forty men on the oarlocks (see also Chapter 13 in this volume).

The underlying assumption, again, was that, at some point, one of the kingdoms would have the wherewithal to reunite Alexander's empire. That meant two areas of activity for the Ptolemies: against Antigonid Macedonia and against Seleukid Asia. Both of these required a fleet. Ptolemy I had established possessions in the Aegean islands and on the Asia Minor coastline, following the collapse of the Antigonid kingdom after the Battle of Ipsos in 301. These were organized into naval districts, each under its own nauarch, and assigned marines and a squadron to hold it. It is with this fleet that Ptolemy II kept probing

Greece for weaknesses against Antigonos Gonatas, an effort thwarted by Antigonos' victories in the battles of Kos and Andros.

The other area of Ptolemaic involvement was their rivalry with the Seleukids over the control of the land bridge area between Asia and Africa, what is now Lebanon, Israel, and Gaza. Ptolemy I had occupied the entire region up to the great bend of the Euphrates River immediately following the battle of Ipsos. But Seleukos claimed it as his territory. Quick communication with this area was necessary for Ptolemy and was facilitated by the Ptolemaic fleet, with their garrisons at ports like Sidon. Over the next century and a half, the Seleukids and Ptolemies would fight eight "Syrian" wars to try to settle the matter of control. For both of them, the ultimate goal of this was the first step in reuniting Alexander's empire. Success swayed back and forth between them, Egypt sometimes moving as far as Syria at several points and the Seleukids getting as far as the suburbs of Alexandria at one point late in the game.

So Ptolemaic Egypt remained in the hunt for empire. Its chief drawback was that it did not have a sufficient Greek population base to recruit an army that could challenge either Antigonid Macedonia or Seleukid Asia. In this regard, it was the weakest of the three kingdoms. But it held a secure territory and was immensely wealthy, advantages that saw it through to be the longest lasting of the all Hellenistic kingdoms.

SELEUKID ASIA

The last of the great Hellenistic monarchies was the House of Seleukos I Nikator, the longest lived and most successful of the Diadochoi. The Seleukids inherited the lion's share of Alexander's empire: Asia Minor, Syria, and Iran. This meant that the Seleukids had immense economic resources, both from dominating the traditional silk and spice routes to eastern Asia as well as from their own natural resources. They also had a much larger population, some fifty to sixty million people, and supported a much larger military establishment than the other kingdoms. Further, it was into the Seleukid territories that the vast majority of immigrants from the Greek homeland poured, settling into some eighty cities in Asia Minor and Mesopotamia. Equally, this meant that the Seleukids had a more massively diverse population than the other kingdoms.

The Seleukid approach to their large native population was the reverse of the Ptolemies. Of all the Macedonian officers who had married Iranian noblewomen at Alexander's great wedding feast at Susa in 324, only Seleukos had kept his bride, Apama, and she bore him his heir: Antiochos I. When Seleukos was assassinated in 281, Antiochos was already serving as joint king and now simply did so solely in his own name. Though the royal family did not continue to intermarry with native elites, a large part of their power base rested on intermarriage. When Alexander sent his 10,000 older veterans home to Macedonia with Krateros, he ordered them to leave their native wives and children behind so as not to cause undue turmoil among the families that awaited them in Macedonia. But Alexander promised to take care of these native families and raise the children as Macedonians. Seleukos kept that pledge and added newer Greek and Macedonian settlers to both of these groups. And others among the 10,000 Macedonian common soldiers who also had married at Susa stayed on in Asia as well. A population that can be identified as "Macedonian," but made up of the descendants of these groups, appears in the sources on the Seleukids down through the time of Antiochos III. From them, the Seleukids could field a phalanx armed and trained in the Macedonian fashion of up to 35,000 men, though of varying quality.

For the rest, the Seleukids likewise followed Alexander's lead more than either of the other two kingdoms. Natives served in the administration and the armed forces, just as they had under Alexander. Altogether, the Seleukids could employ a field army of around 80,000 men by the time of Antiochos III. The core of the army was the 35,000 man phalanx, the rest were native units serving in traditional fashion as linen-clad light infantry, archers, slingers, javelin men, or whatever. This meant that, overall, man for man, the army was not as effective as the Antigonid forces, but usually better than the Ptolemaic armies. And regardless, there were many more of them. On the other hand, Seleukids rarely ventured far into naval activity, with the notable exception of Antiochos III. Their need for a navy was almost nonexistent.

The problem for the Seleukids, both in terms of the economic and military resources, was that the kingdom was so large and required so much. It stretched from the Mediterranean to the Indus Valley in the beginning and had three capitals. The first was the old royal Persian residence at Susa, at the main pass through the Zagros Mountains to the Iranian Plateau, and from which they sought to govern Iran proper. The second was Seleukeia-on-the-Tigris, at the old site of the military camp at Opis, just above Babylon. This was the capital for the Mesopotamian heartland of the Seleukid monarch. The third was Antioch, in Syria, named for Antiochos I. It was the western center of administration for the kingdom and the territories claimed by Seleukos after the battle of Ipsos. It was also the territory in contention with the Ptolemies during the Syrian Wars.

The kingdom was too vast to be governed effectively with the resources the Seleukids had. This was recognized early on by Seleukos Nikator. In 305, Seleukos had negotiated a settlement with Chandragupta, an Indian adventurer who founded the Mauryan Empire. Seleukos gave up all claims to the three satrapies Alexander had envisaged for the Indus Valley, in exchange for a stable of war elephants and their breeding stock. Those elephants had helped win the day at Ipsos, but the settlement was a practical admission that Seleukos could not hold India any more than Alexander could. For that matter, the Seleukids came to the conclusion they could not maintain much of a presence in Iran proper either. They simply set up native satraps who paid tribute and made ceremonial obeisance to the Seleucid monarchy.

It was the drive to increase their manpower resources that prompted a massive resettlement and immigration program by the Seleukids, bringing people from Greece and Macedonian into Asia. There were dozens of city foundations throughout Asia Minor and Mesopotamia; some were named for the kings and queens of the dynasty, such as Seleukeia, Antioch, Apameia, and Laodikeia. Others reflect the areas from which the settlers came, such as Pella, Aigai, and Bottiaia (named for cities and districts in Macedonia). A few, such as Dura-Europus, were totally new foundations and wholly Macedonian initially. But most were based on existing communities, which were renamed, and the settlers were encouraged to intermarry with the local elites, following again the initial policy of Alexander.

Regardless of which particular method or origin, these settlers brought with them the basics of Greek culture, art, and education. Town councils were established in these cities along with gymnasiarchal education. Theaters were built along with temples, gymnasia, stadia, hippodromes, and Greek-style market places. The adaptation of Attic Greek known as Koine (or Common) Greek joined Aramaic as the language of trade and was the language of government as well. Macedonian traditions were kept intact. Citizenship was defined as holding land from the king in exchange for military service, and it was the definition used for the groups from which the phalanx was drawn. There are even vague references to an assembly (*hoi Makedones* – "the Macedonians"), but it was one that could have had not much more than a ceremonial function. The Seleukids themselves, as with the Ptolemies, continued to employ the Macedonian symbols of kingship and ceremonial dress. The court was filled with officials bearing the traditional Macedonian titles and functions. Unfortunately, for the Seleukids, this came with a penchant for court intrigue, dynastic plotting, and murder, which frequently destabilized the kingdom.

Despite all this, the essence of kingship here more than anywhere else was personal. For many of their subjects, the only thing they had in common was that they were governed by the Seleukids and were bound together only by the existence of the monarchy. This fostered the practice of ruler cult among the Seleukids. As mentioned earlier, this can be traced back to Alexander. It shows up among the Ptolemies as well, but there the native Egyptian strain is stronger. Pharaoh derived his legitimate rule from being the living incarnation of Ammon Ra. For the Ptolemies, therefore, to be legitimate in Egyptian eyes, they had to and did maintain this.

The Seleukids had to take a slightly different tack, and initially ruler cult grew out of the civic foundations of the Seleukid colonizing program. The cities recognized the king as their founder, much as Archaic Greek colonies had established hero cults for their founders (oikistai). By extension, the wider practice recognized the ruler for the same reasons as being a benefactor to his people. But it went a step further. For the Seleukids, it acknowledged the ruler as the very symbol of the state and established public services of thanksgiving celebrating the benefits of his rule. The form, as with Alexander, was to worship the ruler "as if he were a god," usually dropping incense on a burner before the royal image. Equally, crowns and other dedications served the same purpose. The practice of ruler cult will carry over to Rome and Augustus in the East for much the same reason as the Seleukids employed it. The act was, in fact, more patriotic than religious. But as Seleukid power waned in the second century, it was pushed to extremes by rulers such as Antiochos IV Epiphanes.

Actually, events began to chip away at Seleucid power from the point of Seleukos I's death. Philetairos, a eunuch and keeper of Lysimachos' treasury at Pergamon, transferred his loyalty (and the treasury) to Seleukos in 282. But with Seleukos' death, Philetairos became virtually independent, though nominally under Seleukid suzerainty. Pergamon was located about fifteen miles up the Kaikos River valley, and the region came to dominate the northwest area of Asia Minor, the old Troad. Having a treasury of as much as 80,000 talents was a good start, but Pergamon was equally a rich agricultural area specializing in fruit, wine, and sheep. Philetairos ruled it for seventeen years, building a fabulous royal residence in the upper citadel and a thriving city below it.

Philetairos was succeeded by his nephew, Eumenes I. With the aid of the Ptolemies, Eumenes formally broke from Seleukid control. When Eumenes died in 241, he was succeeded by his cousin, Attalos I, who will actually found the ruling dynasty: the Attalids. Pergamene policy was to imitate the kingship in the larger states in everything from cults to cultural politics. But the Attalid kingdom had been carved from Seleukid territory, and the Seleukids never forgot that nor accepted it. Further, the Seleukids had never fully established their authority over the interior of Asia Minor. Native monarchies, largely Hellenized, likewise adopted or adapted the Greek model of the Hellenistic monarchies. States such as Bithynia, Nikomedia, Cappodocia, and Pontos emerged along with Pergamon.

Equally, at the eastern end of the Seleucid dominions, there were similar problems. From Seleukos' time onward, control of the Iranian Plateau was nominal. But by the middle of the third century (traditionally by 247), a Scythian tribe called the Parni took over the satrapy of Parthia and began to extend their control over the Plateau. Though a problem in itself, this also cut off the area of Bactria. From Alexander's time on, there had been a heavy Greek settlement in the region. Alexander had founded as many as two dozen cities as part of his way of ending a bitter guerrilla war there. By the 230s, the Greek satrap of the region, Diodotos, had established an independent kingdom, buffered from the Seleukids by the Parthian kingdom.

Bactria was a rich agricultural region. It was watered by the Oxus and Jaxartes rivers, as well as a canal system (*qanat*), which carried water from the mountains. The Greek Bactrian kings built on this (and Alexander's foundations) a brilliant kingdom. Archaeological remains from this region are rich and extensive, the crown of which is Aï Khanum. These are the remains of a Hellenistic city on the Oxus that was probably the capital of the kingdom. Like Pergamon, and the Hellenized kingdoms of Asia Minor, Bactria became a small-scale model of the great Hellenistic monarchies.

At the end of the third century, Antiochos III the Great sought to reestablish Seleukid control of the region by driving out the Parthians (Parni), at which point the Bactrian king Euthydemos acknowledged Seleukid suzerainty (around 206). But control was still only nominal. After Antiochos III left, the Arsacid dynasty that ruled the Parni managed to take back their control first of Parthia, then of the whole Iranian Plateau in the second century. Euthydemos remained as king of Bactria throughout all of this. Barbarian invasions would displace the Bactrian kingdom further south in the second century and further west in the first century but the monarchy lasted at least to the end of the first century.

Despite the size of the Seleukid realm, then, their power was not so nearly as overwhelming as it might seem. For all intents and purposes, both the eastern and western ends of that realm established their virtual independence. The dynasty had to maintain and defend their far-flung dominions, which limited how much attention they could concentrate at any one time on Ptolemaic Egypt or Antigonid Macedonia. Still, the Seleukid heartland of Mesopotamia and Syria was a power to be reckoned with. It was prosperous, populous, and had the largest army in the Hellenistic East.

CONCLUSION: A BALANCE OF POWER

What emerged after the Wars of Succession was a rough balance of power among the three great Hellenistic monarchies. The Antigonids held the Macedonian homeland and maintained the traditions of Philip and Alexander, as well as their claim to empire. It was a goal, which at one point under Antigonos the One-Eyed, they had almost achieved. But the Antigonid economic resources couldn't compare with those of their rivals. Further, the Macedonian army, though excellent, was matched on the one hand by the disposable wealth of Egypt and the resources it could buy and on the other by the greater numbers of the Seleukid forces.

The Ptolemies held the most strategically secure territory in the Hellenistic World. They had immense treasuries and the means to renew them continually. This gave them an advantage, especially in the technological realm of naval warfare. But their overall manpower resources were small militarily, and they could neither match the Antigonids in quality nor the Seleukids in numbers.

The Seleukids had the greatest population and income. But their territories were so exposed and their internal lines of communication so extended that those resources were stretched too thin. Normally, they could not hope to challenge the Ptolemies at sea. As for the Antigonid Macedonia, it was too far away and at the end of a tenuous line of communication, as the events after the murder of Seleukos Nikator demonstrated, to be an effective target.

But the dream of Alexander's empire was still alive. All of these dynasties saw themselves as the direct heirs of Alexander. None of them had forgotten what Alexander had achieved, nor presumed that the balance of power would last forever. Indeed, by the end of the third century, it was arguably resolving itself. But the smaller Greek Hellenistic states, for whom the balance of power meant freedom and autonomy, sought to prolong things by asking for Roman aid. Ultimately that changed everything.

Bibliographical Note

For basic topics and bibliography, a good place to start is *The Cambridge Ancient History*, 2nd edn., Vol. VII.1, edited by F. W. Walbank et al., Cambridge, 1984. See also Will (1979–1982) and P. Green, *Alexander to Actium: The Historical Evolution of the Hellenistic Age*, Berkeley, 1990.

For the period of the Diadochi and individual figures in the formation of the kingdoms: Anson (2004); Billows (1990); Ellis (1994); Gabbert (1997); Tarn (1913, reprint, 1969); Grainger (1990); Landucci Gattinoni (2003); Lund (1992). On the formation and history of the kingdoms, and related topics: Allen (1983); Hansen (1947); Bagnall (1976); Bevan (1927, reprint, 1989) and (1902), dated but useful; Billows (1995); Cohen (1978) and (1995); Fraser (1972) and (1996); Holt (1999); Hölbl (2001); Lerner (1999).

Notes

1 Unless otherwise noted, all dates in this chapter may be assumed to be B.C.

2 The exact nature of Arrhidaios' problem has never been satisfactorily explained. Plutarch variously refers to him as of "unsound mind" (*Alex.* 10.2), a "half wit" (*Alex.*77.5) and "acting like a child" (*De. Fort. Alex.*,337 DE). Diodorus refers to an incurable mental illness (18.2.2).

3 Through Antipatros, virtually all of the dynasts were bound in marriage. His daughter Phila married Krateros, and after his death, Demetrios Poliorketes, the son of Antigonos the One-Eyed. Her son by Demetrios was Antigonos Gonatas, who established the permanent Antigonid hold on Macedonia. Another daughter, Eurydike, married Ptolemy, only to be put aside and have her son by him (Ptolemy Keraunos) disinherited. Ptolemy Keraunos would assassinate Seleukos I Nikator. A third daughter, Nikaia, was married to Perdikkas and later to Lysimachos of Thrace.

4   Neither Seleukos nor Kassandros remained long at the court, certainly not after 322, as neither was caught up in the coming struggle between Antipatros and Perdikkas.

5   Kleopatra was the widow of Alexander of Epiros. She had offered her hand, probably at the suggestion of Olympias, to Leonnatos in 322, but he died that same year. Olympias was clearly the instigator of the offer to Perdikkas. After Perdikkas' death, Kleopatra lived quietly at Sardes in Asia Minor until 309. In that year, she quarreled with Antigonos the One-Eyed and tried to flee to Ptolemy. Antigonos captured and killed her.

6   Following the siege of Pydna, Kassandros put Olympias on trial for the murder of his brother and over 100 Macedonian nobles. She was found guilty and executed by the victims' relatives. Recent excavations at Pydna may have revealed the bodies of her victims. Later that year (316), Kassandros married a daughter of Philip II, Alexander's half sister Thessalonike.

7   The ancient sources are unanimous in stating that the murder was done in secret (probably in 311) and kept secret for an indefinite time (Diod. 19.105.2–3; Paus. 9.7.2; and Justin 15.2.2). That lasted at least until 310/9 based on the listing of Alexander IV's death on the *Marmor Parium* (Jacoby, *FGrH* II B n. 239 F B 18, p. 1008). The burial at Vergina must have occurred shortly after the death became public knowledge. The identification of the remains in Tomb III as Alexander IV is speculation, as there is no inscription or literary source, but there really is no other candidate and the forensic evidence makes it likely.

8   He had previously been married to Kassandros' sister, Nikaia. Now Lysimachos married Ptolemy's daughter Arsinoe, whose mother, Berenike, had displaced Antipatros' daughter Eurydike and her children at Ptolemy's court. It was Arsinoe's goal to do the same for Nikaia's children.

9   Agathokles was Lysimachos' son by Nikaia. This was the culmination of the plotting by Arsinoe.

10 Pyrrhos of Epiros would normally have been a viable choice, but he was fighting the Romans in Italy in 279 and would not return until 275. As a result Pyrrhos was temporarily out of the picture. When he did return, he and Antigonos fought for three years up and down the length of Greece until Pyrrhos was killed in 272 at Argos.

11 An inscription with the formula "King Antigonos [III Doson] and the Macedonians decree...." has been found at Delos [*Syll.*³ 518=*IG* XI.3, 1097], and four other inscriptions refer to the ruler as "king of the Macedonians" rather than "king of Macedonia." The exact meaning of this phase has been debated in the secondary literature, but this is outside the scope of this chapter.

12 Philip had established a "hero" cult for his father, Amyntas III, and was "flirting" with divinity in the Festival of the Olympians at which he was murdered. Alexander, of course, had issued a decree at the Olympic Games in 324 requiring that he be worshipped as if he were a god. As I noted earlier, the Athenians had accorded "divine" honors to the Antigonids as "Savior Gods" after the liberation of Athens.

13 Quintus Cicero, the great orator's brother and Roman governor of the province of Macedonia, remarked in a letter to Marcus that the northern borders of the province were the very swords and spear points of his legionaries.

14 Most Hellenistic monarchs had nicknames, sometimes given to them whether they liked it or not, such as Demetrios Poliorketes, sometimes with totally obscure meanings as with Antigonos II Gonatas. The Ptolemies chose them consciously, and in this case, "Soter" referred to a traditional appellation for Zeus, "Savior."

15 The Rosetta Stone, which provided the key to translate hieroglyphics, was a thanksgiving dedication honoring Ptolemy V Epiphanes for restoring a traditional Egyptian temple.

16 The key garrison at Elephantine at the First Cataract was Jewish.

3: THE *POLIS* AND FEDERALISM

D. Graham J. Shipley with Mogens H. Hansen

❦

THE *POLIS* IN THE CLASSICAL PERIOD AND AFTER

Classical Hellas – both Old Greece and the wider world of Hellenic colonies in the Mediterranean and Black Seas – has often been called "a world of cities" and with good reason. The *polis* (city-state; plural *poleis*) was one of the central institutions of Greek society. Yet, modern historians have sometimes claimed that there was a fundamental change in the Hellenistic period. It has even been asserted that "the" *polis* ceased to exist – perhaps at the battle of Chaironeia (338), at the end of the Lamian war (321), at some point during the wars of the Successors (323–281), at the end of the Chremonidean war (ca. 262),[1] or after the defeat of the Achaian league by Rome (146).

In the face of these rather black-and-white views, recent scholarship has taken a different line. Greek cities, as physical and social entities, patently remained in use and continued to be built throughout the Hellenistic period and beyond. More importantly, the social entity that was the classical *polis* did not lose all its defining features. Rather, it was transformed in practice. As a model, or concept, of social organization, its components were modified in different ways at different times.

The latter claim applies in different degrees, depending on geographical area. The preexisting *poleis* of "Old Greece" and the Aegean were now mostly dominated (to a greater or lesser degree) by overlords of Macedonian descent, who from the last years of the fourth century were usually styled kings. These men could, if they wished, exercise considerable influence over the future development of a *polis* and restrict its freedom of action. At Athens, this was clearly the case during phases of unfreedom. The inhabitants of new *poleis*, however, that had been built on the orders of a king or dynast (mainly in western

Asia but also in Greece) would have less power to shape their physical form or formulate high-level policy. Other *poleis* again remained outside Alexander's former empire (such as in the Black Sea, Sicily, and southern Italy) and were generally no more and no less free than before – at least, if it was so, it was not because of the new Macedonian kingdoms far away in the eastern Mediterranean. In Sicily, the Greek *poleis* were dependencies of the dominant one, Syracuse. In southern Italy, though the *poleis* may have remained independent, several lost their Hellenic status in the course of this period and came to be regarded as "barbarian" communities.[2] There were perhaps three or four different "worlds of the *polis*," not one. The idea that there was such a thing as "the hellenistic city" is an oversimplification.[3]

To characterize the degree of change in the reality and the concept of the *polis* in the hellenistic period, we should first define what a *polis* was in the preceding, "classical" period. Examination of classical sources reveals great consistency in the use of the term *polis*. The Greeks regarded a community as a *polis* if it had a distinct urban centre (however small) and was organized in conformity with a particular sociopolitical model.[4] When he was away from home, a free Hellene was defined in terms of the *polis* of which he was a member. He used an *ethnikon* (ethnic or *polis* name) alongside his given name: *Xenophôn Athênaios*, "Xenophon of Athens." In his home *polis*, his private and public life revolved around other members of the *polis*. He took part in its life in virtue of his status as *politês*, "citizen" (plural *politai*). He was subject to its laws and had, in principle, some say in framing them. In some cities, he was likely to have to be a landowner to be a citizen at all; in others, citizenship extended further down the economic ladder. Women and children of the citizen family were defined in relation to their menfolk.

Cities were thus, in most important respects, the organizing social principle of Hellenic society, the setting for many of the cultural innovations we associate with ancient Greece – philosophy, drama, poetry, participatory politics, and so on. It is true that art and architecture did not develop exclusively in and for *poleis* but also in formal cult places outside *poleis*, as did sporting competitions between members of different communities. These cult places, however, were part of the world of the *polis*, because each belonged to one particular *polis*, even if that *polis* belonged to a larger unit, such as a federal union of *poleis*. Even the few cult places, such as Olympia and Delphi, that we recognize as "international" – their use being shared by all *poleis* – were located in the territory of one *polis* (Elis in the case of Olympia, Delphi itself in the other case) and to a greater or lesser extent were under the control of that *polis*.

There were, of course, rural populations in the classical Greek world, for agriculture was the foundation of the economy. Traces of many anonymous outlying settlements have been found by archaeological field surveys. They tend to be small, however. Contrary to what is generally believed about the classical *polis*, it is likely that a majority of the population lived in urban units (often rather small ones). In small and middle-sized *poleis*, the vast majority of *poleis*, many people who worked the land had their home in the town and spent only part of their time in the countryside, often walking several miles to their fields each day.[5] This situation is typical of what historians call "city-state cultures."[6] Agriculture was supplemented by pastoralism and other means of exploiting the rural landscape.[7] From a human–geographical or ecological–historical point of view the town–country divide may be regarded as artificial, because it is perfectly possible to analyse the ancient world as a single, discontinuously peopled landscape.[8] It remains the case, however, that most or all of the communal institutions that had most influence on social life, politics, and economic activity were located in towns.

In older *poleis*, the element of continuity between classical and early Hellenistic times is strong.[9] Gender relations, attitudes to non-Greeks, commercial practices, art, architecture, philosophy – all these sides of life and culture evolved, but evolution was not a new characteristic: They had been changing in the fourth century and long before that. It is not the fact of change as such that distinguishes the early Hellenistic period. Politics within the *polis* continued much as before. In most *poleis*, whether strongly democratic or less so, the landed élite dominated political society and public office, just as they had in classical Athens. There were few revolutionary upheavals (the main example is Sparta in the 220s), and there is no evidence that the Macedonian rulers of Greece attempted to reshape *polis* societies and economies for their own ends. The old cities negotiated their relationship with kings formally on the basis of equality: They were effectively states within states.[10] Rather, it is the *context* of the *polis* that makes the difference. What had been – ideally – autonomous and free *poleis* became more or less subject communities that a king might try to bend to his will. In new *poleis*, too, there were strong similarities in institutions and physical form between them and their older counterparts; indeed, many new cities were more advanced.[11]

PHYSICAL LAYOUTS

One familiar characteristic of newly built, or rebuilt, Hellenistic *poleis* is the formality of their street plan.[12] This is true, for example, of towns with a primarily military role, such as Halos in Thessaly[13] or nearby Gorítsa, built by Demetrios Poliorketes as a military strongpoint.[14] At Aï Khanum in Afghanistan, perhaps founded by Alexander himself as one of his Alexandrias, Hellenic and local architectural styles were combined within a basically Greek town plan.[15] The most famous of the Alexandrias, the one in (or "by") Egypt, is an example of town planning on a grand scale (see following discussion). It seems that town builders – who may have been military men as often as they were architects – were working from a sort of pattern-book, a template of how a town should look. Often, they had an eye to security, not just building a viable urban community; often, in such places, the new citizens may have been retired soldiers or reservists. It is important to acknowledge, however, that Hellenistic grid-planned layouts evolved out of classical designs.[16] Sometimes, an earthquake or violent destruction may have given an opportunity to lay out a town on a new alignment with new buildings, as happened at Samos.[17] Although new or rebuilt *poleis* were sometimes more advanced in their design than others, the fundamentals of town planning had already been created in the Archaic and Classical periods.[18] In some smaller towns (e.g., Kassope, Gorítsa, Halos), there was a reversion to the elongated grid units of early western Greek colonies. This may indicate that, in these instances, a lower priority was given to urban amenity and a higher priority to maximizing the number of defenders who could be housed in a given fortified area.

Conversely, in towns whose military function was not predominant we often find an increasing elaboration of private houses. Until the fourth century, a rich citizen was generally expected not to show off his wealth by building a grand mansion, but from the later fourth century onwards we find that the private dwelling becomes a status symbol.[19] The house evolves into the late Hellenistic "peristyle" house, with a colonnaded courtyard, as in many examples from Delos and the notable courtyard house on the harbour *akropolis* at Samos.[20]

Grid planning and élite houses were increasingly accompanied by monumental public buildings, particularly in large towns. The market-place or *agora*, for example, was often framed with monumental stoas and made into a rectangular space, as at Miletos[21] or Athens (see following discussion). Yet stoas also became a regular feature of middle-ranking and small *poleis*, too. The author of a third-century travelogue of central Greece (possibly Herakleides "the Critic" or "the Cretan"), in a possibly tongue-in-cheek description of central Greece, notes that Boiotian Anthedon "has an *agora* all planted with trees and enclosed by double stoas" (ch. 23), whereas Chalkis on Euboia is articulated with "*gymnasia*, stoas, shrines, theatres, paintings (*graphai*), statues, and the agora incomparably arranged for professional business" (28).[22] Stoas had been part of the Greek urban and religious landscape since the seventh century (e.g., at the archaic Heraion at Samos),[23] though the earliest built for political purposes may have been the Royal Stoa at Athens (ca. 500).[24] Now, however, they became *de rigueur* for a *polis*, and a grand city might have many. Athens had at least twenty-two, mostly built during the Hellenistic period.[25]

The council-house (*bouleuterion*) became a specialized variety of building for the first time.[26] Approximately half of the permanent stone theatres attested in written or archaeological evidence from across the Greek world are of Hellenistic date.[27] During the late Classical and Hellenistic periods, the *gymnasion* was moved from the suburbs into the urban centre and monumentalized.[28] Its importance as a *polis* institution can be judged by a lengthy second-century inscription from Beroia in Macedonia (*SEG* 27.261),[29] which preserves a detailed law about the *gymnasion* and its personnel. The law implies clear status divisions between citizens and noncitizens and defines distinct entitlements for different age groups and severe penalties for infringements. An additional resolution of the assembly stipulates that "since … in *poleis* in which there are *gymnasia* and anointing (*with olive oil*) is an established practice, the gymnasiarchic laws are laid up in the public things (i.e., *in the archives*), it is well that the same should be accomplished among us (lines 6–9)." The concern with emulating other *poleis* shows that a well-regulated *gymnasion* was essential if a city was to keep its reputation high.

Some changes in the urban fabric reflected the city's relationship with outside powers. City walls continued to be built in the third century, though fewer than in the fourth. In the Peloponnese, for example, urban fortifications were built at Sparta;[30] Argolic Asine; Arkadian Psophis, Teuthis and probably Thisoa; Lakonian Geronthrai; and probably Achaian Leontion. In some cases, they were erected by outside military powers as part of a military strategy. Some rural towers and forts were also built. The notable change comes in the second century, when almost no urban or rural fortifications were constructed.

Relationships with outside powers were also reflected in more peaceful alterations to urban layouts. The Athenian *agora* and even the

Akropolis increasingly became the site of competitive benefaction by
rich foreign statesmen (see following discussion). We do not know
where exactly the Macedonian garrisons at Chalkis or Corinth had
their quarters; probably on the fortified akropolis of each place. No new
structures may have been necessary to accommodate them. But if the
polis was the residence of a prince or governor, there would be a palace.[31]

Other changes in urban form become apparent after the Roman
takeover. The differences between the early Hellenistic and the late
Hellenistic to early Roman *polis* are obvious in terms of physical appearance. In the first century B.C., city walls were no longer built and normally not even repaired.[32] The reason is probably the more peaceful
conditions after the Roman conquest: Walls were no longer needed.
It may be that such changes reflected the financial hardship suffered by
many Greek *poleis* in the first century B.C., as well as perhaps the beginnings of more restrictive rule by Rome after the mid-second century. In
Athens, however, the elaboration of the city centre may have continued
right down to the Mithridatic war and the siege by Sulla (87–85), if
the Tower of the Winds is rightly dated to the second half of the second century.[33] The *pax Romana* may also explain the growing number
of villages in Greece in the Hellenistic period: People did not have to
cluster together behind the walls as they did in Archaic and Classical
times. The *polis* was now less important as a source of protection.

INTERNAL POLITICAL AND CIVIC INSTITUTIONS

To generalize about "the Hellenistic city" is difficult, but one area in
which we can legitimately do so is in the matter of constitutions. During the late fourth and third centuries, in new *poleis* and in old *poleis*
reorganized at the behest of a liberator or conqueror, standard-issue,
Athenian-style institutions were usually installed: assembly, magistrates,
and probouleutic council. These constitutions were often called democratic. Arrian, for example, says Alexander abolished oligarchies in Ionia
and replaced them with "democracies" (*Anabasis* 1.17.8, 1.18.2). Thus,
the former spectrum of constitutions was almost reduced to a single
type: *demokratia* prevailed, whereas *tyrannis* and *oligarchia* were eclipsed.
The early Hellenistic period was thus, at least in a formal sense, the
heyday of democracy.

It is true that there were episodes of tyranny. The historian Douris
was tyrant of Samos for a time, probably acting on behalf of the

Antigonids and later Lysimachos.[34] A number of *poleis* in the northern Peloponnese endured "tyrannies" under Macedonian domination in the early third century.[35] These regimes, however, were probably in most or all cases short-lived governorships given to men who exercised power on behalf of Macedonia. They were probably not politically oppressive; Douris outlived his patron, Lysimachos, apparently continuing to reside in Samos, and in the mid-third century Peloponnese, several former tyrants were rehabilitated as respected public figures and military leaders. It is a reasonable guess that, during the years when they acted as tyrants, they did not seriously interfere with the constitution.

Moreover, it is increasingly accepted that, in most *poleis*, most of the time, the assembly was sovereign and magistrates were popularly elected.[36] Where there were working assemblies, they continued to deal with finance, food supply, defence, international relations, and legislation – the very areas of jurisdiction Aristotle had defined as most important for a citizen assembly (*Rhetoric* 1.1359b–1360a).[37] In Athens, the democracy remained alive and well, though with interruptions, down to the early first century B.C.[38]

In most other cities, however, it seems that democracy was not necessarily the same in practice as the universal, popular, once radical democracy of Athens. In the late fourth century, Aristotle (*Politics* 4. 8–9) advocated a mixed constitution, which he called *politeia* (meaning simply "constitution" or "constitutional government"). It combined the better features, as he saw them, of both democracy and oligarchy, including a (low) property qualification for admission to the assembly and to public office but also including, for example, payment to the poor for jury service. Though he does not call his system "democracy," it seems probable that in the third century the term was no longer limited to "pure" democracies, those with universal citizen franchise. Indeed, P. J. Rhodes has remarked that in the Hellenistic period "it is not apparent that states which use the word *demokratia* are necessarily more democratic than states which do not," and that from the second century "there are cases in which the word *demokratia* has been debased."[39]

Some *poleis* explicitly claimed to be democratic. Smyrna (*IK Smyrna* 573 = *OGIS* 229; shortly after 243 B.C.), at the time when it absorbed its neighbour Magnesia, stated that its democratic constitution would admit all free Greek Magnesians. Some *poleis* explicitly distanced themselves from oligarchy. A decree of Ilion (*IK Ilion* 25 = *OGIS* 218; early third century or ca. 197) was designed to protect the democracy against both oligarchy and tyranny. Similarly, Kos, when absorbing

Kalymna (*Tituli Calymnii* pp. 9–10 T XII; ca. 205–200 B.C.,) made the citizens forswear both oligarchy and tyranny. The Erythraians referred to a previous regime as an oligarchy (*IK Erythrai* 503 = *Syll.*[3] 284; ca. 300).[40] So did the Athenians, in documents referring back to the time before 287, when they were ruled oppressively by Demetrios Poliorketes.[41] In such circumstances, we can reasonably assume that "democracy" means full democracy with no wealth qualification. In other cases, perhaps the majority, it may not be so, and we may be seeing the extension of the word "democracy" to embrace what an Athenian might have called a (broadly based) oligarchy.

One problem is that, even when a decree has been made by an assembly, we cannot tell whether participation in the assembly was open to all citizens or whether the *polis* had a property qualification. Rhodes (1997) however, thinks we can assume the assembly is usually open to all "even if access to the council and to offices was formally restricted" (p. 533). More seriously perhaps, it is not usually possible to tell whether the assembly was a forum for real debate or merely an instrument for "rubber-stamping." Even if assemblies were open, we may suspect – particularly in the Peloponnese, whose *poleis* were mostly oligarchic at earlier times[42] – that richer citizens exercised undue influence. In certain places, such as the *polis* of Elis, there is no evidence at all for an assembly.[43] Even in democratic Samos, we can observe a narrow group of families dominating the list of proposers of decrees, holders of public office, and so on; the political class may also have become narrower through the third century.[44]

Despite these qualifications, Gauthier denies that democracy in the Hellenistic period was a bastardized (*abâtardie*) form.[45] Élite domination of politics is not necessarily a derogation from democracy, for even in fifth-century Athens, the higher offices had been dominated by the élite and most orators were from the upper class. Neither a passive assembly nor the monopolization of public office by the wealthier members of society detracts from democracy as such. The change that took place in the early Hellenistic period may be that people were prepared to call a *polis* democratic, even if it excluded the poor (often a minority of free men) from voting.

Decrees from many cities show that the political traditions of a *polis* could remain vital under the domination of the post-Alexander monarchies. Although cities might find themselves constrained in their foreign policy, they could continue to function as decision making communities in almost exactly the same way as before. Despite the apparent dilution of "democracy," there appears to have been a much wider diffusion of formalized public decision making. This only changed with the Roman takeover in the second century.

POLIS SOCIETY

Hellenistic *poleis* no longer organized their own military forces as a means of putting state policy into practice. They contributed to the military forces of their overlord and subsidized his garrison if he installed one in the city. They maintained defence forces and fortifications, both urban and rural, primarily for purposes of defence or, with royal support, as part of a king's strategy. The institution of the *ephebeia*, unknown before the fourth century, was therefore now the most important public institution. It existed at Athens in the first half of the fourth century (Aeschines 2.167)[46] and was redesigned and extended in 336. It had probably existed in a less defined form earlier, both here and in other *poleis*.[47] In Athens, it was a system for giving eighteen- and nineteen-year-old boys two years' military training, concluding with a period of service in the frontier forts that were an increasingly important feature of Attic "forward defence" in the fourth and third centuries. In Athens and probably elsewhere, the *ephebeia* became élitist and was focused on intellectual training, reflecting the increased visibility of élites who were no longer subject to the restraints of the classical period, when they had tended to veil their wealth, not flaunt it.[48] The *ephebeia* was centred in the *gymnasion*, a structure that became one of the standard institutions of a new or modernized *polis* in the Hellenistic period.[49]

Socioeconomic change in the *polis* is not directly documented with statistical records, but can be inferred from a number of indicators. In various parts of Old Greece, more land and wealth seem to have been concentrated in the hands of the élite, in tandem with a probable limitation of the franchise (though not usually at Athens) and the changes in rural settlement attested by field survey data. In the former Persian empire, a similar process left control of the landscape, directly or indirectly, in the hands of a new nonindigenous élite. They were probably more numerous than the non–native military and administrative class had been under the Persian imperial system, because the new monarchs habitually founded military colonies. The economy of the Hellenistic world was in general more integrated by long-distance trade,[50] which ought to imply that a greater proportion of the population was involved in maritime trade and, perhaps, earning a good livelihood from it. These potentially upwardly mobile persons, however, may not have enjoyed high status or political influence, except at cosmopolitan centres such as Athens and Rhodes or in traditional trading towns like Samos and Thasos.

Archaeological field survey in Greece points to a change in relations with the *chora*, evidenced by a fall in the numbers of small rural sites in many parts of Old Greece, though at different times in different regions, between 300 and 100 B.C.[51] This change need not indicate a reduction in the use of the agricultural landscape, but it could be evidence of an alteration in how it was managed: larger estates, fewer owners, a change in the balance of crops grown, and an increase in dependent labouring groups, perhaps free or semi-free. The latter groups may have lived in residences too poorly equipped to be archaeologically visible today or in rented accommodation in towns from which they travelled out to the fields to work (perhaps residing in the countryside at certain seasons). Again, this fits the picture of economic polarization and political exclusion. In Attica, a particular version of the change is seen, with a diminution in the epigraphic record, and perhaps the prosperity, of the major demes and an increasing focus on defending the agricultural territory using forces deployed from border forts.[52]

During the Hellenistic period, women's place in the *polis* came to be no longer confined to religion. In many *poleis*, rich women made public benefactions in their own name or held public offices that entailed expenditure by the individual on behalf of the *polis*, particularly when no citizen male of adequate means was available to do the job.[53] Women's names in inscriptions are more commonly accompanied by subethnic names (including demotics or "deme names"), indicating a greater degree of integration in the *polis*. Changes in a woman's relationships within her marital family appear to be evidenced by grave-goods from Athens.[54] By Roman times, élite households appear to have had a more relaxed attitude about controlling women as shown by the way domestic space was arranged.[55]

The *polis* was not a society of adult male citizens to the same extent as before. A cosmopolitan society was no new thing, at least in large *poleis*; the general population of Athens, for example, had included many noncitizens and non-Greeks ever since the days of its imperial hegemony in the fifth century. In many *poleis* during the Hellenistic and Roman periods, however, a significant number of free foreigners were admitted to the *ephebeia*; examples include Athens (*IG* ii² 1961, etc.), Eretria (*IG* xii. 9.234), and Sestos (*OGIS* 339.85–6).[56] The coexistence of different ethnic groups and their religions was normal in Greek *poleis*, though it might be going too far to suppose that those differences were celebrated. In Delos, at any rate, non-Greek cults were frequently permitted to take a monumental form. The largest of three sanctuaries of Sarapis on Delos, dating to the second century, had a colonnaded courtyard more than 70 m long.[57] Cults of other Egyptian deities were located in the same area, and nearby stood a sanctuary of several Syrian deities, built in the Greek style[58] and having its own priest. Epigraphic evidence shows worshippers with both Greek and non-Greek names making dedications to both Greek and other deities. Besides other non-Greek sanctuaries, the Jews had a synagogue on Delos. Delos, with its cosmopolitan atmosphere and thriving port, was a very untypical *polis*; but in many other cities, there were non-Greek cults (which had begun to be brought in from abroad long before the Hellenistic period). To the cults of the old gods and heroes were now added new cults of monarchs and deified abstractions, such as *homonoia* or Tyche.[59]

The civic subdivisions into which the citizenry had been organised had faded in importance.[60] Now, however, citizens and noncitizens within a *polis* often formed associations united by commercial, cultic, or ethnic interests.[61] International associations flourished, such as the actors' union, "the artists (*technitai*) of Dionysos."[62]

EXTERNAL RELATIONSHIPS

Several of Alexander's Successors, perhaps starting with Polyperchon in 319 (Diod. 18.55–6), proclaimed their support for Greek "freedom"; but behind such proclamations there often lay the actual or implied threat of coercion. As Diodorus reports elsewhere (19.61), the successive declarations by Antigonos and Ptolemy in 314 that the Greeks should be "free, exempt from garrisons, and autonomous" were a recognition that one could not advance one's cause without the support of the Greek cities – "to gain the goodwill of the Greeks would carry no little weight," he says. A city's relationship with the Successor, or eventually a king, was the most important relationship it could have. Royal power was not absolute; kings often had to earn the support of cities, and cities could sometimes turn this to their advantage.[63]

In the Classical period, independence (*autonomia*) was not an indispensable feature of the concept of the *polis*.[64] Now, at the very time when most *poleis* were dependent rather than independent,[65] *autonomia* became the explicit ideal and goal of the *polis*. Kings often declared that cities were free and autonomous; therefore *autonomia* no longer meant independence but something like self-government or, as we might say, "autonomy" in the limited sense in which we refer to "autonomous regions" of European Union states. Kings claimed the right to bestow freedom or take it away, just as they could impose taxes on a city or waive them. The formalized transactions of a city–king relationship both institutionalized the empire and enshrined the protection and privileges that a city would enjoy.[66]

One important change in the relationship between the *polis* and its landscape is that, by the late Hellenistic period, we see a greater prominence of village-type settlements in the territories of many *poleis*. Authors such as Strabo and Pausanias refer to many more *komai*, second-order urban settlements, than archaic and classical sources do.[67] Partly this is a reflection of an increase in the quantity of evidence for formerly outlying parts of the Greek world, such as northwest Greece or Asia Minor, where villages had always been common. Partly, however, it embodies a change in the significance of the *polis*, which for many Greeks was no longer the principal community in a landscape.

A growing cooperation between *poleis* resulted in an institutionalised network of relations, such as mutual citizenship or *isopoliteia*, or the use of arbitrators from another *polis* to resolve disputes between citizens or between two *poleis*.[68] There was increased participation in the growing number of international festivals that were accompanied by contests. Cities would recognize one another's festivals, appointing *theorodokoi* ("envoy-receivers") to entertain sacred envoys (*theoroi*) sent out by the organizers in advance of a major festival. This practice had begun in the fourth century but became more frequent in the third.[69] The mutual recognition of sacred inviolability (*asylia*) was another diplomatic institution that increasingly brought cities into contact with one another, often at great distances.[70]

A particular variety of interstate association was the federal league (*koinon*, literally "common thing," i.e., community). Several notable leagues rose to prominence as a means of securing protection for small city-states against larger powers. The Aitolian and Achaian leagues played major roles in the Romans' wars during the later third and earlier second centuries. There were classical precedents for regional leagues, such as the long-lived Boiotian confederacy and the Arkadian league of the 360s.

The Aitolian league itself existed by the 360s and, like the others just mentioned, was based on the preexisting ethnic unity asserted by the *poleis* of a region. By the early Hellenistic period, the league had an annual *strategos*, a standing council made up of representatives from each *polis* in proportion to their size, and a central committee of *apoklêtoi* ("men called out"). There was a central cult place for the league, at Thermon.[71] The league came to dominate the Delphic amphiktiony, the ancient board of management for the sanctuary and a source of great prestige and influence. In expanding its membership to include ethnic groups other than Aitolians, using the device of *isopoliteia*,[72] the league set a precedent for others (one inscription, for example, details the incorporation of Chios).[73] The league receives a bad press from hostile writers who view it from the standpoint of more prosperous parts of Greece, but its reputation has been restored in recent times. Although some scholars (surely with the benefit of hindsight) regret that it did not develop further, others point out that it was noted for resolving internal disputes by negotiation, and it maintained internal peace for many decades.[74]

The Achaian league, likewise based on an earlier association, was refounded around 280 (Polybios 2.37–8)[75] and rapidly grew from its original membership of twelve small *poleis* in the northern Peloponnese that were bent on driving out the Macedonians. By the early second century, it included the majority of southern Greek *poleis*. Polybios, the son of an Achaian league statesman from Arkadian Megalopolis, exaggerated the degree of unification between its members, even comparing it to a single *polis*. It had central institutions similar to those of the Aitolians,[76] but although the members issued currency on a common standard, they also kept their own laws, as is common in confederations in later periods. A closer look reveals that some members were coerced into joining and that its leaders were particularly concerned about the possibility of land reform spreading from Sparta to the rest of the Peloponnese. This suggests that the league, like other federal unions throughout history, reflected the class-based character of its member states and was used by élites as a means of maintaining their social position.[77]

Examples of many of the changes outlined thus far can be seen in two "megapoleis"[78] of the Greek world, one old and one new. Without dwelling on every detail, a closer look at Alexandria and Athens will allow slightly more rounded sketches of living urban societies.

CASE STUDY: ALEXANDRIA

Alexandria, whose foundation was reportedly a personal project of Alexander's, replaced Memphis as the centre from which Egypt was administered and became the greatest city in the eastern Mediterranean.[79] Though, like Pergamon, it is hardly a typical *polis*, it exemplifies on a grand scale many of the changes that took place in *poleis* across the Hellenistic world. It was a Greek city in a non-Greek landscape, though officially it was not in Egypt but "by Egypt." Its civic structure was based on Athens, with hereditary citizenship, deme membership, an assembly, a council, and elected magistrates. Ptolemy I claimed for it preeminence in the world by kidnapping Alexander's mummified body and putting it in a spectacular tomb, subsequently elaborated by Ptolemy IV into the Sema ("monument") where both Alexander and the Ptolemaic kings were buried.

The showpiece capital for the Macedonian successors to the pharaohs grew rapidly in both size and population. Its areal extent, and those of its harbours, overshadowed all other Greek cities,[80] and its urban plan was the grandest in the contemporary world. Set out according to the most up-to-date urbanistic principles, apparently to Alexander's own specifications (Arrian, *Anabasis* 3.1), its plan comprised some 120 large rectangular blocks of varying shape.[81] A typical block was approximately square, with sides measuring ca. 400 m and an area of ca. 16 ha (40 acres). Some blocks were reserved entirely for public precincts and royal buildings, and even the grandeur of Alexandria's main streets excited admiration (Strabo 17.1.8). Until recently, its detailed layout was imperfectly known,[82] but knowledge is now being amassed through an active programme of investigation on land and under the sea.[83] This has revealed specific monuments, such as the foundations of the famous lighthouse (the Pharos) and parts of the harbour complexes. We know that the city was larger than was previously thought, having possibly been inundated by the seas in Roman times.[84]

Under Ptolemy II, Alexandria became a centre of high culture (see Fig. 13 in Chapter 8). Under royal patronage, the Museum and library fostered many new kinds of literature,[85] scholarship, and science.[86] Festivals such as the Ptolemaieia (initially in honour of Ptolemy I, posthumously deified; later in honour of all the kings and queens of the dynasty) attracted participants from all over the eastern half of the Mediterranean, including Ptolemies' many Greek subject territories (see, e.g., the decree of Samos for its envoy Boulagoras, *SEG* 1.366).[87] The Ptolemaieia were recognized as "isolympic" (see the decree of the league of Islanders ca. 280, *Syll.*[3] 390). The late Greek author Athenaios, using contemporary information, described in great detail Ptolemy II's procession in 271/0, which cost over 2,000 talents (5.201b–f).[88]

The population was partly made up of Greek émigrés, as well as those who had done well in royal service and were rewarded with fine houses in the city. As well as Greeks, there were many noncitizen groups, such as Egyptians, Syrians, and Jews, the last of whom had special privileges. It is hard to know how typical are the sentiments voiced by a Greek woman in Theokritos's fifteenth *Idyll*, who expressed casual disdain towards Egyptians *en masse* ("ants, numberless and uncounted").

The city was founded on the spoils of war, but was kept alive by trade through what was now the greatest harbour in the Mediterranean. Inward trade brought imports from the Greek world and the entire eastern Mediterranean world, presumably mainly for a non-Egyptian market. Out of Africa, down the Nile, came the surplus grain extracted from the labour of the Egyptians. Under the later Ptolemies, Alexandria's position was not so fortunate, for the Greek citizens' often influential intervention in dynastic conflicts led to the removal of some of the city's democratic institutions and a reduction in its autonomy. It remained, however, one of the world's major cities, and a twelfth-century source reports that the city had 48,000 households.[89]

CASE STUDY: ATHENS

One would expect Athens to be an unusual *polis*, in view of its spectacular Classical past. Like Alexandria, it exemplifies some of the most characteristic changes of the period; unlike Alexandria, it started with traditions and a history.

Cradle of democracy – a constitutional form rare in the Classical period – and institutional model for most *poleis* in the Hellenistic period, Athens struggled to preserve its democracy. At times, democracy was curtailed or even suspended: in 322–318 under Antipatros; in 317–307 under Kassandros' governor, Demetrios of Phaleron; from ca. 300 to 287 or 286 under Lachares and then Demetrios Poliorketes; and most seriously in 262/1–229 under Antigonos II Gonatas and Demetrios II. From 297 to 229, the Peiraieus was directly ruled from Macedonia. Despite these setbacks, the *demos* bounced back each time, honouring its former leaders once an opportunity presented itself (e.g., in the decree of 261–246 honouring Glaukon, who had served Ptolemy II).[90] Athens continually threw up leaders of ability and vision, such as Glaukon's brother Chremonides, author of the decree confirming the alliance of ca. 268/7 which led to the (unsuccessful) war of liberation against Antigonos Gonatas. Most observers would agree that, for Hellenistic Athens, "[t]he most lasting impression produced by a study of the inscriptions is that of a community regulating its affairs in exemplary fashion."[91]

Just as there was a democratic tradition to preserve, so too in the management of space Athens was not a blank canvas. The author known as Herakleides, cited earlier, says (1.1) that alongside its impressive monuments, Athens has a poor water supply, narrow and winding streets, and mainly second-rate houses, in contrast to newly rebuilt Thebes (1.12) with its modern street plan.[92] The Athenians were fortunate, however, not to be required to lay out their city anew; instead, we see a process of monumental modification. After the new stoa at the Asklepieion (300/299), the next major building programme was delayed until liberation in 229, which included a gymnasium complex in honour of Ptolemy III.[93] Royal intervention in the urban landscape is exemplified by Eumenes II of Pergamon in the early second century, who paid for a huge stoa on the south slope of the Akropolis. Some years later, the Seleucid Antiochos IV attempted to complete the sixth-century Olympieion (Vitruvius, 3.2.8). Around the middle of the century, Attalos II of Pergamon donated the (now-reconstructed) stoa that gave the Agora a new eastern definition. Around the same time, the "South Square" of the Agora was created by the addition of further stoas. All these changes formalized the Agora and made it more like *agorai* in new *poleis* like Miletos, but the city had had to rely on outside benefactors to do it. In the first century, the process continued with the "Roman Agora" (really a forum with colonnades) built by Caesar and Augustus. Athens retained the prestige that its history merited, but the actions of foreign potentates and donors marked a departure from the heyday of Athenian hegemony, when the Athenians' own imperial achievements had paid for new temples. The *demos* repeatedly honoured its liberators by reorganizing civic institutions or naming them after them; Attalos I was honoured with an extra tribe and was even allowed to dedicate a statue group on the summit of the Acropolis.[94]

Evidence for depopulation and economic crisis in Attica has been exaggerated,[95] and a declining number of inscriptions from outlying demes cannot necessarily be a "tracer" for declining activity in the countryside.[96] There is no evidence that the Peiraieus was in decline, even while under the control of the Macedonians; and there is every reason to see Athens as still a thriving, cosmopolitan city attracting immigration from all around the Mediterranean. The notorious hymn to Demetrios Poliorketes, wrongly taken as evidence for irreligiousness and cynicism on the part of the populace, is in fact evidence of the contrary.[97] As they did when honouring royal personages who had done good to the city, the Athenians appropriated its rulers and their worship by allocating them a place within a ceremonial code that was all its own. It would be wrong to see Athens as a shadow of its former self, as living in the past. On the contrary, it continued to be looked to as an economic heavyweight and a centre of high culture. The New Comedy enlarged the range of political discourse to embrace the domestic.[98] New philosophies arose in Athens as before. The difference from Alexandria lies chiefly in the fact that Athens was the locus for competitive display between several monarchies, not just under the control of one.

CONCLUSION

The changes just outlined in two "megapoleis" are mirrored in large and small towns across the Greek world, from Massilia to Marakanda. Many small *poleis* in Old Greece appear to carry on as before, but this may be an illusion created by lack of detailed evidence. The closer one looks at individual communities, the more one sees fundamental, if gradual, change resulting from the interplay of local and global factors. One of the most welcome trends in the recent study of Hellenistic history has been the proliferation of local and regional studies.[99] Research on individual communities serves both to extend the field of view when we consider widespread developments and to provide a check on overgeneralization.

As in the Classical period, *poleis* varied in different parts of the world and evolved continuously. Naturally, there were strong continuities between the late Classical period and the two centuries after Alexander's death; but there were significant changes, too. During the early Hellenistic period, roughly one Peloponnesian town in ten disappeared, was rebuilt, or changed its status (either ceasing to be a *polis* or becoming one).[100] The third- and second-century *polis* in general was a dependent *polis*, less able than before to formulate independent military or diplomatic goals. It was less centred on a single settlement and more connected to other *poleis* through economic and ceremonial links. Concomitantly, it was less exclusive in its membership, more cosmopolitan, more pluralist in its religious and ethnic make-up, and perhaps slightly less restrictively masculine. It was also more élitist, albeit within a democratic structure. After the transition to Roman rule, the changes were more radical: the step-by-step abolition of democracy, the abandonment of urban fortifications, the increasing proportion of the population that lived in small villages or élite estates, the exploitative presence of foreign entrepreneurs, and frequent interventions in the territorial and internal organization of cities.[101]

BIBLIOGRAPHICAL NOTE

There is no recent full study of the Hellenistic *polis*. Works on particular *poleis* and regions are listed in the footnotes. General orientations may be found in Shipley (2000), ch. 3; Hansen (2000b) [the latter mainly classical, with pointers to later changes]. There are excellent selections of documents in Austin (1981); Bagnall & Derow (2004). Important discussions of politics include Larsen (1968); Gauthier (1993); Habicht (1997a); on a more technical level, Ma (1999). For an overview of the social formations of Greek *poleis*, mainly in the Classical period, Gehrke (1986) is illuminating. The Hellenistic monuments of Athens are illustrated in Wycherley (1978).

NOTES

1 Gomme (1937).
2 Hansen (2000b) 143 and n. 26 on p. 174.
3 Gauthier (1993) 212.
4 See, for example, Hansen (1997a), Hansen (1998).
5 Hansen (2004) 16–8.
6 See generally Hansen (2000a); Hansen (2002).
7 Forbes (1996).
8 Horden and Purcell (2000) 89–101.
9 Gauthier (1993); Shipley (2000), ch. 3.
10 For the validity of this notion, see, Hansen (1998) 46–7.
11 On the new cities in general, see, for example, Cohen (1978); Cohen (1995).
12 Martin (1974); Owens (1991); Shipley (2000), ch. 3; Wycherley (1962).
13 Reinders (1988).
14 Bakhuizen (1992).
15 Bernard (1967).
16 Hoepfner and Schwandner (1994).
17 Shipley (1987) 203.
18 See, for example, Shipley (2004).
19 Hansen and Fischer-Hansen (1994) 81, 84–5.
20 Delos: Bruneau and Ducat (1965); Ling (1984) 108–14. Samos: Tölle-Kastenbein (1974).
21 Wycherley (1962) 69–74.
22 Müller (1965), i. 97–110; Pfister (1951); translation and notes in Austin (1981), no. 83.
23 Walter (1976) 56–7.
24 Hansen and Fischer-Hansen (1994) 79.
25 Hansen and Fischer-Hansen (1994) 79.
26 Hansen and Fischer-Hansen (1994) 37–44, esp. 42: most are Hellenistic.
27 Frederiksen (2002), table at 111–20.
28 Hansen (2000b) 165 with nn. 267–71 (on p. 180) collects ancient references; see also Delorme (1960).

29 Cf. *SEG* 47. 890; full translations in Austin (1981), no. 118 (date 167–148 B.C.); Bagnall and Derow (2004), no. 78 (200–170 B.C.).

30 Kourinou (2000) 35–66, 277.

31 Nielsen (1996) 51–71; Nielsen (2001). For the absence of palaces in classical Greece, see Hansen and Fischer-Hansen (1994).

32 McNicoll (1997); Camp (2000) 50.

33 Kienast (1997).

34 Kebric (1977); Shipley (1987) 175–81; Lund (1992) 15–7.

35 See, for example, Walbank (1984) 231, 243–56.

36 Sherwin-White (1978) 176; Rhodes (1997) 531–6; cf. Gauthier (1990) 99, quoted by Rhodes (1997) 532.

37 Gauthier (1993) 219.

38 Habicht (1997a).

39 Rhodes (1997) 534, 535.

40 These examples are all cited by Rhodes (1997) 534.

41 Habicht (1997a) 90.

42 Gehrke (1986).

43 Rhodes (1997) 95.

44 Shipley (1987).

45 Gauthier (1993) 218.

46 Cf. Hansen (1999) 89.

47 On the *ephebeia* in Eretria, see Chankowski (1993).

48 See Gauthier (1990).

49 For the *ephebeia*, see also Chapter 13 in this volume.

50 Davies (1984). See Chapter 4 in this volume.

51 Alcock (1994); Shipley (2002a); Shipley (2002b).

52 Parker (1996) 264–6; Oliver (2001).

53 van Bremen (1996) 9–40; Blundell (1995) 199–200.

54 Houby-Nielsen (1997).

55 Nevett (2002).

56 Cf. Chankowski (1993) 23–4.

57 Bruneau (1970) 460, fig. 7.

58 Bruneau (1970) 469.

59 Homonoia: Thériault (1996). Tyche: Shipley (2000) 173–4.

60 Jones (1987) 22–5; for Athens, see Whitehead (1986) 360–3.

61 Baslez (1996); Gabrielsen (2001); Jones (1999); Kloppenborg and Wilson (1996); Leiwo (1997).

62 Lightfoot (2002).

63 Shipley (2000), ch. 3.

64 Hansen (1995a).

65 Hansen (1997b).

66 Ma (1999) 150–65, who makes some fine distinctions between various types of dependent *polis*. He sometimes exaggerates the importance of *autonomia* (= *eleutheria*), but on 163, he admits (hesitatingly) that "even the autonomous ones were *de facto* exposed to the demands of the ruling power."

67 Hansen (1995b); Schuler (1998) 17–32; Hansen (2000b) 155; Hansen (2004).

68 Isopolity: Buraselis (2003). Arbitration: Ager (1996).

69   For examples from the Peloponnese, see Perlman (2000).
70   Rigsby (1995).
71   For details, see Larsen (1968) 195–215.
72   Larsen and Rhodes (1996).
73   Austin (1981), no. 52 = *Syll.*³ 443.
74   Scholten (1997) and Grainger (1999), respectively.
75   Translation and notes in Austin (1981), no. 53.
76   Walbank (1979) 406–14.
77   Shipley (2000), chs 4, 10; Buraselis (2003); Larsen (1968).
78   I anglicize the neologism *mégapole* employed by Nicolet, Ilbert, and Depaule (2000).
79   See generally Fraser (1972).
80   Empereur (2000a) 232, fig. 1.
81   See Figure 13 for city plan of Alexandria.
82   Tomlinson (1995).
83   Results since the early 1990s are drawn together in Empereur (1998a).
84   Overviews: Empereur (1998a), (2000a). Preliminary reports: Empereur, Hesse, and Picard (1994); Empereur (1995), (1996b), (1997), (1998b), (1999b), (2000b), (2001), (2002). Popular reports: Clayton (1996), (1998); Empereur (1996a), (1996c), (1996d), (1999c), (1999a); Schuster (1997), (1999). Underwater epigraphic discoveries: Goddio, Bernard, and Bernard (1998).
85   See also Shipley (2000), ch. 7. See also Chapter 9 in this volume.
86   See also Shipley 2000, ch. 9. See also Chapter 12 in this volume.
87   Translated with notes in Austin (1981), no. 113; Bagnall and Derow (2004), no. 76.
88   For a detailed discussion, see Rice (1983).
89   Nicolet (2000) 248–9, citing the *Chronicle* of Michael the Syrian. Two figures are given, 24,296 and 47,790 (or 47,789), the larger perhaps including suburbs.
90   Étienne and Piérart (1975).
91   Habicht (1997a) 2.
92   See note 22.
93   Miller (1995) 202–9.
94   Stewart (1990), i. 210, ii. 685–91.
95   Shipley (2000) 30–1; Oliver (2001) 137–42.
96   For a discussion of the many fourth-century and fewer third-century inscriptions, see Hansen et al. (1990) 27–8.
97   Shipley (2000) 160–1.
98   Salmenkivi (1997).
99   Attempts at what might be called *histoires totales*, partly or wholly Hellenistic in scope and to a greater or lesser extent making use of both historical and archaeological evidence, include: Tomlinson (1972) [Argolid]; Griffin (1982) [Sikyon]; Shipley (1987) [Samos]; Garland (2001) [Piraeus]; Cartledge and Spawforth (2002) [Sparta]; McInerney (1999) [Phokis]. Other local and regional studies, often more narrowly focused on political–military or institutional history, include Sherwin-White (1978) [Kos]; Reger (1995) [Delos]; Figueira (1993) [Aigina]; Labarre (1996) [Lesbos]; Habicht (1997a) [Athens]: Scholten (1997) and Grainger (1999) [Aitolia]; studies on Rhodes with various aims and of variable quality [Berthold

(1984), Bilde et al. (1991), Gabrielsen (1997), Gabrielsen et al. (1999), and Wiemer (2002)]; together with parts of Berktold, Schmidt, and Wacker (1996), [Akarnania]; Perlman 2000 (several Peloponnesian *poleis*). I leave aside the much longer bibliography of archaeological field survey publications, which is growing all the time.

100 Shipley, work in progress.
101 See generally Alcock (1993) and (2002).

4: HELLENISTIC ECONOMIES

John K. Davies

❧

PRELIMINARIES AND PROBLEMS

The kingdoms, cities, and other political institutions described in earlier chapters give shape and meaning to our geographical and cultural ideas of the Hellenistic era, whereas the creation, expansion, decline, and eventual extinction of the monarchies provide a chronological framework, even if it is hard to define closure more narrowly than (say) 150–131 B.C. Economically, however, no such tidy delineations are possible. The economic historian is concerned above all to trace and explain change over time, and variation by locality, in such human behaviour as involves the use of resources – supply and demand, access, institutions, security, and technologies, as well as social values and attitudes towards getting and spending. Political and institutional boundaries, therefore, matter only insofar as they affect the movement of goods and persons, or generate differing levels of taxation and redistribution, whereas cultural boundaries and conventions matter only insofar as they influence patterns of production and consumption or as they inhibit or encourage that elusive process that economists call "growth." Similarly, just as there is no intrinsic reason why a particular epoch, defined politically, should show a distinctive type of economy, so too there is no reason why a single kingdom, region, or city should show only *one* type of economic behaviour: indeed it cannot, for otherwise change would be impossible. All the more is that true when the ecologies of the areas controlled or influenced by the Hellenistic monarchies varied so enormously, from the baking deserts of Saudi Arabia or southern Iran via the intensive irrigation agriculture of Mesopotamia and the dry-farming Aegean–Anatolian region to the Alpine habitats of northern Macedonia.

This chapter,[1] therefore, has a serious problem at the descriptive level. By chance, but in a form likely to subsist through the effective lifetime of this book, it has a second problem at an analytic level, for debate about the nature of the "Hellenistic economies" has never been livelier. Very briefly and oversimply, although pre-1940 historians (above all Heichelheim [1930] and Rostovtzeff [1953]) were perfectly well aware of the preponderant economic power of the monarchies, they were sufficiently influenced by the "modernising" activities and assumptions of nineteenth-century colonialist powers to see in the Hellenistic world, via its newly available inscriptions and papyri, evidence of similar modernisation, investment, and market-oriented behaviour by the (as it were) "European" monarchies and constructed their major works accordingly. Postwar historians, whether (rightly) detecting anachronistic assumptions in their predecessors' work or influenced by Marx's identification of an "Oriental" or "Asiatic" mode of production, saw instead a far more slow-moving, disarticulated, and technologically backward world, wherein "the economy" could not be separated conceptually or practically from social practice and political expectations: the term "royal economy," first coined by Claire Préaux to characterise Ptolemaic Egypt, gained wide application, and for good reason. More recently, however, that picture has itself become vulnerable. Egypt itself is emerging as much less uniform than was once thought; detailed studies of the manufacture of certain artefacts (metals as well as various genres of ceramics) are revealing the extent of technological innovation; shipwrecks and find-spots illustrating distribution patterns are beginning to show how much really travelled, and how far; and the effects on transaction costs of institutions such as banks or of installations such as harbours are starting to be reassessed. The eventual yield of such current and future detailed work, and of the conceptual debate that it has stimulated, cannot yet be predicted. All this chapter can do is to put the reader in the picture.

There remains a third problem: evidence. Inevitably, there are no "statistics"; population levels, gross natural product, productivity, tonnages shipped, tax yields, and the rest are all beyond reliable quantitative reach and are imaginable only via best guesses of orders of magnitude.[2] Literary sources help little, save for a text of the early Hellenistic period surviving as book II of Aristotle's *Oikonomika*, which begins (II.1, 1–8, $1345^{b}7$–$1346^{a}30$) by listing the revenue sources for four types of "oikonomiai," that of the king, that of the satrap, that of the city, and that of the individual: Whether "oikonomia" here means our "economy" rather than "management framework" and whether the classification suits the economic historian's purposes are much disputed topics. Documentary papyri help more, at least within Egypt, for their various relevant genres, ranging from private letters through leases and estate accounts to royal decrees and handbooks for administrators, give us a picture of economic activity and management surpassed in Antiquity only by Babylonia and by Roman Egypt. However, that picture may mislead, partly because official documents show what should happen rather than what did happen, partly because documents in Greek from Egypt are very sparse until the 250s, whereas those in demotic Egyptian are only gradually becoming accessible via transliteration and publication, and those in hieroglyphic Egyptian are stiffly formal. The recently published Babylonian astronomical diaries are the most directly useful, for they cover (with gaps) the years from 652 to 61 B.C., and their monthly records report *inter alia* the prices of six basic commodities (barley, dates, mustard, cress, sesame, wool). However, much work still needs to be done on them, both to elicit their full value and to assess how much information is specific to Babylon, how much applies to Mesopotamia, and how much more broadly to the Seleukid Empire.[3]

The two remaining genres – physical evidence and inscriptions – yield the most. The physical evidence provided by surviving artefacts, excavated sites, and surface survey increases yearly and has almost reached the point where a chapter with the present title could be informatively constructed without using written evidence at all. Three examples of such material must suffice. First, recent studies of Hellenistic palaces have provided the first real portrayal of one of the period's defining institutions and architectural forms, while also allowing a tentative evaluation of their economic costs and roles.[4] Secondly, building on earlier classificatory work, more recent quantitative studies of the coinages of the period have begun to disclose how much silver was coined by which power, and when, and have thereby triggered the sorts of questions, both of "economic policy" (if that is the right phrase) and of economic transformation, which could not previously even be posed in numismatic terms, let alone answered.[5] Thirdly, although huge efforts were made in the last century to identify and classify the many thousands of surviving amphorae, the foodstuff-transporters of antiquity, only recently has it become possible to move with any confidence beyond the tasks of compilation, or of linking find-spot to place of production, to trace the fluctuations of commodity flows.[6]

In these as in countless other respects, tentative and precarious processes of quantification help to fill out the qualitative picture dimly provided by our best source, inscriptions. It is they, perhaps more than any other single artefact or activity, that define our period chronologically and geographically, for not only did they proliferate after the late fourth century in the older Greek-speaking regions, but they also came to be an invaluable trace element in the areas of conquest. If inscriptions would only be written in Greek if someone could read them, their spread after Alexander – into the Balkans and the Black Sea, through Asia Minor into the Levant, the far south of Egypt, even into Afghanistan[7] – reflected the presence of Greeks (or at least of "culture Greeks"), with their landowning ascendancy, their purchasing power, and their economically dominant cultural preferences. The most directly useful genres for the economic historian are perhaps temple accounts, notably those from Delos, which provide a near-continuous backdrop to Aegean affairs and events,[8] the decrees of Greek city assemblies and councils, which again and again illustrate the complex relationships between inadequate public revenues and the goodwill of internal or external benefactors,[9] and above all royal letters and decrees.[10] By showing in some detail how the kings ran their financial administrations, these last both start and feed debate about whether royal attitudes were predatory, managerial, or developmental.

As with all surveys of a *longue durée*, one must separate what remains more or less stable from what changes. The Environment and Stabilities section embraces the former aspect, The Main Processes of Change the latter. The reader will sense a difference of tone, for although the Environment and Stabilities section reflects general agreement, the topics surveyed in The Main Processes of Change are matters of lively (but amicable) current contention. Though this chapter has no business being sectarian, it will lean towards the view that the world which the Romans overran had advanced economically well beyond that which Alexander knew.

ENVIRONMENT AND STABILITIES

Landscape and Environment

One component of our primary evidence is still there for all to see – the landscapes of the eastern Mediterranean, Anatolia, Arabia, Mesopotamia, the Gulf, and the Iranian plateau. They have changed since antiquity, mostly from erosion, silting, and desiccation,[11] but not enough to subvert our reading of them, or of their rivers and seas, as the bases of human livelihoods. Three aspects are basic. First, ecologically, as much recent work emphasises,[12] this whole vast region comprises a range of diverse micro-regions whose exploitation was determined purely by what would and what would not grow. That meant grain above all, not just in the old Greek world where it probably provided about 80 percent of normal nutrition[13] but also in all other regions of stable and dense population such as Egypt, Syria, and Mesopotamia. Though some pastoral or semi-nomadic populations will have had a different nutritional regime, the predominant pattern was undoubtedly an agrarian subsistence economy, each locality relying on a limited range of seasonal foodstuffs. Their yield (especially of grain, but also of vines, olives, fruits, beans and other vegetables, or forest products) depended on rainfall, whether directly or via the use of irrigation with the seasonal floodwaters of the Nile, Tigris, or Euphrates. By modern standards, such yields were mostly very low[14] and showed a high level of variation from year to year, so that the threat of famine, never remote,[15] generated expedients such as long-term storage or the acceptance that to exploit several physically separated land-holdings, though wasteful of time and energy, offset risk by using differing microclimates.

Use of Complementary Habitats and Resources

Parallel to such small-scale risk avoidance lay much larger-scale patterns of exchange and complementarity, whether between plain and mountain, between agrarian and pastoral, between land and water, or between one country and another. Many such patterns were centuries – even millennia – old, such as the seasonal movements of flocks to and from summer mountain pastures, or the need of Egypt or Mesopotamia to pay directly or indirectly with primary products such as corn for the supplies of the timber or metals that they lacked, or the need of the Aegean communities to offer acceptable commodities such as timber, slaves, agrarian produce, or silver for the iron of Etruria and elsewhere, which they came to require when the supply of tin for bronze became precarious. Of course, though needs were constant, supplies and access were not, so that patterns of multisourcing grew up, such as the disposition of Athens and other Aegean states in the fifth and fourth centuries to seek corn supplies from all over the place – from Thessaly, the Black Sea, Egypt, Libya, or Sicily.[16]

Communications

No product is useful unless it can be brought to the user: The efforts needed should not be underestimated. Roads in Old Greece were still rudimentary, save near certain wealthy sanctuaries, and remained so until the Roman conquest, whereas the network of way stations on roads linking the satrapies of the Persian Empire, which had so impressed Herodotos (5.52–54) and was an essential instrument of communication and control,[17] was far from being the kind of continuous engineered all-weather surface that the Romans began to develop for Italy after 312 with the construction of the Via Appia from Rome towards Capua. True, wheeled transport could be used in limited contexts for heavy haulage, but otherwise the backs of men or of equids were the only resource, though in Arabia at least but not in Egypt till the Roman period, camels were already being used as pack animals.[18]

In contrast, the use of sea and river was ingrained and well developed, for the spread of the Greek-speaking peoples before Alexander had been determined almost totally by seaborne access to areas where vine and olive would grow and that of the Phoenicians by maritime outreach to metal-bearing regions of the Mediterranean and the Atlantic. As a result, installations at ports such as quays and warehouses were already commonplace in the Greek world (e.g., at Peiraieus, Thasos, Corinth, Rhodes, or Byzantion), just as they were in Phoenicia and elsewhere in the eastern Mediterranean. As surviving lawcourt speeches of the 330s and 320s from Athens make clear,[19] this network was already well used and well organised by the late fourth century B.C. Its effects can be seen in the existence of the "main lines" of Mediterranean exchange: (a) between the Egyptian, Syrian, and Phoenician ports along the south coast of Turkey to the major ports of the Aegean; (b) between Aegean Greece and the heel and toe of Italy, eastern Sicily, the northern Adriatic, and Etruria; (c) between the Phoenician city-states, especially Tyre, and their colonial states of the western Mediterranean, above all Carthage; (d) between the Aegean and the Black Sea through Bosporos; and (e) between Syracuse and the Adriatic. Though we cannot yet construct a full picture of what was exchanged along these corridors in the fourth or later centuries, still less quantify the flows, commodities certainly included iron from Etruria, timber, salt, and silver from Iberia, grain from Egypt, the Black Sea, and Sicily, slaves from the Black Sea, silver (as coin or plate), ceramics, and wine from the Aegean, and spices and luxury craftsman goods from Arabia, the Levant and further east.[20]

At a minimum, therefore, economic activities in the Mediterranean by the late fourth century B.C. have to be visualised on two levels: the local, that of production and movement by land or small boat within the radius of a day's journey; and the longer distance, largely by sea or river and with larger ships that involved more complex systems of finance and management[21] and had already stimulated state action and investment via their need for harbours and quays. Even within the second level, there were differences, for the movement of high-value low-bulk luxury goods, such as spices or gems, generated less political sensitivity than that of low-value high-bulk goods, such as corn, but the complexities and the interactions cannot be explored further here. What matters is that, though the self-sufficiency of the individual holding or estate was still a Greek cultural norm, reflecting the practical limits of what could be carried on human or animal backs without disproportionate expense, it was being increasingly complemented by more complex exchange patterns, at least for such micro-regions as were accessible by sea or river. Philosophers who advocated self-sufficiency (Arist. *Pol.* 1.2.8–9, 1252^{b}27–1253^{a}1) planted their ideal cities well away from the coast to minimise evil influences (Plato, *Laws* 4.704d–705b) or delegitimated merchanting habits, and profit-making attitudes (Arist. *Pol.* 1.8–11, 1256^{a}1–1259^{a}36) were not living in the real developing world of the fourth-century Mediterranean.

Land and Land Ownership

Yet, the land and its products remained primary, for they generated not only the means of subsistence but also the surpluses that could be converted from produce into more durable containers of value – and could be taxed. The routes of such conversions lay through an array of ownership patterns and of modes of linkage between man and soil, which is still far from having been mapped satisfactorily for all regions of the Hellenistic world. However, the range of possible patterns was not infinite. One mode, that of the peasant proprietor of an allotted share (*kleros*) of inheritable family land within a *polis* framework, may have been more central in theory than in practice, even in its alleged homeland of Attika,[22] once the military necessity to maximise the numbers of amateur citizen-proprietor soldiers had yielded to the use of mercenary professionals, but remained embedded in the language and was extended to the citizens of the new Greek-style city foundations created by the royal regimes. Close to it was the Egyptian category of "privately held land," especially but not only fruit-tree and garden land, where "the rights to the land were freely conveyable though the institutional interest in the land, either of the pharaoh or of a temple estate, was always retained."[23] Indeed, not only in Egypt but throughout the entire region under review, land in some sense "owned" by temples but worked by lease-holders, share-croppers, or sacred slaves comprised a very major category, not least in Asia Minor and Babylonia[24] but also in traditional Greek lands, the temple estates of Delian Apollo being the best-documented and best-studied example.[25] Another major mode was that of landlord and tenant farmer, a mode that embraced a variety of tenant-statuses including that of tied serf, as surviving land-grants from Asia Minor make clear.[26] However, it was royal power and prerogatives that principally moulded the land-owning regime, alike in old Macedonia and in the newly conquered lands. The debate[27] has been whether the royal lien on land derived from its status as "spear-won land" (*doriktetos chora*), a phrase much used in the two generations after the conquest, or whether it was conceptually indistinguishable from private landownership. Because kings saw themselves as able to sell royal land[28] and to will their territories,[29] practice in effect remained as it had in Achaemenid times, when the King claimed to be able to do as he pleased with his own land (Thuc. 8.52.2).

Left to themselves, these four longstanding aspects of life in the newly conquered world were unlikely to change significantly save as a reaction to environmental impact. However, significant changes can be identified over the period nonetheless. The main portion of this chapter therefore attempts to describe them and to evaluate their collective impact.

THE MAIN PROCESSES OF CHANGE

Monetisation

First in time, and perhaps primordial in importance, was the gradual release into circulation, after Alexander's capture of Persepolis in 331, of the stupefying hoards of bullion accumulated by the Persian kings. The contradictory figures in our sources[30] seem to reflect a total of 180,000 (silver) talents – nearly twenty times the Athenian maximum accumulation of 9,700 talents of the early 440s. What mattered, however, was not the violent shift of ownership but the need to use it, as coin, to pay troops, a need that drove the foundation of mints all over Alexander's Empire, even in areas where Persian darics had circulated little and the creation of a massive flow of coinage. Nor was this a one-off monetisation, for Alexander's Successors had the same need to mint coin to pay the troops whom they had to attract from the Aegean region to hold down their new conquests and repel their rivals. Though some Greek and Macedonian soldiers came to accept payment for military services in the form of land by becoming settlers, most remained mercenaries, recruited for shorter or longer periods into a professional army and hoping to return home intact and wealthy. Because military costs by land and sea were by far the largest component of Successors' budgets,[31] all the kingdoms had to seek out and control supplies of silver, to insist that taxes were paid in coin, and to continue minting or re-minting what accrued.

Albeit driven purely by fiscal and military considerations, this massive shift towards monetisation had significant economic effects. Though efforts to estimate the total quantity of silver in circulation at any one time have yet to deliver agreed results,[32] and though we lack later evidence for interest rates to juxtapose with the data from fourth-century Athens, there is little doubt that the basic measure of money supply (M1) increased very significantly, whereas the general adoption of the Athenian weight standard for the coinages of the Successor states (except for Egypt) went some way to create a single monetary system. Nor were the kingdoms the only minting powers, for some Greek republics continued to coin, notably Rhodes (Ashton, 2001) and Byzantion throughout, whereas Athenian production, spasmodic and small-scale during the third century, showed a notable second flowering after ca. 164 with a so-called New Style coinage,[33] which in effect if not in intention replaced the supply from the Macedonian mines that the Romans had closed after 168. By the late second century, the Delphic Amphiktyony could instruct "all the Greeks" to accept the main Athenian coin, the tetradrachm, at full value.[34]

Royal Economies

A few figures may serve to bring out the overwhelming preponderance that the kingdoms immediately came to have as economic actors. The annual income of Alexander's kingdom is reported as 30,000 talents, of Antigonos's area of control in 316 as 11,000 talents, of Egypt in the mid-third century as 14,800 talents, and of Egypt in the mid-first century as 12,500 talents.[35] Though none come from a contemporary source, these figures, consistent in their orders of magnitude, are plausible. They, along with much other evidence, suggest not only that kings could and did tax very heavily,[36] as indeed they had to for survival, but also that the proportion of the annual gross national product that passed through their hands was nearer modern levels (± 40 percent) than the 5 to 6 percent of eighteenth-century European monarchies. That did not prevent individual rulers from extracting extra resources when under stress, as when Antiochos III leant heavily on Gerrha or stripped the temple of Anaitis at Ekbatana of its remaining cladding,[37] but it did give them the power to dispose of resources at levels that no one in pre-Alexander Europe could reach. Besides the costs of the army, we can see monarchs buying in the services of individuals who possessed exceptional or much-needed skills, such as the intellectuals whom the Ptolemies maintained at the Museum in Alexandria, the artists, architects, and sculptors who built and decorated Pergamon and thereby helped to legitimate the upstart Attalid monarchy, the naval engineers who built floating juggernauts for the Ptolemies,[38] the diplomats who negotiated peace treaties and royal marriages,[39] or the soldiers who commanded royal armies in battle.

The Rise and Fall of Egypt as a "Royal Economy"

As the Hellenistic kingdom that we know most about, Ptolemaic Egypt has come to be seen as the extreme case of a "royal economy."[40] Though closer study of the Seleukid Empire is modifying that view, the Ptolemaic regime did undoubtedly create a new kind of economic machine, imitated elsewhere (as by third-century Syracuse). Its ultimate purpose was to mobilise the resources of Egypt and her overseas possessions so as to allow Egypt as an independent power to compete politically and militarily on equal terms with her rivals. To that end, Egypt's assets – above all her agrarian fertility and her peasant population – were to be squeezed to the uttermost in two ways: first, directly to extract a grain surplus that could be exported in exchange for silver and other commodities (wood, metals) that Egypt lacked, and second, indirectly, by maximising other taxes and requiring that they be paid in, or converted into, coined silver (cf. von Reden 2001). That basic strategy allowed the regime to buy in the materials to build and maintain a very substantial navy, which itself could then not only secure Egypt's hold on Cyprus (invaluable for its copper) but also extend Egypt's military reach into the Aegean via a string of naval bases. It also allowed the construction and adornment of Alexandria, with her multiple functions as capital city, naval base, monopoly port for all import-export trans-shipments, craft centre, and Greek cultural beacon. Two supplementary strategies completed the package. One comprised the creation of a coinage on a lighter standard than the Athenian, so that the movement of silver out of Egypt could be prohibited in law and minimised in practice. The other again involved land, this time being offered as "lots" (kleroi) to immigrant Greek "lot-holders" (klerouchoi) who would hold the land in return for army service: The echo of fifth-century Athenian practice and terminology is no accident.

This "Egyptian system" served the Ptolemies well for a century, though naval defeats in the Aegean in the 260s and 250s damaged its overseas effectiveness, whereas signs of strain have been detected within Egypt in the 240s. Its essentials survived the weakening of royal competence, power, and authority from ca. 210 onwards, as well as military defeat, civil war, and foreign occupation, to provide the Romans after 31 B.C. with a ready-made instrument of exploitation.

Population Movements

Egypt was not the only overseas landscape where Greeks after Alexander might hope for a welcome, high status, and land, for what became the Seleukid Empire offered equal opportunities. True, here prospects took a different form, for successive rulers of the Seleukid dynasty followed Alexander by founding Greek-style cities all over their empire in locations selected for their defensibility, strategic value, and ability to control and exploit agricultural land. Though there is continuing debate about foundation dates, about the mix of motives for each settlement, and about their relationship to preexisting urban nuclei, the effect and intention of the new cities and colonies, as of Ptolemaic land-grants, was undoubtedly to attract thousands of Greeks and Macedonians, as well as their culturally similar neighbours from Thrace and Karia, to the new lands during the third and second centuries, so that they and their descendants could form a reservoir of military manpower, create bastions of domination over an indigenous population, and assure a flow of agrarian production. Their economic effect was therefore twofold. Some transformation of the economies of the newly conquered territories did ensue, though immigrant numbers should not be exaggerated [Davies (1984) 265–6], while the scale of depopulation of rural areas of old Greece by the late Hellenistic period is becoming ever clearer from the consistent message of surface surveys.

However, the evidence of counter-flows precludes us from imagining old Greece as being entirely like late nineteenth-century Ireland after the emigrations of the 1840s and after. Some flows were voluntary, such as those of Syrians to Delos, Demetrias, and Corinth, of Jews to Asia Minor, Greece, and Cyrene, or of Egyptians towards the major Aegean ports. Others were forcible, the products of the slave trade. They formed a continuous low-level Brownian motion throughout the Hellenistic world and beyond, punctuated by occasional peaks, such as the influx of Italian slaves into Greece during the Second Punic War, the deportation of 150,000 Epirotes into slavery in Italy in 167 (Polyb. 30.15), the massive recruitment needed to restart silver-mine production at Laureion after 164, or the glut after 146.[41] Though, as usual, we cannot quantify them, such shifts (and no doubt others we cannot yet even detect) not only gave the late Hellenistic world, especially its cities, a much more ethnically mixed population, but also enlarged those cities dramatically, creating at least three new mega-cities (Alexandria, Antioch, Rome, and perhaps Seleukeia), each large enough to equal if not surpass Babylon. Public order, the demands of the construction industry, and above all the logistics and control of food supply combined to generate wholly new patterns of supply and demand.

Seaborne Transport

Indeed, few transformations in economic history can be documented with such clarity, albeit indirectly, as the growth in the seaborne move-ment of goods in the Mediterranean in the Hellenistic period,[42] for the bar graph of known shipwrecks in the Mediterranean period by period (Figure 1) says it all. Nor is it hard to account for, in gen-eral terms at least. Stimulated partly by the Ptolemaic system that had grain exports as a prime structural component, partly by the effective demand for Greek-style cultural goods (not least of which was wine and olive oil) on the part of emigrant Greeks, partly by the convenience of coin minted to a common standard throughout much of the eastern Mediterranean, such movements benefited everyone who lay within their range and made those Greek states that had significant merchant fleets into influential political players. Placed as she was astride one of the principal routes (see earlier discussion), Rhodes was the principal beneficiary,[43] both via the hulls owned by its residents and via the tolls paid by those who used its port facilities, but others such as Chios, Taras, Syracuse, Epidamnos, Miletos, and Byzantion (cf. Polyb. 4.38) benefited too, whereas Carthage's power stemmed as much from such activity as from its agrarian hinterland. Nor was the growth of seaborne exchange confined to the Mediterranean, for just as the Seleukids explored the Caspian or invested in installations on the shores of the Gulf to protect and milk traffic with India,[44] so too the Ptolemies pushed exploration and settlement down the Red Sea and into the Indian Ocean. Their objectives were partly military, to procure African elephants with which to counter the Seleukid stable of Indian elephants, but then were also

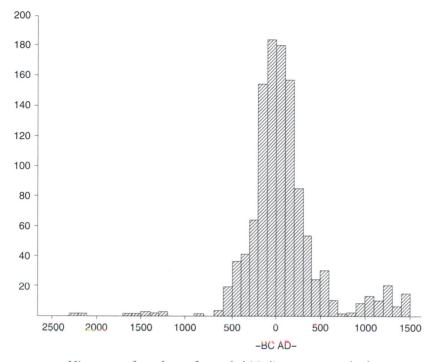

FIGURE 1. Histogram of numbers of recorded Mediterranean wrecks, by century [Z. H. Archibald, J. K. Davies, V. Gabrielsen, G. J. Oliver, eds., *Hellenistic Economies* (London, 2001) 279, fig. 10.2. Reprinted with permission of Routledge Press].

economic, focussed both on protecting the spice trade from Yemen [cf. Kitchen (2001)] and (especially after the discovery of the monsoon winds allowed direct sailings) on creating a route to and from India that obviated the expensive passage of goods through the Gulf and overland.

New Institutions and Installations

Indeed, the Ptolemaic port installations down the Red Sea formed part of a major investment in infrastructure that continued throughout the Hellenistic period. Though roads were neglected, improved maritime facilities came to include lighthouses at Alexandria and Rhodes, beacons, wharves, and warehouses. Even more central to economic life, conspicuously so at excavated towns such as Delos or Priene, were the stoas that came to frame town agorai, serving a multiplicity of commercial and administrative purposes; here, as with other urban amenities such as baths and gymnasia,[45] the institutions had developed in the

Classical period, but it was after Alexander that their wider adoption came to characterise the new world and to define its extent. Less visible, but necessary as instruments with which to manage monetised public and private economies, were banks.[46] Some (as in Egypt) were royal, primarily serving the fiscal interests of the state via tax receipts and conversion of produce, whereas private banks came to supplement temples by offering services such as money changing, lending, and deposit.

Knowledge Transfer

Also common across the whole region of the post-Alexander kingdoms were patterns of knowledge transfer. This could comprise literal transplantation, as with the earlier naturalisation of alfalfa in Greece attributed to Darius (Pliny, N.H. 18.144) or the attempts made by the Ptolemies to make Egypt more nearly self-sufficient in agrarian produce, enterprises that exploited the kind of awareness of which unfamiliar crops grew in newly conquered regions that Theophrastos showed in his two treatises on plants. More common was the transfer of ideas and techniques. For example, just as the disposition to improve the productive environment via drainage or irrigation, and to maintain the installations in good order, had characterised the main riverine civilisations of the Near East for millennia, so too smaller-scale improvements had long been made in old Greece itself, continuing in Alexander's own lifetime.[47]

Luxuries and Lifestyles

Above the subsistence economy of the majority as delineated earlier, and largely obscuring it, lay a far more visible layer of elegance, luxury, and ostentation.[48] Of course it was not a new departure so much as an enhanced continuation of fourth-century tastes and purchasing power, wielded by a tiny minority. The royal or princely palaces of the Hellenistic period noted earlier, for example, simply took further the kind of investment in space and decoration that had been indulged in by Cypriot or Sicilian tyrants, Macedonian monarchs, or the gentry of Athens and Eretria [cf. Kiderlen (1995)], whereas the fifth-century taste for Near Eastern fashions at Athens had evidently packed an economic punch, at least among an elite. Yet, there was a significant change. Whereas some fourth-century men, partly out of puritanism, partly to avoid costly public obligations, had tended to hold their wealth in "invisible" form [Cohen (2003)], such inhibitions gradually faded, opening the way to patterns of conspicuous consumption. Here, the frustration of the economic historian reaches its extreme. We can identify some of the main kinds of expenditure, such as mosaics, perfumes, spices, wine, gastronomy, silverware, sexual services, fabrics, and textiles, jewellery, hunting paraphernalia, or slaves, and we can be reasonably confident, whether from surviving sites and artefacts or from the literary tradition in Athenaios, that the fashion had taken root and spread, but there is currently no means of estimating its economic impact, whether in local and regional terms (which is more likely for gastronomy) or in generating long-distance exchanges (which was certainly the case for perfumes).

The Polarisation of Wealth

Behind the changed behaviour just described lay the wreckage of another discarded inhibition. The Archaic and Classical periods of Greece had had to accommodate an ideology of equality, however contested, or limited to a (free male) minority, or trivialised in practice. Its roots lay in the military need of each state to maximise its heavy-armed field force, a need that in turn had shaped inheritance rules and land-owning patterns so as to maximise the number of minimally viable land-holdings. Powerful until the mid-fourth century, it lost force once states could buy in professional armies when needed because controls over inheritance and land-owning could be flouted more openly. In turn, although a comparatively large polity such as Athens had been able to devise elaborate systems to minimise political patronage and to maximise public revenues,[49] smaller polities with less public revenue (and perhaps with less administrative expertise among their politicians) found themselves in increasing financial difficulty and seem to have come increasingly to depend on the goodwill and deep pockets of benefactors and patrons. Probably the preferred option, because it spread the burden and protected the polity from excessive subservience to a specific individual, was to open a subscription list to raise money, whether to construct public works or to pay off a debt.[50]

Less attractive, but evidently often unavoidable to judge from the number of extant decrees, was the expedient of turning to a wealthy and benevolent citizen. The most illuminating single example is the decree of Samos in honour of Boulagoras, which describes in detail his financial and other services to the state. Passed in ca. 246–243, it first describes how, appointed as ambassador to Antiochos II, he travelled to Ephesos and then Sardis to seek the return to the Samians of estates on the mainland opposite Samos, which were in the hands of the Friends of the king, and secured letters from Antiochos that ensured their return (lines 5–20). It then notes with thanks his services as state advocate in public trials and as emergency superintendent of the gymnasion because the expenses of the post proved beyond the means of the official originally appointed (lines 20–26) and narrates at length how, when the state needed to send a delegation of sacred envoys to Alexandria to honour Ptolemy III and Queen Berenike but there was no money for their travel expenses, Boulagoras advanced to the state the required sum, nearly 6,000 drachmai (lines 26–35). There then follows the longest section, which describes his services as corn commissioner on three occasions "when the people was suffering from a shortage of corn," on the first occasion advancing all the money for the deposit, on the second "promising a sum equal to that provided by the most lavish contributors," and on the third not only again advancing all the money for the deposit but also, "since there were no (civic) resources available to refund the money," repaying from his own pocket the loan that the city had raised for grain purchases together with accrued interest (lines 35–48). After a general reference to his giving good advice to the people publicly and privately and advancing loans to many of the needy, and after an explicit statement that it was being proposed so as to encourage others to do the same, the decree ends with provisions for proclaiming and inscribing it.[51]

Few documents encapsulate so briefly so many themes of Hellenistic civic and economic life – the dependence on royal goodwill, the hand-to-mouth state of civic finances, the perennial anxiety about grain supplies, the roles of assembly and lawcourts, the need for civic officials who were wealthy as well as competent, the linkage between private benevolence and public gratitude, and the multiple roles that a wealthy citizen might be called on to play.[52] One should not, of course, be seduced by the roseate language, for although the kings were undoubtedly the greatest potential benefactors (some, such as Ptolemy III himself, even taking the corresponding Greek word *Euergetes* as a personal title), they were remote and elusive, so that the real everyday power relationships that mattered most were those with the likes of Boulagoras. Here, line 51, with its reference to his loans to the needy, hints at the darker side, for debt and its consequences were at least as much part of this monetised world as they had been in earlier centuries.[53]

West Central Italy as an Economic Actor

The last, and ultimately the most far-reaching of all the processes and agencies of change, was the growth of Roman economic power. This was a growth in degree, not in kind, for economic links between Italy and the eastern Mediterranean, themselves reaching back for centuries, had taken on renewed importance from the Early Iron Age onwards in the wake of Greek colonisation, Phoenician trading activity, and the Aegean's increasingly urgent needs for grain and iron, and had generated a set of east–west exchange routes that supplemented earlier north–south routes. What changed was the focus, nature, and scale of demand. Earlier Greek and Phoenician economic relations with non-Greek areas of Italy had mainly been with Etruria and the Adriatic, and were supplemented by the third century, if not well before, by what seems to have become significant traffic within Italian waters along the southern coastal corridor from Syracuse to Lokroi, Taras, Epidamnos, and the northern Adriatic.[54]

However, as the third century progressed, Roman political and military predominance increasingly overlaid such established patterns with new ones. Some, such as the accumulation of booty and slaves after campaigns and conquests, were just as purely violent and predatory (and therefore, by modern criteria, "noneconomic") as the exploits of Alexander and his Successors, but had equally forceful effects on, for example, the market for slaves, the local construction industry,[55] or the availability of coin and bullion in the eastern Mediterranean. Others, such as the (perhaps still intermittent) need for longer-distance grain imports to sustain a rapidly increasing urban population or the desire to acquire Greek and other Eastern Mediterranean cultural and luxury goods, had even more far-reaching knock-on effects, and it may even be possible to date their emergence. Significant pointers are the creation of a specifically Roman silver coinage on the Ptolemaic standard ca. 269, the foundation of Brundisium as a Latin colony in 244, the cultural outreach to Greek literature as soon as the First Punic War had ended in 241, the concern for the protection of Italian shippers against Illyrian piracy in the 230s, and the decision to treat Sicily as a formal provincia after 227. At latest by 220, if not a generation earlier, Latium-plus-Rome had joined the economic mainstream of the Hellenistic world.

THE DRIFT TOWARDS INTEGRATED ECONOMIES

Notwithstanding all the detailed scholarly work carried out for over a century, no firmly delineated overall picture can yet be drawn. Military and fiscal considerations apart, change had been unplanned even within a single polity, whereas investment for identifiably economic purposes barely extended beyond maritime installations. Though some innovations such as larger ships, navigational aids, and more permeable citizenship statuses had reduced transaction costs, the efforts made by states and monarchs to control the biggest threat to free movement, piracy and brigandage, were ambivalent at best, pirates and regimes sharing a mutual interest in providing slaves and a reservoir of mercenaries and sailors hireable at need.[56]

Likewise, although some regions such as northern Egypt, western Syria, or Asia Minor showed significant economic transformation, others such as Crete showed little or none [Chaniotis (1999b)]. Structurally, we are dealing with a complex set of processes of interlocking between the fiscally exploitative command economies of the monarchies, price-setting market mechanisms in certain commodities and contexts, a major role attributable to "merchants" as being essential though perhaps ancillary to, and indirectly employed by, the monarchs, and above all, as the vertiginous rise in maritime traffic reveals, the pressures for change exerted by urbanisation and monetisation. Those processes cannot yet be measured, let alone modelled. What can be said, nonetheless, is that the economies of the region do seem to have experienced some degree of development and integration during the Hellenistic centuries, however patchy and untidy the process may have been.

BIBLIOGRAPHICAL NOTE

Outdated and vulnerable to criticism on several registers though it is [cf. Archibald et al. (2001)], Rostovtzeff's magisterial three-volume treatise of 1941, best consulted in the lightly revised edition of 1953, remains the only full-scale conspectus of the topic, complemented for Egypt by Préaux (1939). Partial updates on a smaller scale were provided by Moretti, Bogaert, and Parise in Bianchi Bandinelli (1977) 319–419, Préaux (1978) 358–388 and 489–524, Davies (1984), and Foraboschi (1998), but until recently, the main advances came from site publications, newly discovered inscriptions, and study of the making and distribution of classes of artefacts such as silverware [Rotroff (1982)], mould-made bowls [Bilde (1993)], and above all amphorae [summary in Davies (2001) 27–9; Lawall (in press), whereas the various monograph series devoted to the period offered until recently little that was directly relevant. However, stimulated by the newer documentation from Babylonia (see note 3) and by the palmary new start given to the discourse about regional economies by Reger (1994), the economies of the period have featured prominently in the renewed and currently lively debate on the nature of the economies of the classical world in general. In addition to major monographs such as Migeotte (1984) or Gabrielsen (1997) and to imminent or recently published survey chapters [Reger (2003); Manning, Reger, and van der Spek, all forthcoming in the *Cambridge Economic History of the Greek and Roman World*], the proceedings of two Liverpool colloquia devoted to Hellenistic economies are published [Archibald et al. (2001); or in press (Archibald, Davies, and Gabrielsen)], and those of a third colloquium (at St Bertrand, 2004) are likely to follow, whereas further colloquia are planned.

NOTES

1   I thank Gary Reger and the Editor for help towards formulating this chapter.
2   For example, Aperghis (2001).
3   The diaries are published in Sachs and Hunger (1988), (1989), (1996). Fuller discussions in Andreau et al. (1997); van der Spek (2000); Sartre (2001) 204–30; and Aperghis (2004).
4   Hoepfner and Brands (1996); Kutbay (1998); von Hesberg (1998) 182–86; Nielson (1999); Davies (in press).
5   De Callataÿ (1995); Ashton (2001); Panagopoulou (2001); Bresson in Archibald et al. (in press); de Callataÿ in Archibald et al. (in press).
6   Davies (2001) 27–9; Lawall in Archibald et al. (in press).
7   Notably at Aï Khanum and (by the Indian Emperor Asoka) at Kandahar: Thapar (1997) 232; 271–82; *SEG* 48.1842.
8   Reger (1994); Rauh (1998).
9   For example, Austin (1981), nos. 97 (Protogenes at Olbia) and 113 (Boulagoras at Samos).
10 Principally Welles (1934), plus the Skythopolis dossier (text in *SEG* 29.1613 and 41.1574: translation in Sherwin-White and Kuhrt (1993) 48–50; Lenger (1990) for the Ptolemaic regime.
11 Vita-Finzi (1969); Potts (1990) I.22.
12 Brice (1978); Sallares (1991); Horden and Purcell (2000); Grove and Rackham (2001).
13 Foxhall and Forbes (1982).
14 Yields of 1:4 to 1:8 were standard for the Mediterranean, whereas yields of 1:12 or more might be expected in Babylonia.
15 Garnsey and Whittaker (1983); Garnsey (1988); Gallant (1991).
16 Garnsey (1988); Whitby (1998).
17 Briant (1996), ch. 9.
18 Zarins (1992): McDonald in Bienkowski and Millard (2000), s.v. Camel.
19 Especially Demosthenes 52, 56, and 58; Cohen (1992) 121–83.
20 Miller (1997); Reger in Archibald, et al. (in press).
21 Bogaert (1968), but also Gabrielsen in Archibald et al. (in press).

22   Burford (1993) 15–55; summary of more recent debate in Foxhall (2002).
23   Manning (2003) 195.
24   Cf. van der Spek (1987); van der Spek (1995); Dignas (2002).
25   Kent (1948); Reger (1994).
26   Main references in Davies (1984) 300, n. 265.
27   van der Spek (1995); Schuler (1998) 167 ff.
28   *RC* 10–12 = Austin (1981), no. 185.
29   Thus Ptolemy VIII in 155 and Attalos III in 133 [references in Shipley (2000) 210 and 212, with 448, n. 60].
30   Assembled in Bellinger (1963) 68, n. 148 and in Bosworth (1980b) 330 and 336, on Arrian, *Anab.* 3.18.10 and 19.7.
31   Austin (1986); Davies (2001) 36–9.
32   But cf. de Callataÿ (1995); de Callataÿ in Archibald et al (in press).
33   Thompson (1961); Lewis (1962); Habicht (1997a) 243, n. 81.
34   *Syll.*³ 729=Austin (1981), no. 107.
35   References and discussion in Aperghis (2001) 78.
36   Evidence from pre-Maccabaean Judaea even suggests one third of grain crop: Aperghis (2001) 88.
37   Polyb. 13.9.4–5, with Potts (1990) 85–97; Polyb. 10.27.11–13.
38   Athen. 5.203–204; Casson (1971) 107–16.
39   Olshausen (1974); Savalli-Lestrade (1998).
40   Préaux (1939); Turner (1984) 133–59; Hölbl (2001); Thompson (2003); Descat (2003).
41   Gabrielson (2003) 391, citing Strabo 14.5.2.
42   Parker (1992), with updated figures in Gibbins (2001) 306, n. 18.
43   Berthold (1984); Gabrielsen (1997); Gabrielsen et al. (1999).
44   Pliny *N.H.* 6.58 (Caspian); Salles (1987) and Potts (1990), II. 10–196 (Gulf).
45   Coulton (1976) [stoas]; Yegül (1992) 6–29 [baths]; Delorme (1960) [gymnasia].
46   Bogaert (1968); Gabrielson in Archibald et al. (in press).
47   Lewis (2000) [general]; Oleson (2000) [irrigation]; Wilson (2000) [drainage].
48   Schneider (1967–1969), II. 3–69 and 208–21; Davies (2001) 33.
49   Millett (1989); Faraguna (1992).
50   For example, Austin (1981), nos. 101 (*Syll.*³ 544: Oropos) and 103 (*ISE* II 99: Krannon).
51   *SEG* I 166=Austin (1981), no. 113.
52   General sketch in Veyne (1990) 101–200; Bringmann (2001).
53   Cf. the laws assembled in Asheri (1969). *SEG* 33.679 may be another example.
54   Cf. Marasco (1986); Marasco (1988); Bandelli (1999).
55   Cf. the 14 temples built between 302 and 264 [Cornell (1995) 381].
56   De Souza (1999) 43–96; Gabrielsen (2003) 395–8.

5: THE HELLENISTIC FAMILY

Dorothy J. Thompson

∽

In the seventh year of the reign of Alexander son of Alexander, when Ptolemy was satrap for the fourteenth year, in the month of Dios. Marriage contract of Herakleides and Demetria. Herakleides from Temnos takes as his lawful wife Demetria from Kos, a free man a free woman, from her father Leptines from Kos and her mother Philotis. She brings into the marriage her clothing and jewellery worth 1,000 drachmas. Herakleides shall provide Demetria which all that befits a free woman and we shall live together wherever seems best to Leptines and Herakleides conferring together in common counsel. If Demetria is found to be doing any harm to the shame of her husband Herakleides, she shall be deprived of everything which she brought into the marriage, but Herakleides must prove whatever he accuses her of before three men, approved by them both. Herakleides is not to be allowed to bring in any other wife to the insult of Demetria, nor may he have children by another woman nor do any wrong to Demetria on any pretext. If Herakleides is caught doing any of these and Demetria proves it before three men whom they both approve, Herakleides shall return to Demetria the dowry which she brought with her of 1,000 dr. and in addition pay a fine of 1,000 dr. of the silver coinage of Alexander. This deed shall carry the force of law for Demetria and those acting with her in their levy on Herakleides and all Herakleides' property both on land and water. This contract shall have force everywhere and in every respect, just as if it had been drawn up there, in whatever place Herakleides may produce it to bear against Demetria or Demetria and those acting with her may produce it against Herakleides. Herakleides and Demetria are to have the right each to keep their own contracts and to bring them to bear against each other. Witnesses: Kleon from Gela, Antikrates from Temnos, Lysis from Temnos, Dionysios from Temnos, Aristomachos from Cyrene, Aristodikos from Kos.

P.Eleph. 1 = M.Chrest. 283 (311 B.C.)

The marriage contract of Herakleides and Demetria, drawn up little more than a decade after the death of Alexander the Great, may serve to introduce the subject of this chapter. Demetria came from Kos, the husband with whom she now set up home in this "contract for cohabitation" (synoikisia) hailed from Temnos in Aeolis. The contract itself is from the island of Elephantine, close by Aswan on the southern border of Egypt. Indeed, the findspot of the text and the varied origins of the witnesses suggest that this was a forced marriage, that father and son-in-law served together in the garrison stationed on Elephantine. For a citizen of either Temnos or Kos who lived at home, with the citizen status of children in mind, a marriage partner would normally come from the same city.[1] In the world that followed Alexander, however, with the movement of people and the setting up of the different Hellenistic kingdoms, life was changed for many. So when Herakleides married Demetria, still known by the ethnic labels of their home of origin, they were in no position to pass on citizen status to any children. It is their status as free persons that they stress. Following regular Greek practice, Demetria is represented by her father Leptines because Greek (unlike Egyptian) women were held to be legally incapable; the record of her mother too is regular Koan practice.[2] For these immigrants in a foreign land, the contract employed is a Greek one, though the prohibition of a second wife may allude to current Egyptian practice.[3]

The relevance of this contract to the present chapter is in the questions it raises as to how changes in the post-Alexander world affected family units and the individuals within them. How typical of the period was this transaction? How did Greeks adapt to their new role in a world that was now far extended and one in which overall they formed a minority, even though they represented the ruling class? What, in contrast, do we know of the majority populations of the different Hellenistic kingdoms? What can we find of the "Hellenistic family," and how useful can such a concept ever be? In what follows, we examine various ways in which change within the family reflected and affected changes in society at large. And, in the end, it should be clear that no single model for the Hellenistic family can cover all the evidence.

FINDING THE FAMILY

> The whole city is made up of households. . . . and the full
> household consists of slave and free.
>
> Aristotle, *Politics I* 1253b

Aristotle was quite clear on the importance of the family as a building
block of the state but, for him, a family consisted of more than just
related family members; it was the *oikia* of which Aristotle writes, and
his picture of the household – with slaves as well as free individuals –
was a very Greek one. In our search for the family, definition is crucial. In this chapter, the term "family" is used for those members of a
household who are related, whereas a "household" includes other nonfamily household members. Not all household dependents, however,
were slaves because there were many forms of dependency, not all of
which involved chattel slavery. The household in turn may be viewed in
many ways: as a family group involved in the continuation of the family
line, as a legal entity, as a demographic, or as an economic unit.[4] The
Hellenistic household functioned in both public and private spheres,[5]
though the former role differed greatly in the different kingdoms and
states. It is, as always for the ancient world, the private sphere that is the
most difficult to enter, yet for most individuals most of the time, this was
surely the more important in terms of personal identity and definition.

In a world that lacks the court speeches of earlier Athens, where
historians were few and where those writings that do survive are largely
concerned with politics and international affairs, sources for family study
are scattered and inevitably partial. Literature is one such partial source.
New Comedy presents the same problems of typicality as does Old
Comedy[6]; the Greek Anthology, like the recently discovered poems of
Poseidippos,[7] contains many epigrams of a private nature, but the typicality of these will always be debated. Inscriptions on stone (especially
those with scenes as well as words), both public and private, as earlier,
also provide unparalleled information and insights on particular individuals, usually those enjoying a reasonable level of wealth, and on the
practices and values of different communities.[8] Epitaphs, in particular,
both literary examples and those inscribed on stone, form a challenging
dataset.[9] From Egypt comes the fullest information, because the dry
climate there has preserved in large numbers papyrus texts of both an
official nature – royal rulings, tax registers, administrative memoranda,
and so on – and the private papers of individuals – contracts and more
intimate material[10] – of particular interest to our subject.

It is from Egypt, more than any other state, that we may begin to answer questions about relations within and between families and households from different ethnic groups in the population and how these changed according to time and place. It is hard too to be sure of the degree to which conclusions based on this material are applicable elsewhere. Where Egypt differs the most is in the small number of its Greek cities. (There were more in the area of Cyrene to the west, which for much of the period formed part of the Ptolemaic kingdom.) The Seleukid empire boasted many more cities, and in mainland Greece, despite the domination of Macedonia and later development of the Aitolian and Achaian Leagues, the Greek polis remained the regular home for most of the population. Experiences, therefore, will have varied depending in part on the different political contexts where Hellenistic families may be found. In this respect, the most striking new feature was the predominance of the monarchic system. The first form of family to consider, therefore, is the royal family, and the question at stake is its typicality. To what degree were the Hellenistic royal families exceptional in type, and how far might they serve as models in their different kingdoms?

Royal Families

When Alexander's generals divided his empire up between themselves, they struggled each to control the largest area. In these struggles, dynastic marriage and support played a crucial part in determining family strength and survival; details of these upheavals may be found elsewhere in this volume.[11] The "House" of particular monarchs was central to their ambitions and the continuation of their rule, and in the case of the "house (*oikia*) of the Macedonians" (of the Argeads, that is, and of the Antigonids), this was both recognised and named.[12] The prime importance of the royal household was clear to historians of the time. In many respects, of course, the royal experience in the post-Alexander world was very different from that of others in their kingdom. As the pieces settled and the various kingdoms were established or redefined, the position of the different royal families was often bolstered by the establishment of royal and dynastic cult.[13] This lay outside normal commoner experience, though the cult association of Epikteta on Ptolemaic Thera which, with its Mouseion, statues and shrines, marking the heroization of her husband and two sons (and later herself), appears to be a case of a family cult.[14]

The marriage patterns of some royal families represent a further mark of difference, because royal marriages were regularly contracted within a limited family circle.[15] Whether it was Macedonian, Achaemenid, or other local practices that were followed is less relevant here than the results of this pattern, which in the case of the Ptolemies in Egypt, from the reign of Ptolemy II Philadelphos and Arsinoe II, offspring of Ptolemy I and Berenike I, involved the regular marriage of full brother and sister as king and queen. Here, even nonrelated queens might be known as "sister and wife" and such sibling terms for unrelated couples are also found elsewhere.[16] Other dynasties were less inbred, but the importance of family solidarity for a royal family is highlighted in this Ptolemaic practice, which is only found within the general population of Egypt in the Roman period.[17] Nevertheless, in the monarchies of the Hellenistic world, the royals themselves might set the tone for society at large in some respects. How the family on top might affect the value structure of the kingdom as a whole and of individual families within it may be illustrated in two examples, one public and the other concerned with a more private aspect of family life.

One important influence of the royal family may be charted in the form of the bureaucratic structures that developed in the different kingdoms. In Macedonia, the king had his "companions" (*hetairoi*), who formed his cavalry and on whom he relied for military support. And in the kingdoms of the east, the administrative class responsible to a king for running his kingdom was increasingly tied to the monarch by a court honorific structure, which, in the names it employed, presented an ideology of family and friends. In terms of chronology, friends came first, and "friends of the king" played an important role in most Hellenistic kingdoms.[18] But during the second century B.C. in both the Seleukid and Ptolemaic kingdoms, the title of "relative (*syngenês*) of the king" extended the family aspect; those who bore this title might address the king as "brother."[19] And, as within the royal family, the use of family terms of address was standard in the bureaucracy. Not all "brothers" should be understood as such.

On the private front, too, kings and queens played a part in promoting family values more widely in society. When in 213 B.C. Queen Laodike III wrote to the council and people of Sardis about honours for herself, her brother the king, and their children, she refers to the latter as "little ones" (*paidia*).[20] A similar term (*teknia*) is employed for their young children by Ptolemy III and his queen when dedicating a temple to Isis and Harpochrates on the island of Philae.[21] An open

affection for children is here on display, and this royal emphasis on familial tenderness was reflected lower down the social scale. The sympathetic
depiction of children on tombstones, their half-size epitaphs in Smyrna,
and the record of their toys and the lives that they led are all features
of the period in which royal practice may have set or mirrored the
trend.[22]

The emphasis on children as a notable feature of Hellenistic royal
family ideology is matched by that on queens, now regularly included
with their royal husbands in dedications made by those who sought
their favour. Queens, too, might actively promote a family ideology, as
in the case of Laodike just mentioned; on a later occasion, the same
queen provided dowries for the daughters of poor citizens in Iasos.[23]
Phila, wife of Demetrios Poliorketes, did the same for the daughters and
sisters of needy soldiers.[24] The royal family was thus actively involved
both in setting an example to others and in promoting the families of
those, like the troops, on whom they relied.

The rulers of Hellenistic kingdoms traced their ancestry to
Macedonia, but the Greek peoples of their kingdoms came from many
other areas, too. There were those who belonged for many generations
to the cities where they lived, in Greece, the Aegean, Asia Minor, and
elsewhere, and there were those Greeks who came to new homes, in
cities or in the countryside of the kingdoms of the East, as soldiers or
as traders, as those who sought their fortunes as immigrants, or who
simply hoped for a better life. And all the time, besides the Greeks,
there were the long-established inhabitants of the new areas of Greek
rule, earlier subjects of Persia in the East and natives of the lands in
which they lived. In our investigation of family experience in a time of
flux, these are the two main groups we next consider, starting with the
Greeks.

Greek Families

The character of Greek families in the Hellenistic world was multifarious, depending on where they were. For many in the cities of Greece
proper and the islands, or along the coast of Asia Minor in the old Greek
settlements of Asia, the changed political circumstances will have made
little difference. As for Aristotle, the *oikia* remained a building block
of the state, which for Greeks was their polis. Citizenship in the polis
regularly (but not invariably) involved descent from full citizens combined with political recognition – inscription in a civic subdivision, as in
Athens a deme and a tribe – and membership of social organisations like

the phratry. Rules differed according to city; the Athenian two-parent rule for citizenship applicable for a limited period from the mid-fifth century B.C. lay at one end of the spectrum, though even here there were exceptions and, over time, the rules were relaxed.[25] In the Greek cities of the Hellenistic world, not much was changed, at least in theory; marriage between citizens within the community remained the norm. New city foundations adopted similar practices. In Alexandria, a deme and tribal system formed part of the city's new political structure; both there and in Hellenistic Rhodes, the dual-parent rule continued to define full citizens.[26]

Rhodes and Alexandria, however, were large and flourishing Hellenistic cities. It is elsewhere, often in smaller states under the control of the new kingdoms, that different political arrangements affecting citizen families are found. States might merge their citizen bodies in various acts of union.[27] Agreements like these, known primarily from inscriptions, were not new to the Greek world and now, as earlier, the need to strengthen citizen numbers would appear to lie at their base.[28] Elsewhere, citizenship was for sale[29] or grants of citizenship might be made to specific groups (of Greeks), with the aim of increasing the citizen body.[30] Sometimes, it was simply the right to marry (*epigamia*) with Greeks from elsewhere that was granted, so ensuring the legitimacy of future children, but often this was linked to a range of different rights, involving political rights, access to land, legal procedures, contracts, market privileges, and so on.[31]

The data on these developments, whose frequency is hard to assess, is mainly epigraphical, and scattered in publication. It is the family implications of what were essentially political acts that interest us here. Marriage in Hellenistic Miletos, for instance, involved an exciting range of options for citizens of that city. Although for most, a husband or wife from an old Milesian family would be standard, the possible choice of marriage partners was forever widening, as we learn from the grants of citizen rights inscribed in the sacred enclosure of the Delphinion. Already in the fourth century B.C., an agreement of *sympoliteia* was recorded for Miletos and its colony Kyzikos,[32] and in the early second century, the small neighbouring city of Pidasa was incorporated into the city under an act of *sympoliteia*.[33] And there were many others similar grants. Milesians might now contract a marriage with citizens of such states without prejudice to their children's status. Groups of individuals were also granted citizen status, like the Cretan mercenaries in 234/3 and 229/8 B.C., some of whom came with their families and some without,[34] or the bastards registered as new citizens of Miletos.[35] These, too, might now function as an extended source of marriage partners. Like the Greek families of its constituent cities, the Hellenistic world was strikingly diverse.

There were many reasons individuals moved home in this as in any other period, but a feature of surviving inscriptions is the importance to new citizens of rights to a house and a plot of land (or other means of livelihood) in their new home. There was no one blueprint for such grants, and the variety of provisions forms an interesting comment on the different economic features of the various areas and their populations. So, for instance, when Pidasa was merged with Latmos sometime in the period 323–313 B.C., the Latmians were required to provide sufficient quarters (*stathmoi*) for those from Pidasa.[36] The six-year requirement for intermarriage between these two communities was an exceptionally prescriptive clause in this agreement, but the concern for somewhere to live was reasonably standard. When the Cretan mercenaries were settled in Myous by Miletos, they were granted minimal equipment (*sk[eua]rion*) and shelters (*stegna*) to contain this.[37] In the later *sympoliteia* agreement of Pidasa and Miletos in 182 B.C., tax details were specified for olives in the territory of Pidasa, along with the livestock and hives. For Miletos, it was the produce of vineyards and harbour taxes that was detailed. Miletos was to build a road for Pidasa and provide 390 dwellings (*oikêseis*) for their new citizens.[38] Other contemporary decrees specify grazing rights (*epinomia*) along with other rights and local details.[39] Political, private, social, and economic aspects of life were intertwined for the citizens of a Hellenistic city.

So far, the picture has been of Greek cities broadening their scope and citizenship that was likely to result in families with broader connections and (possibly) outlook than found in earlier generations. Cities, however, now functioned in a world of larger power blocs that might intrude on the lives of the citizen. The names of new tribes and demes form one example of the overarching influence of kings, queens, and others of influence. In Athens, new tribal names reflect dynastic change: Antigonis and Demetrias 307–200, Ptolemais from 224/3 and Attalis from 200 B.C.[40] So, when under Ptolemy III and Berenike II Antiphilos was inscribed in the citizen rolls of Ptolemais, the new city foundation of Upper Egypt, it was the *Ptolemais* tribe and *Berenikeus* deme to which he was assigned.[41] Similarly, when in 186 B.C. on the recommendation of Seleukos IV the city of Seleukeia-in-Pieria incorporated a friend of the king, Aristolochos, as a new citizen, he was registered in the Laodikis tribe.[42] Both the nature of the benefactions that earned them their citizenship and the names of their new civic affiliations remind us that, even in Greek cities, citizen life was now played out in the shadow of kings and queens.

Greek Families in Foreign Lands

Not all Greeks, however, lived in cities, and as a result of the conquests of Alexander and the wars of his successors, large numbers of Greeks came to fight in lands that were barely known to Greeks before. The expanded scope of the world had repercussions also on their family situations. It was the Greeks settled in foreign parts who more than any others represented the new Greeks of the Hellenistic world. What do we know of their families?

Perhaps not surprisingly in the changing fortunes of the period, family was sometimes more important to an army man than was his commander. Successful rulers exploited this fact. In January 316 at Gabiene in Persis, Antigonos captured the baggage-train (*aposkeuê*) of Eumenes, including the soldiers' children, wives, and other relations. Eumenes' phalanx, in response to this capture, deserted their previous commander, joining up instead with Antigonos.[43] In 306 B.C. on Cyprus, "baggage" again played a decisive role. When Antigonos' son Demetrios defeated Menelaos, governor of Cyprus and brother of Ptolemy I, at Salamis and captured his troops, he at first re-enrolled these troops in his own units but, when they started deserting back to the defeated Ptolemaic side, he shipped them off elsewhere. The reason, Diodorus reports, for their desertion was that their *aposkeuai* had been left back home in Egypt.[44] Because it is clear from the Gabiene events that the term *aposkeuê* included family, this incident highlights the success of Ptolemy's policy of settling soldiers with land (as cleruchs) in his new kingdom. Scattered through the villages of Egypt, though more in the north than the south, land-holding cleruchs formed a reserve force for the king and a Greek presence in the Egyptian countryside. Papyri from Egypt tell us much about this key group in Ptolemaic society, whose rural settlement reflects the lack of Greek-style *poleis* in this major kingdom, where Naukratis, Alexandria, and Ptolemais Hermeiou in Upper Egypt were the only such cities.

In Seleukid Asia, in contrast, troops were settled together in groups, regularly attached to existing cities, as may be illustrated from the inscription recording an agreement made between the loyal city of Smyrna and Magnesia near Mt. Sipylos after the latter had deserted during the early phase of the Third Syrian War.[45] Seleukos II had returned to the area, demonstrating "his piety towards the gods and his affection in respect of his parents" (l.6). Guaranteeing autonomy and democracy, he now requested asylum status for the temple of Aphrodite Stratonikis (his grandmother as Aphrodite); he addressed this demand to the "kings, dynasts, cities, and peoples (*ethnê*)" of the area. In turn, the local officials (*stratêgoi*) contacted the settlers (*katoikoi*) in Magnesia, the cavalry in the field, and the (foot)-soldiers, offering them friendship (ll.11−14). It later becomes clear that both cavalry and infantry were numbered among the settlers in this new city foundation (ll.43−45).[46]

For settlers, the experience differed according to where they were, and it is the Egyptian scene that is documented best. Here, Greek papyri record a total of over 160 different designations of origin (known as "ethnics"), ignoring the feminine and other related forms.[47] A handful of these denote Africans, Arabs, various Semitic groups, and a few from within the country, but the vast majority designate Greeks from all parts of the Greek-speaking world, providing a fair measure of the degree of migration in the early Hellenistic world. Many of those from elsewhere who ended up in Egypt originally came as military men; yet others were seeking their fortune. There is more work to be done in separating out the contexts in which these ethnics occur according to the occupations of their holders − as cleruchs, serving soldiers, or civilian immigrants.[48] We may expect a varied pattern and one that changes over time.[49]

Once the immigrant families were settled in Egypt, salt-tax registers allow further investigation of family and household make-up. Alexandria and the Delta, where the moister climate means that papyri have not survived (except occasionally in carbonised form), remain uncharted territory, but from Middle Egypt in the third and second centuries B.C., we now have reasonably clear information on settlement and household patterns.[50] A database of 427 households containing 1,271 adults from the Arsinoite and Oxyrhynchite nomes in the second half of the third century B.C. allows some detailed conclusions. The first feature to stress is the different picture found in Greek and Egyptian households, households, that is, differentiated according to the name of the household head. These were differences primarily of size. Overall two-adult households were the most common form, accounting for 38 percent of all households; for Egyptians, they formed 46.5 percent, but for Greeks, only 24.5 percent of households. Of Egyptians, just 13 percent lived in households of over five adults; the comparable figure for Greeks was 35.4 percent. No Egyptian household contained more than eight adults, whereas one Greek household had twenty-two adults in it. Allowing for children, the average size of a Greek family was 4.4 compared with 4.0 for Egyptians; if non-kin household members are included, the figure rises to 5.0 for the average size of a Greek household but remains at 4.0 for Egyptians.

Non-kin dependants are found mostly in Greek families. The contrast with Egyptian households is striking, and Aristotle's definition of a household as one containing slaves is found to be peculiarly Greek. The presence of chattel slaves represents a real feature of ethnic difference. On the tombstones of Hellenistic Smyrna, which given the expense involved are likely to represent the better-off slaves, their low social status denoted by the small scale of their depiction, standardly accompany both men and women.[51] For Greek households in Egypt, the tax registers record slaves in one of seven Greek households. More were female than male, 1.75:1, and the larger households tended to contain more slaves. Some female slaves (known as *paidiskai* or "maids") were clearly household slaves; others, especially groups of "boys" (*paides*), may have been employed in forms of household production.

Other non-kin household members in the Ptolemaic material include nurses, grooms (for cavalry settlers), cowherds, goatherds, shepherds, and a variety of agricultural workers who lived with the families for whom they worked. The larger the family, the more likely it was to contain such nonfamily members. Wet-nurses also occur in more Greek (5.5 percent) than Egyptian households, particularly in the homes of cleruchs. In Smyrna, nurses were shown on gravestones as larger in size than servants, reflecting their somewhat higher status.[52] As with slaves, it was the larger Greek menages that tended to employ a nurse; the only two nurses known from Egyptian families in our database served in professional homes (one working for a brewer, the other for an urban policeman).

The Greek military settlers of Ptolemaic Egypt were, on the demographic evidence of the tax registers, among the better off in terms of the size and diversity of their households. The greater scale of their households is matched in the records also of the livestock they owned and the size of their farms. These, it is clear, were the elite of the Ptolemaic countryside, as reflected in this pattern of family strength and wealth; their standard of living contrasts strongly with that of the smaller families of the Egyptian villagers and peasants among whom they lived.

One final feature of difference needs mention, and that is the statistically significant lack of females apparent among the Greeks. In demographic terms, there is an imbalance in the sex ratio among Greek families not found among the Egyptians. In those families with adult children still living at home, there are more sons than daughters, more brothers than sisters resident in extended families, and more men than women overall. In part, this situation may reflect the pattern of immigrant settlement, with more males than female settlers in the countryside, though by the time of these records, the major wave of immigration was probably over. In part, faulty recording practices may be responsible, though in a situation where women were liable to the salt tax as well as men, this is less plausible than when, as in Roman Egypt, women did not pay the poll tax. An explanation, as argued elsewhere, in terms of female exposure appears to be most likely.[53] This practice would seem to be implied by those somewhat later authors who commented on the Egyptian practice of rearing all their children.[54] Other reasons may, of course, be suggested – the preferential treatment of males, for instance – but whatever the explanation, this is a notable area of ethnic difference.

The problem of finding wives is a feature of most colonial settlements; the most usual solution to this problem has probably been intermarriage with the existing population.[55] That this was also the practice in Egypt under its new rulers is supported by the evidence of our database where nine per cent of Greek husbands had wives with Egyptian names but not a single Egyptian husband had a wife whose name was Greek. Such a pattern has important implications for ethnic relations and for the long-term mix of a population. For what this meant in human terms, it is necessary to go beyond the tax lists and look at family archives.

Many groups of family papers shed light on family relations. Wills, like the collection of military wills in the Petrie papyri from the third century B.C. or the Cretan cavalryman Dryton's three consecutive wills, made in 164, 150, and 126 B.C., catalogue an individual's wealth and how this should be disposed of.[56] Family relations are named and Dryton certainly bucked the trend in rearing five daughters by his second wife Apollonia, also known as Senmonthis, in a family that had four slaves, whereas the cavalrymen of the Petrie wills belonged to a strongly Greek milieu. Dryton's family is interesting in that up country in Pathyris at a later date, it formed part of a far more mixed community. The women in this archive have Egyptian or double names; Egyptian demotic might be used for everyday transactions and, although Dryton's wills were in Greek, the marriage and divorce contracts of his daughters and granddaughters were written in demotic.[57] Apollonia herself was from an Egyptianised Cyrenean family, and it is primarily as a Greek that she presents herself, working in either Greek or Egyptian, depending on the availability of relevant notaries, in her quite extensive business dealings. Her girls, however, tend more towards the Egyptian side, perhaps reflecting their home life.[58] Different families had different experiences, but overall, the tendency over time is towards a greater ethnic mix, and in this, mothers, like nurses, seem likely to have played a key role.

The Non-Greek Family

It has already proved impossible to discuss Greek families living in the Egyptian countryside in isolation from the Egyptian population. In directing the spotlight in turn on family life among the majority populations of the different Hellenistic states, again it is Egypt where the wealth of evidence demands that we concentrate.

For Egyptians, as indeed for Greeks, marriage was sometimes virilocal, but conjugal menages were more standard. The typicality of the nuclear family extended well up the Nile into Middle Egypt (and probably beyond). In demographic terms, what has been identified as a Mediterranean family pattern applied also in Egypt. As among Greeks, resident mothers were a standard feature of extended families; 7.5 percent of all families had mothers resident in them, in most cases, presumably widows.

In other important respects, there were notable differences. Slaves are rarely found in Egyptian households, and in the very few cases where they occur these are urban families, particularly those of Egyptians who were upwardly mobile or who gained Hellenic tax status. Slave-holding, it seems clear, was part of "going Greek,"[59] joining language, food, dress, the legal system employed, and family structure as a clear ethnic denominator.

For Egyptians too, the key moments of birth, marriage, and death were all marked by practices that differed from those among the Greeks. We have already noted the full complement of girls to survive among Egyptian families. On marriage, those Egyptian women who were the subject of prenuptial contracts were well protected; once children were born, further support was regularly laid down in case of divorce.[60] Prior to marriage, clitoridectomy is known to have been applied, a practice that places Egyptian families firmly in the realm of Africa. It is an Egyptian, Harmais, who refers in passing to this as "the practice among Egyptians."[61] Polygamy was another Egyptian practice.[62] On death, of course, mummification was the norm for those Egyptians who could afford it. The vocabulary of close-kin relationships is yet another way in which differences may be seen. In Egyptian demotic, for instance, words existed for "parents-in-law" (/sm and /sm.t), which was not the case in Greek.[63]

A further real difference between the two main populations concerns the legal rights of Egyptian women. Unlike Greek women, who could not act without a guardian, Egyptian women needed no guardians and could inherit or bequeath property separately from their husbands. Inheritance then becomes an even more complex matter, and the archives of Egyptian families, often covering many generations, allow us to identify the multifarious nature of family property and to trace its dispersal and concentration over time and the role of different family members in this process. There was a premium on the preservation of family papers. Contracts within family archives often survived for hundreds of years. So, for a family of Memphite necropolis workers, demotic contracts allow us to trace family property – much of it in the form of prospective mummies – for eleven generations within the same family; the contracts themselves date more closely to the period from 203 to (at least) 65 B.C.[64] The change over time in this case, as in other similar examples, is towards the Greek side, with double names and the later use of the Greek language and legal system. Potentially, this was a destabilising tendency, possibly involving a new system of inheritance. As so often, we lack the evidence to evaluate the extent of change, but in this particular Hellenistic kingdom, there were both real and significant differences between the two main groups in the population and evolution over time of indigenous practices.

There were other groups within the population of Egypt, as indeed of other Hellenistic kingdoms; these often retained their local ways. The *timouchoi* of the Ionian settlers, Arab elders (*presbyteroi*), or the *archontes* and *politarchai* of the Jews show the degree to which others' structures were accepted in this kingdom.[65] In third century B.C., Elephantine Aramaic might still be used; other Jewish communities of Egypt practised their own family law, with Jewish contracts of marriage and separation.[66]

How far this sort of variation was found elsewhere is generally unknown. Traces of adjustment in respect of native peoples are occasionally documented, as in the integration of children of Libyan women from within a designated area into the early Hellenistic constitution of Cyrene.[67] If on the whole, in the Hellenistic world, a high degree of tolerance appears the norm, on occasion, non-Greek practices were rejected. When the Indian prince Keteus died fighting with Eumenes in the battle of Paraitakene in 317 B.C., his two wives fought for the privilege of accompanying him in death. The younger wife won out – the elder was found to be pregnant – and the troops watched this case of suttee with amazement and approbation. Not all of the Greeks, however, shared their sentiment; some considered the practice hard and inhuman.[68] Here, at least, we find some comment on the clash of custom and values. How common this may have been eludes us, though the question is surely worth asking.

The Hellenistic Family in Focus

So far, it is variation that we have found with different family practices according to time, place, and different groups within the population. To integrate this information into the wider history of the Hellenistic world is not an easy task. Is it possible to see any one tendency at work in respect to family history? Was there a move towards Droysen's "Mischkultur" in family matters, or a "Hellenistic relaxation" as affirmed by Daniel Ogden?[69] How far was Greek still Greek, and non-Greek something other? To what extent did subject peoples take on the manners and customs of those who ruled?

No firm answers are clear, but these are the questions to ask, and in some places, some of the time it is possible to begin to answer them. In the context of the Greek city, it seems clear that while holding on to traditional principles and the expectation of endogamy, in practice, there were many places where, as earlier, local compromise was the reaction to problems of manpower. Big cities were more able to hold on to their restrictive practices; elsewhere there was some relaxation. Sales of citizenship, grants of marriage rights (epigamia), and a range of different forms of partnership or amalgamation with other states are found of types less frequently documented for the earlier classical world. One feature, however, is clear. There were limits in all of these grants and, although the boundaries were stretched, for citizens, free Greek descent remained a serious issue, at least in the third and second centuries. So, in the agreement between Magnesia and Smyrna already mentioned, those able to partake in the citizenship of the other city were specified. In each case, the limit applied was: "as many as are free and are Greeks."[70] We remember Herakleides and Demetria ("a free man, a free woman"), with whom we started this chapter. A similar limit is found in the sympolity agreement between Miletos and Pidasa which, among other clauses, allowed marriage with citizen women from the other city. In the case of Milesians, those now available for marriage are described as: "by birth (physei) women of Pidasa or citizens of a Greek city."[71] It is clear from the earlier record of Pidasa that this small state needed coalitions to survive; a less strict regime in terms of marriage partners for their citizens had been allowed and was now taken over by

Miletos. But again there were limits. Only Greek citizen women were legitimate.

Greekness was important, and in the Hellenistic world where, in practice, boundaries became more fluid and Greek status might be claimed by those who were not ethnically Greek, the role of Greek culture and Greek education played an important role in the definition of Greekness. On the Smyrna tombstones, book rolls are commonly shown, Greek terracottas from Alexandria include two girls with texts outstretched on their knees, and the royal encouragement given to education in many Hellenistic states points in the same direction. Whether living in a self-governing Greek city or as a subject in a kingdom, Greeks stuck together and cultivated their Greekness.

At the same time, some preferred to go native; mixed marriages and close contact in everyday life with the many different peoples of the Hellenistic world allowed a range of different options. Dryton's wife might, as we saw, present herself as Greek in her dealings with those around her, but her daughters, more normally known by their Egyptian names, preferred to function in Egyptian.[72] Of the two sons of the Macedonian soldier Glaukias detained in the Memphite Serapeum in the middle years of the second century B.C., the elder, Ptolemaios, consistently presented himself as Greek, whereas his younger brother Apollonios was equally at home in an Egyptian milieu, even using Egyptian for the record of his dreams.[73] There was no one rule, and within a single family, different members might react to the circumstances in which they lived in very different ways. On the whole, however, this was a tolerant world in which individuals at different times aligned themselves with different sides depending on personal whim or occasion. It was a world in which a Greek poet Poseidippos could write an epitaph for an Asian woman.[74] In family matters and experiences, this was indeed a diverse and multicultural world.[75]

BIBLIOGRAPHICAL NOTE

The study of the family has not, until recently, been a standard part of Hellenistic history. Older studies – Préaux (1978) and Davies (1984) – even when encompassing social history, rarely mention the family as such. Studies of the Greek family and its members – Golden (1990), on children, Patterson (1998), Pomeroy (1997) – break off with little more than a final chapter on the period. Pomeroy (1984), with earlier studies, is concerned with the female side, and Ogden (1996), on bastardy, treats another aspect of family history. With van Bremen (2003), family history has entered the Hellenistic mainstream (see her recommended reading, p. 330). This is now the best introduction to the subject, concentrating particularly on the cities of Asia Minor and the Seleukid kingdom.

Further reading might start with the excellent collections of sources in translation: Austin (in press), Bagnall and Derow (2004), and Burstein (1985), with Rowlandson (1998), especially Chapter 3, for Egypt. Lewis (1986) introduces family archives from Egypt, and Clarysse and Thompson (forthcoming, 2005) vol. II, Chapter 7, provide a demographic analysis with family studies. On marriage, see Vatin (1970), Vérilhac and Vial (1998), and the older standard studies of Pestman (1961) and Wolff (1939), on marriage in Egypt. Mélèze Modrzejewski (1999) discusses changes in legal practice, focussing on marriage, divorce, adoption and inheritance; this work is based more on the evidence of papyri (from Egypt) than on inscriptions (from a broader area). There is much work still to be done in exploiting the archaeological material; for a start, see Nevett (1999) 114–23 and Cahill (2002) 84–193, 281–8, on housing; Zanker (1993) on tombstones.

NOTES

1 See Vérilhac and Vial (1998) 24 and 60, for Temnos and Kos requiring citizen status for both parents.
2 Vérilhac and Vial (1998) 60–1. For the (new) responsible role of the partners themselves in this marriage, see Mélèze-Modrzejewski (1999) 266.
3 Cf. Pomeroy (1996) 253, n. 22; for bigamy, see Clarysse and Thompson (in press) II, Table 7:25 with discussion.
4 Production and reproduction are the concerns highlighted by Goody (1976) in his classic study. Patterson (1998) 67–8, surveys the early Greek family; Parkin (1992); Bagnall and Frier (1994); and Saller (1994) stress the demographic aspect, but for later periods.
5 See van Bremen (2003) 329–30.
6 Golden (1990) 169–80, Patterson (1998) 180–225 and Cox (2002) aim to incorporate this material.
7 See Chapter 9 in this volume.
8 See, for instance, Pfuhl and Möbius (1977–1979), exploited for Smyrna by Zanker (1993). Most studies of the Hellenistic family and social institutions are heavily dependent on epigraphical evidence.
9 See Saller (2001) 97–8, on epitaphs.
10 See Lewis (1986). Pomeroy (1984) and (1997) Chapter 6, is at home among the papyri; Rowlandson (1998), provides an historical overview of translated material.
11 See Chapter 2 in this volume.
12 See Walbank (2002) 131–6.
13 See Chapter 10 in this volume.
14 *IG* XII.3.330 (200–195 B.C.); cf. Davies (1984) 318, for other examples.

15 Vérilhac and Vial (1998) 92–8, discuss the phenomenon of close-kin marriage among royal families but stress the atypicality of Ptolemaic practice (followed also by the kings of Pontos).

16 For example, *OGIS* 56.8 (238 B.C.), Berenike II, daughter of Magas, termed "sister and wife" of Ptolemy III Euergetes; *SEG* 39. 1284.B.13–14 (213 B.C.), Queen Laodike III, daughter of Mithridates of Pontos, refers to the Seleukid Antiochos III as "our brother the king."

17 Vatin (1970) 57–114, with Gauthier (1972) 209–10, stressing the political aspect; Vérilhac and Vial (1998) 97–100 with earlier bibliography; see, too, Bagnall and Frier (1994), 127–33; Scheidel (1995), (1996b) 9–51, (1996a), (1997); of the three Ptolemaic examples given by Bussi (2002) 20, none is certain.

18 Mooren (1975) and (1977); Savalli-Lestrade (1998).

19 Mooren (1977) 36–41; cf. van Bremen (2003) 327.

20 *SEG* 39. 1284.B.14, cf. A.4, *tekna* = Ma (1999) 285–6, no. 2, with 287 on royal *philostorgia*.

21 *OGIS* I 61 = *I.Philae* I 4.3, cf. Bingen (1997) 89–90, for the reading and date.

22 On Smyrna, see Zanker (1993) 221–2, liveliness, 228, half-size *stelai*, fig. 18, toys; Posidippus 47, ed. Austin and Bastianini (2002), Onasagorastis who died at age 100 with eighty children and children's children, cf. 59; 44 (the youngest of twelve), 51, and 54, child epitaphs; *Palatine Anthology* IV 312, children's games; Pollitt (1986) 128–9, for Roman copies of child statues. For earlier, see Humphreys (1980) 113, on *lekythoi*, including one depicting a child with his go-cart; 121–2, on post-classical commemoration.

23 Ma (1999) 329–5, no. 26A.18–25 (ca.196 B.C.), specifically mentioning the royal *oikos* (1.26).

24 Diod. 19.59.4; cf. van Bremen (1996) 140–1; (2003) 326–8, on the civic context.

25 So Aristotle, *Pol.* 1275b, but cf. 1278a. Exceptions: Perikles, son of Perikles and Aspasia from Miletos (Plut. *Per.* 37.2–5), granted citizenship in 429 B.C., as were metics who joined in the restoration of democracy in 401 B.C., *RO* 4; for block grants of citizenship by Athens, see [Dem.] LIX 104, Plataia in 427 B.C., cf. Isoc., *Plat.* 51, for *epigamia*, and *ML* 94 (405/404), Samos; M. J. Osborne (1981–1983) I, 15–24, records changing formulae and lists decrees.

26 Savalli (1985) 394–6, argues against the existence of halfway citizens; Vérilhac and Vial (1998) 65–70, survey the evidence. On Alexandria, see Fraser (1972) I, chapters 2–3; on Rhodes, Gabrielsen (1997), especially chapter 5.

27 Through *sympoliteia*, *homopoliteia* or *isopoliteia*; Savalli (1985) investigates the procedures involved in many of these.

28 For earlier mergers, see *Staatsverträge* II no. 297 (ca. 360–350 B.C.), Orchomenos and Euaimon, cf. ll. 40–43 on generous marriage provisions; *IPArk* 9 (mid-fourth century B.C.), Mantineia and Helisson; cf. Xen. *Hell.* 5.2.18, on *epigamia*.

29 [Aristotle], *Oec.* II 2, 3, at Byzantion 30 minas bought citizenship for those with one citizen parent only; *Syll.*³ 531 (third century B.C.), Dyme in Achaia provides for the sale of citizenship to free settlers (*epoikoi*); in Miletos, some offspring of citizen fathers recorded as new citizens may have had this privilege purchased for them, Vérilhac and Vial (1998) 63–5; cf. Tenos where payment of 25 dr. (perhaps a supplementary tax), allowed the registration of bastards in a *patra*, *IG* XII *Suppl.* 303 (fourth century B.C.); 355 (early third century B.C.), Thasos sells citizenship to three individuals for 100 staters a person.

30   Cf. *Syll.*³ 543 (215 B.C.), translated Bagnall and Derow (2004) no. 32, urged by
     Philip V, Larisa extends its citizenship.
31   See Vérilhac and Vial (1998) 68–9, for some examples.
32   *Milet* I.3, 137 (323 B.C.).
33   *Milet* I.3, 149, cf. VI.1, pp. 184–5 for translation (182 B.C.); for the history of Pidasa
     and its earlier union with Latmos, see Wörrle (2003); van Bremen (2003) 313–15.
34   *Milet* I.3, 33–5 and 36–8, with Merkelbach and Stauber (1998) 01/19/03, 01/19.04,
     01/20/33.4; cf. Savalli (1985) 424–6.
35   See aforementioned n. 28; Ogden (1996) 304–10.
36   Wörrle (2003) 122, ll. 19–20.
37   *Milet* I.3, 33e.11–14; houses are mentioned in l.12. Savalli (1985) 425–6, follows
     Cohen in understanding *stegna* as housing for troops; their description as "attached"
     (*epî*) is against this.
38   *Milet* I.3, 149.18–25, Pidasa, ll.28 and 41–45, Miletos.
39   For Gonnoi in Thessaly, see Helly (1973) II, index *s.v.*
40   Will (1979–1982) I, 73, 363–4; II, 130–1.
41   *OGIS* I 49.10–15, in gratitude for the games he endowed "worthy of the king and
     the city."
42   Holleaux (1942b) 199–200, lines 24–7.
43   Diod. 19.43.7–9; see Bosworth (2002) 157–8, and cf. Athenaios XIII 607f– 608a,
     Parmenion gets flute-girls from the *aposkeuê* of Darius III. On Gabiene, see also
     Chapter 13 in this volume.
44   Diod. 20.47.4, with Holleaux (1942a).
45   *OGIS* 229 (ca. 242?), translated in Bagnall and Derow (2004) no. 29; Austin (in
     press) no. 174.
46   See Cohen (1995) 216–17.
47   See now La'da (2002); demotic forms are not included in these figures.
48   Cf. the interesting analysis of Bagnall (1984), from a more limited database than
     now available.
49   La'da (1996), chapter 3, Tables 1–3, documents greater ethno-geographical diver-
     sity in the third century B.C. than later.
50   Clarysse and Thompson (in press); tax registers do not record children.
51   Zanker (1993) 216, 223.
52   Zanker (1993) 223.
53   See Thompson (2002) and Clarysse and Thompson (in press) chapter 7, under "Sex
     ratios." On the variability and consequent unreliability of the Milesian material
     exploited by Pomeroy (1993) and (1997) 205–6, for infanticide, see Vérilhac and
     Vial (1998) 62, n. 68.
54   Diod. 1.80.3; Strabo XVII 2.5 (C824).
55   Chaniotis (2002) 110–3, discusses the apparent preference for traditional marriage
     partners found within Greek garrisons of this period.
56   *P. Petrie*² I. *Wills*, ed., Clarysse; *P. Dryton* 1–4, with translations, ed. Vandorpe.
57   *P.Dryton* 5–9.
58   See Vandorpe (2002) and Rowlandson (1998) 105–12; cf. *I.Fay.* I 2.8–13 (244–
     221 B.C.), two Cyrenean daughters of Demetrios and his Egyptian wife Thasis,
     Eirene/Nephersouchos and Theoxena/Thaues, dedicate a shrine to the
     hippopotamus-goddess, Thoeris.
59   See Thompson (2001) 307–12.

60 See Pestman (1961); Thompson (1988) 181–5, examines some specific cases; Rowlandson (1998) 312–35.

61 *UPZ* I 2.11–13 (163 B.C.), translated with discussion in Rowlandson (1998) 78–100, no. 78; cf. Strabo XVII 2.5 (C824).

62 Clarysse and Thompson (in press) II, Chapter 7, under "Marriage."

63 *P.Count* 10.36; 53.426 (second century B.C.).

64 Thompson (1988) Chapter 5.

65 Thompson (1988) 97; *PSI* V 538, Arab dekatarchs and elders; Honigman (2003b) 62.

66 Aramaic salt-tax receipt (252 B.C.), Porten and Yardeni (1999), D8.13, but cf. Honigman (2003a) 00 (23 in proof). *P.Enteux.* 23 = *C.Pap.Jud.* I 128.2–3 (218 B.C.), marriage by Jewish law; *P.Polit.Jud.* 4 (134 B.C.), a broken betrothal, with Honigman (2003b) 97 and 101–2.

67 *SEG* 9.1 = *SEG* 18.726.1–4 (308/7 B.C.).

68 Diod. 19.33–34.6, with an improbable explanation for the origin of suttee.

69 For Droysen, see Momigliano (1977) 307–23; Préaux (1978), I 5–9; Austin (in press). Ogden (1996), Chapter 11.

70 *OGIS* 229.45, 52 (ca. 242? B.C.), *eleutheroi kai Hellênes*.

71 *Milet* I.3, 149.11–12 (182 B.C.).

72 See aforementioned nn. 56–7.

73 Thompson (1988) Chapter 7, and Rowlandson (1998) 98–105, for the mixed environment of the Memphite Serapeum.

74 56.7.

75 I should like to express my thanks to James Roy, Lene Rubinstein, and Riet van Bremen for helpful comments on this chapter.

6: History and Rhetoric

Graham J. Oliver

∽

Introduction

I s there something different about how history was written in the
years after the death of Alexander up to the first century? What
similarities or continuities characterise writers of history in the
Hellenistic era compared with their predecessors? How does history
writing relate to the development of other aspects of literary and intellectual culture – philosophy, oratory, literature, and education – in
general? How does history writing fit in its own political and historical
environment when the territorial kingdoms that were established after
the reign of Alexander and that characterise the Hellenistic era gradually
succumb to the power of the Roman empire? This chapter attempts to
answer these questions.

The chapter's title, history and rhetoric, offers a particular slant to
a study of history writing in the Hellenistic period. For rhetoric influenced not only writers of history but also makers of history. History
and rhetoric offer two interconnected approaches to the Hellenistic
world and, indeed, other periods of history. On the one hand, one
could write about the role of rhetoric in history or, in the context of
this book, how Hellenistic kings or politicians used oratory, for example. Or how Greek cities employed rhetorical skills in their relations
with the kings and other Greek *poleis* and later Rome, in particular
the Senate, and the Romans, in particular Roman magistrates, generals, and individuals operating in the eastern Mediterranean. On the
other hand, one could consider the influence of rhetoric on history
writers. Historians use speeches. They put spoken words into the historical figures that appear in their narratives. Historians are also writers
who employ rhetorical manners, which comes as no surprise. In other

words, they compose in a self-conscious way. They use rhetorical techniques that had developed or been developed by a society in which the spoken word and argument were part of regular (intellectual) life. For those writing in the Hellenistic period, the context is multifaceted. In the eastern Mediterranean, Greek education and culture (*paideia*) were dominant among the mobile elite and the diffusion of *paideia*, and all that this upbringing entailed had an enormous effect on the development of what we might loosely call Hellenistic civilisation. In turn, the adoption in Italy of many of these cultural practices saw an assimilation of Greek *paideia* in the Roman world. History writers were working in a tradition from the late fourth century onwards. A tradition of history writers (Herodotos, Thucydides, Xenophon, Theopompos, and Ephoros, for example) and an intellectual tradition (e.g., philosophical, rhetorical, poetic, etc.).

There are then several important themes that need to be considered. This chapter is necessarily selective. It offers neither a fully detailed survey of history writing nor a complete synthesis on the history writing and rhetoric. Instead the chapter weaves together two strands – history writers and history makers. One man in the Hellenistic era above all others identified himself as such a figure – Polybios. This Greek writer from Megalopolis (in the Peloponnese) embodies the tension between the theory and practice, between history making and history writing. For Polybios chose to emphasise the importance to the history writer of both personal experience as a history maker and the direct participation and observation of other history makers.

This chapter draws largely on the history writers of Hellenistic era, but it should be noted that often the writers of history were also producing works that might be identified as other genres. Twenty-five years ago, genres – geography, ethnography, antiquarianism (a term that can cover local history and mythography) – were treated separately.[1] Recent studies have preferred to explore the relationships between such genres, emphasising for example the interaction between geography and history or history and ethnography.[2] This trend is part of a wider movement that puts less emphasis on building up the connections between ancient and modern historiographical practices.[3] Instead, greater attention is given to the cultivation of ideas and intellectual changes that preceded and also that marked the age in which ancient history writers were working. There is behind this chapter, therefore, a desire to see the writing of history in several contexts, three of which provide the framework for what follows: Polybios and history writing; history, rhetoric, and Greek *paideia*; and rhetoric for history writers and history makers.

POLYBIOS AND HISTORY WRITING

Of the historians writing during the Hellenistic period, Polybios is the most important largely but not exclusively because he is the best preserved. His work attempted to explain why Rome was such a successful power, and he offers an important analysis of how the Roman constitution functioned. He was much admired by the Romans, although he never made it into their list of the top-rated historians, a canon of authors almost impermeable to those writing after the fourth century.[4] Polybios was born ca. 200 and died in ca. 118.[5] His *Histories* cover events from 264 to 146 in forty books, of which many have survived only in a fragmentary state except for Books 1–6. Polybios' work was the basis for the relevant parts of the history of Rome written by Livy (Books 31–145). Polybios' other works have not been preserved.

Among the lost writings was a biography of Philopoimen, divided into three books in which Polybios described Philopoimen's upbringing (his education) and his greatest achievements (Polyb. 10.21.5–8). Philopoimen (ca. 253–182) was a politician but also a general, and on two occasions he had served as the chief magistrate of the Achaian League (*stratēgos*). Polybios' father (Lykortas, a close friend of Philopoimen), and Philopoimen himself, like Polybios, came from Megalopolis, a relatively new city founded after the battle of Leuktra (371) some time around 370–367 (Diod. 15.72.4). The city became the capital of the Achaian league in which Philopoimen was instrumental in maintaining it as a major power in Greek politics in the late third and early second century. Like Philopoimen, Polybios also served a magistrate in the Achaian League (170/69; Polyb. 28.6.9), as hipparch, the position one level below that of *strategos*. So Polybios was a politician. He had been appointed to an embassy to Alexandria in 180. He had also carried the urn containing Philopoimen's ashes at the latter's funeral a few years earlier.[6] His other works included an account of the Numantine War (Cic. *ad fam.* 5.12.2) written after 133, when the war was won by Scipio Aemilianus. *Memoirs on Tactics*, a work mentioned by Polybios (Polyb. 9.20.4) and later by authors of other similar books (e.g., Arrian, *Tactics* 1.1), was dedicated to matters that also assume some importance in the *Histories*. Polybios may also have written a separate work on the habitability of regions around the equator, mentioned by Geminus (writing ca. A.D. 50; Polyb. 16.32–8), although it has been suggested that the work may in fact have been part of the *Histories*.

This necessarily brief description of what little we know about Polybios' other works is important because it amplifies our image of him as a historian and a writer. Certainly, he was interested in geography and space, concerns that are expressed most clearly by his emphasis on the need to understand topography, particularly on the battlefield.[7] But his geographical interests, fuelled no doubt by his own travels in the company of Scipio Aemilianus to the Alps, Gaul, Spain, and North Africa, also allowed him to observe the customs of others.[8] Book 6 of the *Histories* extends such concerns and mirrors the ethnic digressions in the earliest *Histories*, such as Book 2 of Herodotos on Egypt or, on a much smaller scale, Thucydides on Sicily (Thuc. 6.1.1–6.53).[9]

As a writer of history, geography and ethnography, and as a biographer and author of a manual on military tactics, Polybios operated in a tradition.[10] Biography, for example, developed in the Hellenistic era but was regarded as different from history in genre. Polybios described his *Philopoimen* as an encomium of the man in which he exaggerated the man's achievements, as suited the form. He contrasts that work with his *Histories*, "a work which shares out praise and blame, seeks a true account with a demonstration also of the reasons followed for such allocations [of praise and blame]" (10.21.8). Like biography, history writing had a purpose. Polybios was interested in the educational functions of his work. In the *Histories*, this is a feature of his treatment of individuals, for example. Great men were to be emulated (10.21.4). Polybios therefore felt it useful to describe both their upbringing (formation) and their character (10.213–5). Such concerns echo the interests of those writing *encomia* and early forms of biography and are reflected in contemporary epigraphical sources (see following discussion).

The growth in biographical *encomia* and the interest in individuals are marked by fourth-century works such as Xenophon's *Agesilaos* and *Cyropaedia* and Isokrates' *Euagoras*.[11] Theopompos' (378/7 to ca. 320) *Philippika*, a history of Philip II in fifty-eight books, advanced biographical history further.[12] Such early interest in biography accelerated in the wake of Alexander the Great and the Successors: Kleitarchos, Ptolemy, and Aristoboulos wrote about Alexander; Timaios about Pyrrhos; and Demetrios of Byzantion about Antiochos I Soter and Ptolemy II Philadelphos. At the same time, as such writers focused on the individual, interest in the upbringing or education of such figures intensified. Symptomatic of such concerns are Onesikritos' "How Alexander was educated"; the "Education of Alexander"; written by a companion of the Macedonian, Marsyas of Pella; and Lysimachos' "About the Education of Attalos [I]."

Such interests in historical writing stem from a more individualised perspective of history writing that not only the sponsorship of history writing but also shifts in intellectual culture help explain. Polybios wanted his *Histories* to be useful. Utilitarian sentiments are found repeatedly in Polybios *Histories*, but the opening words make clear the priorities for the work was intended not only as an accurate narrative but served in broadest terms an educational purpose. "The truest education and training for political achievements is an understanding from history, and . . . the surest and only way to teach the capacity to support with nobility changes in fortune is the recollection of the calamities of others" (Polyb. 1.1.1).[13]

However, the choice of subject matter was particular to Polybios' age, and in his eyes made his work exceptional. Who would not want to know, Polybios asked, "how and with what kind of political system (*politeia*) almost everything in the inhabited world was overpowered in almost fifty-three years and fell under a single empire, that of the Romans, an event which has not been seen before?" (Polyb. 1.1.5; 31.25.7). Polybios was writing a history that dealt not only with the contemporary era but also the recent past. Such concerns allow ready comparison with Thucydides. Although Polybios mentioned the Athenian historian only once (8.11.3), he aligned himself in a tradition that looked back to the fifth-century historian.[14] A historian was no doubt expected to claim the importance of his subject matter by the Hellenistic age, and Polybios' own justification is typical of such statements found also in his predecessors' work. However, as a writer of contemporary history, his own use of polemic may have been more excessive than is found in either Thucydides or Xenophon.[15]

The fact that Polybios' *Histories* anticipated the Roman domination of the inhabited world allows his work to be described as "universal history" (Polyb. 2.37.4).[16] However, strictly speaking, such a term applies spatially but not temporally to the *Histories*. Universal history can describe the work of a Greek historian for the first time in the fourth century, Ephoros of Kyme (ca. 405–330). He wrote an account of Greek history from earliest times to the present (340 B.C.) and arranged his work spatially, allocating one book to one region. Polybios was writing in terms of that recent tradition, and the ambitious scale and the global theme of his *Histories* – Roman domination of the known world – justified the claim to universality. Although some have suggested that Polybios' claim to universality is neither clear nor justifiable, the geographical extent of the universe not only justifies Polybios' claim but also sets his work in a long tradition that can be traced back to Herodotos.[17]

However, unlike Ephoros, Polybios' narrative spanned a much shorter period. The final forty-book version of the *Histories* extended in both directions beyond the central fifty-three years of 220 to 167. The summary coverage in the first two books from 264–220 explained the rise of Roman power. But apart from the explanatory function of these books, that 264 B.C. start allowed Polybios to place himself, as other historians before him had done, in relation to his own predecessors. Timaios of Tauromenion had ended his *Wars Against Pyrrhos* in 264, and so Polybios saw himself continuing where Timaios left off (Polyb. 39.8.4). Xenophon had established the practice when he continued Thucydides' *Histories* (Xen. *Hellenica* 1.1.1), and Diyllos had followed on from Ephoros.[18] Polybios' first two books cover a forty-four-year period that suggests another parallel with Thucydides, whose Pentakontaetia, a survey of the growth of Athenian power in the fifty years leading up to the outbreak of the Peloponnesian wars, served a similar function.[19]

Polybios' second critical date, the 140th Olympiad (220–217, Polyb. 4.1.3) marks the opening of his fifty-three-year period of Roman rise to world domination but was also both the final year described by the *Memoirs* of Aratos.[20] That year may have been the end of Phylarchos' *Histories*, which had probably been a continuation of Douris of Samos or possibly Hieronymos of Kardia.[21] Aratos had established the Achaian League as an important power in Greek history, was certainly a figure of some importance to Polybios (magistrate of the Achaian League), and was also used as a source (Polyb. 2.56.1). Polybios did not admire Phylarchos, not only because of the latter's style but also his hostility towards the Achaians (2.56–63 esp. 2.56.6, 61.2).

At the other end of his work, Polybios' choice of first 167 and second 146 were to him and remain for us important moments in Mediterranean history. In June 168 at Pydna in northeast Greece, the Romans led by L. Aemilius Paullus, defeated Perseus, the Macedonian king. The Roman victory marked a massive change, not least because it ended the line of Macedonian kings that had largely dominated mainland Greek affairs since the Antigonid dynasty (Polyb. 31.25.6). On a more personal note, too, Roman success at Pydna inevitably affected the Achaian League. Some Achaian politicians had been careful to support the victors, whereas others had been visibly less than zealous in their enthusiasm. In the first instance, Pydna indirectly changed Polybios' own life for he numbered among the second group of Achaians. He served as hipparch in 170/169 and clearly operated at the highest level. The Romans extracted hundreds of Greeks as hostages and moved them to Italy (Polyb. 30.32.1–12).[22] Among those taken from Greece were 1,000 Achaians, including Polybios. Unlike the other hostages, Polybios stayed in Rome and became close to the family of the victorious general, Lucius Aemilius Paullus (consul in 182) and, in particular, his two elder sons, Q. Fabius Maximus Aemilianus and P. Cornelius Scipio Aemilianus (Polyb. 31.23.1). They had evidently urged that Polybios should stay in Rome. Polybios formed part of Scipio's entourage (Polyb. 31.24.12–25.1). The selection of the final terminal date, 146, marked the Roman destruction of Carthage and Corinth. Polybios was not alone in seeing this point as a watershed, for it served as a real marker in the contemporary Greek world. From 148/7 the Macedonians began a new era and counted dates from this point onwards for several centuries. Ten cities from the Peloponnese, who had been members of the Achaian League until its dissolution in 146, began their own era from 146/5. Even at Athens the creation of a new list of archons starting from 146/5 reflected the change.[23]

Historical writing took many forms. Polybios' history emphasised politics and the recent past but excluded myth, local histories, and foundation stories, forms of writing that also thrived in the Hellenistic period. Moreover, Polybios' history was more than simple narrative. It had a didactic: Truth took precedence over what was probable "for the benefit of those who wish to understand" (2.56.12; 6.2.8). Utility in general overwhelmed but did not deny the *Histories'* potential to entertain. There is an underlying function or purpose (*telos*) for Polybios' *Histories* (2.56.11–13). Walbank said that Polybios "admits that the historian is entitled to entertain. . . . Both aims, the useful and the enjoyable . . . have their proper place in history. But in practice . . . the scales should come down decidedly on the side of utility."[24] Polybios may not indeed have been typical of history writers of the Hellenistic period.[25] Polybios does value the utility of history and clearly had in mind as his primary audience the reader who wanted to learn rather than the reader who wanted to be thrilled.[26] "There is no need for the historian (*syngrapheus*) to thrill by rendering into marvels those people who happen to feature in history nor to seek out speeches that might possibly have been made nor to enumerate the (possible) consequence for those events that under consideration" (2.56.10). Polybios' own *Histories* identified politics and the recent past – the world-changing rise to power of the Romans – not only as world-changing events but as the best vehicle for his paideutic ambitions. Writing about the contemporary and recent past allowed a degree of precision and provided the reader who wished to understand with accuracy or truth (2.56.11–12).

Can the audience of Polybios be identified any further? It was largely but not exclusively Greek. For the first two books of the *Histories* informed an essentially Greek audience because it knew little about the early history of Rome and Carthage (Polyb. 2.35.9). Book 6 on the Roman constitution, the funerary customs, and military organisation allowed Polybios to show more clearly with what sort of *politeia* the Romans were able to gain world domination (Polyb. 6.1–2) and was clearly targeted at a non-Roman audience. It allowed those who wished to understand "the investigation of causes and the selection of the better choice in each case" (Polyb. 6.2.9). Polybios assumed that such readers were unaware of the features peculiar to public and private Roman life and that the *politeia* (the constitution and organisation) of the Roman state was particularly complex (Polyb. 6.3.3). Nevertheless, a Roman audience was not excluded. In reality, Polybios expected that "in particular Romans will take up the book in their hands because it includes the most outstanding and the vast number of Roman achievements" (Polyb. 31.22.9).

If Polybios' vision of history was clearly a didactic aim one, which targetted a readership yearning to understand, it did prevent him from recognising that the history need not give pleasure.[27] In Book 7, Polybios criticised other writers (historians), whom he called *logographoi* (Polyb. 7.7–8). Thucydides had used the same word to describe some history writers who had preceded him (Thuc. 1.21.1). Polybios may have had specific writers in mind as *logographoi*, such as Baton of Sinope and Eumachos, who both wrote about the tyranny of Hieronymos of Syracuse.[28] These *logographoi* had not only written at length but also stressed the marvellous.[29] Polybios thought that such writers lacked facts and wrote about events that were too narrow in scope and importance. The limited importance of their subject matter contrasted strongly with Polybios' choice of what he considered as great events that affected the inhabited world (Polyb. 7.7.6). These writers who treated Hieronymos not only made small affairs seem more important (than they really were) but also devoted much to matters that were not worthy of such record. Polybios recommended, in fact, not only that the Syracusan tyrants, Hieron and Gelon, were worthy of historical treatment but that Hieronymos should be ignored. On the former two, it was possible to fill up books and measure out, at length, a narrative (*diêgêsis*). If a writer followed Polybios' instincts, the product would be "both more enjoyable for those who love to listen to stories and more useful in every respect for those who desire to understand" (Polyb. 7.7.8). It is important, therefore, not to overstress Polybios' desire that history be "useful" as opposed to "enjoyable."

Polybios criticises his predecessors not least for their tendency to stray from facts or overinflate the subject of their work. The history of Hieron and Gelon that Polybios imagines has much pleasure to offer the lover of good stories because of the richness of good stories (which do not need to be padded out) and at the same time offers something for the individual who wants to understand (from) the past. One can learn from the history of Hieron and Gelon but not from Hieronymos' brief career. This tyrant may have been a violent one, admits Polybios, but he came to power as a boy and ruled only for thirteen months. Hieron reigned for fifty-four years and came to power exceptionally without using violence (Polyb. 7.8.1–5), whereas Gelon lived very much in his father's shadow. Polybios is opposed to fabrication and the inflation of trivia into matters of overblown importance, but at no point does he suggest that utility need forego pleasure for the listener of stories. This emphasis is best summed up by Polybios' own expression of what his history was – pragmatic history (*historia pragmatike*) or "political and military history written from direct experience and intended to be useful."[30]

Not only was Polybios' subject matter unique, but so too was his position among the Roman elite. However, previous historians, like Polybios, had been participants in history, not only as eyewitnesses but also as agents. Polybios exploited his political career and subsequent life among Romans but also belonged to a tradition of history writers as history makers. Thucydides, of course, had been an Athenian general, and his involvement in the city's affairs in northern Greece and Thrace clearly marked his writings, for example, his regard for Brasidas. Xenophon had been a significant agent primarily in the events narrated in the *Anabasis*. Hieronymos of Kardia served first in the entourage of Eumenes, then with Antigonos Monophthalmos (including the defeat at Ipsos in 301) and later acted as governor of Thebes on behalf of Demetrios Poliorketes after 293.[31] Polybios' own position as a politician in the Achaian League and later as a member of the Scipio's entourage gave him a similar vantage point from which he close to political realities and therefore the practical application of various skills, such as oratorical power and the qualities of charisma. Polybios used his practical experience to distinguish himself from a figure of obvious importance in Hellenistic history writing, Timaios of Tauromenion. Timaios wrote in the early Hellenistic period several works, including *The Olympic Victors*, the *Sicilian Histories* in thirty-eight books from earliest times to 289/8, and an annex on events including Pyrrhos' Italian campaigns to 264.[32] Timaios was the principal target of Polybios' criticism on historical methods that are found in Book 12 and was arguably the most well known of Hellenistic historians in the late third and early second centuries B.C.

The contrast between Polybios and Timaios sheds light on the methodology of the former and the contemporary practice of history writing. Although both Polybios and Timaios were required to leave their native cities, Polybios eventually returned to Achaia. Timaios of Tauromenion, however, had been forced into exile from in ca. 315 and probably spent the whole of the subsequent fifty years in Athens, where he is thought to have died ca. 260 (Polyb. 12.25h). High among the several criticisms made by Polybios of Timaios was the latter's detachment from real political life, a shortcoming that suggested Timaios should be credited with less authority. For although Polybios had been both a politician and roving eyewitness in the company of great Roman figures, Timaios was *de facto* "deskbound" in Athens. Nevertheless, Timaios' work remained popular long after his death and was clearly highly regarded, not only in Polybios' lifetime but much later, too. Timaios had an enormous effect on history writing – Greek as well as Roman.[33] If on no other basis, apart from the nature of the subject matter, Polybios' construction of pragmatic history and personal experience of history making allowed him to distinguish himself from perhaps the most important historian of the Hellenistic era not to have survived. Indeed, the extent of Polybios' criticisms suggest the exiled Sicilian writer's importance. They also illuminate different aspects of history writing in the Hellenistic world. Although the survival only of Polybios' work inevitably threatens to distort our view of Hellenistic history writing, we can reconstruct with some confidence the different interests of his peers and recent predecessors.

Polybios' history is embedded in events or actions (*praxeis*, Polyb. 1.1.1). What was done and what was said are the essence, but this is hardly novel. In history writing, Thucydides had expressed the same interests (Thuc. 1.22.1) as had those who followed.[34] In Greek culture, the achievements of individuals were calibrated as what they had done "in word and in deed." Polybios wished to emphasise his work not only as "pragmatic history" (*historia pragmatikē*) but also as "apodeictic" (referring to the main body of his work, Polyb. 2.37.3). Apodeictic is thought by Sacks to describe universal history but is taken by most others to apply to Polybios' explanation of causes.[35] Polybios clearly understood by "apodeictic" his deployment of statements supported by proof (Polyb. 7.13.2 and 5–6; 12.25k.9) and the apodeictic technique in this sense reinforces the idea of the utility and strong illustrative methods that Polybios adopts.[36]

In antiquity, writers of history, including Polybios and, for example, Phylarchos, presented narratives that conveyed emotion. However, the latter, writing in the third century, is criticised by Polybios not so much for the use of emotive writing itself but for *imagining* rather than reporting emotional moments. Polybios says that, in the description of the execution of Aristomachos, the Argive tyrant in the mid-third century, Phylarchos fabricates or invents the cries made (2.59.2). The criticism is for Phylarchos' fictitious creation of emotion, not his deployment of emotive speech *per se*. Polybios himself dwells on emotive scenes, such as the supplication by the defeated Carthaginian leader Hasdrubal before the victorious Scipio (Polyb. 38.19–21) and the latter's reaction to the speech made by Hasdrupal's wife (reported indirectly by Polybios). Here, there is no doubt in the reader's mind that Polybios has not made up the words, for not only does the historian emphasise the presence of witnesses to this scene (Polyb. 38.20.1), but he indicates, too, that he was among them (Polyb. 38.21). In the midst of such reported emotions, the tenor of Scipio's comment to Polybios could not have been more "statesmanlike" (*pragmatikos*). The emotion of the scene is used clearly by Polybios to emphasise the qualities that he admired in Scipio and wished to project on his readers. The exploitation of such emotional scenarios reveals the underlying purpose of Polybios' narrative technique. Scenes such as Scipio at Carthage are constructed to underline the character of Scipio, so inform the reader, and help him understand the true nature of character. Polybios does not write only to inform in a neutral scientific style but fashions his history in manners typical of writers brought up in Greek intellectual culture, to which we now turn.

HISTORY, RHETORIC, AND GREEK *PAIDEIA*

Rhetoric and history writing are closely connected: "historiography could be seen as part of, or closely allied to, rhetoric,"[37] Recent work on ancient historiography and indeed prose writing in general stress the influence of rhetoric.[38] Agonistic training is linked with a rhetorical education. Polemic is one product of that formation, so criticisms made by historians of their predecessors are a device typical of such background and therefore almost a *topos* in historical writing by the second century B.C. One target typically identified as liable for criticism is the use of speeches. Speeches in history writing offer a double-edged tool for displaying the writer's rhetorical skill (the composition of the speeches themselves) and the historian's personal attitude towards rhetoric.

Diodorus Siculus, writing much later in the first century, criticised previous historians' use of speeches. The comments may well come from the fourth-century historian Ephoros (Diod. 20.1–2), and they echo remarks made by Kratippos against his own contemporary Thucydides in the fifth century (Dion. Hal. *Thuc*.16).[39] Historians did not think of *not* using speeches in their work, for "in disapproving rhetorical speeches, we do not ban them wholly from historical works, for history needs to be adorned with variety (*poikilia*) and it is necessary in some places to seize upon such speeches" (Diod. 20.2.1). Speeches were an integral part of history writing – rhetoric is deeply embedded in history writing. However, the way rhetoric was used could differ from one historian to another.

Polybios reserved particular criticism for the speeches found in Timaios' work.[40] For the Sicilian historian departed from what needed to be said "like someone in a rhetorical exercise attempting to speak on a given subject" (Polyb. 12.25a 5, translation based on Paton).[41] Speeches were as much a part of history writing for Polybios as they were for any ancient writer of history.[42] For Polybios, however, "the man who passes by in silence the words that were spoken and the causes, and instead of this uses false rhetorical exercises and discursive speeches, takes away what is special to history" (Polyb. 12.25b.4). Polybios was interested in rhetoric for its effect rather than for the sake of and the style of rhetoric itself. It has been suggested that Polybian speeches have more value for their documentary qualities.[43]

Indeed, we can see clearly what Polybios valued in rhetoric by reviewing his remarks on Philopoimen. "A single word spoken at the right moment by a man of real credibility not only diverts men from what is worst but also urges them forward to what is best" (Polyb. 11.10.1). Philopoimen is judged by Polybios to have had such qualities; his life supported his words (Polyb. 11.10.2 and 5). So a few words from Philopoimen on many occasions defeated long speeches made by his political opponents (Polyb. 11.10.6). There is a clear preference in Polybios for an individual's actions, his character or personality as shaped by his achievements, than in credibility and persuasion achieved *only* by words. This idea is conveyed in the praise of Scipio, whose actions contested the words of others (Polyb. 31.29.11). Here is the priority of actions over words. Such sentiments probably echo the moral arguments of the mid-second century, not necessarily in Greece but at Rome too, perhaps even those echoed by Cato the Censor (Polyb. 31.25.5a).[44]

Polybios positioned himself in favour of a particular kind of rhetoric. In the early 150s, scarce references from Polybios Books 32 and 33 reveal something of the politics that saw Greek *poleis* vying for position and advantage in Rome (with Paus.7.11.4–8). One of the big issues then concerned the Athenian intervention in and plundering of Oropos, for which they were fined 500 talents in a judgement made by Sikyon, a member of the Achaian League.[45] In the early 150s, the Athenians went to Rome to complain about the unusually large fine. They dispatched three philosophers, Karneades of Cyrene (from the Academy), Kritolaos of Phaselis (Aristotelian school), and Diogenes from Seleukeia on the Tigris (a Stoic) to form what is known now as the "philosophers" embassy' to bring about a change.[46] It is very likely that Polybios was in Rome and witnessed the event – the ambassadors not only used an interpreter but had clearly spoken before large crowds of people. Each philosopher employed a different kind of oratory. Karneades spoke with force and speed, Kritolaos with skill and smoothness, and Diogenes with modesty and sobriety (Polyb. 33.2.10). The effect of the philosophers' embassy was considerable, not least in that they persuaded the Senate to reduce the fine to 100 talents.[47] However, the philosophers' embassy also had an intellectual impact on Rome – a negative one in the view of Cato the Censor, who complained about the philosophers' readiness to argue on successive days completely opposite positions regarding justice (Plut. *Cato Elder* 22).[48] It is likely that Polybios and Cato shared a low view of such philosophical or oratorical wizardry.[49] Polybios (12.26c) decried the benefits that can be derived from learning paradoxical arguments and revealed clearly his own antipathy towards the sort of philosophical skills that the Athenian embassy had probably employed. In Polybios' account of the success of Herakleides (Polyb. 33.18.11), the historian again reveals his dissatisfaction that an audience should be swayed by rhetorical trickery. Clearly, rhetorical flair as exemplified not only by Herakleides but also by the philosophers' embassy exerted great influence and attracted the majority of the Roman (senatorial) audience.

This study of Polybios' implicit attitude towards rhetoric and in particular the near contemporary employment of paradoxical argument puts into context the historian's own use of speeches and attitudes towards rhetoric. An education at the highest level in the Hellenistic period appreciated the art of rhetoric: "rhetorical training was a basic element of all literary education in Antiquity."[50] As a result, not only practitioners of rhetoric (orators and therefore politicians) but also intellectuals (writers, including of course historians) were brought up on a rich diet of literature. That included not only the great poets (Homer, for example) but also the orators and in particular Isokrates.[51] Indeed practitioners and intellectuals were not necessarily mutually exclusive groups. A politician could also be a writer or intellect (e.g., Demetrios of Phaleron) and intellectuals and writers could also have political careers (e.g., the comic poet Philippides of Paiania). In the second half of the second century, members of the Greek elite typically aspired to an education with the best philosophers, and Athens was one of the centres for such activities.[52]

The common feature for the political and intellectual elite in the Greek world was their education and cultural background, wrapped up in the term *paideia*. Rhetoric and philosophy were significant elements in a typical education. But philosophy and rhetoric were not viewed as activities that employed traditionally the same methods, although they shared important features that became very much intertwined in the fourth century under the influence of Isokrates.[53] Plato had objected to rhetoric. Aristotle saw it as an agonistic confrontation in which one person, pitched against an opponent, had to win, whereas philosophy pursued different goals and was not practised simply to win (Arist. *Cael* 294b6–11).[54] Aristotle's treatise on oratory, *Rhetoric*, marked an important shift from Plato's distance from the subject. However, he sought to separate oratory from the identity of the individual. So oratory in its purest form could transcend the individual speaker and be written in such a way that what mattered most were the oratorical arguments themselves. Aristotle thought that the audience's appreciation of an orator's character should not sway their decision. Instead, he felt that the orator's speech should be the only basis on which the audience should decide the orator's character (Arist. *Rhet.* 1.2, 1356a4–8).[55] For Aristotle's desire to separate the orator's personality or character from the character who spoke was a construction but in practice, and certainly in Polybios' view, oratory did not work this way. The character of the orator was required to be *ipso facto* reputable, so a real orator's own personality became increasingly recognised as an essential tool of persuasion (*Rhetoric to Alexander* 38.2).[56]

Aristotle was also a central figure in the promotion of historical research. According to Momigliano, "he tried to stimulate such historical research as he could accept as useful . . . he replaced the narration of unrelated facts by a systematic analysis."[57] The collection of anecdotes by Peripatetics can be included in this process, a practice that was already widespread in the fourth century but which, in the Hellenistic period, gave rise to works such as the pseudo-Aristotelian *Oikonomika*.[58] It was this marriage between the deployment of researched evidence and the integration of rhetoric in philosophical learning that was particular to the developments of the fourth century. Isokrates exemplified this incorporation of rhetoric and philosophy with an eye for the deployment of historical exempla.

The golden age of oratory was the fourth century. All six of Dionysios of Halikarnassos' best orators worked before the death of Alexander the Great. It was in this period that the gap between philosophy and oratory was closed. Isokrates (ca. 436–338) transformed the relationship between philosophy and rhetoric.[59] Marrou described him as "the educator of fourth century Greece and afterward of the hellenistic then Roman world."[60] He is judged to have excelled in his adoption of a greater philosophical approach to oratory, which Dionysios called "philosophical rhetoric" (*philosophos rhêtorikê*, Dion. Hal. *On the orators* 1).[61] In fact, Dionysios said "in the brilliance of his themes and his philosophic purpose, his superiority to all other Orators, not only to Lysias but to all other orators who have won professional eminence in this branch of learning, is greater than (to use Plato's words) that of a grown man to a boy" (Dion. Hal. *Isok.* 12, translated by S. Ussher). But Isokrates was also interested in history and advised Nikokles to study history in order to take the best decisions (Isok. *To Nikokles* 35). Isokrates' work as a whole is a testimony to his interest in the past.[62]

What Dionysios thought of as the peak of Greek oratory has a great deal to do with taste and, in particular, the preference at Rome in the first century B.C. for the Attic orators. When Dionysios describes a decline in rhetorical art after a golden age, therefore, one has to bear in mind that this expressed as much a preference in style as anything else. The style that replaced those popular in the fourth century "actually made itself the key to civic honours and high office" (Dion. Hal. *On the Ancient Orators* 1). Characteristic of this style, according to Dionysios, was a lack of refinement, in short, a vulgarity. That decline was relative. For Isokrates' style was much more elaborate than, for example, the plain style that Lysias had used in the early fourth century. Isokrates "seeks beauty of expression by every means, and aims at polish rather than simplicity" (Dion. Hal. *Isok.* 2). Indeed, a third-century philosopher at Athens, Hieronymos, found fault with Isokrates' speeches because he thought that it was not possible to deliver them "with the appropriate techniques that are used in live oratory" (Dion. Hal. *Isok.* 2).

The criticism voiced by the third-century philosopher echoes Dionysios' observation that Isokrates was in fact a writer of speeches and not a performer. As Dionysios reveals, Isokrates had aspired to a political career but "lacked the most important qualities of a public speaker, self confidence and a strong voice, without which it is impossible to address a crowd" (Dion. Hal. *Isok.* 1). Despite this failure, Isokrates succeeded indirectly though his pupils among whom were the Athenian general and politician Timotheos, the politicians and orators Hypereides and Lycurgos, the orator Isaios, the historians Theopompos and Ephoros, and the Atthidographer Androtion. The fact that this Attic or *stricto sensu* Isokratean style of oratory failed to gain popularity everywhere in the early Hellenistic period is a reflection, reading both Hieronymos and Dionysios, of both its impracticality for the speaker and the ineffectual impact on the audience that its style imposes (Dion. Hal. *Isok.* 13–14). It is perhaps a more pragmatic oratory that Polybios recognised as opposed to the flowery style of Isokrates. Certainly, Polybios thought that a few words spoken well by great personalities should weigh more in the balance than the verbal wizardry of skilled orators versed only in word play.

The intellectual cultures of the Hellenistic period were fundamental to the development of rhetorical techniques. Philosophy obviously influenced rhetoric, and it is fair to say that the two areas enjoyed a rich cross-fertilisation. Isokrates had brought rhetoric to new heights in the fourth century and transmitted to those whom he taught rhetorical techniques. As Dionysios showed clearly, not only orators but historians, too, were influenced by Isokrates (Dion. Hal. *Isok.* 13).[63] Douris of Samos (ca. 340 to ca. 260) criticised both Theopompos and Ephoros for their Isokratean manner (Douris of Samos *FGrH* 76 F 1). He preferred a simpler style to transmit the emotions and complained of his predecessors' use of rhetoric. The tension around oratorical style that revolved around Isokrates already echoed in history writing of the fourth century. When Polybios came to address the function of rhetoric – the use of speeches in history writing – he was critical not only of his own predecessors (notably Timaios) but also revealed his own ideas about the purpose and techniques of oratory of which he approved. Polybios' own history writing and his approval of Philopoimen and Scipio and their use of rhetoric display a preference for the (measured) words of great political figures. He preferred and invested greater credibility in their capacities as history makers who used rhetoric rather than as orators who pretended to be shaping history. However, rhetorical skills were an essential element, not only in Greek education and culture (*paideia*) but also politics. Whatever Polybios' own attitude towards rhetorical flair, the elite of the Mediterranean world were required to address the political institutions of other communities, whether they were other *poleis*, Roman magistrates, Hellenistic kings, or the Senate at Rome.

Rhetoric for History Writers and History Makers

"I realise that there are so many good orators and historians that to write about all of them would be a long task" (Dion. Hal. *On the Ancient Orators* 4, translated by S. Ussher). This chapter has concentrated on the relationships between history and rhetoric in Polybios and explored the background of historiographical, rhetorical, and to a lesser extent philosophical culture in which Polybios, other Hellenistic historians, and indeed Greek notables were immersed. However, that relationship and indeed the emphasis that Polybios laid on "pragmatic history" requires rhetoric to be placed in a broad political and historical context. The audience that Polybios addressed and the possible functions – especially the educational ones – that his *Histories* would have served can be set in the context of Hellenistic history. For Polybios' own work echoes to some degree the civic values of Greek *poleis* and the demands made by such communities on their citizens. In essence, this wider context pursues in a Polybian manner the connection between history writers and history makers – between historians and politicians.

Polybios was at the same time aware of the needs of the history makers and the demands on history writers. Unlike his self-appointed rival Timaios, Polybios pretended to experience of both. In essence, Polybios was typical of many members of the Greek elite in that, at the highest level, service for his community involved activity in the world of politics. In the Hellenistic period, such activity invariably required participation as a religious envoy (*theoros*) or more directly involvement in diplomatic embassies. These roles represent the same sort of functions that the political elite was expected to have fulfilled on behalf of their communities (typically the *polis*) in the Classical period. Thus, there is considerable continuity here in the Hellenistic era. Where there was change, however, was in the number of *poleis* that were concerned by and required to execute diplomatic missions and therefore deliver the ambassadorial speech.[64] In the early Hellenistic era, the rivalry between the Successors of Alexander, the most important of whom became kings, offered communities several possible geopolitical avenues for their communities to pursue. The collapse of the Persian Empire had seen a massive burst in the number of Greek *poleis* who aspired to exercise such capacities with greater freedom than the Persian king had ever allowed. Later, the increasing presence of Roman power from the last quarter of the third century further complicated, or in some cases simplified, depending on a community's or individual's position, that situation. When Polybios died in ca. 118, the geopolitical context for most *poleis* in the eastern Mediterranean was radically different from that when the historian was born just over eighty years earlier.

Nevertheless, although dramatic changes were experienced on the geopolitical level, there remained a consistent need for communities to use individuals to represent their interests before the dominant political powers of the time. For Athens, seeking a reduction in the 500-talent fine imposed for the plundering of Oropos, the *polis* sent the three most important philosophers to speak before the Senate in Rome. The identities of the powers that a community approached had changed. At the opening of the Hellenistic era, Hellenistic kings and, to a lesser extent, other *poleis* or supra-*polis* structures dominated. By the first century B.C., the now-reduced number of Hellenistic kings and the regionally important neighbouring *polis* had been largely superseded by the not-always-common interests of the Senate in Rome and Roman magistrates operating in the east.

That constant need for diplomats and representatives demanded individuals, preferably of some ability in terms of reputation (oratorical, political, or otherwise), to serve the city. The major sources for Hellenistic history – Polybios and the epigraphical documents – are full of examples of such individuals who served communities in such capacities. However, the enormous amount of rhetoric that such diplomacy required has left few traces. For no extensive body of literature survives to allow us to make the sort of judgements on Hellenistic rhetoric that can be made, for example, for Athenian oratory of the fourth century. The closest we can come to experiencing such oratory is in the decrees recorded on inscriptions and to some extent what Polybios records in his own speeches. But as indicated, the latter probably reflect little of the diversity and style of the speeches that many orators were capable of delivering. And decrees reflect frequently a chancellery style that can hardly have been the sum of what was really said nor a representation of positions taken in debate. Nevertheless, something of the real discourse at the heart of Hellenistic oratory may well be gauged by looking at documents such as the letters of Hellenistic kings and the award of honours granted by communities, usually *poleis*, concerned by such royal correspondence.[65] The epigraphical evidence for relationships between Hellenistic communities and, for instance, Hellenistic kings often suggests the product of a dialogue in which the weaker polity negotiated benefits from the stronger power in exchange for honours granted by the polity.[66] Teos and Antiochos III provide a good illustration of how these interactions can be played out in civic inscriptions.[67] The language of decrees does reflect common themes and, in the context of the award of such honours, one can even speak of a language of euergetism.[68]

The *poleis* were certainly not the leading agents of historical change but were still important. They can illustrate the cultural and political context in which one can explore the interaction of history and rhetoric. Kolophon (in southwest Asia Minor) might be used to represent some features of Greek *poleis* in the Hellenistic period. An honorific inscription for Menippos set up by his fellow Kolophonians provides details of one benefactor's career in service of his *polis*, a career that we would not know about were it not for this inscription.[69] Kolophon was famous for its association with the oracle 15 km away at Claros. There, the community had set up the inscription honouring Menippos, and here it was found in excavations conducted by Louis Robert in the 1950s.[70] Most have assumed the inscription was set up just after 120/119 although a date in the 90s is possible and should not be ruled out.[71]

Menippos' political career had begun by the 130s and certainly before the death of Attalos III in 133. After the death of the last Attalid king, Eumenes III tried to succeed to the throne, even though Attalos had bequeathed the kingdom in his will to the Romans. In a career covering as many as forty years, Menippos "carried out many embassies to governors (*lit.* generals) and quaestors (*lit.* treasurers) and those of the Romans present in Asia, and many to the Attalid royalty and not a small number of *poleis*. But the most important embassies concerning the most pressing subjects (*anankaiôtata*) that he completed were to the very Senate of those who have *hegemonia*."[72] The inscription describes the Senate as the critical political organ of the dominant power of the time.[73]

Of immediate importance here is not so much the content of Menippos' complex career but the incomplete opening of the inscription. For the Kolophonians reveal that Menippos had been sent to Athens, the mother city of Kolophon almost certainly as an envoy for religious matters (a *theoros*). There, he stayed "spending time with the best teachers. He offered the best example in terms of his life (*bios*) and his culture (*paideia*)."[74] The Athenians crowned Menippos and granted him citizenship, the second privilege at Athens still valued highly in the second half of the second century B.C.[75] The decree makes clear how the Kolophonians regarded this stage of Menippos' life. The inscription continues: "After coming back from his studies (*schole*), he proved that immediately in early adulthood he conformed to what has been said of him above, going on embassies and giving the best political advice and falling behind none of his fellow citizens in the pursuit of honour (*philotimia*)."[76] Indeed, we discover that Menippos became associated with the most important Romans and even went on embassies on their behalf.[77]

Here, then, is the one of the essential reasons why rhetoric must be seen at the heart of much intellectual activity in the Hellenistic period. Menippos' career consisted not only of important civic offices but he also represented Kolophonian interests and on five occasions that involved embassies to Rome and the Senate itself. How did Menippos perform such tasks of high diplomacy? By giving good counsel. How had he acquired such skills? By good education and by having the best teachers. In this instance, Menippos had been taught at Athens. The inscription makes clear the relationships between education and Menippos' embassies and good counsel. Rhetorical skills were no doubt supplied by his education and required by diplomacy.

Menippos' career was not unusual. Another unfortunately anonymous visitor to Athens also studied at the Akademy under Karneades, left for Asia Minor, and returned to Athens later.[78] This graduate of the Academy, like Menippos, received the honour of citizenship at Athens.[79] Hellenistic notables took advantage of the best learning environments.[80] Menippos' fellow Kolophonian, Polemaios, displays a similar training, although he was educated at Rhodes where, like Menippos, he spent time only with the best teachers.[81] Education and culture (*paideia*) were an essential training for many of the members of the Greek elite, and the eastern Mediterranean boasted some of the best environments for such activities.[82]

Rome dominated the affairs of the Mediterranean in Polybios' lifetime and especially the interests of the Greek *poleis*. Polybios' experience and familiarity with successful politicians underlie his preference for figures, such as Philopoimen and Scipio. But his own practical experience and personal observations placed greater stress on the political credibility of those who had achieved things. Those who could talk or persuade were viewed with greater suspicion. In practice, Polybios was less persuaded by rhetoric in and of itself than by the force of rhetoric supported by personal credibility. It is clear that rhetorical skill could and did produce results and indeed that there were no doubt many individuals in the Hellenistic world with notable oratorical skills. However, Polybios was not satisfied to identify an individual's excellence only on account of rhetorical skills. Not only does his own judgement of historical figures reflect that opinion but so, too, does his approach to history writing.

The honorific decree for Menippos is one of many Greek inscriptions that saw a polity honouring one of its own members, typically individuals who had performed representative actions for the community. Menippos is awarded the highest honours by the Kolophonians, something that was in many Greek communities through much of the Hellenistic period reserved only for the most exceptional citizens.[83] Menippos had performed many services for the Kolophonians, and his ambassadorial roles to the Roman Senate was only one even if perhaps the most exceptional of these. Behind his five visits to Rome will surely be found Menippos' rhetorical skills learnt in Athens. Inevitably, the individual success of embassies depended on many factors, and rhetoric was one of them. It is not certain but surely likely that Menippos' oratory made some use of the training gained in the philosophical schools in Athens, sometime in the middle of the second century or later. However, Menippos' honours inevitably were the product of both word and deed, of achievements in a diplomatic (or rhetorical) context and in action. The two spheres of activity cannot easily be separated and complement each other – history and rhetoric were invariably interconnected. In Polybios' *Histories*, the same might be true. That history writer was at some point a history maker. Polybios did not want rhetoric to overwhelm his history, but his sensitivity to the former allows us see the wider importance of rhetoric and history in the Hellenistic world.

BIBLIOGRAPHICAL NOTE

On Polybios, the best summary treatment is now Marincola (2001) 113–49 with a very full bibliography. For more detail, see Walbank (1972), his magisterial three-volume commentary, *A Historical Commentary on Polybios* (Oxford: Clarendon Press, 1957, 1967, 1979) and chapters in two volumes of collected articles: Walbank (1985) and (2002). Verdin (1990) contains many useful essays on Hellenistic historiography. For the wider context in which to place Hellenistic history writing, Marincola (1997) offers a good view of the continuities in history writing from the fifth century and the self-conscious ways in which successive history writers dealt with their own contributions to that tradition. Rhetoric is treated in various contexts, but still useful are Woodman (1988) and Kennedy (1994). Wiedemann (1990) is dedicated to rhetoric in Polybios. However, more recent studies develop in different directions (cf. Goldhill (2002) in general, Pelling (2000) for the Classical period, and, for example, Rood (in press, for Xenophon). On the study of discourse in Hellenistic epigraphy, Ma (1999) is fundamental, building on Bertrand (1990).

NOTES

1 For example, Rawson (1985).
2 Clarke (1999); cf. Walbank (2002) 31–52.
3 For example, Momigliano (1990).
4 Marincola (2001) 148–9.
5 Eckstein (1995); Walbank (1972) 1–31.
6 Errington (1969).
7 Walbank (1972) 88.
8 Clarke (1999) 78.
9 See in general, Walbank (2002) 277–92.
10 Marincola (1997).
11 Momigliano (1971) 47–53.
12 Flower (1994).
13 For similar interests in generalship, see Polyb. 11.8 and for Scipio's development from an early age, Polyb. 31.30.1–2.
14 Walbank (1972) 40–3.
15 Marincola (1997) 223–4; Walbank (1985) 262–79; for further references, see Marincola (2001) 133 n. 93.
16 Marincola (2001) 121.
17 Polybios' universality is not clear: Sacks (1981) 96–121; Alonso-Núñez (1990) and (2002) on Polybios' universality and its tradition.
18 Marincola (1997) 237–41.
19 Marincola (2001) 118.
20 Walbank (1972) 42.
21 Marincola (1997) 287–8.
22 On the pro-Roman politicians among the Achaians, see Polyb. 30.13.1–11
23 Habicht (1997a) 270.
24 Walbank (1972) 40.
25 Walbank (2002) 231.
26 Walbank (1972) 6 n. 24.
27 Walbank (2002) 236–9.
28 Walbank (1957–1979), ad loc. 7.7.1.
29 The "marvellous" translates the Greek word *terateia* that conjures up portents and symbolism attached to atypical events, so Polyb. 2.56.10.
30 Hornblower (1994) 43.
31 Hornblower (1981).
32 Brown (1958).
33 Brown (1958) 91–106.
34 Walbank (1972) 43–4.
35 Sacks (1981); see Marincola (2001) 125–6.
36 Walbank (1972) 57 n. 153.
37 Rawson (1985) 215.
38 Historiography: Marincola (1997); prose writing: Goldhill (2002).
39 Canfora (1990) 321–2.

40 Pearson (1986).
41 Canfora (1990) 322.
42 Walbank (1985) 242–61.
43 Lehmann in Verdin, Schepens, and De Keyser. (1990) 302: Polyb. 12.25a.3; 25b.1; 29.12.8; 36.1.7.
44 Eckstein (1997) 192–5.
45 Habicht (1997a) 265.
46 Walbank, (1957–1979), III: 545–5.
47 Habicht (1997a) 266.
48 Astin (1978) 174–8.
49 For Polybios' discontent at the success of oratorical skills, Polyb. 33.18.7–11.
50 Wiedemann in Verdin et al. (1990) 64.
51 Wiedemann (1990) 290–2.
52 Habicht (1994).
53 Cole (1991) 139–58.
54 Cited by Marincola (1997) 220.
55 Marincola (1997) 129.
56 Marincola (1997) 130.
57 Momigliano (1971) 67.
58 Momigliano (1971) 72.
59 For a summary of Isokrates' work, see Ussher (1999) 296–323.
60 Marrou (1948) 128.
61 Cf. Dion. Hal. *Isok.* 4 and 12; Isok. *Against the Sophists* 16–8.
62 Nouhaud (1982) 357.
63 Fox (1993).
64 Wooten (1973).
65 Ma (1999) 237–8.
66 Ma (1999) 184–6, 241–2.
67 Ma (1999) 228–30 and Ma (2003) 251–2.
68 The language is studied by Ma (1999) 179–242.
69 For benefactors, see Gauthier (1985).
70 Robert and Robert (1989) 63–104.
71 Robert and Robert (1989) 99; for the later date, see Eilers (2002) 131.
72 Robert and Robert (1989) 63 col. I ll. 14–19.
73 Eilers (2002) 125–7.
74 Robert and Robert (1989) 63 col. I ll. 4–5.
75 Osborne (1981–1983), III–IV p. 105.
76 Robert and Robert (1989) 63 col. I ll. 3–14.
77 Robert and Robert (1989) 65 col. 3 ll. 5–8, Eilers (2002) 124–5.
78 For the philosophical schools at Athens, see Habicht (1994) 231–47.
79 Osborne (1981–1983), III–III, T119 = *FGrH* 244 F 59.
80 Savalli-Lestrade (2003).
81 Eilers (2002) 132–7; Robert and Robert (1989) 11–62; Robert and Robert (1989) 11 col. I ll. 22–4.
82 Perrin-Saminadayar (2003) 388–9.
83 Gauthier (1985); Kralli (1999–2000).

7: MATERIAL CULTURE

Susan I. Rotroff

☙

It's not what you find, it's what you find out.

Thomas (1979) 30

Alexander the Great's favorite sculptor, Lysippos, was a versatile craftsman: He created both the bronze portraits that Alexander so favored and a new form of ceramic vessel (either a drinking cup or a transport amphora) for King Kassandros (Athenaios 11.784c).[1] Both of these seemingly disparate items fall within the catch-all category of material culture, succinctly defined by one authority as "that sector of our physical environment that we modify through culturally determined behavior."[2] This definition embraces both art and artifacts, but also much more: domestic breeds of plants and animals, the flattened skull that results from the use of the cradle board, even, Deetz has argued, the spoken word (the arrangement of air molecules by the oral cavity to produce culturally determined sounds).[3] The role material culture played in the past and its consequence for present-day knowledge of the ancient world cannot be overestimated, even in the realm of the most intellectual of that world's achievements. The stylus Aristotle used to write the *Metaphysics*, the papyrus or writing tablet on which he wrote, the chair or stool he sat on, and the table at which he sat were all pieces of material culture; and without yet more material culture – manuscripts copied and recopied through the ages – we would know nothing about it.

The up-market end of the material culture scale is treated elsewhere (Chapter 8 in this volume). This chapter focuses on utilitarian objects and structures that, were we walking through a Hellenistic environment, we might not particularly notice, but which nonetheless carry important messages about life in that environment. They number in the thousands: in the house, aside from the house itself and its fittings (doors, locks, paving, walls and their decoration, roof tiles,

136

water pipes), furniture, domestic tools (looms, washtubs), textiles, baskets, wineskins, the pottery for storage, cooking, serving, eating, drinking, washing, and bathing, equipment for the household shrine, toilet items and secular ornaments; on ancient bodies, clothing, footwear, and items of personal adornment; in public buildings, ballots and voting machines, public measures, tokens and nametags, inscriptions, papyrus rolls, writing tablets; in the workshop, the potter's wheel, sculptor's tools, kilns, furnaces; on the farm, hoes, plows, grindstones, harnesses, beehives; in the gymnasion and the bath, athletic and bathing paraphernalia (jumping weights, discus, balls, strigils); and at shrines, votive pottery and figurines, offering tables, and sacrificial equipment. Out on the borders, soldiers on patrol would present another collection (armor, weaponry), and the unlucky victims of a siege could view from their walls the approaching material culture of the enemy in the form of siege machines. At sea, the ship, perhaps the most complex piece of material culture of its time, laden with its cargo of commodities and material culture, was also crammed with the nets, knives, cooking pots, crockery, gaming pieces, and navigational devices that sustained the crew and the passengers throughout the voyage.

Much of the material culture of the Hellenistic period has perished, and much of what has survived is not characteristically Hellenistic. The pace of the evolution of utilitarian objects is often glacial; except in small details, the Hellenistic storage pithos, beehive, or loom was identical to its Classical predecessor. Some distinctive items of Hellenistic material culture, however, do emerge, although at first sight, the collection may seem impoverished. Gone are those favorite illustrations of ancient life, the Attic painted vase and sculpted grave monument. There are few snapshot-like images of people at work or play, and it will require more diligence and imagination to make out the behavior behind the objects. The reward, however, is a broader and fuller portrait of ancient life. Unlike literary sources, which almost exclusively express the male, aristocratic viewpoint and treat only subjects of interest to that class of individuals, material culture is no respecter of rank. It tells everyone's story – man, woman, slave, ruler, metic, citizen – if we can only read it.

MATERIAL CULTURE AND CHRONOLOGY

One of the first ways archaeologists harnessed material culture to the study of antiquity was the development of chronologies. Human beings never continue to make objects in exactly the same way over time. Deliberate innovations are frequent – slight improvements in design, moderations to suit changing taste, or new inventions. Even if consistency is desired, small changes creep in during a craftsman's lifetime, and those who follow in his or her footsteps will add something of themselves in the replication of the object in question. Thus, objects constitute a timepiece that can be consulted to track the course of ancient life.

Building a Chronology

For this tool to be maximally useful, there must be a link between material culture and the historical framework as known from the literary and epigraphical sources. Sometimes, this link is straightforward; the portrait of a king on a coin, for instance, should indicate that the coin was struck during his reign. The identification of the royal portrait, however, may be difficult, and some states struck coins bearing the portraits of earlier kings: like Thomas Jefferson on the twenty-first-century nickel, Ptolemy I Soter, founder of the Ptolemaic dynasty of Egypt, continued to grace the coinage of his many successors throughout the Hellenistic period.

In most cases, an accurate chronology for a class of objects has emerged only after prolonged study and frequent revision, based on analysis of thousands of individual examples. Let us take pottery – without fail, the most frequently found artifact on any Hellenistic site – as an example. It is made of a malleable medium – clay – easily molded into new forms and thus highly responsive to changes in taste. Once broken, a pot is nearly useless (though sherds could be reused as knives, scrapers, or scratch paper), but also almost indestructible, and as a result, an enormous amount of pottery has survived. Studying pottery found in layers superimposed over one another, the analyst can track changes in the forms, surface treatment, fabric, and decoration, and thus place vessels in a relative chronological sequence. This would be sufficient for the study of the evolution of the Hellenistic potter's craft, but it could not contribute to the investigation of larger questions that historians may wish to ask. For that, the relative sequence must be linked to the real passage of calendar years, and that requires a body of pottery that can be associated in some way with a dated historical event.

For example, written sources inform us that the Roman general Sulla sacked the city of Athens in the year 86 B.C.E.[4] The event had a substantial physical effect on the city,[5] resulting in, among other things, masses of broken pottery and therefore offers the potential of forging a link between the material and the historical record. Excavations around the edges of the agora of Hellenistic Athens have uncovered hundreds of wells and cisterns that were filled with debris when the water source was no longer needed.[6] Several of these deposits contain Athenian bronze coins marked with a star and two crescents, an emblem associated with the Pontic king Mithridates, whose agents had encouraged Athens' resistance to Rome,[7] which in turn resulted in Sulla's attack on the city. Coins, issued as they are by government authority, often reflect political events, and that is what had happened here; the mint of Athens had expressed the city's political stance – up with Mithridates, down with the Romans – on Athenian pocket change. The association of the coins with the debris in the cisterns and wells tells us that the pottery, roof tiles, and other objects deposited there had fallen victim to Sulla's soldiers in 86 B.C.E. Although we cannot know how long the wreckage lay where it fell before someone swept it up and deposited it in its final resting place (a process during which newer objects may have been introduced), we can postulate that *most* of the objects in the debris were made before 86. Given a large enough number of deposits that can be associated with dated events like this one, it is possible to construct an increasingly accurate chronology for pottery, lamps, terracotta figurines, or any other type of object that has survived in considerable numbers. Association with dated artifacts creates new dated artifacts, which in turn can give dates to further objects, creating a long chain of evidence linking the material world to real time. The resultant tool can be applied to the investigation of both quite specific and very general questions about what happened in the Hellenistic past.

The Specific: The Hellenistic Metroon

On the west side of the agora of Athens stands the Metroon, a substantial building that served as both the shrine of the goddess and the repository of the state archives.[8] Little remains of its superstructure, but the foundations give the plan, and the account of Pausanias (1.3.5) helps to identify the building. No ancient author gives its date, however; for that information, we must rely entirely on material culture.

The physical relationship of the Metroon to other buildings shows that it cannot have been built before the early third century[9]; the materials used in its construction, especially the red conglomerate of its foundations, confirm this conclusion, for this stone is not found in Classical structures. Architectural fragments of the superstructure, though few, can be dated stylistically to the second century, and the date is further narrowed to the second half of that century by the roof tiles. These were made of terracotta and stamped with the name of both the goddess and of the owners of the factory in which they were made: "Sacred to the Mother of the Gods: Dionysios and Ammonios."[10] Coins and inscriptions provide more information about Dionysios and Ammonios, but here a problem arises, for at least two known pairs of brothers bore those names in the second half of the second century.[11] The first set held various magistracies in the third quarter of the century; the second pair, sons of the first Dionysios, were influential businessmen of the later second century, filling the important position of epimelete of Delos in 111/10 (Dionysios) and 107/6 (Ammonios). Which pair got the contract for the Metroon's roof?

To answer that question, we must we return to the debris of the Sullan destruction. In it were found fragments of round-bottomed, handleless, moldmade drinking cups decorated with tall, rounded petals and signed by the potter Apollodoros. Since a delicate cup is unlikely to have survived for decades, these vessels were probably not very old when they were broken and discarded, and Apollodoros was probably, therefore, working no earlier than the last decade or so of the second century. It so happens that a nearly complete cup of this type, also signed by Apollodoros, was found in the trench that the builders of the Metroon dug to lay its foundation (Figure 2). Because the trench was filled at the time of construction, it appears that the work was done in the late second century, when the tile works were under the direction of the second pair of brothers. In this way, several types of material culture – the foundations, building material, architectural members, and roof of the building, along with coins, inscriptions, and pottery – combine to calculate a date for the construction of the Hellenistic Metroon.

The General: Pottery and History

A surprising observation emerges when one compares the centuries-long sequence of pottery and lamps with the sequence of historical events extracted from texts. In very broad terms, material culture reflects the periodicity that has been applied to the historical record. Hellenistic pottery is clearly different from both the Classical pottery that preceded it and the Roman ceramics that followed. The divisions between the periods, however, are not the same as those in the history books.[12] Asked to pinpoint the beginning of the Hellenistic period, most people would probably choose the death of Alexander the Great or some year within his reign (336–323 B.C.E). The pottery and lamps of the last quarter of the fourth century, however, are firmly Classical in appearance; in fact, the Classical ceramic tradition continued almost unchanged for twenty or thirty years into the third century – at Athens, at any rate; on sites in the Near East, where Greek presence was new, the preceding styles lived on even longer.

Historians assign widely varying dates to the end of the Hellenistic period, with a preference for coincidence with a military victory: the sack of Corinth (146), Sulla's attack on Athens (86), and Augustus' victory at Actium (31) are favorites. The potters, however, were unimpressed by these military watersheds. They continued to produce pots and lamps that were fully Hellenistic in appearance until the end of the common era and beyond; it was not until the Flavian period (69–96 C.E.) that Athenian lampmakers produced a lamp of Roman style. Clearly, it takes a long time for military and political events to have an effect on the way people make things, and therefore, we may infer, on the behaviors that lie behind the production and use of those things. Material culture, then, is not a very accurate indicator of the more momentous events of history; its strengths lie rather in investigation of the more slowly evolving social and economic patterns of the Hellenistic world. Although much effort has gone into the study of the chronology and stylistic development of Hellenistic material culture, its richness as a source of insights into behavior and cultural change has been only haltingly explored. The case studies that follow are examples of those explorations.

MATERIAL CULTURE AND TRADE

Although papyri and other documentary evidence provide information about commerce, it was not a subject liberally treated by ancient authors. Consequently, a large proportion of what we know about it must be extrapolated from the study of objects – especially objects found out of place, far from their point of origin. Some of the most significant Hellenistic trade was in commodities (e.g., wine, oil, grain, salt fish, slaves) that cannot be identified in the archaeological record. Liquids (and some dry commodities) that were shipped over long distances, however, were packaged in ceramic containers that have survived in the tens of thousands (Figure 3). These vessels, termed amphoras, are large, sturdy, earthenware jars with two handles and a solid, pointed toe.[13]

The latter provided a third grip for handling the jars, which are very heavy when full, and was well designed for packing in the hold of a ship. Shipwrecks with cargoes of hundreds of amphoras attest to this mode of use.[14]

The transport amphora was a Bronze Age invention, first produced by the Canaanites of the Levantine coast, who also occasionally impressed an identifying stamp into the leather-hard clay of the jar.[15] Subsequently, Greek cities adopted the amphora (the earliest Greek ones were made in the eighth century), many developing their own distinctive shapes, produced in an equally distinctive local clay. Amphoras from the island of Rhodes, for example, are made of a fine, light-colored clay and have a peg toe and sharply canted handles (Figure 3, left), whereas red clay and a ring around a more pointed toe distinguish containers from the city of Knidos, on the coast of Asia Minor (Figure 3, second from left). The variety is staggering, and although many types can be linked with the issuing states, the origins of many others remain unknown. In the Hellenistic period, the practice of stamping became widespread (although by no means universal), apparently signaling increased state interest in control of the commodities trade. Stamps were usually placed on the top of one or both handles and contained a variety of information; often, both the manufacturer of the amphora (the fabricant) and the name of an official (the eponym) indicating the year of production were included (Figures 4 and 5). Analysis of these names and their combinations has made it possible to develop a tight chronology for some widely traded amphoras, such as those of Thasos, Rhodes, and Knidos.[16]

The identification of amphora types, coupled with their find spots, can contribute to the study of ancient trade: If an amphora was made on the island of Rhodes and found in Alexandria, it is highly likely that Hellenistic Rhodians were sending some (probably liquid) commodity southward to the Egyptian port. Such events are documented by something like 300,000 known stamped amphora handles[17] (a type of object usually recorded by excavators) and uncounted unstamped fragments (far less frequently noted by excavators) that must number in the millions. The presence or absence of amphoras from a particular region gives us a general picture of some of the trading arrangements of the Hellenistic period; massive collections of Knidian amphora handles at Delos, for instance, and of Rhodian ones at Alexandria, attest to a considerable intensity of trade (probably in wine) between various cities, although a number of factors make it difficult to draw conclusions about the nature and magnitude of that trade. The Rhodians stamped a very large percentage of their amphoras and stamped them on both handles, whereas other centers stamped far less frequently and on only one handle, practices that can wildly skew statistics based on stamped handles alone.[18] Furthermore, empty amphoras were themselves items of trade; emptied amphoras could be refilled with new commodities and shipped onward, and the distinctive amphora shape associated with one city was sometimes imitated by another. Unstamped amphoras, generally ignored in the quoted statistics, need also to be taken into consideration; on one estimate, these amount to over 90% of all amphora production.[19] In addition, we do not always know what commodity the amphoras contained, and chronologies are not in all cases well enough established to follow fluctuations in the market. Nonetheless, although much detail is missing, some general trends can be followed.

A selective tally of over 125,000 amphora handles of various types found in the eastern Mediterranean and Black Sea[20] shows that Rhodian wine was a significant export; Rhodian handles make up over 70 percent of the whole, an impressive statistic even when divided by two to account for double stamping. Knidos, in second place with just under 20 percent, falls well behind. The patterns are more interesting, though, if one looks at variations over time and space. For example, although Rhodian handles outnumber Knidians twelve to one at Alexandria, Knidian handles are almost three times as numerous as Rhodian ones at Athens and on Delos.[21] Changing proportions over time signal shifts in trading patterns.[22] Although Rhodian handles are common in third- and early second-century Athens, their numbers decline dramatically after ca. 150. The pattern at Delos is somewhat different, with Rhodians predominating through the first half of the second century and then maintaining a more substantial minority down to the end of the century. At Alexandria, however, and on most Levantine sites, Rhodian amphoras dominate until the end of the period. Sudden and marked changes, like the almost total disappearance of Rhodian amphoras at Jerusalem after 145, can sometimes be linked to historical events; control of the city by the Hasmonean rulers, who enforced strict adherence to traditional Jewish practices, apparently extended to the import of gentile wine – whether as an economic and political measure or also as a religious measure remains a topic of debate. The large numbers of Rhodian amphoras recorded there in the preceding fifty years must surely reflect the Hellenizing influence of the policies of Antiochos IV.[23]

MATERIAL CULTURE AT DINNER

What people eat and how they eat it vary intriguingly from place to place, and experiencing the dietary customs is part of an introduction to a foreign culture. Although texts tell us something about ancient eating habits, the information is selective. Fortunately, however, those habits are liberally reflected in the vessels used in the preparation and service of meals.

Ways of Drinking

The symposium – the aristocratic drinking party that followed the meal – dominates descriptions of ancient Greek dining habits. Most famously from Plato's dialogue of that name, but from many other sources as well, we know that these events were hosted by men for other men, who reclined on couches in a room specially designed for the purpose; that they usually included entertainment by women (musicians or prostitutes); and that the wine was mixed with water in a large bowl, then distributed to the drinkers.[24] The custom required an assemblage of pottery that is easily recognized and highly characteristic of Greek culture: containers for wine and water, large numbers of drinking cups, and, most importantly, the krater, the large and elaborately decorated two-handled bowl in which wine and water were mixed. Kraters were already an important part of the Greek ceramic repertoire in the Bronze Age. At Athens, they make up a prominent part of the assemblage throughout the Iron Age and the subsequent Archaic and Classical periods. Modes of decoration and shapes changed, but the vessel remains easily recognizable for what it is, both from its large capacity and from its elaborate decoration, demonstrating that the krater was a piece of "best china," on display as a showpiece to be admired by the guests. It can be traced into the Hellenistic period (again, at Athens), when the most lavish of the prevailing decorative styles were applied to it. Painted wreaths, necklaces, and geometric designs in buff and white on a black gloss background (the West Slope style) decorate third-century kraters, whereas, toward the end of the century, moldmade kraters were introduced, with relief decorations on their walls, along with painted West Slope garlands on the rim and the interior. Around the end of the first quarter of the second century, however, Athenian potters stopped making finely decorated kraters, although they did continue to produce them in coarse ware. Kraters were occasionally imported to the city from elsewhere, but local demand was apparently insufficient to encourage a local artisan to offer the item. It appears that, although literary texts continued to describe symposia, something fundamental had changed in the way communal drinking was organized, at least among those Athenians who normally used eating and drinking vessels made of clay.

Perhaps kraters of some other, more perishable material – most likely metal – took their place, but if so, the custom of fraternal drinking was now restricted to that wealthier segment of the population that could afford metal vessels. In any event, examination of the rest of the ceramic drinking assemblage provides more evidence of change.[25] Drinking cups grew larger, whereas kraters (as long as they continued to be made), grew smaller. Pitchers, used to dip wine out of the krater for distribution to the guests, also grew smaller; instead of holding enough to fill several cups, they were too small to fill even one, and their necks became too narrow for them to be used as dippers (Figure 6). In the second century, a new shape entered the drinker's equipment: the *lagynos*, a delicate one-handled decanter with a narrow neck (Figure 7). It was utterly unsuited to the old communal drinking customs; rather, it seems to have been designed to hold the portion of a single person, and the Greek Palatine *Anthology* records intimate conversations between the solitary drinker and his *lagynos* (5.135, 6.248).

Along with changes in drinking equipment came changes in the drinking venue. Greek houses, at least since the fifth century, had included a room specifically adapted to this form of communal dining and drinking: the *andron*. This was an approximately square chamber, often with its entry off an anteroom, with the door off-center to accommodate the dining couches arranged around its sides. The couches are often attested by the raised border on which they stood, as well as in patterns in the paving of the floor, with the visible, central area more lavishly treated. This is the only room of the Greek house whose function can be asserted with complete confidence.[26] It is designed to accommodate a private drinking party of limited size (few *andrones* could have held more than seven couches, and a couch could accommodate, at most, two diners) among social equals and lends itself to generalized conversation rather than intimate tête-à-têtes.[27] In the later Hellenistic period, however, the *andron* was replaced by other types of public rooms. These are best illustrated in the many houses excavated on Delos, an island under Athenian control from 167 onward, but which hosted a thriving business community of mixed ethnicity from before the middle of the second century through the first thirty years of the first century. There, the intimate *andron* is frequently replaced or augmented by broad rooms, entered on their long sides directly from a colonnaded courtyard.[28] Their size and decoration set them apart as the principal room of the house, and it seems certain that they were the locus of such entertainment as the householders undertook. Although the pattern of paving indicates that they (at least sometimes) held dining couches, both the shape of the room and the many doors that lead into it make it impossible to reconstruct an unvarying pattern of arrangement.

These changes suggest that the private, communal drinking of the Classical symposium was passing out of fashion among citizens of the middling sort. The pottery assemblage indicates that, instead of sharing a mixture from a common bowl, drinkers may have brought their own wine and mixed it to their own satisfaction in their capacious drinking cups. The houses suggest a less intimate party, with more flexibility in the seating arrangements.

Also from Delos comes evidence of a completely new form of drinking. Just to the north of the Agora of the Italians, excavations have revealed the remains of a tavern, a public drinking place of a type familiar, a century and a half later, from Italy, but rarely encountered in Greek lands.[29] Its identity emerges from the shattered pottery that was found there: in one room, wine amphoras stockpiled to supply the customers; in the other, masses of drinking cups and a small collection of pitchers of graduated sizes. There is no krater, but an example of the fashionable *lagynos* is present. Dice and gaming pieces expand on the offerings of the establishment, and cosmetics and jewelry suggest that an upper floor was occupied by a woman: the owner, a prostitute, or both? The tavern may have catered to the many Italians – citizens, freedmen, and slaves – who did business in Delos in the late Hellenistic period.

Ways of Eating

The character and development of the distinctive cuisine of ancient Greece can be read in the pots in which it was prepared. From the fifth century onward, the Greek cook's mainstays were two: a capacious, globular pot, sometimes fitted with a lid, probably to be identified as the ancient *chytra* or *kakkabe*; and the *lopas*, a wider, shallower vessel, always lidded, and resembling a modern casserole. Snippets of ancient text associate the *chytra* with the boiling and stewing of vegetables and soups, whereas the *lopas* was commonly used for cooking fish in oil, water, or sauce.[30] In smaller numbers, but also regularly present, are shallow baking(?) dishes shaped like a modern pie plate. Whatever the precise functions of these different utensils, they are the material reflection of typical Greek culinary habits, and when, in the Hellenistic period, Greeks began to move in large numbers out of their traditional homelands, these characteristic cooking vessels betray their presence. Furthermore, occasional additions to the typical assemblage can point to new ethnic elements in a Greek or Hellenized population.

The small Hellenistic settlement of Tel Anafa, in the Hula Valley in present-day Israel, illustrates the point.[31] Habitation there was concentrated in three phases, two Hellenistic and one Roman, distinguished by stratigraphy, architecture, and distinctive assemblages of objects. The second of phase (ca. 125 to 80 B.C.E.), followed a period of severely reduced occupation and probably represents the arrival of new settlers on a largely abandoned site. A baggy cooking pot with a constricted neck – typical of the Levant and the only cooking vessel documented in the first of the three settlements – was their most common cooking vessel, but the settlers also used the lopas and the baking dish characteristic of Greek cookery. This suggests that Tel Anafa's new inhabitants were a partially Hellenized population, possibly from the cosmopolitan area of Phoenicia to the north. The assemblage also contains another and even more unusual piece of kitchen equipment: a broad pan with vertical sides. Pans of this shape are as foreign to the Greek kitchen as they are to the Levantine one; their homeland is Italy, where they were used to make egg dishes rather like a modern quiche. Only a few were found among the pottery of the second settlement at Tel Anafa, but enough to show that an Italian presence was making itself felt. In the third settlement, a reoccupation in the first half of the first century C.E., the number of pans multiplies sixfold and forms part of the evidence that these newcomers included Italians.

MATERIAL CULTURE AND ACCULTURATION

In material culture as much as in language, there was a Hellenistic *koine*; the same general types of objects, be they lamps, pots, coins, terracotta figurines, or buildings, were produced and used by people all over the Hellenistic world. This is perhaps surprising, in view of the considerable geographical extent of the Hellenistic East, and in view of what must have been a very diverse population, in which Macedonians and Greeks were normally a minority, though a controlling one. We are still in the dark about the mechanisms that supported this *koine*. How did pottery styles in Aï Khanum, in present-day Afghanistan, keep pace with styles in the old Greek homeland?[32] The explanation must lie in the continuous movement of people (including craftsmen) and goods over those long distances, combined with an eagerness, among Hellenic or Hellenized populations, to bolster cultural solidarity through material culture.

There is also, however, enormous diversity within Hellenistic material culture, the expression of the widely different populations that created it. Written sources are not very forthcoming about the indigenous inhabitants of the lands overwhelmed by Alexander's armies. They speak, however, through objects, which provide a glimpse of their reactions – resistance, accommodation, imitation – to this new, enforced contact with an alien culture. One way in which pottery reflects culturally determined behavior was discussed earlier: An ethnic cuisine requires specific and often distinctive equipment for food preparation. But pottery can tell us more. Different populations favored different shapes (often for the same functions, such as drinking) and different styles of decoration and surface treatment. Although no neat formula equates a certain type of pottery with a specific ethnic group, the interplay of different styles allows us to observe intercultural negotiations second hand.

Hellenistic Sardis

The city of Sardis had long been in close contact with Greeks; Solon's sixth-century visit to King Kroisos was recorded by Herodotos (1.29–33), and abundant imports of Archaic and Classical Greek pottery are attested by excavation.[33] These exotic vessels augmented an indigenous ceramic assemblage that was very different, with its own shape repertoire and a preference for a red rather than a black surface, or for reduction firing that left the surface black and the clay itself gray. The conquests of Alexander brought the city firmly into the Greek sphere, and subsequently it was controlled by a sequence of Hellenistic dynasts – the Antigonids, Lysimachos of Thrace, the Seleukids, Pergamon – before becoming part of the Roman province of Asia.[34] The ceramics produced in the city provide evidence of both resistance and accommodation to these new masters.[35]

Attic imports disappeared early in the Hellenistic period, but close imitations, with shiny black glaze, stamped and rouletted decoration for plates and bowls, and painted West Slope decoration for cups and closed shapes are well represented throughout the third century. Some may have been made at Sardis, others imported from cities on the coast. At the same time, however, indigenous pottery continued to be produced: Achaemenid drinking cups (a form introduced long before from the East and by the third century thoroughly naturalized, Figure 8), and pitchers with ridged necks, all partially covered with a typically Lydian red gloss. These shapes are well represented in debris that resulted from the capture of the city by Antiochos III in 213, when Sardis had been a "Greek" city for over a century. Thereafter, however, the two traditions seem to have reached an accommodation. The Lydian shape assemblage disappeared, wholly supplanted by the Greek repertoire; Lydian heritage lived on, however, in traditions of surface treatment and firing. Surfaces are rarely a true black; often they are red (the old Lydian preference) or shades of brown, as though the attempt to imitate traditional Greek black gloss was only halfhearted. The age-old Anatolian preference for reduction firing also survives. A vigorous local industry produced moldmade bowls – one of the most distinctively Greek Hellenistic shapes – but largely with red gloss or in gray ware (Figure 9). This increased hybridization in material culture in the course of the Hellenistic period (which has been observed elsewhere as well, and in a variety of object types)[36] suggests the degree to which accommodation to Greco-Macedonian influence had progressed.

Pottery and Settlement Patterns

A study of Greek shapes within the Seleukid empire, including pottery excavated in Mesopotamia, Iran, and Bactria, has revealed both widespread recurring patterns and striking local variations.[37] Typically, imported black gloss, either Attic or strongly Atticizing, is in evidence in the earliest years of the period but disappears after the early third century. Thereafter, a limited repertoire of Greek shapes was made locally, primarily bowls with incurved or outturned rims, fishplates, and plates with an inwardly thickened rim. Moldmade bowls, so typical of Hellenistic ceramics on the Greek mainland and the western coast of Asia Minor, and enthusiastically adopted at Sardis, are almost totally lacking. Sometimes, the Greek shapes made up part of a special production, as at Dura Europus, in Syria, where they were made in a red painted and a gray ware, in which no indigenous shapes were made. More frequently, however, the Greek shapes were incorporated into the production of local fabrics. So, in central and southern Mesopotamia, in Susiana in Iran, and even at the site of Ikaros, in distant Kuwait, these bowls and plates were made in the local green-glazed ware as well as in unglazed and undecorated plain wares. At the same time, production of the indigenous fine eggshell ware in these areas remained utterly uninfluenced by Greek models. Lise Hannestad has advanced the hypothesis that the degree of Greek influence on local ceramic production is a result of the intensity of Greek colonization and thus can be read as an index of settlement patterns.[38] We would then expect Sardis, with its thoroughly Hellenized ceramic production, to have experienced a massive injection of foreign, colonial population – and both its proximity to Greece and the Greek cities of Ionia and the fact that it served as a regional capital of the Seleukid empire make this likely. The minimal effect of Greek models on the ceramics of western Iran suggests that the Greco-Macedonian element of the population there was numerically insignificant,[39] a small group of controlling officials within an enclave, surrounded by a population whose culture was largely unaffected by their presence.

MATERIAL CULTURE AND THE PAST

One pleasant afternoon in the first half of the first century BCE, the Roman orator Cicero embarked with friends on a stroll from the Dipylon Gate of Athens to the Academy *gymnasion*, less than a mile outside the city (*De finibus* 5.1–5). Cicero describes several evocative landmarks encountered on the way. The village of Kolonos reminds them of Sophocles and, reaching back further, Oedipus. The Academy itself calls Plato to mind, a specific seat recalls one of his successors, Polemon. An Epicurean among them is particularly moved by the Garden of Epicurus, which they pass on the way, and comments that Epicureans favor rings and drinking cups bearing the image of their founder. Summing it all up, one friend observes that "one's emotions are more strongly aroused by seeing the places that tradition records to have been the favourite resort of men of note in former days than by hearing about their deeds or reading their writings." Elsewhere (*De oratore* 2.87.357–360), Cicero expands on the link between places and recollection, describing a form of memory training in which one first chooses a place (public monument, large house, or the like) and then situates within this architectural framework an image for each thing that one wishes to remember. Roman authors give us the fullest description of this method,[40] but they credit Simonides of Keos, a poet of the fifth century, with its invention (Cicero, *De oratore* 2. 86.351–355), and the art clearly flourished in the Hellenistic period. With the connection between the material world and memory so firmly entrenched in ancient thought, it comes as no surprise that ancient people used artifacts not only to stimulate memory, but to manipulate it.

Appropriation: Claiming the Cretan Past

Students of Greek archaeology learn early on that Crete fostered the "first civilization of Europe." During the middle part of the Bronze Age (ca. 2000–1470), a complex society flowered there, complete with beautifully painted palaces and villas, a wide variety of luxury goods, and finely crafted artifacts of all sorts. Crete of the Hellenistic period, however, was far different. The island was divided among dozens of small polities; continuous warfare gradually reduced their number by perhaps a third in the course of the period, making the relocation of populations and the redrawing of boundaries common phenomena. The period also preserves signs of a heightened interest in the past.[41] Survey and excavation have revealed an increase in the number of small shrines, many of them built close to or within the ruins of Minoan sites that were apparently still visible. Cave shrines, an earmark of earlier religious observance that had gone into eclipse in the post-palatial era, flourished anew. Hellenistic cemeteries were deliberately placed atop much older burial grounds, the later interments respecting the positions of the earlier ones. The past was also recalled in three inscriptions that include puzzling symbols that resemble signs in the linear scripts of Bronze Age Crete. Taken together, these finds show a desire to recall and reclaim a heroic past – whether on the part of local elites or of the population at large – perhaps in response to the unsettled conditions of the present.

Creation: A Samothracian Enigma

Those who possess no hoary ruins of a glorious past may be compelled to invent them. This is what happened on the island of Samothrace, in the Sanctuary of the Great Gods, home to one of the most important mystery cults of Greece. The earliest archaeological evidence for ritual activity on the site dates to the seventh century, but significant architectural development did not begin until the fourth century. The charter myth of the Mysteries, however, projected them into the Age of the Heroes; the rites were founded by the hero Iasion-Aëtion, a son of Zeus and brother of Dardanos, the ancestor of the Trojan kings.[42]

An enigmatic piece of material culture within the sanctuary appears to be a response to the need for physical documentation of this mythical history.[43] Set into a long retaining wall that supports a terrace in this hilly site is a peculiar doorway (Figure 10). It is built of roughly shaped fieldstones; a massive and irregular slab serves as its lintel, above which two more slabs form a rough triangle. The doorway frames a passage that ends against the virgin soil of the hillside after only two meters; it is a monumental doorway to nowhere. Fragments of pottery found in its foundation trench date the retaining wall to the late third or early second century; but this does not look like Hellenistic architecture, where regular ashlar coursing is the norm. Its closest parallels lie much earlier, in the monumental tombs and gateways of the Bronze Age, where a characteristic "relieving triangle" protected the lintel block from the weight of the construction above it. The Samothracian door is, in fact, a Hellenistic replica of a Bronze Age doorway and, although its precise purpose can only be guessed at, one likely explanation is that it represented the tomb of the founder, who was said to have met his end on the island, struck by a thunderbolt of Zeus. Hellenistic Samothracians created a spurious antiquity – perhaps on the traditional site of the hero's immolation – to bolster his memory and to demonstrate the high antiquity of the sanctuary.

MATERIAL CULTURE AND GENDER

Greek Women at Home

Because the documentary record of the Hellenistic period was largely written by men, for men, about men, and on subjects of interest to men, material culture is particularly important as a source of information about the lives of women. Recent studies of domestic architecture show how the analysis of material culture can provide a corrective to documentary sources. Literary and epigraphical texts mention a part of the house reserved for women (the *gynaikon* or *gynaikonitis*); such a room or area must have existed, for playwrights and orators knew their audiences were familiar with it (e.g., Aristophanes, *Thesm.* 414–417; Lysias 1.9), and inscriptions record the separate rental of the *andron* and the *gynaikonitis* of third-century Delian houses.[44] Xenophon, whose *Household Management* has been a primer for the understanding of the Greek household, alludes to a locked door between men's and women's quarters (9.5). In another frequently quoted text (Lysias, 3.6), the speaker claims that the women of his household are so sequestered that even to be seen by male relatives is traumatic.

Until serious attention was paid to the plan of the typical Greek house, these texts seemed to support a view of Greek domestic life in which women were cloistered in a harem-like apartment, spinning, weaving, and caring for the young and the elderly, and emerging only rarely for family funerals and weddings. It is clear, even from the texts, that this can have referred only to citizen women (female slaves were another matter altogether) in families of considerable means (poorer wives and mothers had to leave the house to earn a living). Even so, if women were routinely sequestered in the home, domestic architecture ought to show us how this was managed. To the contrary, however, Greek house plans are remarkably open, and individual rooms or apartments of rooms could not easily be shut off from the rest. Artifacts reflecting women's activities – loom weights, toilet items, cooking pots – are found spread throughout excavated houses, not concentrated in a single area. The only solution would be to imagine the women's quarters on the second floor; but the texts make it clear that, although this was sometimes the case, in other instances, it definitely was not. It emerges that, whatever the *gynaikonitis* was, it was not a hermetically sealed apartment. Greek women enjoyed freedom of movement within their own homes, and the image of oriental seclusion must be abandoned.[45]

The Strigil and the Mirror

Not only material objects themselves, but also the ways they functioned together and the contexts in which they have been found contribute to insights into antiquity. Grave gifts are a good example; the associations among the contents of the tomb and their relationship to the deceased express the attitudes of the society toward their dead. The gifts must be, in some way, appropriate, and changes in the nature of those gifts over time may signal changes in social attitudes. The fact that women were chiefly responsible for the care of the corpse and the grave suggests that they played a large part in the choice and deposition of funeral gifts, which consequently may reflect their views of themselves and the world around them.

Two common Hellenistic Athenian grave gifts provide a case study.[46] Both the bronze mirror and the strigil had long been common tools of daily personal care, frequently pictured in the vase paintings and funerary sculpture of the Archaic period and the fifth century. In these images, mirrors are regularly associated with women, usually in bridal or courting scenes; the strigil, a curved bronze or iron implement used in bathing, generally accompanies young men and evokes the world of the palaestra. Both were rare as funerary gifts until the end of the fifth century; then, however, their occurrence increased tenfold, and they continued to be fairly common in Athenian graves throughout the Hellenistic period. The graves also demonstrate that the earlier gender associations of these objects were weakening. Strigils have been found in the graves of older men as well as youths, and also in the graves of women, suggesting a shift in this object as symbolic of the palaestra to a more general association with bathing and personal hygiene. Its presence in female graves suggests a vision of the deceased woman not just as the mother (or potential mother) of legitimate offspring, but as an attractive and erotically desirable individual.

This more liberal interpretation of femininity is also expressed in the terracotta figurines of the Hellenistic period. In the Classical period, these small clay figures most frequently depicted religious subjects – divinities and their devotees – or costumed actors. The second half of the fourth century, however, saw a sea change in both style and subject matter. Women – beautifully dressed, naturally posed, and at their leisure – form a large part of this new repertoire (Figure 11). The style arose in Athens, possibly influenced by the vivid characters of New Comedy, but it was soon exported to Boiotia; hundreds were deposited in graves outside the small Boiotian town of Tanagra, whence they acquired the nickname "Tanagra Figurines."[47] This subject matter became popular throughout the Hellenistic world, and images of attractive women, unencumbered by the trappings of motherhood and housewifery, adorned houses and shrines and accompanied the dead, bespeaking a new image of the female sex. Here again, material culture invites us to consider a story that is otherwise largely untold.

CONCLUSION

In the early 1970s, archaeologists in Tucson, Arizona, initiated the Garbage Project.[48] Applying established archaeological techniques of analysis, they examined the refuse of modern householders, sorting the debris into categories and quantifying what they found. Their aim was to understand the behavior of the householders in a way that went beyond the usual questionnaires used in the study of contemporary social questions. Indeed, it quickly emerged that what people said about themselves in response to such questionnaires quite often did not square with the evidence of their household rubbish, which provided a more unvarnished account of their lifestyles. This is an important lesson for those who study literate ancient societies: texts are crucial for our knowledge of the past, but they can be self-serving, biased, lacunose, or misleading. As the aforementioned case studies illustrate, the material culture that accounts for much of ancient garbage can go far to correct and amplify the written record.

BIBLIOGRAPHICAL NOTE

Lubar and Kingery (1993) and Deetz (1996) provide fruitful ways of finding things out by means of material culture (though their examples are not drawn from the Hellenistic world). An idea of the tremendous variety of objects preserved from the ancient Greek world can be extracted from Davidson (1952), nicknamed "the phone book" because of its bulk, on the so-called minor objects from excavations at Corinth, ranging in date from the Iron Age to the Roman period. Included are figurines, vessels, furniture, locks and keys, tools, utensils, and implements, games, armor, weights and balances, stamps, and seals. Numerous corpora illustrate pottery, the largest class of Hellenistic material culture preserved; for the Greek heartland see Rotroff (1982), (1997c), and (2005) on Athens and Edwards (1975) on Corinth. The range of Hellenization of eastern ceramics can be appreciated from the pottery of Pergamon, on the western coast of Asia Minor [Schäfer (1968)], Tel Anafa, in present-day Israel [Berlin and Slane ([1997)], and Ikaros, in present-day Kuwait [Hannestad (1983)]. Grace (1979) provides an accessible introduction to transport amphoras; see Garlan (2000) for the history and present state of their study, Whitbread (1995) for petrographic studies of the most important types. A regional survey of terracotta figurines may be found in Higgins (1967), with fuller discussion of Tanagra figurines in Higgins (1986); the vast collections of the Louvre give a sense of their variety [Mollard-Besques (1963); Besques (1971)]. The evolution of the Hellenistic house is surveyed by Hoepfner (1999). For Hellenistic funerary customs, see Kurtz and Boardman (1971) 161–9.

NOTES

1 See Lawall (2004).
2 Deetz (1996) 35.
3 Deetz (1967) 83–96.
4 Plutarch, *Sulla* 14; Appian, *Mith.* 5.38–39; Pausanias 1.20.5–7.
5 Hoff (1997).

6   Rotroff (1997c) plan.

7   For the coins, see Kroll (1993) 69–70, 74.

8   Thompson (1937) 172–217.

9   For discussion of the date, see Thompson (1937), 192–5.

10 Thompson (1937), 191–2, fig. 118.

11 Habicht (1990) 574–75.

12 Rotroff (1997a); Rotroff (2001). Adams (1979) has made the same point for a different time and place (Medieval Nubia).

13 For an overview, see Grace (1949); Grace (1979); Empereur and Hesnard (1987); Garlan (2000).

14 For an early Hellenistic example (the Kyrenia wreck, with 404 amphoras), see Bass (1972), figs. 26–8.

15 Grace (1956).

16 For example, Grace (1985) (Rhodian and Knidian); Finkielsztejn (2001) (Rhodian); Debidour (1986) and Avram (1996) (Thasian).

17 Garlan (2000) 2.

18 Empereur (1982) 226–9.

19 Sartre (1995) 73.

20 Ariel (1990) 17, Table 1.

21 Grace and Savvatianou-Petropoulakou (1970) 281–82.

22 See, for example, charts in Finkielsztejn (2001) 286–287; Empereur (1982) 223–25.

23 Finkielsztejn (1995) 291; Ariel (1990) 25–28.

24 Lissarague (1990); Murray (1990).

25 Rotroff (1996); Rotroff (1997c) 14–5.

26 Orlandos and Travlos (1986) s.v. For examples in well-preserved fourth- to fifth-century houses at Olynthos, see Cahill (2002) 180–90, pls. I, II.

27 Dunbabin (1998) 82–3.

28 Dunbabin (1998), 84–9, figs. 2, 3. For example, Chamonard (1922) pl. XIII, room k (Maison du trident), pls. XIV–XVII, room f (Maison de la colline), pls. XXIX–XXII, room h (Maison du lac), XXIII–XXVI, rooms f and h (Maison des dauphins); Bruneau, Vatin, and Bezerra (1970) plan A, rooms N and AE (Maison des comédiens).

29 Hatzidakis (1997).

30 Bats (1988) 43–5 summarizes the ancient citations.

31 Berlin and Slane (1997) 20–32, 104–9.

32 Gardin (1990).

33 Schaeffer, Ramage, and Greenewatt (1997).

34 Hanfmann (1983) 112–4.

35 Rotroff (1997b) 228–32. For Sardian Hellenistic pottery, see Rotroff and Oliver (2003).

36 For example, Colledge (1987).

37 Hannestad (1983) I, 83–120.

38 Hannestad (1983), 84, 118.

39 Hannestad (1983), 119.

40 For example, (Cicero), *ad Herennium* 3.16–24.

41 Alcock (2002) 101–21.

42 For the Samothracian foundation myth, see Cole (1984) 3–4; Burkert (1993) 179–80.

43   McCredie (1994).
44   Hellman (1992) 99–100.
45   Cahill (2002) 148–3, esp 191–93.
46   Houby-Nielsen (1997).
47   Higgins (1986) 117–61; Uhlenbrock (1990) 48–53.
48   Rathje and Murphey (1992).

8: Hellenistic Art

Two Dozen Innovations

Andrew Stewart

⚬⚭⚬

In his second essay *On the Fortune or Virtue of Alexander* (*Moralia* 333D–F), Plutarch presents his readers with a problem. Was it Alexander's good luck that blessed him with such extraordinarily talented artists – Lysippos, Apelles, Pyrgoteles, Deinokrates? Or was it their extraordinary good luck that they lived during his reign, caught his eye, and could profit from his largesse? Was the creation of what we call Hellenistic art ultimately attributable to them or to Alexander?

This is a chicken-and-egg problem, and Plutarch knew it. The fourth century B.C. was not the nineteenth or twentieth centuries A.D., and Lysippos, Apelles, and their peers were not Monet, Rodin, or Picasso. Usually produced on commission, Greek art was the result of four-way negotiation among patron, artist, context, and genre. No innovation appeared out of the blue, the handiwork of a lone, creative genius. All of them had a history.

Yet Plutarch's rhetoric conceals a deeper truth. Greek art did change profoundly under Alexander, and the invigorating combination of an audacious, opinionated, and uniquely successful young king and a set of supremely talented artists certainly had much to do with it. So the fact that some of the period's innovations had important classical antecedents is essentially irrelevant. Antecedents can help us to measure and contextualize innovations, but they can neither explain them nor exhaust their meaning. For no complex human artifact – no painting, building, poem, or symphony – is ever explicable by the sum of its historical conditions. And the Hellenistic ideal, in both art and letters, was to engage the past creatively, not simply to replicate it or repudiate it.

Because some continue to dismiss the Hellenistic period as derivative and sterile even so, a collection of these innovations follows. It makes no claim to be complete or systematic; not everything included is equally important; some items will merit less attention than others; and a few have a long pedigree in the ancient Near East. The list begins where the period itself begins, with Alexander.

THE ARTS OF POWER (FIGURE 12)[1]

Alexander's artists invented the western iconography of power. In addition to portraying the king in every major medium, they explored at least six basic royal scenarios: battles, hunts, rituals, allegories, weddings, and family groups. And before his death, they effectively turned him into a god.

Lysippos invented what a later epoch would call the swagger portrait. His bronzes of Alexander, naked, cloaked, or armored, used a new proportional canon (slimmer, leaner body and smaller head) to make the king seem taller. They showed him as a quasi-Homeric hero – a second Achilles, spear in hand, dashing and youthful, ready to make the world anew. On foot, mounted or chariot-borne, with their eyes fixed on far horizons, his Alexanders burst the narrow boundaries of the classical city-state. Their domain was the world.

Meanwhile, Apelles represented the king with thunderbolt in hand in a colossal painting for the Artemision at Ephesos. His *Alexander Thunderbolt-Bearer* was no mere hero but a Zeus on earth. This hybrid, theomorphic image simultaneously inaugurated a new type of ruler portrait and provoked a storm of criticism, predictably led by Lysippos. Pyrgoteles, Alexander's gem-engraver, apparently reproduced these images in miniature for court and personal use, and the king and his successors soon put them on their coins (Figure 12).

As to royal narratives, Lysippos' bronze groups at Dion and Delphi showed Alexander fighting at the Granikos in 334 and hunting lions in Syria. Alexander himself commissioned the first; his general Krateros commissioned the second, having saved the king's life when the chase went awry. Apelles probably invented the royal allegory, painting the chariot-borne Alexander (1) alongside Nike and accompanied by the Dioskouroi, and (2) alongside Triumph and accompanied by the trussed-up figures of War and Fury seated on piles of weapons. A much later, Ptolemaic example is illustrated in Figure 12.

Royal rituals and weddings are represented by another picture by Apelles at Ephesos showing Alexander on horseback, apparently in procession, and by Aetion's tongue-in-cheek *Marriage of Alexander and*

Roxane, auctioned at Olympia in 324. Aetion illustrated the king's conversion from war to love by a crew of Erotes filching the king's weapons and armor to give them to his bride – a scene famously recreated at Rome in 1516 by the painter Il Sodoma for the bridal chamber of the aptly named papal banker Alessandro Chigi.

Finally, royal family groups are evidenced by Leochares' gilded marble (*pace* Pausanias, probably *not* chryselephantine) quintet of Philip II, Amyntas, Olympias, Eurydike, and Alexander in the Philippeion at Olympia. Commissioned after Philip's great victory over Athens and Thebes at Chaironeia in 338, it was probably finished around the time of his assassination and Alexander's accession, two years later.

TRYPHE I. THE PALACE AND COURT ART (SEE FIGURE 20)[2]

The court was the apex of Hellenistic society. Centered on the palace (*basileion*), it was a world unto itself, with its own special culture and protocols. It was where power was concentrated, favors were curried, crucial decisions were made, and endless intrigues were pursued. Dedicated to conspicuous consumption as a way of proclaiming the kingdom's power and wealth (*tryphe*), it soon generated its own art forms to cater to the privileged and to dazzle visitors.

The palace itself was an early Hellenistic creation. The classical *poleis* had no need for them and generally disdained the luxury arts they spawned. The earliest extant one, at Vergina, perhaps built by Kassandros (r., 316–297), is essentially a colossal fourth-century villa. A vast two-story building 100 m² and built of mud brick on stone foundations, it used marble only for thresholds and accents. Its loggias overlooked the rich Macedonian plain.

Behind a monumental propylon, three successive entrance halls announced a huge colonnaded central courtyard, 2,000 m² in area. Moving clockwise around it, one first encountered a circular shrine to Herakles Patroos, then no fewer than fifteen dining rooms, including a "royal suite" floored with intricately patterned pebble mosaics. The royal and guest apartments were on the second floor, now destroyed.

The palace was thus a multipurpose building. Accommodation aside, it offered numerous private venues for work and play, and its courtyard could host court ceremonies, the endless streams of petitioners, and whispered conversations out of earshot of one's rivals. This plan was soon adopted at Pergamon and elsewhere, and presumably also at

Antioch and Alexandria, where the now-lost palaces of the Seleukids and Ptolemies were surrounded by gardens and parks. Around 210, Ptolemy IV even built a floating version for use on the Nile. The late Alexandrian author Athenaios preserves a description of it (5, 204B–206C).

Palace embellishments included the aforementioned mosaics, wall hangings, frescoes (figured and *faux marbre*), and sculpture (see Art Collecting). Remains of lavish wooden dining couches (*klinai*) with ivory trimmings (figured, animal, and floral) appear in many Macedonian tombs and surely were made for more than funerary use. Engraved and embossed silverware, often probably crafted from Persian spoils, graced both banquet and boudoir.

Women's jewelry included gold tiaras (see Figure 20), hairnets, earrings, necklaces, brooches, bracelets, rings, and even (depending on one's *metier*) more exotic paraphernalia, such as anklets, thigh bands, breast-cups, and crisscross love charms or *kestoi* worn across the naked torso. Men might wear gold rings and garment pins, and gold wreaths at banquets. Both sexes used engraved gems and cameos as ring-bezels and personal seals; favorite subjects ranged from royal portraits to Dionysos, Aphrodite and their retinues. Embroidered and purple-dyed clothing was popular, and Chinese silk was not unknown. King Demetrios Poliorketes had most of his clothes woven with gold and flaunted a cloak embroidered with the solar system.

TRYPHE II. POMP AND CIRCUMSTANCE[3]

Greeks had held open-air religious processions and public feasts – often quite extravagant affairs – since time immemorial. The Athenian quadrennial Greater Panathenaia is the best documented but was far from unique. Hellenistic kings and cities soon recognized the propaganda potential of such events. Impressive spectacles in their own right, they stamped the kings' territories with ritual symbols of dominance.

In 291 (or 290), the Athenians welcomed Demetrios Poliorketes as their liberator with a parade accompanied by paeans, odes, and a specially commissioned ithyphallic hymn comparing him to the Olympians. He then promptly took up residence in the Parthenon. In 279, Ptolemy II Philadelphos inaugurated a splendid festival in Alexandria dedicated to his parents, the Ptolemaieia, which featured a sumptuous procession and a lavish banquet in a specially constructed pavilion. He declared the festival "isolympic" and invited all Greek states to send delegates.

The contemporary description preserved in Athenaios (5, 196A–203B) shows that the procession blended an Egyptian harvest festival, a Greek religious *pompe*, and a political/military parade. Framed by the Morning and Evening Stars, it included sections dedicated to the deified Ptolemy I Soter and Queen Berenike; to Zeus and the Olympians; and to Alexander. Dionysos' section was the richest. Loaded with gold and jewels, it featured hundreds of boys, women, and men dressed as satyrs, dispensing wine, grape juice, and milk from golden vessels for the thirsty crowd, legions of incense bearers, the Dionysiac Artists (the actors' guild), and a menagerie of exotic animals and birds. It included huge gilded and decorated floats bearing colossal golden Nikai; altars; personifications; Dionysiac scenes; a colossal mechanical Dionysos with his nurse Nysa; masses of golden wine jars and sacrificial implements; colossal statues of Alexander, Arete, Ptolemy, Priapos, and Corinth, followed by women impersonating the Ionian cities liberated by Alexander; a 90-foot silver spear (recalling Alexander's "spear-won" territory); a 135-foot golden *thyrsos*; and even a 180-foot golden phallos! Alexander's section featured the conqueror and Nike in gold on an elephant-drawn chariot; floats bearing chryselephantine thrones, a colossal double cornucopia, and 30-ft high eagles (both potent Ptolemaic symbols); and sundry colossal golden objects with dynastic/military overtones, including sacrificial implements, eagles, crowns, thunderbolts, an aegis, a huge suit of armor, and masses of gold and silver plate. A vast army followed.

The festival pavilion, a huge tent accommodating 100 chryselephantine dining couches, was supported by 50-ft poles resembling palm trees and *thyrsoi*, and was festooned with Egyptian fruits and flowers. Its surrounding colonnade was embellished on the inside with purple drapes, embroidered cloaks, exotic animal hides, marble statues, and old master pictures. Above it, golden tripods framed niches bearing Greek theater characters dining off gold plate. At the top was a frieze of golden, heraldically arranged eagles $22^1/_2$-ft high. Costly tapestries covered the couches, and each guest had his own golden table and golden place setting. Further commentary would be otiose.

THE CITY BEAUTIFUL (FIGURE 13)[4]

In Greece, grid planning began in the archaic period and was theorized by Hippodamos of Miletos around 460. But his projects were never completely realized, and the planned City Beautiful – coordinating gates, streets, public buildings, sanctuaries, and temples – is essentially a Hellenistic product.

Priene, founded in 334, bridges classical and Hellenistic city planning. Its grid produced blocks of 48 × 35 m (155 × 116 ft) and streets that alternate between 12 and 15 ft in width. Its agora is a unified central space bounded by a long northern stoa and a *pi*-shaped southern one, and is traversed on its north by one of the town's three main east–west streets. Yet, the others are poorly coordinated with the agora, and for defensive purposes, none of them runs right across town from gate to gate. The *emporion*, Athena sanctuary, *bouleuterion*, *gymnasion*, and theater are all aligned with the city grid and ring the agora, but bear scant relation to the latter architecturally.

Alexandria, founded in 331 and planned by Alexander's architect Deinokrates, was much different (Figure 13). He used a spacious 330-m (1,000-ft) master grid, with individual blocks measuring 300 × 150 ft. The city proper was basically rectangular; the royal palaces and gardens adjoined it to the northeast, and the Sarapeion to the southwest. The main east–west street – the majestic, 100-ft-wide Canopic Way – traversed it from gate to gate, and two equally wide north–south streets apparently crossed it at each end of town. The six grid squares in the town center, bisected by the Canopic Way, contained the agora, emporion, and probably the lawcourts, gymnasion, Museum, and library. Such regularity soon prevailed throughout the Hellenistic world.

Hilltop sites demanded a different, contour-related approach. Pergamon, for example, boasted a spectacular system of terraces rising majestically in a great arc to the top of its 1,000-ft. akropolis. They radiate from the central hub of the theater, and rusticated walls of dark local stone anchor them firmly to the craggy hillsides.

After this, it remained only for Hellenistic architects to invent the arched gateway (first definitely attested in 156 at Priene) and the colonnaded street (in first-century Antioch). With these, the concept of the city beautiful, its graceful arched gates announcing monumental colonnaded boulevards that structured a rationally planned urban environment, was complete.

THE SANCTUARY BEAUTIFUL[5]

Classical Greek sanctuaries are usually informal in plan. At Priene, however, the Athena temple, altar, and ancillary stoa are aligned with the city grid, but the entrance from the upper main street is slightly

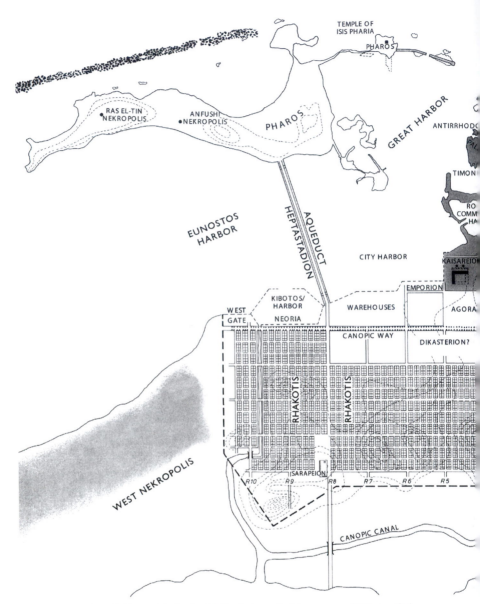

FIGURE 13. Plan of Alexandria in the Hellenistic period (courtesy of Günter Grimm and the Archäologisches Institut der Universität Trier, edited with English captions by Erin Dintino).

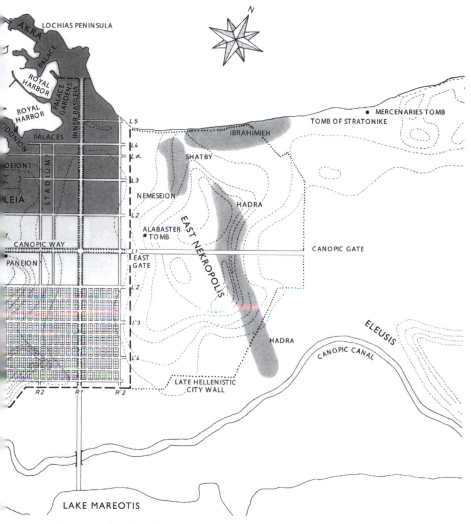

FIGURE 13 (continued).

off-axis. (Classical Greek architects preferred oblique to head-on views.) At Alexandria, the third-century temple of Sarapis was 22.5 m (75 ft) or one-quarter of a city block long and was surrounded by an imposing colonnaded court measuring 82.5 × 165 m (250 × 500 ft) – a quarter grid module by-a-half. Whether this colonnade was one- or two-storied is unknown, but Pergamene architects soon definitely employed the latter in such contexts (see The Two-Storied Colonnaded Façade).

Next, at Lindos and Kos around 150, preexisting temples to Athena and Asklepios were incorporated into axially symmetrical terrace systems marching up the hillside like giant staircases. Bordered by stoas pierced by monumental propylaia and (at Lindos) featuring a screen colonnade across the foot of the main stair, these grandiose, axially planned ensembles not only framed and articulated the temples but now embraced the visitor and directed him inexorably to his goal. Italian builders quickly adopted this innovation, achieving a new monumentality and grandeur. In the Sanctuary of Fortuna, at Praeneste, for example, spacious stone colonnades masked vaulted concrete corridors, galleries, and exedrae, and a theater–temple satisfyingly crowned the composition.

THE HOUSE BEAUTIFUL[6]

Houses with colonnaded courtyards and rudimentary pebble mosaics appear at Olynthos by ca. 400. Within a century, Pella and Morgantina in Sicily boasted houses of a truly impressive size (around 50 × 50 m), often incorporating pebble mosaics of the highest quality. Mural decoration soon evolved from simple bands of color to a quasi-architectural, tripartite scheme at Pella and Delos of dado, paneled wall (sometimes articulated with pilasters), and entablature. They mix stucco relief and illusionistic fresco, anticipating the so-called First and Second Styles of Pompeian mural decoration.

At Delos, where most of the extant houses date to the Athenian colony of 166–88, tessellated mosaics (see Tessellated Mosaics; cf. Figure 17) abound, and figured frescoes appear occasionally. Marble sculpture, rare at Olynthos (destroyed in 347) and Pella, is also plentiful. This Delian domestic decor could include carved altars, reliefs, statuettes, and busts or even full-sized statues of the owners, sited so as to greet the unsuspecting visitor as he or she entered the house.

THE CUSTOMIZED LIBRARY[7]

The customized library was the creation of the fourth-century Athenian philosophical schools. When Plato died in 347, his Academy was probably a quite informal affair, but by ca. 300, a handsome, purpose-built library occupied the site. A 110 m² reading room flanked by book depositories stood at one end of a large (23.4 × 40.4 m) rectangular courtyard whose Ionic colonnades housed over forty reading tables and two small rooms perhaps used for dining. A large statue base, perhaps for the Nine Muses, stood at the head of the courtyard, in front of the reading room.

Because Aristotle's library was far bigger than Plato's, his Lykeion (Lyceum) probably boasted a similar but even larger complex. It may be found someday, but the greatest library of the Greco-Roman world, at Alexandria (see Figure 13), is now completely destroyed. Although Ptolemy II Philadelphos is traditionally credited with founding it and the adjoining Museum – the ancestor of today's research institutes – around 280, his father surely did much of the preparatory work. His adviser was Demetrios of Phaleron, a graduate of Aristotle's Lyceum, but the design also probably drew on the local tradition of temple libraries, too.

Fortunately, a Pergamene version of the Alexandrian library has survived, albeit in ruin. Eumenes II built it around 190. Situated behind the north stoa of the Athena Nikephoros sanctuary, it consisted of a large, airy, 200 m² reading room, three storerooms, a vestibule, a hostel with three bedrooms, and a dining room for sixteen people. The head librarian (a scholar) and his staff lived in the hostel and entertained visitors there, and the books were kept in the four-room complex next door, also accessible from the stoa's upper floor. The big reading room no doubt housed the most popular ones; patrons could either consult them there or take them out into the stoa. The bookcases stood on a stone socle 90 cm high and 1.05 m deep, anchored to the wall by metal ties but placed 50 cm away from it to minimize damp.

Opposite the reading room's main door stood a one-third-scale marble copy of Pheidias's colossal chryselephantine Athena Parthenos at Athens – the goddess of wisdom – now a monument of culture rather than cult. *Plus ça change*: her bust also crowns the main door of the neoclassical Californian library in which I am writing this chapter.

THE CUSTOMIZED CLUBHOUSE (FIGURE 14)[8]

Private associations and clubs, already numerous in classical Greece, multiplied in the Hellenistic period. Religious ones met in the shrine of their patron deity or hero; the Athenian philosophical schools at first in *gymnasia*; and political and "hellfire" clubs in private houses. But evidence for customized facilities begins only in the Hellenistic period.

After the Platonic Academy, built around 300 (see Customized Library), the best surviving example is the Establishment of the

Poseidoniasts of Berytos on Delos (Figure 14). This aptly named association of maritime traders, shippers, and forwarding agents from Beirut in
Lebanon built a large two-story clubhouse on the island around 110. An
impressive 1,300 m, blending elements of a sumptuous private house on
the one hand and a Hellenistic palace on the other, it was a storehouse,
office suite, meeting place, hostel, and shrine all rolled into one.

Business was transacted and goods stored in two extensive suites of
rooms astride the main door; many of them opened onto the street. The
private areas were reached via a corridor leading to a small courtyard.
This opened westward onto a vestibule and row of chapels to Roma,
Poseidon, Aphrodite-Astarte, and Asklepios-Echmoun, and eastward
onto a large colonnaded courtyard, 20 × 27 m. This large courtyard,
its central cistern covered by a mosaic floor, probably served similar
functions to those of the Hellenistic palaces. Three doors in its western
side led to the most private space of all, a courtyard 12 × 15 m, no
doubt the club's open-air meeting place. The hostel was on the upper
floor, now destroyed. The decor included mosaics, painted stucco, and
numerous sculptures: marble cult statues of the club's patron deities,
bronze honorary portraits of its merchant benefactors, marble altars and
herms, statuettes of a classical Herakles and Aphrodite, a satyr disrobing
a nymph, and the famous "Slipper-slapper" group of Aphrodite, Pan,
and Eros, dedicated by one Dionysios of Berytos to his "native gods,"
which surely included Aphrodite-Astarte.

THE TWO-STORIED, COLONNADED FAÇADE (FIGURE 15)[9]

Greek architects had long employed superimposed Doric colonnades
inside their temples, and around 330, the Temple of Zeus at Nemea
substituted an upper Ionic order for the customary Doric one. Soon,
the architect of the early Hellenistic palace at Vergina (see The Palace
and Court Art), realizing that the latter scheme was perfect for an upper-
floor loggia apparently transferred it *en bloc* to the palace façade. The
nearby Great Tomb at Lefkadia concretely documents this innovation
a generation or so later. Its upper Ionic order is about two-fifths the
height of its lower Doric one and frames a series of shuttered windows.

Because this scheme offered a perfect grandstand for ceremonies
and other spectacles, its application to stoas in sanctuaries and agoras
was only a matter of time. In 300/299 a new stoa in the Athenian
Asklepieion, overlooking the god's temple and altar, featured a two-story

Doric order. The upper one, used also for ritual sleep-ins, was between three-fifths and two-thirds the height of the lower, though when the building was published in 1911 only the entablature, one column drum, and no capitals from the latter were extant. Recent restoration work has identified many of the missing blocks, and will enable a more exact calculation to be made. On present evidence, the next step was taken in second-century Pergamon. The L-shaped stoa built around the temple of Athena Nikephoros at Pergamon around 190 resurrected the Doric-Ionic combination; regularized the relation between the two orders by making the upper one exactly two-thirds the height of the lower; and embellished the upper story's balustrade with reliefs of captured arms and armor. Uniquely, though, its Ionic architrave carried a Doric frieze. This both echoed the Athena temple's own Doric order, and spoke to the goddess' own martial character. A century earlier, Kallimachos had written his *Hymn to Athena* in the "manly" Doric dialect, and in the Augustan period Vitruvius (1.2.5), paraphrasing a Hellenistic theorist, declared that the Doric order was particularly appropriate to Minerva, Mars, and Hercules for this very reason.

Yet, the end result was still technically a solecism. Soon, the magnificent stoas donated by Eumenes II and Attalos II to Athens both tacitly corrected it and greatly enlarged the lion's head gargoyles centered above the columns to link the two stories visually. Finally, the Romans equalized the colonnades' heights and often added a Corinthian one above them, creating the magnificent multistoried façades that typify the imperial Roman architectural idiom.

THE EXTERIOR CORINTHIAN ORDER (FIGURE 15)[10]

The Corinthian order was invented around 400. At first it was used only inside temples and *tholoi*, for reasons that remain unclear. It first "comes out" on the sumptuous tripod base erected in Athens by Lysikrates to celebrate his choregic victory in the theatre in 334. Early third-century architects soon took up the innovation.

Around 280, the Propylon of Ptolemy II at Samothrace employed Corinthian for its interior façade and Ionic for its exterior one, thereby using the best of both worlds, and the tomb chamber of an imposing royal mausoleum at Belevi near Ephesos was ringed with thirty-two Corinthian columns. The Samothracian propylon faced the temple, altar, and performances of the sacred mysteries, whereas the mausoleum's colonnade perhaps referenced the custom of embellishing gravestones with acanthus ornamentation. Indeed, the Corinthian capital's inventor allegedly got the idea from an acanthus growing around an offering basket on a young girl's tomb (Vitr. 4.1.9).

The first Corinthian temple façade was apparently that of the tetrastyle prostyle Sarapeion at Alexandria, built by Ptolemy III Euergetes. Now known only from reproductions on coins and gems, it apparently included a Doric frieze. Not until ca. 170 did a full Corinthian peripteros and frieze appear together, on the colossal temple of Olympian Zeus at Athens and another at Olba Diocaesarea (Uzuncaburç) in Cilicia. The patron in both cases was the eccentric King Antiochos IV Epiphanes of Syria. Given the order's special character, it may be no coincidence that both temples were dedicated to the supreme Olympian god and Antiochos' own patron deity, and that the Athenian temple's architect was an Italian, a certain Cossutius. His involvement was prophetic, for in Roman hands, the Corinthian order would eventually conquer the world.

THE VAULT[11]

The post-and-lintel system allowed only limited spans that could bear little additional weight. The alternative is the arch and its offshoot, the vault, though these were seldom used aboveground until the Roman period. The true stone vault using voussoirs (trapezoidal blocks locked in place by a keystone) is a Near Eastern invention perhaps introduced to Greece as a result of Alexander's conquests. It first appears there around 320, in the athletes' entrance to the stadium at Nemea. The barrel-vaulted passage, over 36 m long, was 2.06 m wide and 2.48 m high and employs masonry of the highest quality.

A couple of years later, Tomb II in the Great Tumulus at Vergina was given a barrel vault over twice as wide, but its 4.46 m span was soon surpassed by that of the 6.5 m wide antechamber of the early third-century Great Tomb at Lefkadia (see The Two-Storied, Colonnaded Façade). Buttressed by earth mounds, these vaults simply abut the tombs' traditional colonnaded façades. The widest Hellenistic aboveground vault, 7.35 m across, occurs in second-century Pergamon, and the first ornamental archway, just over 6 m across, on the contemporary agora gate at Priene, was built in 156. Though these seem impressive, none of them comes close to the 24.5 m span of Fabricius' bridge over the Tiber at Rome, built in 62 and still standing today (but renamed the Ponte

Quattro Capi). By then, however, the Roman invention of concrete permitted even greater spans, which in the imperial period sometimes exceeded 40 m.

THE BAROQUE (FIGURES 15 AND 16)[12]

Although often regarded as the most characteristic and even the most important artistic innovation of the Hellenistic period, the baroque is notoriously difficult to define. Its favorite tactic is the use of classical motifs in a nonclassical manner, its main characteristic is flux, and its principal aim is "swaying the soul" (*psychagogia*). On present evidence, two centers contributed most to its development: Alexandria in architecture and Pergamon in sculpture. Curiously, though, each apparently disdained the other's innovations in these media.

Together, Alexandrian tombs, architectural fragments in the local museum, and the indirect evidence of the rock tombs at Petra (Figure 15) and other Jordanian sites demonstrate the existence of recognizably baroque architecture in Alexandria by ca. 150. Roman late republican frescoes, using the same vocabulary and syntax, confirm this from afar. The style's characteristic features include acanthus column bases, Corinthian capitals with S-shaped spirals, modillion cornices, and, especially, curved entablatures, segmental pediments, and half-pediments. Although the former enhance the building's overall exuberance, the latter break up its façade with unexpected curves, setbacks, and voids, and (in the first-century royal tomb at Petra called the "Khazneh," Figure 15) focus attention on the conical-roofed tholos at its center. Here, the static, two-dimensional classical façade becomes three-dimensionally dynamic. Broken pediments announce the thrusting climax of the central tholos, whereas curves, setbacks, and voids open enticing portals to the interior.

In Pergamon, however, sculpture set the pace. Although the baroque tendencies appear in late fourth-century painting (the Hades-Persephone scene in Tomb I at Vergina), third-century sculptors, such as Epigonos (a local Pergamene) and Phyromachos (an Athenian immigrant), were the first to realize its full potential. Commissions included monuments to immortalize the regime's victories over the brutal, invading Gauls and portraits of inspired intellectuals such as the long-dead philosopher Antisthenes. A tragic mode is detectable in some baroque groups: Achilles with the body of his beloved Penthesileia, Ajax with the body of Achilles (the so-called "Pasquino"), and (in Rome) the Laokoon. The baroque's acknowledged climax, however, comes on the

Great Altar of Pergamon around 170 (Figure 16). Its epic Gigantomachy pulls out all the stops, relentlessly mobilizing every classical motif available, adding many new ones, and then cranking up the energy to the utmost in order to "sway the soul" of the astonished onlooker. The result is a panorama of cosmic violence unsurpassed in ancient art.

Baroque architecture and sculpture thrived in imperial Rome and in the provinces and, when rediscovered around 1500, helped to create both the high Renaissance style of Sansovino and Michelangelo and later the counter-reformation baroque of Borromini and Bernini.

Rococo[13]

The baroque sometimes verges on self-parody, but the rococo turns unashamedly to burlesque. It is the satyric mode to the "Pasquino's" tragic and the Gigantomachy's epic one. Its subjects are largely Dionysiac: satyrs inviting girls to dance, courting them, and often molesting them – a hobby also of hermaphrodites and the great god Pan. Erotes, Centaurs, and other mythological small fry also populate the rococo landscape, which is frustratingly difficult to localize.

A satyr molesting a nymph and the famous "Slipper-slapper" group of Pan molesting Aphrodite dedicated by Dionysios of Berytos to his native gods stood in the Establishment of the Poseidoniasts at Delos (see Figure 14; discussed in The Customized Clubhouse), but such provenanced pieces are few. Pliny (N.H. 36.24) and a recently discovered statue base show that another such molestation group and a dancing satyr stood at Pergamon, and Roman coins of Kyzikos in Asia Minor localize the Invitation to the Dance somewhere in that city, but all else is conjecture. Sanctuaries of Dionysos and nymphaia in royal parks are the obvious candidates, but the slate is essentially blank until the Roman period, when copies of these groups frequently turn up in purely secular locations such as villas, private houses, porticoes, and baths.

Realism[14]

Realism is different from naturalism. Greek artists sought a natural look from the beginning, but achieved it by inventing generalized and visually satisfying conventions or *schemata* for muscles, lips, eyes, hair, and so on. The "Greek ideal" is the general and typical, the highest common factor in human and animal.

Sporadic bursts of realism – the faithful transcription of individually specific traits, even of personal quirks – appear from the sixth century on. Some sculptors, like Demetrios of Alopeke (*floruit* ca. 400), even specialized in it, to considerable disapproval (e.g., Quint. *Inst. Or.* 12.10.9). The foundations for an aesthetically satisfying realism were laid only under Alexander, by Apelles and Lysippos, with their commitment to a kind of "phenomenal idealism" that took the king's real physiognomy and discreetly idealized it (see Figure 12).

Apelles capped a long list of representational innovations (shading, perspective, and so on) by inventing *luster* – the glint of light on water, gold, skin, and the thunderbolt held by his Alexander Thunderbolt-Bearer. In sculpture, Lysippos modeled hair and other features with unprecedented finesse, whereas his brother Lysistratos provided technical support. "He was the first to mold an image in plaster from the human face itself, and established the practice of making corrections upon a casting produced by pouring wax into this plaster mold. [He thereby] instituted the practice of making likenesses; beforehand, they tried to make portraits as beautiful as possible" (Pliny, *N.H.* 35.153).

Others soon followed along. Though almost all Hellenistic painting is lost, the Alexander Mosaic shows what it had achieved by 300, and other mid-Hellenistic mosaics continue the tradition. These include a hunting dog from the new Alexandrian library site; the parrot and garland mosaics from the palaces at Pergamon (plus Sosos' Bird-Bath and Unswept Floor mosaics there, known from literary sources and numerous copies); and the superb mask-and-garland mosaic discovered at the author's excavation at Dor in Israel in 2000 (Figure 17).

In sculpture, Polyeuktos's *Demosthenes* (384–322), made in 280 and extensively copied, achieves a powerful blend of intellectual intensity and facial, corporeal, and sartorial realism. A real middle-aged man stands before us, captured in that tense moment before beginning to speak (in his youth, Demosthenes had suffered from stage fright and tended to gesture wildly). And in a recently discovered papyrus, the early Hellenistic epigrammatist Poseidippos of Pella (see Chapter 9 in this volume) praises a now-lost portrait of the scholar-poet Philitas (ca. 340–270) for the same achievement:

> This bronze, just like Philitas in every way, Hekataios
> molded accurately down to the toenails.
> Following a human standard in scale and feature,
> he blended it with none of the form of the heroes,

but modeled the old perfectionist with all his skill,
    holding fast to the straight canon of truth.
He seems about to speak, so characterful is he;
    the old man's alive, even though he's bronze;
and here, thanks to Ptolemy, god and king alike,
    this man of Kos is dedicated for the Muses' sake.
                                (Austin & Bastianini 2002: no. 63)

By around 250, then, Hellenistic realism had come of age, blazing
the trail for Roman republican verism and its late Hellenistic cousins
(Figure 18).

THE GROTESQUE[15]

At one level, the grotesque is a blend of realism, rococo, and the
baroque, pressed to a comic or disgusting extreme, or both. Although
the lifesize Hellenistic "old derelicts" (old prostitutes, fishermen, and
peasants) sometimes meet this description, the term is more usually
applied to miniature bronzes and terracottas. Vast numbers of these
have appeared in the graveyards and garbage dumps of the Hellenistic
east.

Many functions have been suggested for them, some supported
by textual or archaeological evidence, some not. These include: votives
to Dionysos and other divinities; talismans against the Evil Eye; banquet decorations or favors representing jesters, mimers, and mummers;
racist put-downs of the non-Greek underclass; and even doctors' teaching aids! No explanation covers more than a part of the corpus, and
some not even that. Even their ancient nomenclature is problematic,
for although the Greeks and Romans seem to have called some of them
grylloi, the meaning of this term is uncertain and the best English one,
"grotesque," does not describe them all and introduces other, anachronistic connotations.

Fortunately, their aesthetic effect is easier to describe. They lure us
into a double take, first attracting us by their hyperrealism then repelling
us by their ugliness. The antithesis of the upright citizen body – the
myriad statues of civic "worthies" that studded the Hellenistic world –
they offer a chaotic farrago of excess, aberration, convolution, disjunction, discordance, imperfection, mutilation, atrophy, decay, self-
indulgence, and self-loathing. Creatures of both lack *and* superfluity,

they often combine stunted or missing limbs with acromegaly and other pathologies. Repulsive yet fascinating, they provoke reactions akin to the Gorgon's and openly flaunt their otherness like the satyr. They are the reverse side of the civic coin – the Morlocks of the Hellenistic world.

THE HERMAPHRODITE[16]

The hermaphrodite is the grotesque's polar opposite, the mythological third term to the citizen – derelict nexus. The neutered child of Hermes and Aphrodite, combining the sex organs and beauty of both, it is physically godlike but for one thing – its sterility. Yet, like the grotesque, it is a creature of great power. Its erect phallos, often self-revealed in the *anasyromenos* gesture of the street-corner flasher, repels the Evil Eye just as effectively as the grotesque's misshapen body was thought to attract it. This ever-ready organ and the creature's prominent breasts go far toward explaining its strong connection with fertility cults.

Classical authors already list some of these characteristics and func-tions, but their artistic realization is a product of Alexander's age, in the form of a fragmentary clay *anasyromenos* from an Athenian garbage dump. Marble hermaphrodite statues and herms soon appear (some *anasyromenoi*, some not), and two "rococo" groups of satyrs molesting them survive in copy. The most heavily copied hermaphrodite, however, was the sleeping type, often attributed to the Athenian Polykles (*floruit* 156–153 B.C.) on Pliny's authority (*N.H.* 34.80, cf. 52). Like the grotesque, it, too, produces a double take. The (male) spectator first espies a gorgeous, near-naked woman lying prone on the ground, her body twisted in troubled sleep and her head turned toward him with eyes closed, blissfully unaware of his approach. Circling her for the coup-de-grâce, he then encounters a crudely jutting phallos, bluntly signaling "F . . . off!" If a recent identification of this creature as the violent Phrygian hermaphrodite Agdistis could be sustained, then its one–two punch would pack even more power.

NEOCLASSICISM[17]

Neoclassicism is realism's opposite pole: historicist, nostalgic, and staunchly idealist.

Although late classical and early Hellenistic cult images often inclined to conservatism, around 200, a new phenomenon appears: a frankly neo-Pheidian look. In his cult group for the Temple of Despoina at Lykosoura in Arkadia, Damophon of Messene clearly sought to evoke the majesty of Pheidias' great fifth-century cult images, structuring the goddesses' heads accordingly and simplifying their modeling. (The head of the Titan Anytos and the drapery, however, remain purely Hellenistic in style.) Their contemporary, the Athena from the Library at Pergamon (see The Customized Library), copies Pheidias's Parthenos at one-third scale, "modernizing" the drapery and features only slightly.

Athenian sculptors soon jumped on the bandwagon – indeed, may even have set it rolling. At any rate, around 150–125 the Athenians Timarchides and Timokles, sons of the aforementioned Polykles, propelled it one stage further, embellishing the marble shield of their Athena Kranaia at Elateia with a copy of the Amazonomachy on the Parthenos' golden one. Such copies soon underpinned a new industry, the production of decorative marble panels, vases, wellheads, and altars (the so-called neo-Attic reliefs) for the Roman market. Copies in the round soon followed, and bronzes kept pace. Echoing a late Hellenistic critic's backhanded judgement on them, Pliny remarks that after an alleged 140-year lacuna, bronze sculpture "revived" in the years 156–153 under Polykles, Timokles, and others, "far inferior to their predecessors, but still artists of note" (*N.H.* 34.52).

Either inspiring all of this or (more likely) invented by Hellenistic intellectuals to underpin it, the so-called *phantasia* theory sought to explain why Pheidias' vision of the Olympians was so compelling. Thus, Quintilian (*Inst. Or.* 12.10.9) remarks that the beauty of his statues added something to the traditional religion and that he alone captured the gods' majesty. Philostratos (*Vit. Ap.* 6.19) even fantasized that he and Praxiteles went up to heaven and copied the forms of the gods, then returned to earth to inject them with a strong dose of imagination (*phantasia*). "For *mimesis* will represent that which can be seen with the eyes, but *phantasia* will represent that which cannot."

CONTINUOUS NARRATIVE (FIGURE 19)[18]

Continuous narrative tells a story that develops in time. Although earlier Greek artists often included discreet references to cause and effect, they rarely conflated two or more temporally distinct actions within a single frame. And although temple metopes sometimes carried heroic biographies, only a tiny group of works – a dozen Attic red-figure cups showing the Labors of Herakles and Theseus – ever repeated the protagonist within the same pictorial space. Exported to Italy and buried in Etruscan tombs, these had no influence on later Greek art.

By contrast, the mid-second-century Telephos frieze from the Great Altar of Pergamon narrates the hero's life, episode by episode, against a continuous landscape background, switching between Greece and Asia half a dozen times in the process. Even in its fragmentary condition (only a third of its 58 m length survives), Telephos appears no fewer than fifteen times, his mother Auge five times, and his father Herakles and stepfather Teuthras twice each. Episodes vary from 1.4 to 2 m in length, and transitions are marked by a landscape element or prop (usually a tree, rock, or pillar) on one side but never on both.

Similarly conjoined excerpts from epic and tragedy on contemporary ceramic relief bowls (cheap imitations of metal ones), accompanied by brief citations from the actual texts, show that this frieze was no aberration. Monumental painting may have pioneered the technique, which next appears on the first-century Odyssey frescoes from the Esquiline Hill in Rome (Figure 19). Labeled in Greek and thus probably copies, they narrate episodes from *Odyssey* X and XI against a fully continuous landscape background. Figures and scenery are now more naturalistically scaled, and sophisticated perspectival devices (diminution and atmospherically graded colors) enhance the effect.

In one scene, Odysseus and the sorceress Circe appear twice over, at the entrance to her palace and inside it. Roman painters soon embraced this practice, sometimes cramming up to four such episodes into a single panel. Meanwhile, the frieze tradition flourished in such quintessentially Roman "historical" monuments as the columns of Trajan and Marcus Aurelius and blossomed again in the Middle Ages in such masterpieces as the Bayeux Tapestry.

TESSELLATED MOSAICS (SEE FIGURE 17)[19]

The first signs of cut stone or "tessellated" flooring appear in Carthaginian North Africa, where some fourth- and early third-century floors of mortar and crushed terracotta (so-called *opus signinum*) include simple designs of this material. Contemporary Greek mosaicists, however, preferred colored pebbles set in mortar or clay, often using lead strips for contours and sometimes for internal modeling as well. After ca. 300, however, they began to experiment with stone chips recycled from builders' waste. Mostly used as background fillers, sometimes these chips are specially trimmed to render important details, such teeth, eyes, and locks of hair.

The earliest fully tessellated mosaics – made completely of cut stone, terracotta, and sometimes even glass cubes – come from opposite ends of the Mediterranean Greek world. This new technique had many advantages. It produced floors that were flat, damage-resistant (pebbles are easily kicked loose), and easy to clean; it allowed a much wider range of colors; and it enabled the mosaicist to imitate the spectacular chiaroscuro effects of contemporary painting.

A mid-third-century mosaic of hunting Erotes from a villa near Alexandria uses limestone, slate, and terracotta tesserae of red, pink, yellow, gray, beige, black, and white, but still retains lead strips for contours and pebbles for textured surfaces, such as hair, bristles, and manes. At Morgantina in Sicily, the so-called House of Ganymede, built apparently before the city's destruction in 211, boasted three fully tessellated ones. Backgrounds are made of 1 cm² black tesserae, and the figures of smaller ones are in a wide variety of colors: red, brown, yellow, gray, green, blue, black, and white. Specially cut pieces were used for Ganymede's eyes, testicles, and toes.

Although the older techniques never died out, fully tessellated mosaics soon dominated the Mediterranean scene, and virtuoso illusionistic techniques – later called *opus vermiculatum* – became commonplace. Tesserae as small as 1 mm² are not unusual, and the use of colored glass alongside stone produced not only a full palette of colors but also compositions of stunning iridescence, such as the mask-and-garland mosaic from Dor mentioned in the Realism section (see Figure 17). Popular throughout the Roman Empire and revived in the late Middle Ages, the technique remains standard today.

POLYCHROME JEWELRY (FIGURE 20)[20]

This section introduces three innovations in the luxury crafts, specifically in jewelry. Near Eastern and Egyptian jewelers had used colored stones and glass for centuries, even millennia, and the Greeks themselves had practiced the art of gem cutting for stamp seals since the Bronze Age. Archaic and classical Greek goldsmiths, however, preferred homogeneity in materials, creating miniature sculpture enlivened only by some discreet filigree and granulation. In Tomb II at Vergina in Macedonia, however, an intricate gold diadem crafted around 320–300 includes ten tiny buds sprouting from discs of blue cloisonné enamel, together with numerous buds and petals of the same material.

Third-century diadems, earrings, necklaces, bracelets, and rings were often spectacularly inlaid with enamel, chalcedony, cornelian, clear quartz, and, above all, red garnet (Figure 20). Alexander's conquests apparently provided the motive, means, and opportunity for this chromatic extravagance. Earring pendants – especially birds and other creatures – are often dipped in white or blue enamel for polychromatic effect, and emeralds and pearls appear in the second century as direct trade grew with India and the East. By this time, too, another long-lasting polychromatic innovation had been introduced into the jeweler's repertoire: the cameo.

THE CAMEO (FIGURE 21)[21]

Unlike engraved gems, which were regularly employed as stamp seals, cameos have no practical use, but – being bichrome and in relief – far greater decorative appeal and legibility. Made of banded agate or laminated glass (a cheap substitute), they were invented apparently around 200 in Alexandria, for the earliest extant examples are portraits of the middle Ptolemies, particularly Ptolemy VI Philometor, and their queens. (The great St Petersburg and Vienna cameos perhaps representing Alexander and Olympias, once attributed to Ptolemy II, are now convincingly reassigned to early imperial Rome.) The fashion soon spread. Some late Seleukid royal cameos survive, and a cameo of a Bactrian king has appeared in a Kushanic noblewoman's grave at Tillya Tepe in Central Asia.

The so-called Tazza Farnese, a dazzling yellow-banded agate (sardonyx) cameo bowl 20 cm in diameter, preserves the first royal allegory in this medium (Figure 21). Although its subject – the fertility of the Nile under Ptolemaic rule – guarantees manufacture in Ptolemaic Alexandria, its date is fiercely controversial. Current opinion inclines to the mid–first century B.C. Its complexity and sophistication strongly suggest that it was not the first work of its kind. Nor was it the last: In Augustan and Julio-Claudian Rome, the art reached new heights, with such masterpieces as the Gemma Augustea, the Grand Camée de France, the Alexander cameos mentioned earlier, and the invention of the cameo glass vessel. Some of these spent the Middle Ages in church or royal treasuries, rekindling the art in the Renaissance.

THE OPEN HOOP EARRING[22]

Classical Greek earring types include simple hoops, discs, spirals, and pendants (especially the fashionable boat-shaped variety). Open hoop earrings with fancy finials first appear around 330 and remained popular for hundreds of years. Once again, the jewelers' source of inspiration was probably Persia. As today, the pointed end of the hoop was thrust through the earlobe, leaving the finial (usually an animal, monster, fish, or human head) to dangle below the ear, facing either forward or backward.

ART COLLECTING[23]

The origins of art collecting remain obscure and its definition problematic. Do "collections" of fine tableware (Attic red-figure pottery or Georgian silver) count? Or domestic embellishments, such as mosaics (Figure 17), carpets, tapestries, and frescoes? Or icon collections in monasteries? Or artworks acquired as plunder? According to one useful working definition, "true" collectors are: (a) largely uninterested in the practical utility of their collection; (b) generally uninvolved in its production; (c) assembling it not to meet normal living requirements but primarily for personal pleasure; and (d) following some sort of an agenda or theme, however ill defined.

By these criteria, the West's first securely documented art collector was the "Achaian leader" Aratos of Sikyon (271–213 B.C.) – though *inter alios*, Ptolemy I and II, Pyrrhos, and other early Hellenistic rulers may have anticipated him. Fortunately for Aratos, Sikyonians had dominated Greek painting for a century, and it was there that the easel picture had been invented around 400, making collections like his possible. Plutarch (*Aratos* 12–13) tells us that Aratos, "a man not without good taste," collected Sikyonian "old master" paintings and drawings, especially those of the late classic painters Pamphilos and Melanthios. He even used them as diplomatic currency, sending some to Ptolemy III Euergetes to solicit his support as an ally.

Collections of sculpture followed apace. A letter supposedly written by Plato to Dionysios II of Syracuse (Plat. *Epistle* 13.361A) mentions the philosopher's purchase of two Apollos by Leochares for the tyrant and his wife, but is almost certainly an early Hellenistic forgery. It sets the scene, however, for the decorative sculptures and paintings of

Ptolemy II's festival pavilion of 279 (see *Tryphe* II. Pomp and Circumstance), and for sporadic finds of sculpture in apparently decorative contexts in the houses of third-century Pella and elsewhere, in the Attalid palaces at Pergamon, and (though the remains are presently uniformly Egyptian or Egyptianizing) in the submerged Ptolemaic palace gardens at Alexandria. In late Hellenistic Delos such collecting reached epidemic proportions (see The House Beautiful). Roman expansion brought further developments, documented from texts, shipwrecks, and finds *in situ*: mountains of loot (paintings, sculptures, jewelry, metalwork, and tapestries), conspicuous consumption, sumptuously embellished villas, a vast expansion of the copying industry, and an art market not unlike today's – expensive fakes included.

ART HISTORY[24]

Classical Greeks were the first to realize that art has a history, but the writing of that history – as distinct from workshop manuals and *ad hoc* philosophical reflections on art – is a Hellenistic innovation.

Two distinct approaches are immediately detectable: the biographical (a subgenre of historiography) and the formal (perhaps an offshoot of the workshop manual). Douris of Samos (ca. 340–260) pioneered the first and his contemporary Xenokrates of Athens the second. Both are known largely from Pliny, who drew on them for his discussions of metals, pigments, and stones in *Natural History* books 34–36.

Douris, a historian of Macedonia and biographer of Alexander's successors, wrote books on both metalwork and painting. Pliny, *N.H.* 34.65 cites him for an illuminating anecdote on the early career of Lysippos, but otherwise his art writing remains enigmatic. Xenokrates is better understood. A second- or third-generation member of Lysippos' school, he was both a practicing bronze sculptor and a historian of bronzework and painting. A citation from his discussion of the painter Parrhasios (*floruit* ca. 400) in *N.H.* 35.67–68 reveals that he analyzed painting in terms of line and color, human proportion, and fidelity to nature (*skiagraphia*, *symmetria*, and *akribeia*). Similar passages on other artists (both painters and bronzeworkers) include remarks on perspective and composition (*skenographia* and *rhythmos*), and indicate that Xenokrates produced histories of both arts that reduced them to a series of formal and technical innovations culminating in the work of Apelles and Lysippos. But if *N.H.* 34.54–67 truly reflects his ideas on the evolution of bronzework, they were badly askew. Apparently lacking independent dates for Myron and Pythagoras of Rhegion, he placed them between Polykleitos and Lysippos, whereas in reality they preceded both.

The recently discovered poetry collection probably by Poseidippos (ca. 310–240; see Realism), containing nine epigrams on statuary, shows that Alexandrian intellectuals soon noticed these treatises. Other contributions soon followed. A certain Antigonos – the polymath Antigonos of Karystos(?) – revised Xenokrates' book in the late third century, adding biographical and epigraphical material to it. In the late second century, a chronicler, perhaps Apollodoros of Athens, gave the major sculptors and painters *floruit* dates by Olympiads, but wrote off the entire period between Olympiad 121 and 156 (−296/5–156 B.C.) as a time when bronzecasting simply "stopped" (*N.H.* 34.49–52; 35.54, 58, 60–61, 78–79). A diehard neoclassicist (see The Hermaphridite), he evidently disliked Hellenistic realism, baroque, and rococo enough to erase them from history.

By the end of the Hellenistic world, a certain Metrodoros had written a history of architecture, Heliodoros a book entitled *Athenian Votive Offerings*, and Pasiteles (ca. 100–50) five books on world masterpieces of sculpture. With these, the foundations for the work of Varro, Vitruvius, Pliny, Quintilian, and Pausanias – and art history as practiced today – were firmly in place.

BIBLIOGRAPHICAL NOTE

The sites are described and referenced in Stillwell (1976). Useful introductory monographs on Alexandria and Pergamon are Grimm (1998) and Radt (1999), with Ginouvès (1994) on Macedonia.

The best survey of Hellenistic art is Pollitt (1986), with Boardman (1994) on its diffusion. Webster (1964), Onians (1979), Fowler (1989), and Zanker (2004) offer extensive, often impressionistic correlations with literature and philosophy. Beard and Henderson (2001) is resolutely iconoclastic. There is no good architecture survey in English: see Lauter (1986) (in German), with Lawrence (1996) for an introduction; Steele (1992) is unreliable and includes much that is Roman. Sculpture surveys abound: see Bieber (1961); Stewart (1990); Smith (1991); Moreno (1994) (in Italian); Ridgway (1990), (2002); and Andreae (2001; in German; superbly illustrated). Painting and mosaic are almost as badly served as architecture, largely because a continuous history is impossible: see Pollitt (1986) for comments, with introductions to Ling (1991), Ling (1998), and Dunbabin (1999); also, for example, Andronikos (1984); Rouveret (1989; in French); and Westgate (2000). For numismatics, see Mørkholm (1991); and for engraved gems, Plantzos (1999). Hellenistic minor arts are covered only in general surveys of these media, in site reports and in specialist articles; for synopses and selected bibliographies, see *The Dictionary of Art* (London, 1996) under "Greece, Ancient: Pottery: Metalwork; Terracotta; Other Arts."

For a sample of current trends, see Reeder (1988) for an up-to-date exhibition catalogue of a single museum's holdings; Bulloch et al. (1993) on images and ideologies; Zanker (2004) on viewing; Stewart (1996) on the Hellenistic body; Stewart (1993a) and (2003) on Alexander portraits; Zanker (1995) on philosopher portraits; Meyboom (1995) on the Nile Mosaic; Hamma (1996) on Alexandria; Dreyfus and Schraudolph (1996–1997) on the Telephos exhibition; Cohen (1997) and Pfrommer (1998; in German) on the Alexander Mosaic; Mattusch (1997) on the Getty bronze athlete; de Grummond and Ridgway (2000) on Pergamon and Sperlonga; Hellenkemper-Salies (1994) on the Mahdia wreck (in German); and Walker and Higg (2001) on Kleopatra.

NOTES

1   See Stewart (1993a); update, Stewart (2003); for the new gold double daric of Alexander, hinted after the Hydaspes in 326, showing him with elephant-skin cap, Ammon's ram's horn, and Zeus' aegis, see Bopearachchi and Flandrin (2005). For the material of the Philippeion portraits, see Schultz (in press).

2   See Nielsen (1994); Hoepfner and Brands (1996); Nielsen (2001); with Ginouvès (1994) 84–90 and ff (Macedonia); Herman (1997; court society); C. Kunze, G. Zimmer, and W. Sonne, in Hoepfner and Brands (1996) 109–29, 130–5, 136–43 (sculpture, silverware; gardens); Grimm (1998) 51–63 (Ptolemaic pavilion and riverboat); I. Nielsen, M. Hatzopoulos, I. Saatsoglou-Paliadeli, and G. Clarke, in Nielsen (2001) 165–248 (gardens; Pella; Vergina; Jebel Khalid). See also in general Strong (1966; gold and silver plate); F. Naumann-Steckner, in Williams (1998) 95–8, color pl. 13, fig. 123.3 (jewelry); Plantzos (1999; gems and cameos).

3   See Rice (1983); cf. J. Edmondson and A. Kuttner in Bergmann and Kondoleon (1999) 77–123.

4   See Wycherley (1962); Onians (1979) 164–78; Lawrence (1996) 190–204; and Cahill (2002) 1–22; also Hoepfner and Schwandner (1994) 188–292 (Priene; Alexandria; Dura; the East); Grimm and McKenzie in Hamma (1996) 55–74, 109–26; Hoepfner in Dreyfus and Schraudolph (1996–1997) vol. 2, 23–58; Grimm (1998) 14–5, 26–7; Radt (1999); McKenzie (2003).

5   See previous note, with Tomlinson (1976).

6 See Harward (1982); Kreeb (1984); Lawrence (1996) 182–9; Ginouvès (1994); Cahill (2002).

7 See Grimm (1998) 45–51; Hoepfner in Dreyfus and Schraudolph (1996–1997) vol. 2, 40–6, with fig. 18 and foldout 2; Hoepfner (2002); and on the Academy, also Travlos (1971) 42–51, figs. 52–64.

8 See Wycherley (1978) 219–35; Jones (1999); and on the Poseidoniasts, Picard (1921).

9 See Coulton (1976); Ginouvès (1994) 86, 178–81; also Lawrence (1996) 148 (Nemea), 155–6, 197–9; Allen and Caskey (1911) (Athenian Asklepieíon) with Aleshire (1989) 27–28 for the date; Radt (1999); Travlos (1971) 127–37, 505–26.

10 See Pollitt (1986) 248–49, 289–90; Lawrence (1996) 140–1, 154, 159; McKenzie (2003) 50–3 (Serapeion); and on the symbolism, Onians (1979) 72–9; Ridgway (1999) 46–50.

11 See Lawrence (1996) 170–3, 196 (Priene); cf. Miller (2001) 62–89 and frontispiece (Nemea); Andronikos (1984) 97–9 (Vergina; though following Rotroff (1984) 343–54, many now prefer a date in the last quarter of the century and an ascription to Philip III Arrhidaios, killed in 317/16).

12 Architecture: McKenzie (1990) and McKenzie in Hamma (1996) 109–26; also, on Petra, see Markoe (2003). Sculpture: Pollitt (1986) 79–126; Stewart (1990) 205–18; Smith (1993) 36, 99–126, 155–80; Stewart (1993b); de Grummond and Ridgway (2000); Stewart (2004); Stewart (in press). Painting: cf. Rouveret (1989) 228–35, 275–6.

13 Klein (1921); Pollitt (1986) 127–41; Smith (1993) 127–35; Stähli (1999).

14 See Laubscher (1982); Himmelmann (1983); Pollitt (1986) 47–66; Stewart (1990); Smith (1993) 19–50; von den Hoff, et al. (in press); and on Poseidippos, Austin and Bastianini (2002) ad loc., with Stewart (2005); Stewart (in press).

15 See Laubscher (1982); Himmelmann (1983); Stewart (1996) 224–8; and for pre-decessors, see Lissarrague et al. in Cohen (2000).

16 See Stewart (1996) 228–30; LIMC s.v. "Hermaphroditos" (A. Ajootian); Ajootian (1997).

17 See Pollitt (1986) 164–84; Rouveret (1989) 411–60; Stewart (1990) 94–6, 213–4, 219–21, 224–6; Smith (1993) 240–1, 258–61; Fuchs (1999); Ridgway (1990–2002), III 186–261; also Themelis (1996) for a new chronology for Damophon; and on the phantasia-theory, Pollitt (1974) 52–5; Rouveret (1989) 383–411; Halliwell (2002) 305–12.

18 See Pollitt (1986) 185–209; Stewart, in Dreyfus and Schraudolph (1996–1997) vol. 1, 39–52.

19 See Dunbabin (1999) 18–52 and 101–3 (Carthage), with Westgate (2000); for Alexandria, see also Daszewski (1985); Grimm (1998) figs. 38–41, 81c, 102. Dor: Stewart and Martin (2003).

20 See Higgins (1980) 155; Ogden (1982); Pfrommer (1990); Williams (1998), with Andronikos (1984) 196–7, figs. 158–9 for the Vergina diadem.

21 See Plantzos (1996a and 1996b), briefly summarized in Plantzos (1999) 101–2; for the traditional view, see Pollitt (1986) 23–4, 257–9; Grimm (1998) 73.

22 See Higgins (1980) 159–62; Pfrommer (1990); Pfrommer, in Williams (1998) 79–83.

23 See Alsop (1982) 1–32, 68–101, 170–211; on sculpture, Marcadé (1969); Harward (1982); Kreeb (1984); and especially C. Kunze, in Hoepfner and Brands (1996)

109–29; on Alexandria see now Empereur (1998); Grimm (1998); McKenzie (2003) 45–7. On Roman collecting, see especially Chevallier (1991).

24 See Pollitt (1974); Rouveret (1989); on Poseidippos, see Austin and Bastianini (2002) nos. 62–70, with several studies forthcoming. Plato, *Epistle* 13, 361A, purporting to describe the philosopher acting as art agent for the tyrant Dionysios II of Syracuse (367–57), is surely a forgery.

9: LANGUAGE AND LITERATURE

Nita Krevans and Alexander Sens

ℭℐℴ

LANGUAGE: THE RISE OF THE *KOINE*

The army that marched through Asia under Alexander's command included speakers of many regional Greek dialects, but its official, administrative language, spoken by its Macedonian leaders and used in formal documents, was a version of Attic, the dialect spoken at Athens. The evidence for a native "Macedonian" language is shadowy, but suggests that it was either an idiosyncratic variant of Greek or a closely related Indo-European language.[1] Although the Macedonian royal house claimed to have its origins in Argos, where the spoken language was a form of Doric Greek, the political power and cultural influence exerted by Athens made its dialect particularly important for a philhellenic Macedonian court interested in laying claim to a Hellenic heritage. The formal adoption of Attic as the official language of the Macedonian court under Philip II was merely the culmination of a linguistic trend that had already been under way for more than half a century. Its consequences for the linguistic and cultural landscape of the Hellenistic period were monumental.

The version of Attic adopted by the Macedonian royal house differed in some respects from the local dialect spoken by ordinary Athenians. By the late fifth century, the influence of Ionic, a dialect closely related to Attic and spoken in many of the city-states that made up the Athenian empire, had led to the development of a "Greater Attic" dialect in which certain marked local morphological and syntactical features were diminished or eliminated entirely. As a result of Athenian political power and cultural prestige, this dialect, spoken and written (in the Ionic alphabet that the Athenians adopted to replace their own local script at the end of the fifth century) by Athenian elites and used in the official Athenian records, exerted a growing influence throughout the Greek-speaking world even before the intercession of the Macedonians in Greek affairs. It was this Greater Attic that was taken over by the Macedonian leadership, carried with the army on campaign, and consequently inherited as the *koine* ("Common") Greek that became established as the official language of the successor kingdoms.[2]

Before the Hellenistic period, the majority of speakers in any given Greek city-state would have spoken roughly the same local dialect, and this fact helped preserve a fair degree of dialectal continuity in local communities, even in the face of the growing influence of Greater Attic. In the Hellenistic period, the realities of military service, increased migration, and the formation of cosmopolitan cities populated by speakers of a wide variety of Greek dialects contributed to a process in which the various dialects were slowly homogenized, and although inscriptional and literary evidence suggests that regional dialects persisted, it was natural that soldiers and immigrants to Alexandria and the other Hellenistic cities would rapidly learn the dialect spoken by their military and political rulers, even if they continued to speak their native dialects as well.

Two passages of early third-century poetry offer some sense of the linguistic pressures experienced by the men and women who had, for one reason or another, left their native homes to take up residence in the diverse and international Hellenistic capitals. In a poem by Theokritos (see following discussion), two Syracusan women residing in Alexandria visit a religious festival at the Ptolemaic palace and are berated by an anonymous man for "prattling" in their native Doric dialect (15.87–88); one of the women responds that as Corinthians by descent, they have the right to speak Doric. The tone and significance of these verses is debated, but the passage may hint not only at the social stigma that could be attached to the public use of local dialect in Alexandria but also at the pride that dialect speakers could feel for the language of their native land.[3] Something similar may be suggested by a newly discovered epigram by Poseidippos of Pella, a poet active in Alexandria (and elsewhere) in the early third century. This poem takes the form of an epitaph of a dead man named Menoitios, who is imagined to speak from the grave to passersby and who expresses vexation at their supposed interest in conversing with him; he is, he says, a Cretan and a man of few words because he resides in a "foreign" land. That the dead Menoitios "speaks" a "mixed" dialect in which Doric elements appropriate to the language of Crete are juxtaposed with non-Doric elements may be intended to reflect his ambiguous linguistic status.[4]

Despite the resilience of local dialects well into the Hellenistic period, the growth of the *koine* must have seemed a threat to the native linguistic traditions of those who arrived in the new cosmopolitan capitals, and it is reasonable to think that the assimilatory pressures compounded a general anxiety immigrants to these polyglot cities would have felt about the long-term survival of their own local traditions. In such a context, the fervor with which Hellenistic intellectuals undertook the task of recording, ordering, and preserving the Greek linguistic heritage takes on special meaning. We have evidence not only for collections of glosses by men like Simias and Philetas but also for treatises on regional nomenclature, like that of Kallimachos (fr. 406 Pfeiffer). These projects find antecedents in the fourth-century collections of Aristotle and his successors, but the concern of Hellenistic scholars with uncovering and preserving the linguistic and cultural past is a notable feature of the scholarship and literature of the age.

Although the impulse toward linguistic conservation was felt throughout the Hellenistic world, its most monumental expression was the great library constructed at Alexandria under Ptolemy II Philadelphos.[5] In this institution, which dwarfed earlier scholarly and royal collections, the Ptolemies set out to collect every Greek book they could find. The Library, which dominated all intellectual enterprises in the Greek-speaking world for hundreds of years, formed part of the Museum, literally "a shrine of the Muses," where a thriving scholarly and literary community was housed and supported at royal expense. The Museum and its library attracted philosophers, scientists, historians, and poets to Egypt – even residents of other cosmopolitan centers like Athens and Syracuse – and inspired rival foundations, like the library at Pergamon. In addition to producing their own individual scientific and literary work, some of those assembled at the Museum were also commissioned as librarians – collecting, correcting, and classifying Greek texts, and overseeing the translation into Greek of foreign books. Conducted under the direction of a royally appointed head librarian (early incumbents include the Homeric critic Zenodotos, the epic poet Apollonios of Rhodes, and the polymath Eratosthenes), the work of these intellectuals preserved and organized the scientific and literary work of the past and shaped the way it was understood.

As editors, librarians, and critics, Hellenistic intellectuals designated the authors and works to be used as yardsticks for each literary genre, including, for example, nine lyric poets, three iambographers, and three comic poets, among other categories. Such selective classification finds precedents in earlier periods (the notion of seven sages, for example, is pre-Hellenistic), but was a hallmark of the Hellenistic age, in which ranked lists of other sorts proliferated.[6] A telling anecdote reflecting the pervasiveness of the impulse to collect and rank reports is that the scholar-poet Eratosthenes seems to have been called "Beta" (i.e., "number two") – a reflection of his always being ranked second.[7]

In commissioning such a large-scale project of recovering, collating, and preserving the literature of the past while simultaneously supporting the work of contemporary men of letters, the Ptolemies deliberately placed themselves in a long-standing Macedonian tradition. Indeed, patronage of the arts by Macedonian royalty dates back to the end of the fifth century, when Archelaos brought to his court at Pella poets (including Euripides) and artists from around the Greek-speaking world, at least in part to bolster his own claims to Hellenic origins. For Philip II, Alexander (who himself had been taught by Aristotle), the early Ptolemies, and other Successors, patronage served a similar function. It has been suggested that the Ptolemies' foundation of the Library – the recovery, collation, and preservation of the Greek cultural past – was designed in part to show the superiority of Greek culture,[8] but it also served the more fundamental role of casting the royal family as protectors of the Hellenic heritage and thus of calling attention to their own Hellenism.

Literature: Scholars and Poets

The interest that Hellenistic kings and queens showed in establishing their place in a continuous line of Greek leaders finds a close analog in the concern that Hellenistic writers felt about their relationship to their forebears. This is particularly clear in the case of Hellenistic poetry. As we shall see in more detail, these poets were often conspicuously original, but even at their most innovative, a number them explicitly represented themselves as the successors to the earlier literary tradition. To this end, early third-century writers regularly endowed "new" genres with legendary poet-founders or invoked the authority of archaic and classical predecessors for their formal and stylistic practices. This Hellenistic appropriation of the literary past was itself an interpretive act that has been compellingly described as the "archaeological" excavation of Greek literature; with access only to written texts separated from their original performance context, Hellenistic poets reconstructed archaic and classical genres in ways that suited their own interests.[9] This focus on previous literature, however, was not uncritically nostalgic or antiquarian, but selective and self-conscious, calling attention to the unbridgeable gap between past and present.

Such selectivity is most obvious in the treatment that some Hellenistic authors afforded Homeric epic, which had always occupied the central place in Greek culture and which poets like Kallimachos and Theokritos treat as a literary monument that modern writers would be misguided and vainglorious to try to imitate (Theokritos 7.45–8; Kall. *Hymn* 2.105–12). These same writers, however, draw continuously on Homeric epic to illustrate the novelty and accomplishment of their own work. Even Apollonios of Rhodes, whose "heroic" epic appears at least superficially as close to "Homer" as almost any extant Hellenistic verse (see following discussion, p. 200), creates a narrative that must be read as a successor to the Homeric epics and yet relates a story logically anterior to the events of the *Iliad* and *Odyssey*. It, therefore, may be read as both successor and predecessor of the Homeric poems. The relationship of Hellenistic poets to their literary past is thus complex and suggests something akin to an "anxiety of influence" in the broadest sense of the phrase – constantly aware of their place in the tradition, these authors emphasize their own debt to the past while using it to proclaim their own originality.

The intellectual culture created at the Library and Museum fostered this tension between past and present. Perhaps the most striking feature of these institutions was that most of the poets assembled there were also engaged in scholarship on earlier texts. The literary model for the era – even for the relatively unscholarly Theokritos – was Philitas of Kos, who held the royal tutorship, wrote poetry and glosses, and was aptly characterized by Strabo (14.2.19 = T 2 Dettori) as "at once poet and scholar."[10] Already in the Classical period, the poet Antimachos of Kolophon had conducted critical work on the text of Homer,[11] but he is a relatively isolated scholar-poet; in the third century, such figures were so prevalent that it is perhaps easier to list poets who were not scholars: Hermesianax, Herodas, and Theokritos have left us no evidence of critical or scientific activity *per se*, although their verse shows the same sort of learning and sophistication that characterize the work of their contemporaries who are known to have been active scholars.

The other major figures from this period follow the model of Philitas. Apollonios wrote critical treatises. Simias produced collections of glosses. The poets Aratos and Rhianos both edited Homer, whereas Lykophron and Alexander Aitolos edited comedy and tragedy, respectively. Kallimachos produced over a dozen prose treatises on subjects ranging from critical ideals to birds. The most famous of these, entitled *Pinakes*, is an encyclopedic description of all of Greek literature and is often considered the founding work of the Western science of bibliography. Conversely, figures now primarily known as scholars also wrote poetry. Zenodotos, famous for his criticism of the Homeric poems, is said to have written epic, Eratosthenes epic and elegy. The bond between scholarship and poetry was so strong that scholars, rather than Muses or royal patrons, appear in the invocation of one work; Philikos of Kerkyra addresses his *Hymn to Demeter* to the *grammatici* (*SH* 677): "Men of letters, I bring you gifts of a composition of Philikos in a new style."

It is thus hardly surprising that erudition ranks as the most obvious hallmark of the poetry produced by those associated with the Museum and Library, and it has become conventional to describe learned Hellenistic verse as "Alexandrian," even when it is produced by poets whose association with that city is tenuous or nonexistent. The existence of the Library cannot have been the sole factor that led poets to produce such verse, because the work of early writers like Antimachos and poetry composed in other locations show that similar erudition was already evident at other times and places. Aratos, for example, seems to have composed his didactic poem on the heavens (*Phainomena*) under the patronage of Antigonos Gonatas.

Nonetheless, the Library of the early third century provided an unparalleled access to the written record – both prose and verse – and Alexandrian poets exploited this resource fully. Indeed, the book-roll itself became a source of inspiration: Kallimachos, for instance, makes explicit his dependence on a prose history of Kos by Xenomedes and reports that it was from him that the story of Akontios and Kydippe made its way to his "Muse" (fr. 75.74–7 Pfeiffer). Nikander seems to have derived much of the material in his didactic poems on beasts and their poisons (*Theriaka; Alexipharmaka*) from scientific treatises by Apollodoros of Alexandria, much as Aratos made extensive use of the astronomical writing of Eudoxos of Knidos. Other poets, too, drew on a vast array of previous literature. But above all, the Homeric poems were a particular focus of the learning of Hellenistic poets, who strove to make clear their detailed knowledge of the epics while simultaneously demonstrating their own creativity and originality. Homeric words are combined in new ways or combined with un-Homeric elements; standard expressions are used in new or rare metrical positions; familiar epic language is employed in un-Homeric senses. The overall effect is to create the simultaneous appearance of contact and divergence.

Hellenistic poets also frequently referred to contemporary scholarly debates about Homeric usage or about the text of the epics. A phrase from the *Aëtia* of Kallimachos provides a good example: early commentators had disagreed about whether Homer used the masculine noun *aetes* or the feminine noun *aete* for "wind" (cf. scholia to Homer, *Iliad* 15.626); Kallimachos' *thelus aetes* (fr. 110.53), a masculine form, is modified by an adjective (*thelus*) whose basic sense is "female" but which may mean "gentle" and thus appropriately be applied to a breeze.

This learned engagement with earlier poetry, and with Homer in particular, is in many cases not merely empty pedantry. It is surely true that some Hellenistic works – Lykophron's *Alexandra* is a notorious example – seems to have aimed at obscure erudition for its own sake, but the evocation of the literary past often serves more complex poetic purposes. Many passages so precisely and clearly evoke specific passages in earlier literature that it seems clear that Hellenistic poets expected them to be read against the backdrop of their predecessors. The effect of these allusions varies, but in a great number of cases, the reuse of the literary past seems designed to create a gap between what the fictive "speaker" – whether narrator or embedded character – understands and what a well-read reader knows about the literary provenance of the poet's language. Thus, for instance, in Apollonios' *Argonautika*, a poem that tells the story of the Argonauts' pursuit of the Golden Fleece and return home to Greece, the persistent assimilation of Medea to Helen as she was portrayed in the Homeric poems lends poignancy to Medea's uncertainty about how she should respond to a handsome stranger (already in the *Iliad*, Helen had recognized that she was mistaken to leave her home with Paris; Medea embarks on what too will eventually be a disastrous course without the benefit to be gained from a knowledge of the epic tradition, or, for that matter, of the aftermath as it unfolds in Attic drama). Similarly, the song sung by Polyphemos in Theokritos 11, by recalling Odysseus' account of his adventure with that same Cyclops in the *Odyssey*, points out the creature's ignorance about his own place in literary history. Examples could easily be multiplied; indeed, it is fair to say that this sort of irony is another hallmark of Hellenistic verse.

Such allusive erudition raises the vexed question of audience. A much-cited passage of Timon Phliasios, in which the speaker complains that the Museum's inhabitants are overfed, quarrelsome parasites (*SH* 786: "In well-peopled Egypt are gorging many / tame scholars squabbling continuously / in the Muses' bird-cage"), has often been taken to mean that residents of the Museum were ivory-tower intellectuals writing for and debating only with each other. But even though Hellenistic poetry often presupposes an *ideal* intended audience familiar with both the literary tradition and contemporary scholarly debates, the actual audience may have been considerably broader.

An interesting point of comparison in this regard is provided by the work of Matro of Pitane, whose parodies, written late in the fourth century, were likely intended in the first instance for performance before a public audience.[12] In the only substantial fragment that survives, Matro juxtaposes contextually related passages of Homer in such a way that only those with a detailed knowledge of the poems would have recognized the underlying joke, although even those with a more rudimentary familiarity with the *Iliad* and *Odyssey* would have appreciated the application of epic language to an account of a raucous Athenian dinner party. Similarly, the public honors awarded to poets like Philitas and Philikos suggest that their popularity transcended an elite circle. Indeed, papyri from the late third or early second centuries B.C.E. show not only that Alexandrian verse circulated well beyond the confines of the city within a generation or two after it was written, but that it was (at least in some cases) quickly fortified by marginal commentaries designed to aid those outside a narrow circle of cognoscenti. More importantly, several of these papyri – most notably the so-called "Victory of Berenike"(*SH* 254–69) from Kallimachos' *Aetia* and a recently published collection of epigrams of Poseidippos[13] – focus attention on accomplishments of the Ptolemaic family and thus reveal the important role early Hellenistic poets played in the creation and propagation of the image that the Alexandrian royal house presented to a broader public.[14]

It is hardly surprising that the Ptolemies understood the power of poetry in this regard, because Greek thinking had long recognized that verse was the premier medium for immortalizing great achievements. In the archaic and classical periods, wealthy and powerful men – private individuals as well as the rulers of states – commissioned poets like Simonides, Pindar, and Bacchylides to compose songs honoring their accomplishments in athletic contests, and it was inevitable that Hellenistic monarchs would similarly see the advantages to be gained from supporting the arts. In complex and subtle ways, the scholar-poets supported by the Macedonian kings helped establish and promote the image that the ruling house wanted to present to the world. In great part, this poetry emphasizes the continuity between the Ptolemies and the Greek past. Thus, heroes like Herakles and the Dioskouroi, who managed to negotiate the transition between the mortal and immortal worlds, provide a Greek model for the apotheoses of members of the royal house, whereas the marriage of Zeus and Hera justifies the sibling marriages of the Alexandrian dynasty. The celebration of Ptolemaic victories in the panhellenic games shows members of the royal house gaining eternal glory in an activity from which foreigners were excluded and thus underscores their legitimacy as rulers of the Greek world. The Spartan dyarchy provides a model for legitimate Greek kingship.[15] Although much of this encomiastic activity seems to have drawn on Greek literature to emphasize the Greekness of the Macedonian court, recent work, especially by Stephens (2003),[16] has shown that Alexandrian poets also drew on Egyptian material, thereby constructing a portrait of the ruling dynasty as a legitimate bridge between the Greco-Macedonian and indigenous cultures.

Although both elite and popular audiences would still have attended festivals, contests, plays, and recitations, we find in the early Hellenistic period an important shift in the way that poetry was experienced. Originally, Greek poetry was written for performance in specific private or civic contexts, and although there is evidence of written versions of – for example – Attic drama already in the fifth century (cf. Aristophanes, *Frogs* 1114), live performance remained the primary venue for the experience of literature in the Classical period. The gradual shift from a culture of oral delivery to a culture of the book became particularly visible after the death of Alexander, when written texts of, for example, lyric and dramatic poetry were circulating in a cultural context far removed from that in which they were originally performed. In other words, the label "bookish" so often applied to Hellenistic poetry is not simply a description of the scholarly interests of the Hellenistic authors but also a description of the new importance of the written form of literature. The shift is evident in an especially vivid way in the Hellenistic poems known as "technopaegnia," poems whose metrical pattern is constructed to form shapes when the lines are written out on paper. Simias of Rhodes – the author of riddle-poems like "The Egg," whose solution is provided by the appearance of the poem – is the best-known practitioner of this art but was not the only poet to experiment with patterned verse. Only an age self-conscious about the written appearance of poetry could produce these concoctions.[17]

A subtler and far more significant effect of the new "bookishness" is the blurring of traditional boundaries between the different genres of poetry. The transmission of lyric without its accompanying music and the emphasis on writing made previously distinct verse forms seem less obviously divergent. The elegiac couplet, for instance, had always been a versatile meter, used for narrative, lament, exhortation, and epigram, but in the Hellenistic period, it became especially popular, because its association with multiple genres appealed to authors who no longer saw meter and genre as indissolubly linked.[18] Hellenistic poets like Kallimachos used elegiac couplets for victory odes and hymns – poems traditionally composed in lyric stanzas or hexameters. They also reused traditional meters in other new ways – for example, by plundering lyric stanzas for individual metrical units, which they arranged in repeating lines of "stichic" verse.

For these writers, the old associations linking performance context, meter and dialect, and content were gone. As a result, Hellenistic poets could and did play, in exuberant and often sardonic ways, with the conventions that separated the traditional literary forms; this manipulation of generic expectations and characteristics is another hallmark of Hellenistic poetry[19] and is to be found in all the most influential literary products of the age – Theokritos' "bucolic" poems, for instance, derive much of their point from the way in which they place language derived from Homer in the mouths of unheroic goatherds. These games with the traditional intersections of content and form are particularly striking and amusing in literary epigram, which utilizes the forms and conventions of short verse traditionally inscribed on grave markers or dedications for content that was drawn from a wide variety of literary traditions and, in many cases, inappropriate for actual inscription.

For many Hellenistic authors, this new generic freedom was an invitation to write in many different genres and in a variety of meters and dialects. Earlier poets like Simonides and Pindar (among others) composed for a variety of occasions and in a range of meters, but in the Hellenistic period, the "rules" that distinguished individual genres were more clearly defined, and poets' self-conscious understanding of them laid the groundwork for their special interest in "*polyeideia*" (literally, "many-formed-ness"), a phenomenon that must be counted as yet another hallmark of the age. Of the Hellenistic poets now most often discussed, we know that Theokritos wrote hymns in several dialects, epigrams, love lyrics, mimes, and bucolics; Apollonios epigram, epic, and (probably) iamb; Kallimachos a collection of etiological stories in elegiac couplets, a short epic narrative, hymns, odes, iambs, and epigrams.

Indeed, variety is perhaps the single most striking general feature of the literary production of the age, and any selective treatment of individual poets and works runs the risk of being misleading, especially in the wake of the publication of a number of new papyri and of the monumental *Supplementum Hellenisticum* (*SH*), which brings together other texts previously difficult to access. Few literary periods have benefited so much in recent years by the discovery of new texts, including important papyri of Kallimachos and the so-called "new" Poseidippos papyrus, a text containing over 100 previously unknown epigrams by an important third-century epigrammatist. At the same time, it must be said that, although our canon of Hellenistic poetry has been shaped to a great extent by accidents of transmission and by the tastes of modern readers, the focus of Classical scholarship on the works of three major figures – Kallimachos, Apollonios of Rhodes, and Theokritos – at the expense of some other well-preserved and influential texts (including those of Nikander, Aratos, and Lykophron) also reflects the preeminent position these authors occupied in ancient literary history and their importance for later Greek and Roman writers.

KALLIMACHOS

Any discussion of the Hellenistic poets must begin with Kallimachos, whose work is often treated as representative of Alexandrian poetry in general. The use of "Kallimachean" as synonymous with "Alexandrian" reflects the vast shadow that Kallimachos cast over contemporary and subsequent literature, but risks understating the unique brilliance of Kallimachos' witty and often biting verse. Born into an aristocratic Cyrenean family, Kallimachos arrived in Alexandria early in the third century B.C.E.,[20] and by the 270s was well established under royal patronage as a scholar, poet, and, above all, critic. In memorable and sometimes vicious programmatic passages scattered throughout his corpus, Kallimachos attacks his literary enemies (whom, in the prologue to his *Aetia*, he represents as invidious mythological metal-workers known as the Telchines) and lays out appropriate poetic standards for the new linguistic and cultural world inherited from Alexander.

The basic principle enshrined in the Kallimachean literary program is that poetry must be produced with extreme precision and care. In a famous and much-discussed passage of the *Aetia*, Kallimachos imputes to his alleged critics the claim that he has not – despite his old age – written a long, continuous poem on kings or heroes (Aetia fr. 1.3–6). He responds that his poetry is characterized by different standards. In his view, poetry should be judged not by its length, but by its artistry (*Aetia* fr. 1.9, 18), and it must be "slender," as Kallimachos has Apollo, god of poetry, advise: "poet, raise your sacrificial animal to be as fat as possible, but to keep your Muse slender" (*Aetia* fr. 1.23–24).

Such claims have sometimes been taken to be an endorsement of brevity per se, but clearly involve other issues as well. In the new age in which Kallimachos writes, the abundant style of Homeric epic, in which words, phrases, and even whole speeches are regularly repeated, is no longer appropriate. Homer is inimitable, and modern writers must find new directions and forge new paths (*Epigram* 28.1–2). The production of poetry requires tremendous toil (*Epigram* 27.4) and exactitude: If Homeric poetry is like the sea, monumental but turbulent, modern poetry should be like a pure stream (*Hymn* 2.105–12).

These values are everywhere in evidence throughout his substantial corpus, in which he regularly praises those whom he sees as appropriate models – Hesiod, Aratos, Ion of Chios – and skewers those who violate these rules (in particular, Antimachos of Kolophon, a fourth-century polygeneric scholar-poet whose work was highly praised by several of Kallimachos' contemporaries, is criticized harshly).[21] Although any number of Kallimachos' works might be chosen to illustrate his own refined praxis, the *Hekale*, a poem based on one of the adventures of Theseus, offers an especially illuminating example of his concerns and techniques, and in particular of his complex relationship with the literary tradition.

In Homeric diction and elegantly crafted hexameters, Kallimachos presents an "epic" whose deliberately cultivated obscurity is as striking as its relatively reduced scope (1,000–1,300 lines).[22] Theseus, on his way to confront the bull of Marathon, takes shelter for the night with a poor old woman named Hekale. After his conquest, he returns to find her dead and honors her by founding a temple of Zeus Hekaleios and naming a deme for her. Although the poem includes many learned digressions, it is clear that the focus of the poem is not Theseus' heroic deed (second-hand heroism at that: The bull of Marathon is a "leftover" from one of Hercules' labors). The fight with the beast, the best-known and most traditional portion of the tale, is sharply abbreviated. Instead, the emphasis is on Hekale and her laborious, frugal hospitality. A humble old woman who had played a minor role in Kallimachos' sources for the tale (Philochoros *FGrH* 328 F 109) here replaces the hero himself as the focus of attention.[23]

Everything about the *Hekale* reinforces the program outlined earlier. The abbreviated epic form (later called *epyllion*) offers a concise alternative to traditional epic; the carefully wrought hexameters refine the meter inherited from Homer by restricting or avoiding certain rhythmical phenomena;[24] the delicate narrative compresses the obvious and traditional and lingers on the neglected, a favorite Hellenistic technique with obvious utility for poets seeking to distance themselves from the narrative practices of earlier epic. In a larger sense, moreover, the poem reflects contemporary esthetic trends: The attention that Kallimachos directs to an aged, poor, and female protagonist finds a close parallel in the visual arts, especially sculpture, which in the Hellenistic period increasingly represented not only idealized public heroes but also more lowly individuals. In both Hellenistic poetry and sculpture, artists shift their focus away from traditional depictions of heroic figures. In the *Hekale*, Theseus' battle is recounted quickly; the narrator's attention instead lingers on – *inter alia* – the humble meal that Hekale furnishes the hero from a thinly stocked larder. Indeed, the poem's focus on a woman is an index of the increasingly prominent place that women occupied in Hellenistic literature and art, in part because of their visibility in public life and in part because their traditional importance in the private domestic sphere made them appealing subject matter for poets seeking new paths. Though earlier poetry had also depicted powerful women and scenes of private life, the prominence of women as subjects of Hellenistic poetry – in which they are naturally represented in a wide variety of ways – is striking: The Ptolemaic queens figure prominently in the court poetry of Kallimachos, Theokritos, and Poseidippos; Apollonios' focus on Medea's psychological development and on the change in her social status is a notable feature of a poem devoted to an archetypal heroic expedition; and Herodas and Theokritos both focus on rather ordinary female characters in their urban mimes.

A brief survey of some of Kallimachos' other poetic works reveals both an impressive variety of form and theme and a consistent emphasis on the aesthetic principles found in the *Hekale*. The only work to survive intact via the medieval manuscript tradition is a collection of six *Hymns*, which imitate the archaic rhapsodic hymns attributed to Homer but also use meters, dialects, and forms uncharacteristic of those archaic examples. In *Hymn 6*, for instance, the narrator, using a stylized literary Doric dialect, directs the actions of a group of worshippers, whereas in *Hymn 5*, written in elegiac couplets rather than hexameters, the narrator functions almost as a religious officiant who first effects and then describes an epiphany of the goddess. Like the *Hekale*, the hymns contain numerous scholarly allusions to local cults and rare Homeric words and make use of the same Hellenistic narrative features noted in the *Hekale*: In them, for example, condensed and elliptical descriptions of well-known stories alternate with detailed presentations of obscure myths and rituals.

Of Kallimachos' other works, the *Iambi* demonstrate in a particularly striking way Kallimachos' manipulation of genre. The thirteen
poems recovered from papyrus fragments form a designed and unified collection of material adapted from archaic iamb.[25] The first and
last poems provide a programmatic frame by addressing contemporary
critics: *Iamb* 1 resurrects Hipponax from Hades to scold Alexandrian
intellectuals, whereas *Iamb* 13 defends Kallimachos against the charge
of writing in too many genres (*polyeideia*). In the intervening poems,
the collection converts iamb into a "genre" that is itself an example of
polyeideia. The first group is written in conventional iambic meters and
engages in traditional attacks on the poet's enemies (*Iambs* 2, 4), as well
as on a faithless youth and an immoral schoolteacher (*Iambs* 3, 5), but
the remaining poems include other meters, untraditional dialect coloring, and thematic material drawn from a variety of sources, including
lyric, epic, and prose: Thus, *Iambs* 6 and 7 are written in Doric dialect
and in a combination of iambic trimeters and ithyphallic metra; *Iambs*
8 and 12 are also occasional poems (the first a victory ode, the second a
birthday poem); *Iambs* 7, 9, 10, and 11 are aetiological poems that could
easily (save for their form) fit into a prose treatise or into Kallimachos'
own *Aetia*.

We have already had occasion to mention the famous and influential prologue to the *Aetia*, a four-book elegiac poem on "causes" (*aetia*),
reconstructed from extensive papyrus fragments. This work, a series of
learned narratives about the origins of obscure rituals and place-names,
offers two possible methods for organizing poetic collections. In Books
I–II, individual tales are, for the most part, united by a narrative frame
in which the poet interrogates the Muses. In Books III–IV, the narratives have no such connecting device. In fact, several long poems
that almost certainly circulated separately as occasional pieces for the
court are prominently displayed as part of the collection (the so-called
"Victory of Berenike," at the beginning of Book III, and the "Lock of
Berenike," at the end of Book IV). Books I and II emphasize continuity and coherence; III and IV stress variety and independence. Roman
poets eventually found in the *Iambi* and of *Aetia* a range of models for
organizing their own collections. Ovid exploits the Muse-frame in both
the *Fasti* and the *Metamorphoses*; Horace chooses to emphasize individual poems in his *Odes*; the elegists combine features of both options in
their love elegies. These and other late-Republican and Augustan poets,
moreover, seem to have read Kallimachos' response to the Telchines in
the *Aetia* prologue as the definitive description of good poetic practice, and they adapted its central images repeatedly, especially in the

context of programmatic passages in which they assert their resistance to writing epic.[26]

APOLLONIOS OF RHODES

The only work by Apollonios of Rhodes (fl. 270–245) to survive intact, the *Argonautika*, was also a crucial model for later poets, including not only Virgil but also a wide of range of other "epic" writers in both Greek and Latin (e.g., Valerius Flaccus, Ovid, Statius, "Orpheus," and Quintus of Smyrna). The poem, which narrates a heroic story – the Argonauts' quest for the Golden Fleece – is written in dactylic hexameters and borrows extensively from earlier poets, especially Homer. It is thus hardly surprising that already in antiquity scholars raised the question of the relationship between Apollonios' project and the distaste for imitations of Homer expressed by Kallimachos and others. Ancient sources claim that Apollonios was Kallimachos' pupil and was buried near his master (Suda a 3419; Vitae A, B) but also that he departed Alexandria in disgrace for Rhodes following an unsuccessful first edition of his epic (Vitae A, B) and that Kallimachos' vitriolic attack-poem, the *Ibis*, was directed at him (Suda k 227). Modern scholars have increasingly found these tales of a bitter quarrel between Kallimachos and Apollonios implausible; the picture of Apollonios as Kallimachos' pupil is perhaps equally exaggerated.[27]

Our best evidence comes not from the ancient biographies, but from Apollonios' own work. Like Kallimachos, he wrote prose treatises on philological topics, and his scholarship must have been well respected by the Ptolemies, because he was appointed to the prestigious post of chief librarian.[28] Erudition is a pervasive feature not only of the *Argonautika*, in which aetiological material about rituals, place-names, and cult sites connected to minor episodes in Jason's expedition figures prominently, but also in the fragmentarily preserved poems on foundations of cities, which integrate historiography with archaic lyric and epic in a manner very similar to that found in Kallimachos' *Aetia* and *Iambi*.

Indeed, the *Argonautika* is in every way a quintessentially Alexandrian poem, one that accords well with the precepts of the *Aetia* prologue. Relative to the Homeric epics, which by the Hellenistic period were divided into twenty-four books, the *Argonautika* is concise, consisting of only four books (though each of these is relatively long by Homeric standards). As in the *Hekale*, major episodes, such as Jason's contest with the fire-breathing bulls, are compressed, whereas the narrator lingers over purification rituals, the burial customs of the Kolchians, and other details. Moreover, the poem incorporates into epic material drawn from a variety of genres. The portrait of the vulnerable, bewildered, and love-struck Medea in the third book, for instance, takes some of its coloring and content from Euripides, and in fact the poem consistently demands to be read against the backdrop of that playwright's *Medea*. So, too, the form of the opening invocation to Apollo recalls the poems of the Homeric Hymns more than those of the *Iliad* and *Odyssey*, and when Orpheus breaks into song in Book 1 (1.496–511), his composition resembles Hesiodic and philosophical cosmogonies more than it does the inset songs of the Homeric bards Demodokos and Phemios. More fundamentally, Apollonios' diction, though superficially Homericizing, in fact involves the same sorts of linguistic variation as other Hellenistic poets.

For this new brand of epic, Apollonios creates a novel protagonist.[29] Neither an accomplished warrior like Achilles – his only "epic" military victory against humans inadvertently brings about the death of a friend – nor an accomplished liar like Odysseus, Jason takes up the burden of his quest reluctantly and is given to bouts of despondency that stand in stark contrast to Odysseus' resourcefulness: Whereas the Homeric hero bears the epithet *polymechanos* ("of many resources"), the Apollonian narrator describes Jason as *amechanos* ("without resources, at a loss"). Moreover, whereas many of his crew are the offspring of gods and have superhuman abilities, Jason's talents are far less obvious, and he regularly relies on others to perform difficult tasks: Polydeukes, for instance, boxes the brutal king Amykos, whereas the sons of Boreas drive off the Harpies. Medea, too, serves as a foil: It is she who gives Jason magical ointments to withstand the fire-breathing bulls, overcomes the dragon guarding the fleece, and kills the bronze monster Talos with a single glance, and her assistance prompts the blasphemous and hot-tempered Argonaut Idas to fume that it is disgraceful to seek help from women (3.556–63).

Herakles' participation in the expedition sets in particularly stark relief the representation of Jason as a hero. When Jason assembles the crew and asks them to elect a leader, they immediately choose Herakles (1.341–3), who graciously declines the post. Herakles' leadership is nonetheless important while he is with the expedition: It is, for example, Heracles who recalls Jason and the other Argonauts to their task when they are dallying with the Lemnian women (1.861–74). Even after Herakles has been inadvertently left behind at the end of the first book, Argonauts continually wonder how Herakles would have handled various challenges, and throughout the poem, Herakles' own accomplishments stand as a counterpoint to those of the Argonauts.

Much contemporary scholarship on the *Argonautika* has therefore argued that Jason is a fundamentally flawed hero, at least by the standards of early epic. To be sure, as depicted by Apollonios, Jason stands at an unbridgeable distance from the heroes of the *Iliad* and the *Odyssey*, and he sometimes appears indecisive and weak. At the same time, however, Jason's accomplishment may be seen to stand in more favorable contrast to that of both Odysseus – who returns home without his crew – and of Achilles – who sacrifices his comrades to his own quest for glory – and some recent scholars have emphasized the ways in which his concern for the welfare and solidarity of his group might at least be consonant with Ptolemaic self-representation. Whatever one's verdict, however, Jason seems – in a way that anticipates Virgil's Aeneas – to be a hero brought down to size, a man overwhelmed by the epic world in which he finds himself and compelled by circumstance to accomplish tasks that seem to him impossible and mysterious.

THEOKRITOS

The bulk of the extant corpus of Theokritos (fl. ca. 275–260?) consists of poems that the ancient scholia describe as *eidyllia*, "little forms," a term that has generated the modern label "idyll" but whose precise significance remains obscure.[30] These thirty-one poems,[31] none longer than 300 verses and most considerably shorter, are diverse in their content and theme; the bulk of them are in dactylic hexameters, but there are also poems in aiolic meters. Several of the idylls consist of short narratives on the deeds of great heroes of the past (13, 22, 24); one is a wedding song for Helen (18); there is a hymn to Ptolemy Philadelphos (17), a poem in honor of Hieron II of Syracuse (16), and a trio of "urban mimes" (2, 14, 15; see following discussion); the central body of another (11) contains a song sung by Polyphemos, the Cyclops of the Odyssey, here represented as a hapless lover whose words reveal his ignorance of "subsequent" literary history. Two of the idylls treat episodes that also occur in Apollonios' *Argonautika*: 13 tells the story of the loss of Hylas from the Argonautic expedition, a narrative that occupies the end of *Argonautika* 1; 22 recounts the boxing match between the Bebrykian king Amykos and Polydeukes, the episode that opens *Argonautika* 2. It is clear that one poet had the work of the other in mind, and although evidence is not definitive, cumulatively it suggests that Theokritos' poems were written in response to the *Argonautika*. There is, however, no reason to view these short, freestanding narratives based on Apollonios as a hostile critique of the poetic principles enshrined in that poem; it is just as likely that Theokritos' engagement reflects a more friendly rivalry.

There can be no doubt, however, that the most influential and well-known poems in the Theokritean corpus are the so-called "bucolic" idylls. As a group, these poems show the same diversity in tone and content that characterizes the corpus as a whole, but in general, they feature rustics, usually herdsmen but also reapers, who meet in an idealized and entirely isolated natural setting and exchange songs, sometimes in a competition with one another. These poems, which are written for the most part in a stylized, literary Doric dialect and borrow heavily on the language of epic, derive much of their point from the contrast between their form and their content and from their play with the relationship between artifice and nature. Thus, for example, the obscene banter of Komatas and Lakon in *Idyll* 5.39–41 maps onto the most heroic of meters coarse dialogue that represents a stylized version of the way herdsmen might abuse one another "in real life." That herdsmen might be made to speak dactylic hexameters is not itself new – figures like Komatas and Lakon have an antecedent in Eumaios in the *Odyssey* – but now they are the central focus, and the incorporation of brutish vocabulary like *pugizo*, "bugger," creates as much amusing tension as when lowly goat- and cowherds are made to speak in the language of Homeric heroes. Thus, the point of these poems depends in large part on Theokritos' reuse of the epic past and his blurring of its generic limitations, much in the way that the attention that Kallimachos pays to Hekale – whatever its antecedents in scenes like the encounter between Odysseus and Eumaios in Homer – represents a skewing of the traditional focus of epic. After Theokritos, the generic lines were redefined; later writers – Bion, Moschos, Virgil – had Theokritean bucolic as a model to which they could react directly.

This tension between form and content may also be seen in Theokritos' urban mimes (2, 14, 15), short sketches that (like some of the bucolic poems) involve dialogue between multiple, lower- or middle-class characters,[32] but that are set in the city rather than the country. These poems show the influence of Sophron, a fourth-century writer who, like Theokritos, originated in Sicily,[33] and have a contemporary counterpart in the mimes of Herodas (fl. 270–250?), whose works (which survive only on a papyrus) feature many of the stock characters of Athenian New Comedy. Herodas' poems are written in choliambs, and their tone, in keeping with the meter, is often vulgar: in Mime 2, a pimp accuses a customer of assault; in Mime 5, a woman has been having an affair with a slave; in Mime 6, two housewives discuss dildos.

As in other Hellenistic poetry, the apparent coarseness is belied by the studied precision of the language, and indeed several mimes clearly show Herodas' affiliation with Theokritos and Kallimachos. Mime 4, like Theokritos 15, portrays two bourgeois women admiring artwork in a temple; Mime 8 combines the dream framework of the opening of the *Aetia* with the themes of Iambs 1 and 13 as Herodas defends his poetry and claims the mantle of Hipponax. Whether Herodas' mimes were ever performed is a disputed question,[34] though clearly other dramatic poetry was being written and performed in the Hellenistic period.[35] Sadly, apart from the Attic New Comedy of Menander, little of this work has survived.

VARIA

Of other literary forms, we have already mentioned the vibrancy of epigram in the early Hellenistic period; most of the major literary figures of the period experimented with it, perhaps attracted to the challenges as well as the possibilities created by the traditionally limited size of inscribed models. The recent publication of the new Milan papyrus of Poseidippos (cf. previous discussion) has shed important light on the form of ancient collections of epigrams and spurred renewed scholarly interest in the form. Didactic poetry, too, thrived in the third century, as exemplified by Aratos' *Phainomena* and Nikander's *Theriaka* and *Alexipharmaka*. Other, more obscure literary forms, now known only from exiguous fragments preserved in later authors or on papyri, were also produced in great numbers, and it is to be hoped that the coming years will see both the recovery of further texts and heightened critical interest in "noncanonical" Hellenistic literature.

We have deliberately excluded from this essay the historical writings of Polybios and other Hellenistic historians (see Chapter 6 in this volume), as well as other "nonfictional" works, but it is clear that Hellenistic prose was as varied and interesting as was the poetry of the period, even if much of it is now lost. It would be fascinating, for instance, to know more about the work of the humorist and essayist Lynkeus of Samos, who produced, *inter alia*, the obviously jocular treatise *On the Art of Grocery Shopping* mentioned by Athenaios (7.313f).

It would also be interesting to know more about the early history and development of the Greek novel.[36] Complete books survive only from the imperial period, but papyrus fragments suggest that the form was established by the first century B.C.E. and that early examples involved some of the basic plot features found in more "sophisticated" later examples. The novels have features in common with New Comedy, tragedy, and ethnography: The attractive if ingenuous hero and heroine fall in love at first sight; are separated by pirates, war, lustful despots, and natural disasters; travel to distant lands throughout the known world; and, although threatened with death or rape, remain true to each other until the inevitable happy ending. Although these novels are generally considered a "popular" form, in their own way, they are as quintessentially Hellenistic as the far more self-consciously refined works of third-century poet-scholars. Above all, they take as their setting the new, larger geographical space of the Hellenistic kingdoms, from Spain in the west to India in the east and thus stand as a mark of a new era, in which the Greek language and its speakers far transcended the boundaries of the old Hellenic world.

BIBLIOGRAPHICAL NOTE

Hutchinson (1988) offers a broad survey of Hellenistic poetry whereas Bing (1988) considers the new importance of writing. Stephens (2003) addresses the Egyptian context of Alexandrian culture. A revised and expanded English translation (2005) of Fantuzzi and Hunter (2002) should be widely read. Gutzwiller (1998) and Tarán (1979) illuminate the settings and conventions of epigram. Cameron (1995) offers a wide-ranging if controversial portrait of Kallimachos and his relationship to his contemporaries. Rosenmeyer (1969) and Gutzwiller (1991) are important treatments of Theokritean bucolic, whereas Hunter (1996) serves as an excellent introduction to Hellenistic poets' engagement with the literary past in general and to Theokritos' nonbucolic poetry in particular; Burton (1995) treats the "urban mimes." For Apollonios, Hunter (1993a) treats a range of literary questions; Clauss (1993) studies the representation of Jason's heroism. For Hellenistic poets' learned use of Homer, the work of Giangrande (1970) may serve as a useful starting point. Hägg (1983) gives a general overview of the Greek novel. Pfeiffer (1968) is an indispensable guide to the scholarly world of Alexandria. Recent translations of the major authors include Green's *Argonautika* (1997, with helpful introduction), Nisetich's *Callimachus* (2001), and

Verity's annotated *Theocritus* (2002, with introduction by Richard Hunter). Full bibliographies for individual Hellenistic poets are as of this writing maintained online ("A Hellenistic Bibliography") by Martin Cuypers at Leiden University.

NOTES

1   Our discussion of linguistic change draws heavily on the excellent survey by Horrocks (1997); for ancient "Macedonian," cf. Horrocks (1997) 32–3.
2   Horrocks (1997) 70.
3   Cf. Clarisse (1998).
4   Sens (2003) on Poseidippos 102, Austin and Bastianini (2002).
5   The evidence for the precise circumstances of the Library's founding is complex; cf. Pfeiffer (1968) 98–104; Blum (1991).
6   Pfeiffer (1968) 203–7; Radermacher *RE* s.v. "Kanon."
7   Cf. Suda ε 2898, with Pfeiffer (1968) 170.
8   Blum (1991) 103–4
9   Cf. Hunter (1996); Fantuzzi and Hunter (2002).
10 Cf. Dettori (2000).
11 Cf. Matthews (1996) 46–51.
12 Cf. Olson and Sens (1999).
13 Cf. Fantuzzi (2004); Austin and Bastianini (2002).
14 For the function of encomiastic poetry in the Hellenistic period, cf. also Barbantani (2001).
15 Cf. Fantuzzi (2004).
16 Cf. also Selden (1998).
17 Cf. Bing (1988).
18 Cf. Harvey (1955).
19 Kroll's (1924) description of the phenomenon as "Die Kreuzung der Gattungen," "the mixing of the genres," is a useful characterization of the moment of literary production, but must be used with sensitivity; cf. Barchiesi (1997) 65–6.
20 On the family's court connections versus the implausible tale that Kallimachos was a village schoolmaster, see Cameron (1995) 3–7.
21 Krevans (1993).
22 The *Hekale* survives only in fragments, but some of these are substantial. Hollis' edition (1990) provides an excellent picture of the shape and style of the work.
23 Cf. Hollis (1990) 5–10.
24 On Kallimachos' (and other Hellenistic poets') metrical practices, see West (1982) 152–7.
25 On the four additional poems that may belong with this collection, see Acosta-Hughes (2002) 9–13.
26 Wimmel (1960).
27 Both allegations are conventional in ancient poetic biographies; see Lefkowitz (1981) 117–35.
28 *P. Oxy.* 1241; there is no good evidence that Kallimachos ever held this position, in spite of his bibliographical work; see Pfeiffer (1968) 128, 154.
29 Cf. Clauss (1993).

30   Cf. Gutzwiller (1996), who suggests that *eidyllia* may have been the title of an ancient collection of Theokritos' poetry.

31   Thirty are transmitted in the manuscript tradition, another on papyrus. In addition, we have twenty-five epigrams transmitted under Theokritos' name, as well as the fragment of a work known as *Berenike*. Modern scholarship is in broad agreement that at least some of the idylls in the corpus are not in fact by Theokritos.

32   On these poems, cf. Burton (1995).

33   Cf. Hunter (1996) 116–23.

34   Mastromarco (1984) 5–19; Hunter (1993b).

35   Lykophron's *Alexandra* takes the form of a tragic messenger's speech but was clearly never intended for performance.

36   See Hägg (1983); the fragmentary novels are available in Stephens and Winkler (1995).

10: GREEK RELIGION

Continuity and Change in the Hellenistic Period

Jon D. Mikalson

ℭ𝒷

T he social, economic, and political changes occasioned by Alexander's expeditions and the wars and policies of his successors brought changes also to religious traditions and practices, but the extent of these changes varied greatly for Greeks living in different parts of the Hellenistic world and in different kinds of cities.[1] Athenians, for example, very conservatively preserved their centuries-old religious cults, practices, and festivals, and a fifth-century B.C.E. Athenian finding himself in second century B.C.E. Athens would have found the religious environment quite familiar, with only a few new and disturbing elements.[2] In Alexandria of the same period, by contrast, there was a most unclassical heterogeneity of Greek, pseudo-Greek, Egyptian, and Jewish deities and religious practices, all in a multiethnic and multicultural cosmopolitan environment more like that of a modern metropolis than that of the Classical Greek city-state.[3] We have at Alexandria, by design, a mixed population of Macedonians, Greeks, Egyptians, Jews, and others, and for the first time in the Greek world, all the citizens and residents of one city were not expected, as a matter of course, to be worshiping the same state deities in common sacrifices and festivals. This was largely the result of bringing together several nationalities to create one new city and of the nonrestrictive religious policies of its rulers. The changes characteristic of Hellenistic Greek religion largely emanated from this religious multiculturalism in Alexandria and other similar metropolitan centers and did eventually affect all parts of the Greek world but some more so than others, some earlier than others, and some differently from others, all to the extent that it is erroneous to imagine a single form of Hellenistic religion that was practised by all or even a majority of Greeks at any one time.

Perhaps the single greatest cause for change in religion in the Hellenistic period was the increased movement and settlement of Greeks and non-Greeks around the old and new worlds opened up by the conquests of Alexander and the establishment of kingdoms by his successors. Many Greeks left behind the cities where they and their families had resided for centuries and went off to seek their fortunes as mercenary soldiers or as traders and merchants. The new royal courts were heavily staffed by Greeks, and Greek actors, poets, and philosophers were much in demand at these courts. Greek scholars were recruited for the new cultural centers and libraries at Alexandria and Pergamon. Some Greeks emigrated to the many new cities being founded by the Macedonian kings. So, too, native peoples of these areas, Syrians, Egyptians, and others, now moved and settled more freely about the Mediterranean, and this meant that Greeks now were more broadly and for longer periods of time exposed to the deities and religious cults of these peoples. One notable "mixing pot" for these many cultures was Delos, the whole island sacred as the birthplace of Apollo and Artemis but also, in the late Hellenistic period, a major international port and trading center.[4] By the mid-second century, the island was under the control of Athens, and many of Delos' native Greek cults were maintained: of Apollo and Artemis and their family, of Zeus Polieus and Athena Polias, and of Dionysos, Hermes, Pan, and Asklepios. But this small island now also had major cults, with extensive sanctuaries, of the Egyptian Sarapis and Isis and of the Syrian Atargatis and Hadad. By 100, there were additional cults of the Assyrian Ba'al of Babylon and of Astarte of Ascalon in Palestine. On Delos at this time, there was also a Jewish synagogue. Romans, too, were now living and trading on Delos and practised their own traditional cults. This was truly an international community, and, unlike anything we find in the Classical period, Greeks of different cities, Egyptians, Palestinians, Romans, peoples of several other nationalities, and even freedmen and slaves worshiped, sometimes together, in a wide range of Greek and non-Greek cults.

The thousands of Greek emigrees of the Hellenistic period were largely liberated from the all-encompassing religious traditions of their homelands, traditions that had dictated which gods they were to worship, where and on what days, for what purposes, and in which social and political contexts. But these gods were very much tied to local cults and practices in their homelands, and the emigrating Greek could not simply take them with him. He now faced choices in his religious life that neither he nor his ancestors had ever encountered. A Greek injured or sick in Athens virtually automatically would have gone to the Asklepieion. An Athenian resident on Delos in the second century B.C.E. had the opportunity to decide whether to go for healing to the Asklepieion or to the sanctuary of the Egyptian god Sarapis, and most chose the Sarapieion. The Athenian who settled in Alexandria had before him a bewildering set of choices. Should he participate extensively in the cults of the Alexandrian township of Eleusis and other cults seemingly imported by Ptolemy I from Athens? If he was associated with the royal court of the Ptolemies, he would surely be expected to show proper devotion both to the court-favored Sarapis and to the cults of the Ptolemies themselves. Many lower-class Greeks, soldiers, laborers, and merchants, who in their own homelands had been full citizens and had participated extensively in the religious/political structure of their own cities, found themselves as noncitizens in their new lands largely excluded from the political structure and from the cults of deities who supported and were supported by the political establishment of their new cities. Such an individual in Alexandria might well marry an Egyptian woman, have a family, and find himself more drawn to the native cult of Isis, which better served his private needs and those of his family.

Many Greeks joined the new, Greek-style cities founded especially in Asia Minor by the Seleukids. Here, they might be citizen members of a rather small Greek/Macedonian ruling elite, and in such cities, the Greeks often made strenuous efforts through their schools and gymnasia to maintain Greek religious traditions. Many such cities, like established Greek cities at this time, had a one- or two-year program for eighteen- to twenty-year old males, the *ephebeia*, which offered military, cultural, and religious instruction in the Greek traditions. The patron deity of the *gymnasion*, the center of ephebic activity, was usually Hermes or Herakles, but the ephebes' schedule was filled with sacrifices, processions, and other religious activities directed to established Olympian gods. For the citizen members of such states and their descendants, the gods and religious practices of their new homeland would not have differed significantly from what they had left behind. But, again, the Greeks on the margins of the elite, whether in the new cities, in Alexandria, or elsewhere tended to be excluded from the state-sponsored religious cults of the city-state type, and, for their religious community, they often turned to private associations. Such associations were not unknown among citizens in the Classical period, but they were more naturally the community of choice for foreigners like the Egyptian residents in Athens who worshipped their native god Isis. So, too, in the Hellenistic period, traders and sailors from Beirut

FIGURE 2. A long-petal bowl from the workshop of Apollodoros, found in the foundation trench of the Athenian Metroon (Athens, Agora Excavations P 3661; photo: American School of Classical Studies, Agora Excavations).

FIGURE 3. Amphoras from Rhodes, Knidos, Chios, and Italy, destroyed in the Sullan sack of Athens in 86 B.C. (Athens, Agora Excavations, SS 8602, SS 7918, P 19120, and SS 7319; photo: American School of Classical Studies, Agora Excavations)

FIGURE 4. Stamp on a Rhodian handle, with the head of Helios and the name of the eponym, Sostratos (Athens, Agora Excavations, SS 7584; photo: American School of Classical Studies, Agora Excavations).

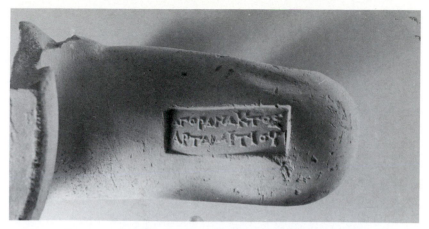

FIGURE 5. Stamp on the other handle of the same amphora, giving the fabricant, Agoranax, and the month, Artamitios (photo: American School of Classical Studies at Athens, Agora Excavations).

FIGURE 6. A Hellenistic drinking assemblage with a large cup and a small krater decorated in West Slope technique, and a small oinochoe (Athens, Agora Excavations, P 15166, P 6289, P 13449; photo: Craig Mauzy).

FIGURE 7. Three lagynoi found in Athens. The one on the left was probably man-
ufactured in Kypros, the one on the right in Asia Minor. The black-gloss lagynos
is a local Athenian product (Athens, Agora Excavations, P 3188; P 7041; P 3375;
photo: Craig Mauzy)

FIGURE 8. Drinking cup of Achaemenid shape, Sardis, third century (Sardis
P65.249:6911; photo: Archaeological Exploration of Sardis).

FIGURE 9. Second-century moldmade bowl made at Sardis (Sardis P98.90:10912; photo: Archaeological Exploration of Sardis).

FIGURE 10. The tomb of Iasion–Aëtion? Pseudo-Mycenaean doorway in the Sanctuary of the Great Gods on Samothrace (photo: Robert Lamberton).

FIGURE 11. Terracotta figurine from Tanagra: draped woman wearing a sun hat and holding a fan (British Museum C245; photo: British Museum).

FIGURE 12. Alexander the Great with diadem and Ammon's horns. Tetradrachm minted by King Lysimachos of Thrace, 297–281 B.C. Silver; diam., 3.0 cm (London, British Museum; photo: University of California Berkeley Archive).

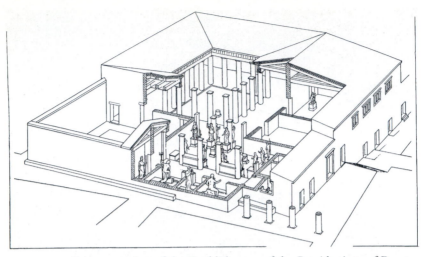

FIGURE 14. Reconstruction of the Establishment of the Poseidoniasts of Berytos (Beirut) at Delos, ca. 100 B.C. [from C. Picard, *Exploration archéologique de Délos*, vol. 6 (Paris, 1921) 32, fig. 26].

FIGURE 15. The Khazneh at Petra. A royal tomb, either of King Aretas III Philhellen (reigned, ca. 85–62 B.C.) or of King Aretas IV Philopatris (reigned 9 B.C.–A.D. 40). Ht., 38.77 m (photo: Andrew Stewart).

FIGURE 16. The "Lion Goddess" from the Gigantomachy frieze of the Great Altar at Pergamon, ca. 160 B.C. Marble; ht., 2.3 m. (Berlin, Pergamonmuseum; photo: Andrew Stewart).

FIGURE 17. Comic mask of a young dandy wearing a fantastic party hat and surrounded by garlands of fruits and flowers, ca. 200–100 B.C. Fragmentary mosaic
border, probably of a banquet room or *andron*, from Tel Dor (ancient Dora), Israel.
Colored stone, glass, and ceramic; ht. of field, 43 cm [Nahsholim (Israel), Centre
of Nautical and Regional Archaeology at Dor; photo: Gabi Laron and Tel Dor
Excavations].

FIGURE 18. Portrait head from Delos, ca. 100 B.C. A merchant or other notable, originally inserted into a (draped?) body. Marble; ht., 41 cm (Delos Museum; photo: Andrew Stewart).

FIGURE 19. Two panels of the Odyssey frieze from a *cryptoporticus* on the Esquiline Hill, Rome, Vatican Museums. Odysseus lands in Laestrygonia; the Laestrygonians prepare to attack his fleet. Fresco; ht., 1.5 m. (Rome, Vatican Museums; photo: DAI Rome).

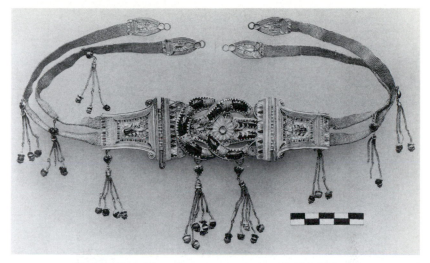

FIGURE 20. Diadem from Thessaly, ca. 200–100 B.C. Gold inlaid with garnet and enamel; ht. of Herakles knot, 4.5 cm [Athens, Benaki Museum; from Berta Segall, *Mouseion Benaki*: *Katalog der Goldschmiede-Arbeiten* (Athens, 1938): plate 28].

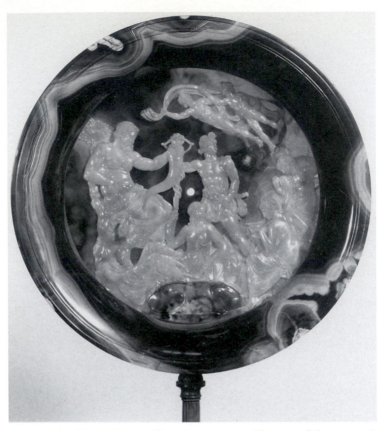

FIGURE 21. The "Tazza Farnese," ca. 100–25 B.C. Allegory of the prosperity of Egypt under Ptolemaic or (possibly) early Roman rule. Features the Nile (left, seated), Horus–Triptolemos (center, standing), Isis–Euthenia (center, reclining), and the Sphinx (below), flanked to the right by the Seasons, with the Etesian Winds above; on the underside (not shown), a Gorgoneion. Yellow-banded agate (sardonyx) cameo bowl; diam., 20 cm (Naples, Museo Nazionale; photo: DAI Rome).

formed a club on Delos, the Poseidoniastai, to worship their native deity Ba'al, but they gave him a Greek name, Poseidon. The professional troupes of actors and musicians who traveled throughout the Hellenistic world providing artistic contests at the festivals favored by the Hellenistic monarchs formed essentially trade unions dedicated to their patron Dionysos. Private clubs devoted to Dionysos, with their many banquets and parties, sprouted up throughout Greek-inhabited territories. Such associations also could provide expatriots what they had formerly received from their extended families at home: financial and moral support in times of crisis and, most importantly, proper burial and tendance of their tombs after death.

For the first time, Greeks were making personal choices about which deities to worship, and as a result, the deities they chose to worship may have been more personal to them. The rising popularity of such deities as Asklepios, Dionysos, and Isis suggest that the expatriate Greeks were turning more to deities who could offer them and their families personally, rather than the state as a whole, health, safety, and the good life. Isis was not the lone foreigner among such deities. Atargatis, a mother-type Syrian deity of fertility with her male consort Hadad, is one of several Asia Minor deities to whom some Greeks turned in the late Hellenistic period. Her temple in her home city of Hierapolis Bambyce was rebuilt by the wife of Seleukos I ca. 300 B.C.E. and became one of the major shrines of the region. But it is on Delos that we can most clearly see how her cult was brought to the attention of and accepted by Greeks. There, in 128/7, a Hierapolitan (with a Greek name) built a temple and served as priest, and the goddess and her consort maintained their Syrian names. These Syrians, importantly, spoke Greek and published their records in Greek, and so their new cult would be intelligible to the Greeks there. By 112/11 an Athenian had become priest, and, for the Greeks, the goddess and her consort had new, Greek names: Aphrodite Hagne ("Pure") and Zeus Hadatos. Athenians made their dedications to Aphrodite Hagne, the Hierapolitans still to Atargatis. The Athenians who participated in this cult, as priests or devotees, were prominent, wealthy men who dedicated over the years costly temples, altars, stoas, a theater, statuary, and furniture. The cult was also multinational, with devotees from Antioch, Laodikeia, Alexandria, Ascalon, Seleukeia, Ephesos, Damascus, and even Rome. Was Atargatis/ Aphrodite Hagne Syrian or Greek to the Athenians who worshipped her? Clearly she remained, despite her new name and Greek priest, strongly Syrian. The Greek names should not mislead us. For centuries Greeks had given their gods' names to foreign deities however slight their similarities, as they did here with Atargatis, but such identifications rarely affected the nature of the indigenous deity. Atargatis, despite her new name Aphrodite, remained known as "the Syrian goddess." The pattern here – the exposure of Greeks, through proximity and the Greek language, to a foreign deity, participation in the cult, giving the new deity a Greek name, and taking positions of leadership in the cult – was repeated by Greeks countless times at the cult sites of various indigenous deities in the Hellenistic world. But for these Greeks, participation in such cults did not necessarily mean giving up their traditional gods and religious practices. An Athenian devotee of Atargatis on Delos might also serve as priest of Apollo or make dedications to other traditional Greek deities. He could simply add Aphrodite Hagne or other exotic foreign gods to his personal pantheon.

It was, however, only the enterprising Greeks who had left their homelands that experienced the new and multicultural religious environment of Delos and other metropolitan centers. Their fellow citizens at home seem to have been little affected by the exotic foreign cults, and even the Greek emigrants and traders, when they returned home, were inclined to resume the traditional religious life of their homeland, rarely introducing the new cults or practices they had learned abroad.[5] The old mainland Greek cities like Athens, Sparta, and Corinth, and even those cities long established on the Anatolian shores like Miletos and Erythrai, were influenced only slightly by the new religious fashions experienced by their more adventuresome and cosmopolitan citizens abroad. At Erythrai, for example, an Ionian city on the north coast of Asia Minor, epigraphical records from the early to mid-Hellenistic period indicate fifty-four cults, nearly all traditional cults devoted to Athena, Zeus, Hera, Poseidon, Apollo, Artemis, Demeter and Kore, Ares, Aphrodite, Dionysos, Asklepios, and Herakles. The Erythraians maintained even their traditional hero cults, including that of their eponymous founder Erythros.[6] But even in the long established, more conservative cities such as Athens and Erythrai, there were some new, characteristically Hellenistic additions to the pantheon. By the end of the second century, the Erythraians had cults also of Eirene (Peace), Arete (Virtue), and Nike (Victory), all personified deities. Such personifications had been common in Greek poetry since Hesiod's time in the seventh century, but they are raised to the status of state deities with priests and sacrifices only in the late Classical and Hellenistic periods. By 335/4 Agathe Tyche (Good Fortune) already had a temple and treasury in Athens, and her cult is soon found at Erythrai and throughout the Hellenistic world. "Fortune" or "Chance" (Tyche) was increasingly thought to be determining many events in the turbulent Hellenistic period, and the Greeks now sought to influence her by religious means. Personified deities and Agathe Tyche arose from within the Greek tradition, and the only truly foreign deities to make widespread inroads into the panthea of established Greek cities in the Hellenistic period were the Egyptian Isis and Sarapis. Their cults might first be established, in a manner like that of Atargatis on Delos, by Egyptians living in these cities. The Athenians before 332/1 granted Egyptians the right to acquire land in Peiraieus for a cult of Isis, a cult intended only for Egyptian worshipers (*IG* ii² 337), and it is not until 133/2 that we have evidence for the Athenians themselves worshiping Isis in Athens (*SEG* 24.225). So, too, the Erythraians have a state cult of Isis by the end of the second century, and by the end of the Hellenistic period, her cult is found in almost every Greek city. The spread of Isis' cult in Greece was initially facilitated by her identification with Demeter, but Isis embraced areas well beyond those of Demeter and, in the late Hellenistic period, included healing, protection of the family, and personal safety amid the dangers of sailing the seas, and the combination of all these powers in one deity appealed to some Greeks. But the Greeks simply added these personified deities and Isis and Sarapis to their traditional panthea, and this seems not to have diminished significantly the role and importance of their traditional deities. In the old cities, Greeks continued to pray, sacrifice, make dedications, and celebrate festivals for their old deities in much the same manner as they had in the Classical period.

New political realities of the Hellenistic period also influenced religion. The once proudly independent and largely self-sufficient city-states were now, in varying degrees, dependent on Alexander and his successors. These Macedonian kings could determine the safety, prosperity, food supply, welfare, and even the existence of these cities. By whim or careful choice they might, as they marched past with their armies, obliterate a city or enrich it with incredible largess. This magnitude of power of individuals to affect their lives and cities was new to the Greeks and appeared virtually superhuman, more like the power of gods than of men, and they responded to it and attempted to influence it by religious as well as political means. They offered, some more eagerly than others, "god-like" honors of sanctuaries, altars, sacrifices, priests, statues, and festivals to these Macedonian powers.[7] In 314, Antigonos I declared all Greek states "free," and in 307/6 his son Demetrios Poliorketes liberated Athens from Kassandros' garrison. The Athenians in gratitude gave various honors to Antigonos and his son, including adding and naming after them two new tribes, just as they had named their original ten tribes after cult heroes. In 224, they similarly made Ptolemy III Euergetes a tribal eponymous hero for his help, and in 200, Attalos I of Pergamon. The cities in Asia Minor that Alexander, Seleukos, Antigonos, Ptolemy, and their successors most benefited established god-like, not "hero-like" cults for them early and maintained them through the Hellenistic and Roman periods. Athens, which was largely hostile to Alexander, established a cult for him as a "god" at his request in 324, but dissolved the cult immediately after his death in 323. By contrast, the Erythraians, who in 334/3 had been granted their independence from the Persians by Alexander, on their own initiative created one of his earliest divine cults and maintained it well into the Roman period. When Seleukos I gained control of their area in 281, they founded a cult and festival for him and then one for his son Antiochos I when he confirmed the autonomy of the city and defended it against the Galatians. Finally, in 188, the Romans made Erythrai a "free and tax-free city," and the Erythraians responded with a cult and festival of the goddess Roma.

The cults of these rulers took a variety of forms and did not displace traditional city gods such as Athena and Zeus. Most were created on the initiative of the individual cities. Individual dynasties and individual members of these dynasties responded differently to these offers of divine honors, some even rejecting them, and only in Egypt did the rulers systematically develop and promote their own cults. Ptolemy II Philadelphos proclaimed his own father the "savior" (Soter) god in 280, one year after his death, and instituted in his honor a major quadrennial festival with games, the Ptolemaieia. About ten years later, Ptolemy II declared himself and his wife/sister Arsinoe deities, the first living royalty in the Ptolemaic tradition to be self-proclaimed gods. After Arsinoe's death in 270, he created for her a separate cult, with its own priestess. Ptolemy III Euergetes and his wife Berenike appear as gods, the *Theoi Euergetai* (Benefactor Gods), just four years after their accession, in 243/2. And so it went on, with ever more Ptolemaic deities. But it is important to note that even their own "divinity" did not prevent the Ptolemies from promoting and even associating with themselves in cult Egyptian deities such as Isis, Sarapis, who was their own hellenized form of Osiris, and the traditional Greek gods, Aphrodite and Dionysos.

The forms of these ruler cults varied significantly, from god to god and from place to place. Sometimes the statue of a ruler or a member of his family was set up alongside traditional gods in a sanctuary, and prayers and sacrifices were made to the gods on the ruler's behalf. Sometimes separate sanctuaries were created for the ruler with their own altars, sacrifices, and festivals. At times, the ruler might even identify himself with a god, with, for example, both Demetrios Poliorketes and Ptolemy XII claiming to be the "new Dionysos." The cults of these rulers and their family members were added to the cities' panthea and became part of their calendars of sacrifices and festivals, but these rulers were never quite "real" gods on a par with the established deities of the state. They were given god-like if not truly "divine" honors of sanctuaries, altars, priests, and festivals, but they did not receive from individual devotees, as real gods did, prayers and dedications, two fundamental forms of divine worship, nor were they expected to perform miracles. Also, as for Alexander, Antiochos, and Demetrios Poliorketes at Athens, their cults could be "disestablished" when political circumstances changed – an inconceivable notion for a real god of a Greek city-state. The introduction of the divine cult of rulers in the Hellenistic period is a major new development in religion, and it is often viewed as an indicator of the debasement of the Greeks and of Greek religion, but it should rather be thought of as genuine expression of gratitude, fear, and respect for a new power affecting human life, a power that was providing what the Greeks traditionally asked of their gods: protection against foreign enemies, economic prosperity, food, and personal safety.

If a human ruler could be considered god-like in cult, lesser benefactors of the state could be given, after their deaths, lesser, hero-like honors. They received the honors of sanctuary and sacrifice that Greek cities traditionally paid to their cultic heroes of old, like Theseus in Athens or Orestes in Sparta. After Demetrios Poliorketes was given divine honors in Athens in 307/6, his friends and generals, Adeimantos, Oxythemis, and Bourichos were granted by the state "hero" cults in 302/1. If the king was to be a god, his lieutenants were to be recognized as "heroes." Once the practice developed, the states, often with the approval of the Delphic Oracle, could give heroic status even to local benefactors, and, as such honors multiplied, eventually even families could declare one of their own recently dead a hero. The formal differences between the cult of the hero and the tomb cult of the common dead had never been great, and eventually, in the Roman period, families commonly termed all their deceased members heroes. In a sense, the ordinary dead man was as much a real hero to his family as the Hellenistic king was a real god to his subjects.

The depressed economic conditions of many Greek city-states during the Hellenistic period also entailed some significant changes in the financing and, as result, in the sociological structure of their religion. In the Classical period, for example, Athens had financed the sacrifices, festivals, and the building of temples from state general revenues, from taxes on various commercial activities, and from income from property owned by the sanctuaries. In Athens, general revenues dropped precipitously after the loss of its empire, and other revenues declined in the third century under Macedonian occupation. From the fourth century on, with some exceptions, city-states no longer could afford themselves to build new temples or to dedicate marble and bronze statues of gods, to say nothing of gold and ivory ones, in their sanctuaries. Many were hard pressed even to finance their annual sacrifices and festivals from state and sanctuary revenues. In many states, as at Athens, priests and other religious officials began to be expected to contribute their own funds to maintain or enhance the religious program of the cults they served. In others, particularly in Ionia and nearby islands, priesthoods were leased by auction annually, with the winner assuming financial management of the cult and reaping in return exemption from various taxes, prestige, and any profits the sanctuary might provide. The increase of individual financial participation in cult life extended also to festivals, with contributions and subscriptions made by wealthy individuals for, as one example, Athenian state religious pilgrimages to Delphi in the second and first centuries. On Delos, individual Athenians even financed the construction of buildings in sanctuaries. In the Hellenistic period, the balance of power in cult affairs was shifting from the state to wealthy citizens, and these wealthy citizens in turn wanted recognition for their contributions. Humans now replaced gods as the most commonly dedicated statues in sanctuaries, and inscriptions proclaimed the religious services that these individuals or their family members had performed.

The Hellenistic kings also devoted some of their vast riches to the support and reinvigoration of established Greek cults, as Alexander did for the oracle of Zeus at Dodona, the Seleukids for the oracle of Apollo at Didyma, and the Ptolemies for the Mysteries on Samothrace. Antiochos IV Epiphanes undertook to complete the grandiose temple of Zeus Olympios at Athens in 174 B.C.E., the temple begun by the tyrant Peisistratos in the sixth century, but on his death, left incomplete. In addition, these monarchs contributed large sums to support established or newly instituted festivals, games, sacrifices, and banquets for traditional Greek gods in dozens of cities around the Aegean. In this atmosphere, many cities naturally began seeking Panhellenic and royal recognition for their major deities, promoting a cult that once had been limited to their own citizens. Apollo of Delphi, Zeus of Olympia, and Poseidon of Isthmia had had, of course, such recognition for centuries, furthered through panhellenic games at their festivals. Beginning in the

260s in Boiotia and eventually spreading throughout the Greek world, individual cities sent out delegations to ask fellow Greek states, the Hellenistic kings, and later even Rome, to grant *asylia*, "inviolability," to their most famous sanctuary or, if the sanctuary was within their city, to designate the city and its territory "sacred and inviolable."[8] Often, especially in the earlier times, this request was accompanied by an invitation to participate in a new set of panhellenic games in their deity's honor. Among the 200 cities that made such requests, Magnesia on the Meander in 208 asked that it be sacred and inviolable because of its sanctuary of Artemis Leukophryene and combined this request with an invitation to her festival and games. The Magnesians received positive responses from the Aitolian, Boiotian, Akarnanian, Phokian, and Achaian leagues, the kings Attalos I, Antiochos III, and Ptolemy IV, and from Delphi (which had motivated the proposal), Athens, Corinth, Delos, Rhodes, Syracuse, and dozens more cities ranging from Iran to Sicily. Such requests for *asylia* apparently were not intended to protect the cities against wars and pirates as the term *asylia* would suggest, but were rather an attempt to bring honor and prestige and perhaps royal attention to their most important deity and their city. Cult centers that did, in fact, secure lasting international recognition and royal patronage in the Hellenistic period, such as the oracle of Apollo at Didyma, the Asklepieion on Kos, and the Mysteries on Samothrace, flourished, with floods of visitors and major expansions of their facilities.

As we have seen, the religion that a person in the Hellenistic period practiced was very much determined by where in the Greek world that individual happened to find himself or herself. Most Greeks no doubt stayed in their home cities, and they continued to worship the same deities with the same rituals and practices that their ancestors in the Classical period had. Those living in established Greek cities in the territories of the various Hellenistic kingdoms or subject to their influence no doubt participated in the state festivals of the relevant ruler-god, and the most prominent politically might even serve as the priest of such a cult. Some were attracted to the exotic new cults of Isis and Sarapis, but, at this time, not to the exclusion of other local deities. Those Greeks who emigrated from their homelands and lived permanently or for an extended time in the new multinational and multicultural centers such as Alexandria, Antioch, and Delos found a much different religious world, with a melange of Greek, Egyptian, Syrian, and other deities. They had to make personal choices as to the deities they chose to worship. Their political, social, and economic position within these communities no doubt determined somewhat the options available to them, but, to judge by the behavior of Athenians on Delos in the middle of the second century, many Greeks even of economic and political means, freed from the traditions of their homelands, embraced the foreign cults they encountered. But, in so doing, they also showed allegiance to the Greek gods they found in their new communities. In these new cosmopolitan centers of the Hellenistic world, men and women of various nationalities now mixed quite freely together, as did the gods of the various nationalities, and the foreign gods, in the trail of the humans, now also moved around the Hellenistic world. But, importantly, it appears that Greeks at all these various places and times in the Hellenistic period were still seeking from their gods, old and new, Greek and foreign, immortal and human, much what they had sought in the Classical period: safety, fertility, health, and national and personal prosperity.

I have described the introduction of foreign cults, the new ruler cults, the increase in personifications as deities, the increasing role and authority of the wealthy in cult affairs, and other distinctive features of Hellenistic religion as "changes," a neutral term. I do so to avoid imposing on these changes the value judgments that have characterized some studies of religion in the Hellenistic period. Some see the period as a deterioration from the religion of the Classical period; others see it as a time of positive changes leading in the direction of Christian conceptions. Both are, I think, misconceptions of religion in the Hellenistic period. Let us begin with the notion that religion in the Hellenistic period is a debased form of Classical religion. The evidence is overwhelming that in most established Greek cities, such as Athens, Erythrai, and many others, the citizens continued to worship, pray, sacrifice, and make dedications in nearly identical ways to the deities that they had inherited from their ancestors in the Classical period. But were they doing so in the same spirit? Or were they now thoughtlessly performing age-old rituals, as is often claimed, while their hearts and minds had turned elsewhere? The deterioration in "quality" of Hellenistic religion has generally been laid to three causes: the loss of the independence of the Greek city-states to the Macedonian powers, the importation of foreign deities, and, lastly, the challenges posed by the new philosophical systems of the late Classical and Hellenistic periods. Let us take each of these separately.

After the defeat at Chaironeia in 338 B.C.E. by Philip II and the later victories of Alexander and his successors, most Greek city-states certainly lost their independence to act as they wished in foreign policy, but that need have had little effect on the religious cults and beliefs

that were directed almost solely to the *internal* needs of the city-state –
to the attempts of citizens to provide fertility, food, health, economic
prosperity, safety, and a sense of national identity for themselves, their
families, and their fellow citizens. The hundreds of city-states of the
Classical world each had, though with broad similarities, their own cult
structures supporting political, social, economic, and personal life, and
these were not dependent on any authority – apart from the occasional
Delphic oracle – outside the city. The isolation of the cities from foreign
affairs, their loss of independence in foreign policy, need not, and, so far
as we can tell, did not diminish either the quantity or quality of religious
activity. In fact, the greatest religious revival of which we have record
in the ancient Greek world occurred under the leadership of Lykurgos
in the decade *after* the Athenians had lost the battle of Chaironeia and
were under the authority of Philip II.

What is new in religious terms is not what was taken from the
city-states by foreign events but what was introduced into them by
these same events. Foremost among these was ruler cult. Whether the
impulse for a ruler cult came from the ruler himself or not, the states in
a complex blend of political and religious strategies and emotions gave
the ruler the trappings of divinity without the full status of a god. The
god-like ruler was, after all, from the outside world providing them with
god-like gifts, but at the same time, the citizens sacrificed, prayed, and
made dedications to the state deities that provided these same benefits
from within the city-state.

By the second century, as we have seen, Delos had a profusion of
exotic cults from Egypt, Palestine, Syria, and elsewhere, but Delos was
the exception. With the exception of Isis and Sarapis, these foreign cults
found little reception elsewhere in the Hellenistic period. And Isis cults
in this period found only a small audience among the Greeks themselves. First usually introduced by Egyptian priests for a small Egyptian
community residing in a port city, they might some decades later be
taken up by a private association of citizens and eventually be supported
by the state. But her cult remained one among many, a cult that one
might choose to participate in or not, offering benefits of healing and
safety at sea traditionally associated with Greek gods, and we find none
of the Isiac mysteries or exclusive dedication by Greeks to this one god
that were features of her developed cult in the Roman periods. If we are
careful to distinguish between the Hellenistic and Roman periods, we
find the Eastern cults appealed mostly to emigrant Greeks who often
were at the fringes of political and social power in their adopted communities, and even when these cults were adopted by the traditional

Greek cities, they attracted relatively few citizen devotees. For most Greeks, they certainly were not a viable alternative to the traditional gods and practices maintained since the Classical period.

Finally, the various Hellenistic philosophical systems of Plato's Academy, Aristotle's Lyceum, Zeno's Stoa, and Epicurus' Garden, offered alternatives to the religious concepts of traditional religion, but we must ask how they affected people and how many people they affected. In the Hellenistic period, Athens was the center of this philosophic activity, and we can best see the interaction of philosophy and traditional religion there. The philosophers, mostly expatriates, formed a relatively closed group, and as non-Athenians they could not at this time, had they wanted to, have participated as citizens did in Athenian prayers, sacrifices, and festivals. Their students, too, were largely non-Athenians, but even some of their prominent Athenian students showed considerable interest and expertise in traditional Greek religion. Lykurgos of Boutadai, a student of Plato, led the religious revival in Athens after the battle of Chaironeia, and the very philosophical Demetrios of Phaleron created for Ptolemy I the Greek liturgies for the new Sarapis. Here we must distinguish three groups – the philosophers themselves, elite members of society who studied and socialized with them, and the vast majority of Athenians and other Greeks who had little or nothing to do with them and occasionally persecuted them for challenging conventional beliefs. Modern scholars are probably led by their interest in innovation in intellectual history to overvalue the influence of the philosophers on their contemporary society. Even in later, Roman times, their influence was limited largely to the educated elite. Finally, the Hellenistic philosophers probably had little if any impact on the masses. In regard to the practiced religion of the time, there is thus not enough evidence from the loss of independence of the city-state, from the foreign cults or from the influence of the philosophic schools, to indicate that the well-documented sacrifices, dedications, and festivals for traditional deities were insincere or in any sense seriously threatened.

Others see in the Hellenistic period in positive terms what they consider movement from state religion to personal religion, away from the traditional Olympian state gods to gods promising personal salvation, to the elevation of one god above all others, and to the dedication by individuals to the exclusive worship of one god – a precondition of monotheism. In so doing, they often underestimate the strong continuity of Hellenistic religion, even in its later periods with the Classical past, and they mistake the seeds of change with the developed plants that appear only in the post-Hellenistic, Roman period. The seeds are certainly there, often first appearing in various spots in non-Greek areas, then transplanted to the cosmopolitan centers such as Alexandria and Delos, where they were hellenized for and by Greek worshipers, and then, finally, only in the Roman period experiencing a spread throughout the Mediterranean world. These seeds are the result of innovations in the cults of certain Greek and non-Greek deities, especially Asklepios, Dionysos, and Isis who all broke the usual tight local connections of ancient deities and developed a universal appeal. Each, characteristically, served exclusively personal and familial interests instead of those of the state. Although the cults even of these deities varied significantly from one another and the cult of the same deity might differ from one city to another, we find in the late Hellenistic period that their devotees, as missionaries and often at the gods' requests, now founded new sanctuaries, promoted their gods by descriptions of their miracles and powers (aretalogies), and actively proselytized. These deities were credited by their devotees with an increasing range of powers, with Isis in particular claiming the competencies of virtually all Greek gods and even authority over Fate and the underworld. As such, she could fulfill all the religious needs of her devotees, and the concept of monotheism is established in practiced cult, not just in literature or philosophical theology. The members of some of these cults were formally initiated, formed separate religious communities, and were expected to maintain prescriptions of dress, diet, and moral behavior. And, eventually, such deities, especially Isis and Dionysos, were thought by their devotees to offer not only earthly benefits in the old Greek tradition but also the means to a blessed afterlife. Cults with some or several of these features are attested at scattered places in the late Hellenistic period and appear to have had a relatively small following. But the attestations are sufficiently common and widely dispersed to indicate that new forces were present, forces that became much stronger in the Roman Empire and contributed to the religious and cultural environment in which Christianity found its place.

BIBLIOGRAPHICAL NOTE

For full studies of Hellenistic religion in terms of Classical precedents, later developments in the Roman Period, and economic, historical, and intellectual contexts, see Nilsson (1961), II, 1–309; Schneider (1967–1969), II, pp. 765–959; and Z. Stewart in Bianchi Bandinelli (1977), vol. 8, pp. 503–616. For more general and recent accounts, emphasizing continuity of Classical religion in the Hellenistic period, see Chamoux, (2003) 323–52; Shipley (2000) 153–76; and Mikalson (2005), Chapter VIII.

Notes

1 On the type of demographic, economic, and social changes that affected religion in the period, see Davies (1984) 257–320.
2 For religion in Athens in this period, see Mikalson (1998).
3 For the religious environment of Alexandria, see Fraser (1972), I, pp. 189–301.
4 On the religious environment of Hellenistic Delos, see Bruneau (1970) and Mikalson (1998), chapter 7.
5 For this phenomenon in Athens, see Mikalson (1998) 238, 275–9.
6 For the religious cults of Erythrai, see Graf (1985) 147–375.
7 On ruler cult, see, in addition to the general studies listed in Bibliographical Note, Habicht (1970).
8 On the Hellenistic practice of asking for and granting *asylia*, see Rigsby (1996).

11: Philosophy for Life

Robert W. Sharples

∽

A New Type of Philosophy?

In 323 B.C., Alexander the Great died. It was also – and not coincidentally – the year in which Aristotle left Athens, allegedly saying that he did not want the Athenians to sin against philosophy a second time.[1] He was clearly identified with the Macedonian cause (even though the story later grew up that he had arranged for Alexander to be poisoned); and the fortunes of his school, the Lyceum, in the rest of the century (flourishing under Demetrios of Phaleron; forcibly closed for a time in 307/6 after Demetrios of Phaleron was driven out by Demetrios Poliorketes), show the ways in which political allegiances impinged on philosophy.

The coincidence of date has helped to further a myth, which like many myths contains a partial truth. From late antiquity onwards Plato and Aristotle have been studied more than any other ancient Greek philosophers; many university philosophy courses have jumped from Aristotle to Descartes without as much as a glance at the intervening eighteen centuries. And in some quarters, it has been thought that ancient philosophy after Aristotle, beginning with the Hellenistic period, was inferior or decadent. Sometimes the objection has been to materialism – a charge that can itself be traced back to late antiquity and which, like many charges, reveals as much about the views of those who make it as about its target. (Others, indeed, have praised Epicurus for his allegedly atheistic materialism.)[2] But more generally, Hellenistic philosophy has been criticised for being concerned not so much with argument as with teaching people how to live – sometimes with the addition that this was necessary because the certainties of the city-state had been swept away and because the expansion of the Greek world

223

by Alexander meant that many were torn away from their traditional cultural roots.

This picture is not entirely false. Hellenistic philosophy did indeed have as its overriding concern how a person might best live his or her life.[3] But that, as much recent research has shown, did not mean a lack of sophistication in philosophical argument. Stoic formal logic anticipated discoveries that had to be made again independently by modern logicians, and even as these discoveries were being repeated, philologists who knew nothing about contemporary logic were removing the evidence from the ancient texts on the grounds that "if, if the first then the second, and the first, then the second" was clearly textually corrupt (no one, after all, would write "if" twice in succession, would they)?[4] And Socrates and Plato would have been amazed to hear that either philosophical argument and concern with how life should be lived were in some way antithetical or they did not have the latter as their primary concern. (They might also have been surprised by the notion that the Greek city-state provided certainty and security, Plato's *Crito* notwithstanding.) Hellenistic philosophy in fact continues a much older tradition; that of the "wise man" as the guide to life. What distinguished Socrates was his belief in the *power* of knowledge; not only was "the unexamined life not worth living,"[5] but all wrongdoing is the result of ignorance – which amounts to saying that knowledge or understanding is sufficient for virtue. Hellenistic philosophers were not all equally happy to acknowledge Socrates' influence,[6] but that philosophy can teach people how to live and that reason is the key to living well is a common theme in Hellenistic philosophy. Philosophers, after all, have a vested interest in rational solutions. Plato in *Republic* 10 criticises tragedy for stirring up emotions, which in real life are not helpful; when disaster strikes, what we need to do is not to lament but to work out calmly what to do next (604c). If that sounds hard-hearted, even inhuman, there are aspects of Hellenistic philosophy that are very similar, and the reason is the same, the assumption that life should be lived logically – though the initial impression of insensitivity should not necessarily be our final verdict.

Hellenistic philosophers also shared the common presupposition, formulated by Aristotle in *Nicomachean Ethics* 1 but with roots in earlier Greek thought,[7] that the individual's concern is with living the best life for himself or herself, that is, achieving happiness, *eudaimonia* (which need not, it should be emphasised, imply disregarding the interests of others), and that the fundamental moral question is how this is to be achieved. The starting point of Hellenistic ethics is not therefore how we can determine which ways of acting towards other people are right and which wrong; the emphasis is rather on what sort of life I should aspire to for myself.

The emphasis on the practical was not indeed universal. For Aristotle, ethics had been only one of a range of areas of enquiry. Indeed, he regarded theoretical enquiry – "contemplation" or *theoria* as he called it, "research" as we might now call it – as the highest form of human activity. It has been well suggested that the rapid decline of Aristotle's school in the Hellenistic period has not a little to do with the fact that it had no distinctive message about how life should be lived, other than this one, which was as little to the general taste then as now, coupled with the fact that for those who did want to spend their time in research, sponsorship by the Ptolemies meant that the opportunities were in Alexandria rather than in Athens.[8]

The contrast between Plato and Aristotle on the one hand and their Hellenistic successors on the other is also misleading in another way, in that it can suggest that the philosophy of the fourth century can be identified with that of Plato and Aristotle. Others, too, were active at the same time; they were of less interest to later antiquity, and so we are even less well informed about them than we are about philosophers of the Hellenistic period. And one of the topics of debate in recent scholarship has been how far the Epicureans or the Stoics were reacting to Plato or Aristotle and how far they were developing their own thought largely independently; here, it is useful to remember that it may still be helpful to compare a Stoic position with an Aristotelian one even if they were developed independently.[9]

SCEPTICISM AND HEDONISM

Pyrrhon of Elis (ca. 365–275 B.C.) was claimed by later Sceptics as the founder of their tradition. Scholars differ on whether he derived the unreliability of our senses and opinions from the indeterminable nature of things or vice versa; the former view, involving an *assertion* about the nature of reality, would put him at odds with the later sceptical tradition.[10] In any case, it seems that what he primarily rejected was ethical dogmas; his follower Timon may be responsible for emphasising the implications of his views for knowledge more generally.[11] Suspension of judgement, Timon asserted, brings freedom from disturbance (*ataraxia*). Much of what became known as "Pyrrhonism" is strictly neo-Pyrrhonism, developed in the last century B.C. and the first two centuries

A.D. and attributed anachronistically to Pyrrhon himself; in particular, the development of the "modes," types of argument that could be used to cast doubt on dogmatic claims, is due to Ainesidemos (first century B.C.). Pyrrhon is said to have accompanied Alexander the Great to India, and conversations with Indian philosophers may have influenced his thought. Stories were told that Pyrrhon's suspension of judgement meant that his companions had to restrain him from walking over the edge of cliffs (because he could not be sure that they were there); the stories are probably invented, but they highlight a general problem for scepticism to which we will return later. (The eventual neo-Pyrrhonist answer, as we find it in Sextus Empiricus, ca. 200 A.D., is in effect that we suspend judgment but follow our instincts.)

The issue of the relation of fourth-century and Hellenistic philosophies to Socrates is highlighted by the example of the Cyrenaic school, founded by Aristippos. Aristippos' grandfather, also named Aristippos, was one of the associates of Socrates; the reported attitudes of the grandfather to some extent anticipate the doctrines of the school founded by the grandson. The Cyrenaics taught the hedonistic view that the goal of life was pleasure. An account of choice and error based on this view was notoriously placed in Socrates' mouth by Plato in the *Protagoras*, whether or not we are to suppose that it was actually endorsed either by the historical Socrates or even by Socrates the character in the *Protagoras*; he may adopt it only for the sake of argument. The point that Socrates in the *Protagoras* uses hedonism to make, however, is the entirely Socratic one that understanding is needed to judge the best course of action; it is not always immediately obvious that a short-term pleasure is outweighed by its more painful long-term consequences. The Cyrenaics on the other hand held that our knowledge is limited to our immediate awareness of pleasure and pain; alone among ancient philosophical schools, they rejected any attempt to see human life as directed towards anything other than immediate goals. The Cyrenaic Hegesias was allegedly banned from lecturing by Ptolemy II Philadelphos because his description of death as an escape from pain was driving his pupils to suicide.[12]

Much more significant and influential were the teachings of Epicurus (341–270 B.C.), whose views on pleasure are presented in ancient sources as contrasting with those of the Cyrenaics. Epicurus came from a family of Athenian settlers (*klerouchoi*) in Samos; he founded a school at Mytilene and then at Lampsakos, and subsequently set up his school or community, the Garden, in Athens in 307/6. His teachings are known to us from three letters and a collection of "Principal Doctrines"

quoted by the biographer Diogenes Laertius; from his other volumi-
nous writings, preserved in fragmentary form among the papyri buried
in an Epicurean library at Herculaneum by the eruption of Vesuvius
in A.D. 79; from the extensive inscription set up by another Diogenes
at Oenoanda in Turkey in the second century A.D.; and from their
exposition by the first-century B.C. Latin poet Lucretius.

Epicurus adopted the explanation of all physical reality as made
up of atomic particles of different shapes and sizes moving in an infinite void, originally advanced by Leukippos and then by Demokritos in
the fifth century B.C. The differences between atoms and differences in
their arrangement explain the differences between the perceptible bodies that they more or less temporarily go to make up. Epicurus' adoption
of the theory was not a piece of antiquarianism; the atomic tradition had
continued alongside the work of first Plato and then Aristotle during
the fourth century B.C., and Epicurus had been taught by the Atomist
Nausiphanes. However, whereas Demokritos had emphasised the sceptical implications of atomism − what really exists is atoms and void,
and these we can only reason about, not experience directly − Epicurus emphasised the reliability of our senses; error is not due to failures
in sense-perception itself, but to our erroneous interpretation of the
evidence it provides. Where the evidence of the senses, however carefully examined, cannot decide between rival explanations, as in the
case of heavenly phenomena, we should accept all the possible explanations as true; to prefer one to another in such cases would be engaging
in "mythology."[13] This might at first glance seem an anticipation of
enlightened modern science, and that impression need not be altered
by its connection with the atomist belief in a universe infinite in both
space and time, with an infinity of "worlds" − systems like that in which
we live, including the earth, sun, moon, and stars, on the basis that in an
infinite universe every possible explanation will be true somewhere. We
may, however, hesitate in such an assessment, first because Lucretius lists
as possible explanations some theories that were already outmoded in
Epicurus' own time (such as that the days are longer in summer because
the air through which the sun is moving is thicker, listed alongside
the explanation, correct if one supposes that the sun moves round the
earth, that more of its daily path is above the horizon in summer),[14] and
second, by the fact that the *impossible* explanations are those that reason shows to be impossible on theological grounds, namely those that
involve divine intervention, which would be incompatible with divine
tranquillity. This is not the only occasion on which we will see what
looks like a scientific thesis in fact being used for theological purposes,

though that is not a phenomenon confined to Hellenistic philosophy. In the case of the fundamental theory of atoms and void itself, Epicurus argues that it is the only theory that can account for our experience of the world; for example, the existence of motion requires the existence of void. Others (e.g., Aristotle) had already argued otherwise and would continue to do so.

Epicurus modified the physical theory that he inherited in various ways, the most significant of which for the present discussion is his introduction of the atomic "swerve." Demokritos had thought of each atom as moving in a straight line until it collided with, and hence was deflected by, another atom. In this purely mechanistic system, there was no purpose, although from one point of view the movements of atoms, and hence everything else, were necessitated by what had preceded; from another point of view, everything was due to chance rather than design. Epicurus accepted the denial of purpose in nature, but not what he at least saw as the deterministic implications of Demokritos' system for human action; so that our actions would not all be predetermined by prior movements and configurations of the atoms that go to make us up, he argued that atoms can deviate from straight paths, thus introducing indeterminacy into the system. The question whether randomness in the movement of (as we would now say) subatomic particles has any relevance to the question of human free will and responsibility is still a topic of philosophical debate today; so, too, is the problem that random indeterminacy seems an inadequate foundation on which to build any theory of responsibility worthy of the name. Epicurus insisted against Demokritos that the objects of our experience are as real in their own terms as the atoms that go to make them up, and this suggests that his answer would have been along the lines that what is random in the context of individual atoms becomes responsible in a human mind;[15] but exactly how these two aspects are to be related remains unclear.[16] For Epicurus, the study of the natural world is explicitly only a means to an end, that of enabling us to live a happy life.[17]

How far this was a totally new development in Atomism is unclear; we have insufficient evidence to determine whether we can speak of Demokritos and his successors as already having an ethical system. Epicurus' message – for that is the appropriate term – is summed up in the first four Principal Doctrines, summarised even more concisely by his followers as the "Fourfold Remedy" or "Fourfold Amulet" (*tetrapharmakos*). First, "god is not a thing to be feared"; the gods, who are examples to Epicureans of the calm and tranquil life to which they should aspire, are not concerned with our world or with our doings, and so we should not fear them. (The gods are themselves composed of atoms; it is disputed, and may have been disputed already in antiquity, whether they are spatially located in the gaps between world systems or whether they are in some sense located in our minds, but even if the latter is the case the nature of the gods is not a purely subjective matter, for some views about them are right and others wrong.)

Second, "death is not a thing to be feared"; human beings like everything else are temporary combinations of atoms, and our souls, that is, the parts of us that explain sensation, movement, and thought,[18] do not survive the death of the body; we should not therefore fear either torments in Hades after death or even our future nonexistence, for that is irrelevant to us, and, it is claimed, should cause us no greater anxiety than the fact that we did not exist before our birth. Our present life is all we have, and it is foolish to spoil it with anxiety about what is inevitable anyway. Epicurus arguably fails to take due account of a natural human desire for achievement and of planning for the future in a way that may be thwarted by death. Indeed, Martha Nussbaum has well argued[19] that the ideal life for a human being in Epicurus' view is all too like the tranquil impassivity of the Epicurean gods (not itself an idea alien to earlier Greek thought; Homer's gods are, precisely, "blessed" because no real harm can come to them). Readers of Lucretius' attack on the fear of death in Book 3 may well feel that it succeeds in part by minimising the attractions of life and activity. Freedom from disturbance or anxiety had been Pyrrhon's goal, too; but although Pyrrhon based it on the impossibility of knowledge, Epicurus holds that it requires a right understanding of the nature of the world and of human existence.

Third, "the good is easily obtained." The limit of pleasure is the removal of pain (which includes both physical pain and mental anxiety); after that, pleasure can be "varied" or "seasoned," but not increased. Exotic foods do not give us any *more* pleasure than a simple diet, provided the latter is sufficient to keep us healthy. Epicurus does not argue that we should reject exotic foods and luxuries in general, as being intrinsically bad for us; but he does insist that we should recognise that these things are not necessary and that becoming habituated to them may well lead us to the mistaken view that they are and to consequent anxiety about how we are to obtain them. Just *because* all pleasure in itself is good, some pleasures are to be rejected, because they involve pain that exceeds the pleasure gained. And although some desires are natural but not necessary, others are unnatural, above all, that for political status and power. Lucretius, in terms worthy of (and influential on) Juvenal, explicitly traces the political ills of Rome in the first century

B.C. (3.59–86) and indeed the history of human political development (5.1117–1150) to misplaced ambition reflecting an unconscious fear of death; and Epicurus asserts that "safety from people" is best achieved by withdrawing from public life and living in obscurity with a circle of like-minded friends[20] – the Epicurean community. Such communities regarded Epicurus as others would regard divine benefactors, displaying statues of him and celebrating his birthday as a festival; after all, he had not only shown how human beings could live like the gods – with both the positive and negative connotations that we have seen – but also himself provided an example of such a life.

Fourth, "What is terrible is easily endured." No physical pain is both great and long-lasting; and, just as mental anxiety (such as fear of the gods and of death) is worse than bodily pain, so mental pleasure can more than compensate for bodily pain, as Epicurus himself on his deathbed said the memory of philosophical conversations did.[21] Physical pain and pleasure are confined to the present; the mind can consider the past and the future, too. This may provide an answer to the charge that Epicureanism is a philosophy only for an elite who are reasonably secure and comfortable; it is all very well to stress that our necessary desires are more limited than we may think, but what about those who cannot even be sure of sufficient food to live on or of a minimal level of security? The Epicurean answer would seem to be that, if they survive, they will have nothing to worry about, and if they die, that is nothing to worry about either.

There are other difficulties, too. Pleasure and pain are among our sensations, which, as we have seen, are in themselves entirely reliable; and observation of infants confirms that our primary instinct is to pursue pleasure and avoid pain. However, Epicurus is also committed to the view that the ambitions of those who engage in public life are unnatural. It is not clear whether he thinks that the fulfillment of such ambitions (never complete, as Lucretius emphasises)[22] in fact brings no pleasure at all or whether he thinks that any pleasure it does bring is exceeded by the consequent anxiety. More generally, any attempt to justify a particular view of how humans can achieve happiness on the basis of what is "natural" is open to the objection that views on what is "natural" differ; similarly, appeal to the common opinion shared by almost all human beings, which Epicurus uses to support the claim that gods are immortal and blessed,[23] runs into the difficulty that common opinion certainly did not agree with *everything* Epicurus held about the gods. Ultimately, the only way in which Epicurus could justify his view about the best life for a human being would be to claim that experience shows that it works in practice. Nor should the connections between his views and some aspects of traditional Greek thought lead us to underestimate the extent to which he rejected a culture that he saw as based on false assumptions, writing to Pythokles "flee from all culture (*paideia*)" (Diogenes Laertius 10.6).

Epicurus lays such emphasis on friendship within the Epicurean community that some have thought that he saw it as valuable in itself without any reference to the pleasure it brings. This would however introduce a fundamental inconsistency into the whole Epicurean ethical system. The objection that friendship may bring more anxiety than pleasure, because of emotional involvement, can be met by the argument that human nature is such that friendship is indispensable for happiness, even if there are costs attached to it; the objection that we cannot really be concerned for our friend's interests if our own happiness is paramount can be answered by the fact that, at least according to Diogenes Laertius (10.120), Epicurus held that the wise person will sometimes die for a friend and presumably on the ground that friendship of its nature requires confidence that others will actually do this *in extremis*. Epicurus can still be charged with regarding friends as replaceable; but it is arguable that here he is simply being realistic, as when he says that the members of the Epicurean community will not grieve at the untimely death of a friend.[24] After all, death is not an evil. But a logical approach to life can have something chilling about it.

Epicurus regards justice as a social contract; the laws of states are manmade agreements neither to harm or to be harmed, aimed at the mutual benefit of the citizens, which is the criterion by which they are to be judged; if circumstances change, a law that was just formerly may cease to be so. Those who do not recognise the benefits of this arrangement should still obey the laws, because the fear of punishment if they are found out, which they can never be sure will not happen, produces anxiety that exceeds any possible benefit from the crime.[25] This argument for behaving justly has the advantage that it does not appeal to unverifiable beliefs about punishment in the afterlife; it is questionable, however, whether it will influence anyone who is not already a committed Epicurean. Diogenes of Oinoanda describes a future situation when everyone will be an Epicurean and laws will no longer be necessary[26]; strikingly, Karl Marx, who anticipated a similar future withering away of the state, wrote his first published work (his doctoral thesis) on the differences between the physical theories of Demokritos and Epicurus, though he could not have known about Diogenes' then undiscovered inscription. But until this situation becomes reality, Epicureanism has nothing in particular to say about the existing order of society; Epicurus' message to his followers is to disengage from that society as far as possible – which raises the question, which lies at the root of Cicero's objections to Epicureanism, whether they cannot be accused of taking advantage of social arrangements without playing their part in contributing to them.

THE SUFFICIENCY OF VIRTUE

Rejection of conventional society, though in a very different way, was also the distinguishing feature of the Cynics, traced by later writers to Socrates' follower Antisthenes, but really founded as a philosophical tradition by Diogenes of Sinope in the fourth century B.C. Diogenes took the rejection of normal behaviour to the extremes of living in a barrel, telling Alexander the Great that the only thing he wanted from him was to get out of his light, and performing private bodily functions in public in the marketplace. The point was to demonstrate that the conventions of society were just that, conventions, contrary to nature, that could be discarded. The contrast between convention and nature was not new – it can be traced back to the Sophists in the fifth century; but the way in which the Cynics lived it out in practice was new. The Cynic ideal was self-sufficiency. The Cynic tradition continued into the early centuries of the Roman Empire, covering a spectrum from the more extreme forms of asceticism to a "refined" cynicism, which overlapped with Stoicism; particularly significant is the incorporation of one strand of Cynicism into a tradition of popular moral preaching, especially in Bion of Borysthenes (ca. 335–ca. 245 B.C.).

The Cynic interpretation of "life according to nature" seems to have been essentially negative, rejecting convention, though this is disputed.[27] Zeno, who founded the Stoic school in ca. 300 B.C., was originally a Cynic; both he and the third head of the school, Chrysippos (ca. 280–207), wrote *Republics* which, unlike Plato's work of that name to which their titles alluded, described imaginary communities consisting *entirely* of wise men and women, rejecting conventional institutions even more than Plato had done, to the extent that Chrysippos argued that there was no rational ground in nature for rejecting incest or cannibalism. Not surprisingly, these treatises became an embarrassment to later Stoics. More significantly, however, the Stoics gave "life according to nature" positive content. Like the Epicureans, they believed that only what is bodily exists; but they regarded all bodies as the product of two principles, themselves both bodily, the active principle – God, nature, reason, fate, providence, Zeus – being present everywhere in the passive principle and thus fashioning the whole world, which for the Stoics is a single, finite, closed system. The active principle was identified by Zeno with fire; Kleanthes, the second head of the school (331–232), invokes it in his *Hymn to Zeus*[28] with imagery taken from the Presocratic philosopher Herakleitos. Chrysippos regarded the active principle as present in the world in the form of spirit or *pneuma*, a mixture of fire and air, which takes various forms, but in living creatures constitutes their souls. Human soul and human reason are thus literally physical parts of the cosmic reason that governs the entire universe; and living in accordance with nature for the Stoics means living in accordance with reason, because nature is itself rational. Periodically, the entire world is converted to fire – assimilated into God, in other words; then the whole process begins again, repeating itself exactly, at least as far as all significant aspects are concerned. Nothing for the Stoics happens without a cause[29]; but this principle, which at first glance looks like a principle of scientific enquiry – differences in experimental results must be accounted for – is in the Stoic context more a theological assertion of the power of divine providence. Belief in the predetermined and rational sequence of events is the basis of the Stoic acceptance of divination and astrology; indeed, the (alleged) effectiveness of divination was used as an argument for the existence of this predetermined sequence. Human actions are as predetermined as everything else; but – the Stoics argued – we are still responsible for our actions, because they are *our* predetermined responses influenced by our psychological state, and, because they have consequences, they play a part in the predetermined course of events. Whether such an account is sufficient to establish responsibility or not is a topic on which philosophers are still arguing. Although we are all responsible for our actions, only the wise person – the sage – is free; this freedom consists in accepting the course of events, not in the sense that one should not act to influence it in the way that seems best (on the contrary, one must do this) but in the sense that, if the intended result is not achieved, one should accept that divine providence knows better than we do what is actually for the best.[30] The most distinctive Stoic ethical doctrine is that moral virtue is sufficient for happiness. That it was necessary for happiness was widely accepted, being agreed by Socrates, Plato, Aristotle, and Epicurus; that it was sufficient was denied by Aristotle and asserted by the Cynics. Whether it was regarded as sufficient by Plato, and by Plato's Socrates, is debated. For the Stoics, virtue is the only good and wickedness the only evil; everything else – health, sickness, wealth, poverty, and the like – is "indifferent," though the orthodox view within the school allowed that some indifferents were preferred and others dispreferred. Thus, in normal circumstances, one should act in a way that will achieve wealth rather than poverty; but sometimes there are exceptional circumstances. The correct selection among indifferents in a particular situation is an "appropriate" action, translated by Cicero as a "duty" or *officium*; appropriate actions are virtuous actions if they are performed for the right reasons and on the basis of a settled disposition, which can be done only by a wise person or sage. In particular, the sage will be aware that what matters is performing the right action; the outcome is beyond our control. Stoicism is thus not, as it is often mistakenly said to be, a philosophy of fatalism, quietism, or resignation; on the contrary, the sage will, as the Stoic Poseidonios put it in the early first century B.C., join in establishing the good order of the universe,[31] but will do so recognising the limitations of human knowledge and human power. The sage always acts virtuously and that indeed is in effect the definition of a sage; all other human beings, and all their misdeeds, are equally evil; there are no degrees of wickedness. Clearly, this is a paradox intended to make the point that perfection is of its very nature absolute. Sages rarely exist in practice; no Stoic philosopher ever claimed this status for himself, though Socrates was regarded as having been a sage. The reaction of some modern readers is that the rarity of sages itself shows that Stoic moral theory is out of touch with reality; that ideals should be extremely difficult to live up to may not however seem surprising. The Stoic Panaitios (ca. 185–109 B.C.),[32] an associate of Scipio Aemilianus (though the picture of the "Scipionic circle" seems to owe more to Cicero's literary imagination than to historical fact) is often said to have made Stoic ethical doctrine more realistic and practical; he certainly made a distinctive contribution in emphasising the difference between individuals in their characters and inherited or chosen positions in society and careers, but it is not clear that he made any fundamental change to the Stoic position in ethics, rather than a change of emphasis. He did, however, apparently treat ethics as self-sufficient, having little to say about the physical theory that had provided its background, and he rejected divination and astrology, about which others had already had doubts.

More problematic than the positing of a virtually unattainable ideal is the question why moral evil should be so prevalent in a providentially ordered universe; here, the Stoic answer seems to have been that the necessary conditions of human and animal life – specifically, the shock experienced at birth and exposure to the cold air (which is necessary to convert the plant-like *pneuma* of the embryo into animal soul), and the attempts of nurses to compensate for this – all too easily encourage the mistaken belief that the pursuit of pleasure and avoidance of pain are important, and such beliefs and others based on them are then transmitted to subsequent generations.[33]

The most basic animal instinct, the Stoics argued, is nevertheless not for pleasure, as Epicurus supposed, but for self-preservation. In a process described as "appropriation" (*oikeiosis*) Nature causes all living creatures to be aware that certain things are proper to them and others not – the first proper thing being the creature itself. (English has no term in current use that really renders *oikeiosis*; its opposite, "alienation," is familiar enough.) It is this realisation that certain things are proper and others alien that enables us to distinguish between preferred indifferents and dispreferred ones, and is also the basis of domestic and political communities; but the sage has come to realise that what is actually most proper to a human being is reason, displayed in action, rather than the preferred indifferents that ordinary people mistakenly think are relevant to their happiness. Critics objected that this introduced a fatal discontinuity into the Stoic account of human moral development and that it was absurd to say that what had supreme value was the attempt to achieve things which in themselves had no value; to the latter point, the Stoic response would simply be that this is a correct understanding of their position, however paradoxical it may seem. Virtue is the art of living; as with dancing, the important thing is to achieve a virtuoso performance.[34]

As for the Socrates of the *Protagoras*, so for the Stoics all human behaviour is rational, not in the sense that it is based on correct judgements – usually it is not – but in the sense that how we behave reflects our judgments, correct or mistaken. Passions, or mistaken emotions (*pathe*), are the result of, or (for Chrysippos) simply *are*, mistaken judgments; in the case of anger, for example, the belief that something bad has happened (which is mistaken, because the only thing that is actually bad for me is my own wickedness) plus the belief that I should react in a particular way. The sage will feel no such passions; he will experience "good emotions" (*eupatheiai*), for example, joy in his own virtue and those of other sages. Many have thought that this restriction of emotion, together with the belief that outcomes do not matter, makes the Stoic sage a cold and repellent figure, acting correctly towards others indeed but doing so always with a focus on his or her own virtue; once again, what we see is the effects of the interpretation of human life in purely rational terms. Poseidonios rejected the orthodox Stoic view of emotions as judgments and argued rather, with Plato, that the human soul has both a rational and an irrational aspect, arguing that the ortho-dox account could not explain what seemed to be an innate tendency in children to misbehave or the features such as spirited behaviour, which humans share with irrational animals.[35] In other respects, too, Poseidonios was not an orthodox Stoic; his interest in a wide range of subjects, notably geography, led to him being described as more like an Aristotelian.[36]

CERTAINTY AND SCEPTICISM

The Stoics, like the Epicureans, were empiricists. Whereas Epicurus had argued that we should avoid jumping to hasty conclusions from unclear perceptions but wait until we could obtain a "clear vision" of an object, the Stoics went a stage further and developed the doctrine of an "apprehensive presentation," an impression that was such that it was self-evidently correct, such that it "*could not* have come from what is not that existing object."[37] Sages and non-sages alike, it seems, would assent to such impressions – though the rider had to be added, "provided there is no external obstacle," as in the case of Admetos failing to recognise his own wife in the unusual circumstance that she had been brought back from the dead.[38] Where fools – that is, everyone who is not a sage – go wrong is rather in assenting to nonapprehensive presentations, where the wise thing to do would be to suspend judgement. Assenting to a nonapprehensive presentation results in holding an "opinion," the distinctive feature of which is precisely that it is unreliable; consequently for the Stoics the wise person will never hold mere opinions.

Although Plato's immediate successors in the Academy were dog-matists, Arkesilaos (316/15–242/1 B.C.) adopted scepticism – which is, after all, one natural reaction to the fact that in many of Plato's dialogues, Socrates' questioning leads to general perplexity. Arkesilaos turned the Stoic argument against the Stoics themselves, because there are no impressions that simply could not be misleading (given suffi-ciently bizarre circumstances: for example, in one notorious story [LS 40F] Ptolemy Philopator offered the Stoic Sphairos a bowl of wax fruit; when Sphairos realised the trick, too late, he responded that he had only assented to the impression that it was *reasonable* [*eulogon*] that the fruit be real). Consequently, by the Stoics' own argument, suspension of judg-ment is *always* the wise course. Arkesilaos indeed seems to have argued that we still have a guide to action in impressions that are "reasonable," even if not certain, though this is controversial and some have suggested that Arkesilaos was not advocating what is "reasonable" as a criterion himself, but simply offering it to the Stoics as a substitute for the "apprehensive presentation."[39]

A similar question arises for a later head of the Academy, Karneades, one of the three philosophers sent on an embassy from Athens to Rome in 156/5 B.C. to argue against a fine imposed for the destruction of Oropos, when he shocked Cato the Elder by demonstration of the claim that there are equally strong arguments on both sides of every question by speaking in favour of justice one day and against it the next.[40] Karneades modified the notion of the "reasonable impression," speaking rather of that which is "persuasive" (pithanon), "undiverted" – that is, not called into question by other evidence – and "thoroughly explored." But his pupils already disagreed about his own position; Kleitomachos interpreted Karneades as saying that the wise person would suspend judgment rather than holding opinions, Metrodoros as allowing the holding of opinions provided it was realised that they were fallible. Kleitomachos' successor as head of the Academy, Philon of Larisa, initially adopted the same view as Metrodoros, but subsequently, after moving from Athens to Rome in 88 B.C., argued that, although things could not be known according to the Stoic criterion of the "apprehensive impression," they could nevertheless be known in themselves, and that this had been the consistent view of all members of the Academy throughout its history. Philon's pupil Antiochos of Askalon claimed to be scandalised by such a claim and made it his occasion to break with Philon altogether, return to dogmatism, and claim to be restoring the true doctrines of the Academy. Philon's most influential pupil was Cicero, whose own philosophical position is one of moderate scepticism, expressed in the appropriate form of dialogues in which different speakers present competing views (though in ethics he indicates a clear preference for Stoicism over Epicureanism). Another of Philon's pupils, Ainesidemos, left the Academy altogether and developed extreme neo-Pyrrhonist scepticism. The future of Platonism itself, however, lay in the return to dogmatism, which eventually in the third century A.D. gave rise to Neoplatonism. Antiochos' adoption of the Stoic criterion of the "apprehensive impression," basing knowledge on the senses as the Stoics did, put him so much at odds with the views suggested by Plato's own writings that he must be seen as a dead end in the history of Platonism rather than as marking a new beginning.[41] His most distinctive doctrine was that, although virtue was sufficient indeed for happiness, as the Stoics had claimed, the addition of other goods can increase happiness even further,[42] a view that can be seen as a commonsense compromise, but perhaps for that reason was not adopted by any successors.

PHILOSOPHY AND SOCIETY

What difference, finally, did Hellenistic philosophy make to Hellenistic society? In intellectual circles, the influence was considerable; for example, there is interaction between philosophy and medicine both in physiological theories (such as the role of *pneuma* as a vital force) and in such areas as the theory of causation.[43] This in itself is hardly surprising. But beyond that, we must look to individual influence. This might be on the level of encountering an itinerant Cynic preacher; it might be on that of a philosopher as adviser to a king – even Epicurus, if we can believe Diogenes Laertius 10.120, held that the wise person will be the courtier of a king "if it is opportune" (*en kairoi*), and the Stoics held that a philosopher will take part in politics when reason so indicates (LS 67W). Before arriving at the Ptolemaic court, Sphairos had been an advisor of the reforming Spartan king Kleomenes III. Antiochos of Askalon accompanied the Roman general Lucullus.

Hellenistic philosophy did not however offer anything like a theory of politics or a critique of society. Attempts to connect adherence to a particular philosophical tradition with a particular political agenda have generally failed.[44] The Stoic response to slavery is not to challenge the institution but to argue that even a slave can be virtuous and therefore happy; this was radical enough in terms of traditional Greek thought and to be contrasted with Aristotle's view that some people are naturally fitted only to be slaves[45] – but it characteristically focuses on the individual rather than on the institution.[46] Epicureans and Cynics, as we have seen, in different ways rejected conventional social arrangements altogether. The original Stoic notion of an ideal state populated only by sages was replaced by the notion that all sages, wherever they may be, are fellow citizens of the one true cosmic city and by the idea – already present in Herakleitos – that the human laws of individual states derive from the single divine law; but the idea that the world as a whole is a single community, the home of gods and men, and the combination of this idea with the indigenous Roman concept of the "law of nations" seems to be a distinctively Roman development, appropriate to a state that had geopolitical ambitions beyond those of any Hellenistic monarchy, and due above all to Cicero.[47]

BIBLIOGRAPHICAL NOTE

The ancient evidence for Hellenistic philosophy is most easily accessible in Long and Sedley (1987) [LS]. Accounts for the general reader can be found in Long (1986) and Sharples (1996). For comprehensive reference, see Algra, Mansfeld, and Schofield (1999). On some specific aspects, see Annas (1993); Brunschwig and Sedley (2003) in Sedley (2003) 151–83; Inwood (2003); Nussbaum (1994); Sorabji (2000); and Warren (2004).

NOTES

1 Aelian, *Varia Historia* 3.36.
2 For example, Farrington (1967).
3 On the place of women in Hellenistic philosophy, see Nussbaum (1994) 53–4, 117, 322–4.
4 Cf. Mates (1961) 76.
5 Plato, *Apology* 38a.
6 Cf. Long (1996) 1–34.
7 Cf. on this Irwin (1989) 7–10.
8 Cf. Glucker (1998) 313–4; Annas (1992) 27.
9 On the importance of Plato, see Sedley (1998) 75–82.
10 On this issue, see Brunschwig (1999) 246–7.
11 Brunschwig (1999) 248–9.
12 Cicero, *Tusc. Disp.* 1.83.
13 Epicurus, *Letter to Pythocles* 87.
14 Lucretius 5.680–698.
15 Cf. Long and Sedley (1987) [henceforth LS], i.109–11, and for the general principle of antireductionism, Lucretius 2.886–990; 3.262–287.
16 The claim of LS loc. cit. that choice causes swerves runs into the objection that on a physical level swerves caused by choices and others not caused by choices will be indistinguishable.
17 Epicurus, *Principal Doctrine* 11.
18 A modern analogy would be the brain and nervous system, except that Epicurus, like most ancient Greek thinkers with the notable exception of Plato, placed the mind in the chest rather than in the head. On Epicurus' arguments concerning death, see Warren (2004).
19 Nussbaum (1994) 192–238.
20 Epicurus, *Principal Doctrine* 14.
21 Diogenes Laertius 10.22.
22 Lucretius 3.995–1002.
23 Epicurus, *Letter to Menoeceus* 123.
24 Epicurus, *Principal Doctrine* 40. Cf. Lucretius 3.894–911.
25 Cf. Epicurus, *Principal Doctrines* 31–8.
26 LS 22S.
27 Cf. Moles (1995) and (1996).
28 LS 54I.

29 Cf. Plutarch, *On Stoic Self-Contradictions* 15.1040b.

30 Our evidence for Hellenistic Stoicism is even more fragmentary than for Epicurus. Consequently, it is best consulted in collections of testimonia; for the physical theory outlined in this paragraph, cf. LS 43–55 and 62, and for the ethical doctrines of the following paragraphs, cf. LS 56–64.

31 LS 63J.

32 For Panaitios, cf. LS 66CDE.

33 Cf. Calcidius, On Plato's *Timaeus* 165.

34 A way of putting the point that I owe to Becker (1998) 106–7.

35 For the orthodox view and for that of Poseidonios, cf. LS 65.

36 Strabo, *Geography* 2.3.8.

37 LS 40D, E, H.

38 LS 40K.

39 On the question whether Arkesilaos and Karneades (next paragraph) advocated a criterion of their own or were simply arguing *ad homines* against the Stoics, cf. LS i.455–460 (adopting the latter view), Schofield (1999) [adopting the former].

40 LS 68M; Plutarch, *Cato Maior* 22.

41 Cf. Tarrant (1985) 10–11.

42 Cicero, *On Ends* 5.81; *Tusc. Disp.* 5.21.

43 For a judicious account of the extent of such interaction, see Cambiano (1999) 599–613.

44 See Griffin (1989). The most notorious alleged example has been the Epicureanism of Cassius the assassin of Julius Caesar.

45 Aristotle, *Politics* 1.5.

46 Cf. the criticism by Williams (1993) 115–7.

47 Cf. LS 67.

12: SCIENCE, MEDICINE, AND TECHNOLOGY

Paul T. Keyser and Georgia Irby-Massie

୶

S cience, medicine, and technology seek knowledge to understand or control the natural world. This chapter draws together science and medicine, occupations primarily of the educated elite, with technology often practiced by slaves or foreigners. Some scholars bridged that gap, particularly those treating architecture, mechanics, poliorcetics, or medicine. A greater number of scientists and engineers, particularly ca. 320–200,[1] accumulated more new knowledge than during any other three centuries of antiquity, and more scientific documents survive from this era than any other kind of writing. But, owing to disproportionately larger losses both of Hellenistic material and of works from all ancient eras on science, medicine, and technology, we consequently rely heavily on fragments quoted or paraphrased by writers in the first centuries of the Roman era.

The kingdoms of Alexander's successors promoted science and engineering due both to governmental patronage and multicultural context. Warfare, trade, and prestige elicited or even demanded the growth of science and engineering. Greeks like Herodotos and Ktesias had admired the ancient civilizations of Egypt and Mesopotamia, and now elite members of the new Greek kingdoms – rulers, merchants, and scholars – found fresh material to contemplate and adapt in the ideas and practices of the conquered peoples.

The best-known work of Ptolemaic patronage was the Museum and its Library at Alexandria, which Ptolemy I founded to be a universal library and school, appointing Demetrios of Phaleron its organizer. Archives and scholarship, however, accompany the earliest writing, and libraries founded by autocrats in their capitals are attested in sixth-century Babylonia, Persia, Athens, and Samos. Moreover, victorious rulers had taken books as booty since the days of Ashurbanipal (d. 627). Hekataios of Abdera (*fl.* 300) recorded the Egyptian library of sacred books in the Ramesseum at Thebes (Diod. 1.49.3–4). The Athenian schools (*infra*) were each dedicated to a divinity, so Ptolemy placed his library in a shrine to the Muses, the *Museum* (see The Customized Library, Chapter 8 in this volume). The king appointed the Librarian, who was also often the royal tutor, and about three dozen scholars, living and teaching there in a community. They served at the pleasure of the king, who occasionally imprisoned or even executed some for malfeasance (Vitruvius 7.*pr*.8–9). The earlier Ptolemies vigorously augmented the collection, confiscating, copying, and translating books from everywhere. They sought both legitimacy as heirs of Alexander and rulers of the Greek world, as well as links to the Greek past by creating a symbol of Greek culture.

The Library's early endeavors included a 120-volume catalog of all writers and their works. Composed by Kallimachos of Cyrene (*fl.* 270–240), the catalog was similar in purpose but grander in scope than those of Babylonian libraries. Another central activity was the production of standard editions of Greek literature beginning with Homer. This Library grew to include perhaps 100,000 works (in half a million scrolls), and Ptolemy III founded for public use a daughter library, one-tenth the size, in the temple of Sarapis (ca. 240). Funding was cut after Ptolemy VIII expelled the Librarian Aristarchos of Samothrace and the scholars in 145/4 (Ath. 4 [83]). The post of librarian was thereafter a sinecure awarded to courtiers, and its scholars turned to the systematic study and criticism of existing literature. The aggressive acquisitions policy had encouraged the proliferation of forgeries, and arguments about authenticity occupied the scholars.

Not all scholars worked in, or even visited, Alexandria. Such visits were unnecessary because similar libraries were founded at the Macedonian capital Pella by Antigonos ca. 270, at Antioch by the Seleukids before ca. 200, and at Pergamon by Eumenes II ca. 190. Those rulers also patronized scholars, scientists, physicians, and engineers. Many towns, such as Athens, Kos, Rhodes, and even Mylasa (modern Milas in southwest Turkey), possessed libraries that were often funded by local elites and held a few thousand scrolls. By ca. 350, booksellers were common in cities, where literacy appears to have remained widespread (and important to the bureaucratic Ptolemaic regime), while inscriptions reveal that both boys and girls attended school.

Roman conquests from 168 to 48 damaged or emptied the Macedonian, Pergamene, Athenian, and Alexandrian libraries, and long subterranean storage allegedly wrecked Aristotle's library. Three riots during the late Roman Empire destroyed the remains of the Alexandrian collections, so that only works in local and personal libraries survived.

Extant treatises are mostly school texts, copied in great numbers, whereas advanced or esoteric works were rarer and therefore perished more easily. Doxographers focused on major figures, thus deepening the neglect of lesser known writers. Fewer technological texts than scientific or medical texts survive, because theories usually had greater philosophical cachet than applied practices. Byzantine copyists and their patrons preserved scientific works suited to their tastes, preferring writers of the Greco-Roman period and emphasizing mathematics, astronomy including astrology, medicine, and poliorcetic works. Only books transcribed from papyrus-roll to codex, and then from majuscules to miniscules, survived. Some works survived because they appealed to the 'Abbasid Arabic translators in Baghdad (750–950 C.E.).

Modern scholars, persistently regarding this era as somehow inferior to the Athens of Perikles and Demosthenes, have often disregarded Hellenistic science and technology in favor of later Roman achievements or earlier Greek work. Studies of earlier Hellenic philosophy (ca. 650–325) have often concentrated on reconstructing the earliest text on a given topic, a quest for origins seen already in Aristotelian doxography. Classical scholars continue to debate well-studied topics, rather than to explore new questions.

The complex traditions of science and technology demand a topical approach. For medicine, however, we offer a chronological narrative, because surviving texts show how successive theories and practices depended on prior ones.

SCIENCE

Scientists and natural philosophers often worked within one of a few distinct schools of thought proffering a complete, systematic account of philosophy. Four were founded in Athens ca. 385–305: Plato's Academy, Aristotle's Lyceum, and after Alexander's death, Zenon's Stoa and Epicurus' Garden (see Chapter 11 in this volume). Around 360, Pythagoreanism was revived. Academics and Pythagoreans sought explanations through mathematics, emphasizing cosmology and astronomy. For two centuries (ca. 270–90), however, Academics tended to doubt any attempt to offer definite views on anything. Aristotle explained all phenomena using four causal categories: material, formal, efficient, and final. But his followers, the Peripatetics, neglected teleology, emphasizing instead empirical investigation of individual phenomena, whereas Stoics and Epicureans argued that only physical bodies can mediate causation. Zenon of Kition (d. 263) taught that matter was continuous, finite, and passive, whereas the active principle was the pervasive, divine *pneuma* (meaning both spirit and breath), which propagated changes from one part of the organic *kosmos* to others, and established *sympatheia*. Epicurus of Athens (d. 270) hypothesized two fundamental principles, atoms and void, on which to base naturalistic explanations of phenomena, but advocated offering multiple explanations and suspending judgment between them (Epicurus, *Ep. ad Hdt.*, *Ep. ad Pyth.*).

Some scholars trace the skeptical tendency of contemporary Academics and Peripatetics to Pyrrhon of Elis (d. ca. 270), who argued that the irreconcilable dispute of the philosophers showed that no positive knowledge was possible, so the wise man should withhold judgment. He advocated *stochasmos*, a procedure that stressed observation, as broad as possible, and inference from empirical data through arguments based on signs. This method of inquiry emphasized passive absorption and accumulation of individual experiences in three ways. The best experiences happened of their own accord, whereas less reliable experiences were improvised at need. Least reliable was to repeat either of the two better kinds of experience.

Scientific thought is marked both by debate between these philosophical syntheses and productive investigation on their margins. Writers and practitioners focused on narrower topics, as natural philosophy grew from a subdivision of philosophy into a discrete discipline. Empedokles, Aristotle, and others had attempted synoptic or even totalizing accounts, but Hellenistic scientific writers typically wrote often extensive monographs, in some cases, on a wide variety of topics. Fundamental notions include: the four elements fire, air, water, and earth; the eternity of matter; the orderliness of the *kosmos*; and the comprehensibility of the *kosmos*. Epicureans explained the four elements in terms of their fundamental concepts of atoms and void, whereas Aristotle added a fifth element, later called *quintessence*, to explain eternal circular planetary motion.

Greek mathematics was primarily geometrical, and scholars debate the extent of a possible lost arithmetical tradition. Unlike the place-value numerals of modern arithmetic, their most common numeral system was aggregative (cp. Roman numerals), *alpha* through *theta*, representing 1–9 (the sixth position being filled by the obsolete letter *digamma*), then *iota* to *xi*, plus obsolete letter *qoppa*, representing 10–90, and finally *rho* to *omega*, plus obsolete letter *san*, representing 100–900. Most fractions were represented as unit fractions, like 1/6th. Tables in astronomical papyri show a symbol "ŏ" for zero, sometimes wrongly thought to be an abbreviation for "*ouden*," nothing.

Hellenistic natural philosophers often took mathematics as the paradigm of science and sought to mathematize their study, that is, to ground all its claims in mathematical theorems and procedures, a goal shared by modern scientists. Pythagoreans and Plato had also done so, and the trend may reflect their influence or the successes of Eudoxos of Knidos (*fl.* 350). There were, however, plentiful novel approaches and questions. Practitioners regarded astronomy, geography, mechanics, harmonics, pneumatics (the study of fluids), and optics as mathematical sciences, *because* each of them possessed fundamental mathematical rules. Only Epicureans rejected a key role for mathematics.

Six writers active in the third century, whose works survive intact or in significant fragments, show the wide range of scientists. Euclid (*fl.* 290?) offered a systematic compendium of geometry and number theory, probably including many of his own advances, in his textbook *Elements*, used for over two millennia. He proved the long-known Pythagorean Theorem, demonstrated the endless sequence of primes, and constructed the five Platonic solids. He also wrote on astronomy, harmonics, and optics. Straton of Lampsakos (head of the Lyceum 287–269) sought to construct a cosmology explaining the universe on a solely natural basis, so that, opposing Aristotle, he admitted the void and eschewed prime movers and natural places. Notable is his empirical demonstration that falling bodies accelerate. The renowned astronomer Aristarchos of Samos (*fl.* 280) published the first known *geometrical* determination of the distances of the sun and moon, and hypothesized a heliocentric planetary system. Archimedes of Syracuse (d. 212/1) studied astronomy, mechanics, optics, and pneumatics, which he first mathematized, distinguishing density from weight and establishing the principle that an immersed solid is buoyed up by a force equal to the weight of the displaced liquid. He also invented the worm-gear, explained the operation of the lever, computed approximations to π (between 223:71 and 22:7), invented a place-value numeral system in base 100,000,000, and developed what amounts to integral calculus. Eratosthenes of Cyrene (Alexandrian Librarian 245–194) was admired for his wide-ranging talents, writing on mathematics, geography, harmonics, chronology, and even literature. His most influential work, the *Geographika*, applied mathematics to geography, to describe regions geometrically and locate sites astronomically, and determined anew the

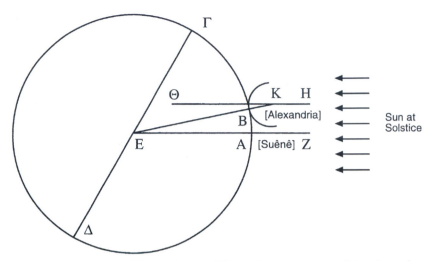

FIGURE 22. Diagram of Erastosthenes of Kyrene's measurement of the circumference of the earth [G. L. Irby-Massie and P. T. Keyser, *Greek Science in the Hellenistic Era. A Sourcebook* (London, & New York, 2002) 121, fig. 5.1; reprinted by permission of Routledge Press].

circumference of the Earth (Figure 22). His mathematical work included the prime-sieve, still the most efficient algorithm for calculating primes less than 10,000,000,000.

Philon of Byzantion, Apollonios of Perge, and Diokles, all active around 200, represent the end of the most productive period of science. Philon wrote a practitioner's encyclopedia covering mechanics, pneumatics, and optics, in which he offered an unusual theory of liquid motion and a discussion of falling weights. Apollonios constructed an automaton flute-player,[2] contributed to the epicyclical model of planetary motion that replaced Eudoxos' model (Ptol. *Almagest* 12.1), and advanced the theory of conic sections to levels not surpassed for two millennia. Diokles' treatise on burning mirrors (those designed to focus the sun's rays on a given set of points) included a proof of the focal property of the parabola, the basis of telescopes since Newton.

Hipparchos of Bithynian Nikaia, active on Rhodes 147–127, explored combinatorics,[3] probably invented plane trigonometry, and exploited Babylonian astronomical observations. All the fundamental parameters of his lunar model are derived from contemporary Babylonian data. His model of solar and lunar motion enabled prediction of lunar (but never solar) eclipses. His observations and models were sufficiently precise that he discovered the 26,000-year precession of the equinoxes. He also wrote on the mechanics of falling bodies, optics, geography, and astrology – to which he was the first Greek to apply mathematics, based again on Babylonian data and ideas.

The goal of earlier astronomy was to establish a mathematical model to explain the observed celestial phenomena, considered fundamentally orderly, and to account for the consequences of the model. Archimedes called this "fitting the demonstration of the phenomena to a hypothesis" (*Aren.* 1), whereas Poseidonios of Apameia designated it "saving the phenomena" (fr. 18 EK). Astronomers now also had many practical motives, from regulating the complex Greek luni-solar religious calendars, to constructing sundials, producing tables of planetary positions, and applying Babylonian data and models. Sosigenes (*fl.* 50), employing the quadrennial leap-day pioneered in 285 by Dionysios, designed for Caesar the calendar that still underlies the Western calendar.

From the time of Hipparchos, astrology coupled with Stoic cosmology increasingly served as the grand unifying theory of nature. Scholars assign a mix of four causes for the development and reception of astrological theory: the mythic significance of constellations, the Stoic doctrine of *sympatheia*, geocentric planetary theory, and, most crucially, the introduction of late-Babylonian horoscopic astrology. Aratos of Soloi (*fl.* 280–240) had versified Eudoxos' account of celestial topography and earthly events portended by celestial risings and settings, whereas Eratosthenes described dozens of constellations with attention to their mythic significance. The book attributed to Nechepso and Petosiris (ca. 145) connected occasional portents with political events. Despite its influence, later astrologers, such as Teukros of Babylon (*fl.* 50), predicted individuals' lives from planetary positions at birth or conception. The earliest extant Greek horoscopes are contemporaneous.

Greeks never applied mathematics to alchemy, biology, or physiognomy, and only partially to geography. Therefore, these studies were seen as less certain and philosophical, and writers preferred catalogues, descriptions, and applications. Nonetheless, the lack of mathematical foundation for these disciplines neither invalidated them nor weakened the general desire for such a foundation. Theophrastos of Eresos (head of the Lyceum 323–287) covered all these areas, whereas later writers were specialists.

Practical understanding of materials and their transformations is pervasive and ancient in human culture. Alchemy is a medieval term for the Greek science that emerges from these practices. Aristotle's *Meteorologika* 4 analyzed composite bodies and their sensible qualities, a foundation for later theories. Theophrastos' contribution is preserved in his works on stones (giving recipes for changing stones to metal and for altering colors) and on fire (explaining some transformations). Bolos of Mendes (*fl.* 200), possibly influenced by Egyptian practices, contributed profoundly to the development of alchemical theory and practice in his books on gold and silver, stones, and dyes, especially purple. Bolos' fundamental alchemical principle was based on the long-persisting idea that color, weight, and all other perceptible properties of materials were secondary accidents, and so could be altered, removed, or added by suitable processing that exploited *sympatheia*. Alchemists succeeded in producing (*sc.* imitating) purple and other desirable dyes, precious stones, and even silver, but their attempts at gold were never as efficacious.

Descriptive geography attempted to explain local features and peculiarities. The spherical shape of the earth (doubted only by Epicureans) and its size, as well as latitude and longitude, were topics of mathematical geography, latitude explaining climate and its effects. Theophrastos' work *On Winds* is in part descriptive geography, whereas Eratosthenes and Hipparchos augmented their mathematical geography with descriptions. Historians such as Polybios (*fl.* 140) inserted descriptions into their narratives, and poets such as Pausanias of Damaskos (*fl.* 85, known as pseudo-Skymnos) versified descriptions of the world. Kallimachos (*supra*) and his student Philostephanos of Cyrene (*fl.* 210) accumulated anomalies of remote places, contributing to the development of paradoxography.

Alchemy and descriptive geography, the sciences of the mineral kingdom, remained descriptive; studies of plants and of animals remained similarly focused on data collection. Theophrastos described and classified plants, but later botanists were mostly pharmacologists seeking effects based on *sympatheia* from botanical sources for medical or dietetic use. Galen credits Mantias the Herophilean (*fl.* 175) as the first to prescribe pharmaceutical compounds (although Babylonian pharmacists had long done so), whereas Krateuas' (*fl.* 80) book on botanic pharmacy undergirded all later work. Plato, *Tim.* 90e–92c, and Aristotle, *de Partibus Animalium* 4.10 (686a25–687b25), theorized that animals were respectively degenerate or incomplete humans, which encouraged anthropocentric biology. The Alexandrian Museum included a zoo for research. Archelaos (*fl.* 250) wrote a paradoxographical book on animals, and Leonidas of Byzantion (*fl.* 100) wrote on ethology. Apollodoros of Alexandria (*fl.* 280) wrote on venemous beasts, Bion of Soloi (*fl.* 280) on farming and animal husbandry, and Nikander of Kolophon (*fl.* 130) versified those and other topics.

Pre-Socratic discourse included physiognomy, the science of deducing character from bodily signs, to which Theophrastos' work *Characters* also contributed. The Aristotelian corpus contains a physiognomic work (probably three documents), contemporary with the physiognomic authors Loxos and Melampous (*fl.* 250). Just as the soul, whether composed of atoms or quintessence, revealed itself in affecting the conformation of the body, so too the soul was affected by external events through *sympatheia*.

MEDICINE

Physicians regarded medicine as a kind of philosophy and explained their theories and practices in philosophical terms. Health was understood to be a balance of humours (*chumoí*) in the body, and healing was sought by gross manipulation of these bodily fluids. Because invasive procedures like cautery, emetics, enemas, laxatives, phlebotomy, and surgery were risky, some earlier physicians preferred the noninvasive technique of regimen (*diaita*), diet, and exercise. The *Hippocratic Oath* (ca. 350) prohibited drugs for suicide and surgery for any reason, preferring dietary to pharmaceutical treatment. Although probably Pythagorean, those tendencies reinforced the lexical ambiguity of *pharmaka*, meaning both medicines and poisons (compare English "drugs"). Treatment by surgery was reserved for wounds and fractures, the removal of arrows, and sometimes the excision of excruciating bladder stones or gallstones. Pain is rarely mentioned, and apparently few analgesics or no anesthetics were used.

Whereas early physiological models of the body emphasized the role of blood- or food-bearing tubes, later Hippokratic treatises seem more committed to a model of four humours: bile (*chole*), blood (*haima*), phlegm (*phlegma*), and black bile (*melaina chole*). Phlebotomy was employed because excess blood was the cause of fever and redness. Alkmaion of Kroton (*fl.* 500) recognized the central significance of the brain, in contrast to Mediterranean traditions locating the soul in the liver, heart, or elsewhere. Other texts, including the Hippocratic *Sacred Disease*, and Plato's *Timaios*, followed his insight, but Aristotle's notion of the brain as a somnifacient refrigerator prevailed. The two Hippocratic theories of spermatogenesis derived seed from the male brain or spine (*Airs, Waters, and Places*) or else from all parts of the male and female body (*Sacred Disease* and *On Seed*).

The figure who mediates the transition from Hippocratic medicine is Praxagoras of Kos (*fl.* 300), from a family of religious healers, who taught Herophilos (*infra*). Praxagoras proposed eleven humours to explain health and disease: sweet (*glukus*), mixed (*isokratos*), clear (*hualoeides*), sour (*oxus*), soapy (*nitrodes*), salty (*halukos*), bitter (*pikros*), oniony (*prasoeides*), yolky (*lekithodes*), corrosive (*xustikos*), clotting (*stasimos*), and blood (*haima*). Just as we commonly refer to four or five flavors (bitter, sweet, salty, sour, and umami, the meaty flavor) but acknowledge that they scarcely explain the taste of carrots, Praxagoras' system seems intended as a trenchant criticism of the four-humour theory, which, however, prevailed.

Praxagoras offered several innovative theories on physiology, two of which became standard. Egyptian medicine offers the same two theories, probably parallel responses to similar problems, rather than any diffusion of ideas. Empedokles and Anaxagoras had sought to explain nutrition by positing the presence in food of essential elements (the four "roots" of Empedokles, the infinitesimal powder of all things in Anaxagoras). Praxagoras took another approach entirely, suggesting that the nutritional principle was inhaled *pneuma*, wheseas digestion, although necessary, was essentially corruption.

Praxagoras made a number of connected discoveries and suggestions related to the role of the heart and blood in movement and life. Galen and others cite him as the first to direct attention to the pulse as a diagnostic tool, examining arterial pulsations and specifying varieties of pathological movements. He also was the first known to distinguish veins from arteries, perhaps initially because the pulse could be sensed only in the arteries. He theorized that veins contain blood, but the arteries contain *pneuma*, and create the pulse. The heart is the seat of the soul and thought, whereas the brain is an appendage or excrescence of the spinal cord. The *neura*,[4] originating at the heart, are a refinement of the arteries, which control the movements of the fingers and hands. The whole is a sensible and coherent theory: The soul resides in the heart, the source of arteries filled with *pneuma*, pulsing with that contained life and tapering to the *neura* that control motion.

Herophilos of Chalkedon (*fl.* 275), seemingly the first court-sponsored physician in Alexandria, was a pioneer in dissection and in studies of the pulse. The efficacy of Ptolemy's patronage was not based on funding, because surely fees covered most expenses, but it lay in the resulting intellectual ecology of early third-century Alexandria. The temporary relaxation of the inveterate Greek taboo against mutilation of the corpse was crucial to Herophilos' work; this relaxation was surely supported by the claims of Pythagoreans and Academics that the body is just a bag of meat confining an immortal soul. Herophilos went further, vivisecting criminals condemned by Ptolemy for the benefit of improving anatomical knowledge and surgical practice. Herophilos founded an eponymous sect that endured for three centuries. His followers, perhaps no longer finding dissection in favor at Alexandria, shunned Herophilos' anatomical researches but continued his work on pharmacy and the pulse.

Herophilos continued to use established methods, such as regimen, phlebotomy, and purgatives. He rejected the therapeutic relevance of the Aristotelian concept of homoiomerous parts (e.g., blood, marrow, or sinew) and limited his treatment to remedies suited to instrumental parts (i.e., organs and limbs).

Herophilos' work is marked by an unusual accuracy of observation indicative of autopsy. The reconstruction of the structure of his book, *On Anatomy*, shows that his presentation was systematic: He proceeded from the brain to the digestive organs, to the generative organs and finally to the vascular system. His cranial dissections distinguished features not previously noted, so that his nomenclature partly survives in modern medicine. He also first perceived the nerves as distinct organs and their connection to the brain, and also distinguished between motor (*proairetika*) and sensory (*aisthetika*) nerves. Moreover, it is the nerves that contain *pneuma*, which is what allows them to mediate sensation and motion.

Herophilos provided the earliest accurate description of the human liver, unsurpassed before Galen. Our *duodenum* is the Latin translation of Herophilos' name *dodekadaktulon* for that organ. He investigated other organs, including the lungs and their breathing action, and wrote a monograph on ocular anatomy. His investigation of the generative organs confronted theory with anatomy for the first time. Herophilos provided precise and accurate descriptions of the male *epididymis* and *vasa deferentia* and of the female ovaries and Fallopian tubes. He explicitly compared the ovaries to testicles (calling each pair "twins") and coined the term *epididymis* ("on the twins") still in use. Herophilos sided with Aristotle (*de Generatione Animalium* 1.16–20 [721a26–729a33]) against Hippokratic theories of spermatogenesis, advocating a hematogenic theory by which nourishing blood is cooked up into semen. He also composed *Midwifery*, a treatise on childbirth and gynecology that attempted to demystify the female generative organs.

Herophilos' detailed researches on the anatomy of the vascular system replaced previous merely speculative models, and he amplified the work of his teacher Praxagoras in his own monograph on the pulse. Herophilos refined and delineated the rhythms to be observed and correlated those observations with diagnoses. The cause of the diastole and systole of arteries lies not within the arteries but flows to them from the heart. He borrowed musical metaphors from Aristoxenos (*fl.* 330) to describe the diastole-systole of various pulse types: Infants' pulses are *pyrrhic* (⌣⌣), adolescents have a *trochaic* pulse (‒⌣), those in their prime are in a *spondaic* stage (‒‒), and the old are *iambic* (⌣‒). Herophilos built a calibrated *klepsydra* (water-clock) to time the pulses of the four age groups.

Erasistratos of Keos studied in nearby Athens, probably before ca. 308, was a well-known physician by 294/3, and worked in Alexandria contemporaneously with Herophilos. He contributed less to anatomy than did Herophilos, but offered an experimental outlook and a mechanical theory, consonant with the work of his contemporaries Straton (*supra*) and Ktesibios (*infra*). He restricted the use of humoural pathology and entirely avoided phlebotomy. He preferred prevention to remedy and wrote a separate treatise on prevention. Erasistratos founded an eponymous sect that survived for over four centuries, known especially for eschewing phlebotomy.

Erasistratos' physiology was based on a theory that particles of void pervade all bodies and account for transparency, compression, and mixing (Aristotle *Meteorologica* 4; Thphr. *CP* 1.2.4, 2.5.4; and Straton in the preface to Heron *Pneum.*). Physiological events result from bodily liquids following the void. His metaphors for bodily structure are likewise mechanical: Each part is a three-fold weave (*triplokia*) of vein, artery, and nerve, growing while nourished by the arterial *pneuma*. Nutrition occurs analogously: The stomach compresses nutriment out of food. To demonstrate metabolic loss of matter, he placed a bird and its food in a container, and, while collecting the droppings, monitored the steady decrease of the total weight.

Based on comparative dissections, Erasistratos correctly inferred that the degree of convolution of the brain correlates with the relative intelligence of species; he also distinguished the cerebrum (*enkephalos*) from the cerebellum (*epenkranis*). Moreover, he conceived the heart to function like a pump, analogous to the force pump invented a few years later by Ktesibios: The left ventricle contains *pneuma*, the right contains blood, and the semilunar valves prevent reflux, whereas the bicuspid and tricuspid valves control efflux.

Erasistratos maintained that veins and arteries originate from the heart and that veins contain blood, but the arteries only *pneuma*. Cut arteries bleed because the escaping *pneuma* draws blood from the veins via something like capillaries (*sunanastomoseis*), too small to be seen. Most diseases occur because excess blood in the veins leaks through to the arteries, where it obstructs the free flow of, and therefore is compressed by, the *pneuma*. Many symptoms, especially fever, ensue.

Herophilos had made the phenomena the first matter: Now the Empiricist medical sect emerged and made them the only matter. Based on the thought of Pyrrhon and influenced by Philinos of Kos (*fl.* 250), a student of Herophilos, the Empiricists rejected the growing medical consensus. They offered no new theory or practice of healing but held that observation and recording of repeated experiences brought a measure of assurance. It was neither valid nor necessary to seek hidden causes, because one cannot experience the invisible or know hidden causes. Instead, the physician treated individual cases, minimizing inference and guided by manifest and significant symptoms, that is, any unnatural features of the patient. Those symptoms were the sole valid basis of inference. A disease was a concurrence (*sundrome*) of symptoms, and remedies were applied to symptoms. Anatomy and physiology were excluded altogether, because they rely on intervention or theory and so are invalid as a basis for inference. The Empiricists also accepted transmitted records of experience (thus encouraging scholarship) and analogical inference: Treat a leg wound as one would an arm wound.

In this way, they sought to evade the diagnostic paradox that the untrained eye cannot see. Diagnosis requires the recognition of symptoms, which itself presupposes a theory of health and disease, which they eschewed. As is common with deliberately extreme forms of skepticism, there is an ironic and unquestioning acceptance of numerous common notions: that two instances of a given herb will have in fact the same potency or that two instances in different patients with the same symptom will be amenable to the same treatment.

Local traditions, especially in Egypt and Mesopotamia, continued to be woven into the tapestry of medicine in the Greek eastern Mediterranean for the next two centuries. One significant strand of traditional medicine was the herbalist: From the earliest times, people have believed, often rightly, that in the world of plants, medicines can be found for mortal ills. Many plants do provide medically useful compounds, as modern tests show, so that experimentation by trial and error would surely have revealed numerous herbal medicines in antiquity. Already Homer records the use of the magic herb *molu* (*Od.* 10.302–306) as an antidote and of the Egyptian painkiller *nepenthes* (*Od.* 4.219–232) – probably opium. Theophrastos' *History of Plants* [*HP*], book 9, the earliest known Greek herbal book, gives much practical and prescriptive information on the medicinal uses of plants. Botanists after Theophrastos were primarily pharmacists (*pharmakopolai* or *rhizotomoi*) or else agricultural writers (see above).

Asklepiades, from the Bithynian city Kios or Prusias, came to Rome ca. 120 as an orator but soon transferred to medicine, of which he proved an apt but heretical pupil. Two main medical contributions are recorded, a simple theory and a correlatively simple therapy. He claimed that no physician worthy of the name should ever be seriously ill, and he never was, dying by a fall downstairs in "extreme old age."

Asklepiades advocated a theory according to which disease is caused by a disturbance in the normal and healthy free motion through bodily pores of the microscopic divisible corpuscles (*onkoi*) of which the body and the world are made. Disease was mostly a blockage of this motion, which was to be relieved by treatment causing the *onkoi* to move freely again. Normally, the *onkoi* moved toward rarefied zones (just as the bodily liquids follow the void according to Erasistratos), and the arteries pulsed, dilating because they were filled with *pneuma* drawn in with the air breathed into the lungs. The *pneuma* itself was drawn inward by the rarefaction of the finest pores in the lungs. In a disorder, the corpuscles moved toward and crowded around the affected part, resulting in blockage and dissolution of the corpuscles and consequent disease: infection or bruise, as we would say.

Asklepiades' therapy veers away from a strongly interventionist approach. He prescribed a famously mild regimen involving moderate use of drugs, drinks of wine and water, and remedies such as diet, massage, and exercise. His drugs included a wide variety of ingredients, so that his moderation was in application not in selection. The recipes include a cough syrup, containing expectorants and opium, and an aromatic throat lozenge, containing licorice and tragacanth, which are still used today. He avoided surgery almost entirely and denounced the excessive use of purges, but retained the use of phlebotomy and enemas. He treated mental derangement by the use of music, among other therapies.

TECHNOLOGY

Science is knowledge applied to understand the world – technology is knowledge applied to affect the world (cp. Epicur., fr. 227b Usener;

Polyb. 3.4.10–11). Technology becomes more effective as its practitioners accumulate knowledge, acquire economic power, and achieve sociocultural acceptance. Practitioners were called *architekton*, *mechanopoios*, or *technites* and were highly innovative in water, warfare, ship, and machine technologies. Aristotle argued that inventors were admired "not merely because some ... inventions were useful, but as being ... wise and superior ... ," that is, for understanding *causes* (*Metaphysica* 1.1.14 [981b13–17]), and writers admired technologies behind which lay some theory or account, such as medicine or architecture (cp. Panaitios of Lindos, in Cic. *De officiis* 1.151). Demokritos and others, however, praised innovations prompted by human needs (Diod. 1.16; Lucr. 5).

Some modern scholars of ancient technology, relying on false assumptions, puzzle over an apparent lack of innovation. Technological innovations do not always increase industrial output, nor are inventions, obvious or necessary in retrospect, always obvious or necessary in foresight. Innovation builds on existing knowledge, and larger populations will, all other things being equal, produce more innovations than smaller ones, hence the rate of innovation will normally seem to have been slower in earlier less-populous times. Scholars influenced by Marxist interpretations of history assert that slavery impeded innovation, but it never prevented innovations that rendered slaves more efficient (compare the cotton gin in the American South). Others, quoting remarks in Plato, Aristotle, and even Plutarch, about banausic workers and citing the Greeks' ideological preference for traditional economic and social practices, argue that upper-class disdain for handiwork dissuaded attempts at innovation. Such elite attitudes, however, now weakened[5] and were balanced by praise for technological benefits to civilization,[6] an enduring topic.[7]

The primary technology of any human culture provides water, food, and clothing. Although novel foodstuffs entered cookery and new clothing styles became fashionable, food and clothing technology changed little. In contrast, water technology developed new methods to lift and transport water, and water power was applied to mill grain. (For more on material culture, see Chapter 7 in this volume.) Molded glass was occasionally used, and blown glass was invented near Sidon ca. 50.

Staple crops were grain, grapes, lentils, and olives; numerous fruits, herbs, nuts, and vegetables, as well as fish and meat, were *opsa* ("delicacies"). Barley was parched before grinding to bake *maza*, but wheat needed no parching and made better bread, baked unleavened on ashes or leavened in containers. The vine symbolized peace and was labor-intensive, not capital-intensive. Grapes were trod (filtered through wicker for white wine), and the must was collected into fermentation vats (up to 2,000 liters). Wine was sold new or aged, by locale of origin, and often flavored (with perfume, salt, or pine resin). Shipped in cork- or clay-sealed amphorae, it was served chilled from a *psykter*. Lentils were served as soup, unbaked cereals as porridge. Olives were crushed in a mortar and pestle, by treading in clogs, or under stone rollers. The pulp was squeezed under a five-meter-long lever powered by weights, a winch, or even a screw, and the residue was employed as plaster (Cato *Agr.* 92).

Two innovations are first attested at Olynthos (destroyed in 348 and never resettled): the rotary crusher described by Cato (*De agricultura.* 20–22) and the pivoted-handle hopper mill (45 by 45 cm). The latter allowed continuous grinding and is depicted as male-operated, evidence of the increasing industrialization of flour production. Innovation continued in flour production: by ca. 250, rotary mills (60 cm diameter) had been imported from the West, the larger ones being animal-driven, and by ca. 50, some were water-driven.

Other foods were produced and processed by traditional methods. The mostly vegetarian diet required salt, produced under state monopoly by evaporating brine in salterns and sometimes by mining. Common fruits included apples, figs, pears, plums, pomegranates, and quinces; typical nuts included acorns, almonds, chestnuts, filberts, and walnuts; characteristic vegetables included beans, cabbage, lettuce, onions, radishes, and squash. Beehives were horizontal wide-mouthed terracotta jars with a removable sleeve holding the hive, and the honey was marketed in the combs (*skhadones*): cp. Arist. *Historia Animalium (HA)* 8(9).40 (623b15–627b21). Cheese was made from sheep's, goat's, and even cow's milk, curdled by fig juice or rennet. The curds were often pressed and dried to make hard cheeses, which were grated for consumption. Eggs of chicken, geese, or other fowl were eaten raw and cooked. Fish were salted or sauced, in *garos*, or in brine, and shipped like wine in amphorae. Seafoods also included ascidians (sea squirts), bivalves, cephalopods, and crustaceans. Meat was consumed fresh during the temple-sacrifice of young animals, often sheep, sometimes goats, pigs, geese, or chickens, and, rarely cattle. The butchery began by slashing the carotid artery, the blood being sprayed onto the altar. The heart, liver, and some other organs were excised, cooked, and eaten first, the bones and other uneaten portions were combusted and then the flesh boiled or roasted (Hesiod *Theogony* 535–557). Game such as deer, hare, and even fox was also eaten, as were nonsacrificial animals like dog, donkey, and horse (Hipp. *Vict.* 2.46). Meat was made into sausage or pickled in wine, vinegar, or brine (Hipp. *Vict.* 2.56).

Animal skins were purchased from temples or butchers, cured, and tanned by smoke, oil, or plant juices to produce leather, which was used for shoes, belts, and hats, as well as armor, shields, and scabbards, not to mention sacks and parchment. Dyeing and earlier steps in leather processing, which used urine, produced odors that generated social constraints on workers. Wool was felted to produce clothing, armor, and padding. Cloth was woven from linen, wool, and Egyptian or Indian "tree-wool" (cotton); luxury garments were also made from Koan silk (Arist. *HA* 5.19.6 [551b9–16]). Hemp and goat hair were rarely used for clothing, but hemp was used to make rope. Usually, the women of the family producing the fibers also spun them, and they wove the yarns on upright warp-weighted looms, working elaborate patterns into cotton and woolen fabrics via twill, tapestry, brocade, or other weaves, whereas simpler weaves were used for hard-to-dye linen. Mineral and vegetable dyes colored yarns red, brown, yellow, green, blue, and purple.

Greeks collected, stored, and transported water multifariously and developed significant new approaches to collection and transport. Water served not only as a beverage (preferably flavored with wine) and for bathing and irrigation, but also in industries such as pottery, fulling, dyeing, tanning, and mining.

Cisterns under the whole peristyle courtyards of houses collected roof runoff; bottle-cisterns (2.5 m tall by 1.25 m diameter) stored water in other locations. Wells bored to a 30 m depth (0.5 to 2.0 m diameter) augmented rainwater. Aqueducts brought water from remote sites through terracotta pipes (up to 20 cm diameter). They followed terrain contours, buried a meter deep, or were laid along tunnels. The earliest known siphon (*koilia*), a closed pipe drawing water through a declivity, is at Pergamon (ca. 180). The Pergamene siphon descends 180 m (so the maximum pressure was 18 times atmospheric), and its lost pipes were probably bronze. Other siphons, however, were shallower and usually built of bored stone or stone-reinforced terracotta. Within towns, terracotta pipes distributed water from the fountain house (at the aqueduct's outlet or where the spring flowed). Drains were more often open than closed (Diod. 11.25.3 Akragas, 19.45.1–8 Rhodes). By the fifth century, however, Athens had a large covered drain (Arist. *Ath.Pol.* 50.1) often renovated during the Hellenistic era.

Water pumps or lifting devices include the millennia-old *kelon(eion)* (swape or shadouf, ps.-Arist. *Mechanica* 28 [857ab]), with a maximum 2 m lift, the possibly-Persian *polukadia* (bucket-wheel) described in Vitruvius 10.4, and perhaps the *cherd* (Ktesias in Plu. *Cleverness of Animals* 21 [974e]). Early inventions were the *tumpan(i)on* (the compartmented or "drum" wheel) and the *halusis* (the bucket-chain), described in Philon and Vitruvius 10.4–5. The latter was an improvement on the rope and pulley (giving greater flow) and on the bucket-wheel (allowing operation in a restricted space). Around 260, Ktesibios of Alexandria invented the two-cylinder force-pump, whose greater lift saw service in bilge-pumps and fire-engines (Philon; Vitr. 10.7; Heron *Pneum.* 1.28). A generation later, Archimedes invented the *kochlias* (auger), used where irrigation required low lift and high flow (Diod. 5.37.3–4; Vitr. 10.6).

Water wheels to drive mills were designed by ca. 50 (possibly based on the *polukadia*). The undershot wheel was better suited to fast streams (Vitr. 10.5), whereas the overshot wheel (described by Antipatros of Thessalonike, *Palatine Anthology* 9.418) served where slower streams could be channeled down on the wheel (cp. Strabo 12.3.30, Lucr. 5.509–533).

Greek cities also used water for baths, smaller and shallower than the Romans' (Vitr. 5.10–11). The *balaneion* or *loutron* often had freshwater inlets above one-person basins and sometimes had a larger pool, circular or square (about 10 m diameter and over 2 m deep). Baths had been heated at Sybaris (Ath. 12 [518]), at Athens (Aristoph. *Nubes* 1044–54, *Plutus* 951–3), and at Olympia (ca. 350); new heated baths were built at Arkadian Gortys (ca. 275) and at Chios (ca. 235).

People possessing adequate water, food, and clothing normally also develop the technology of shelter and safety, which includes the production of fire, construction of buildings, and means of defense. Engineers oversaw the rapid development of artillery and warships, as well as continued use of long-established techniques. Without increasing productivity, these innovations greatly altered society by providing new possibilities.

Furnaces, kilns, and stoves were fueled with wood or charcoal (*anthrax*) produced by the partial combustion and carbonization of various woods, especially *aria* or *phellodrus* (holm-oak), in covered pits (Thphr. *De igne* 28–31, *HP* 5.9.1–4; Strabo 3.2.8). Such fuels sufficed for food-cooking, lime-burning, silver-cupellation, pottery-firing, copper- and iron-smelting, and rarely even for making steel (*chalups* or *sideros*: Arist. *Mete.* 4.6 [383a32–b5]). Lignite coal was known and burnt (Thphr.

De lapidibus 12–17; ps.-Arist. *Mirabilia* 33, 41,115; Nic. *Theriaca* 45–50). Lamps were fired with olive oil.

Greeks built houses for themselves and their gods originally of wood, later reproducing wooden post-and-lintel designs in stone (see The Sanctuary Beautiful, The House Beautiful, and The Vault in Chapter 8 in this volume). Metal cramps and wooden or metal dowels ensured tight yet quake-resistant joints. Roofs were untrussed wooden frames, and thus buildings lacked large open interiors; the roof-beams were covered with easily removed tiles. Heavy members, weighing 20 tons or more, were transported in wheeled wooden frames and lifted into place by single-, double-, or triple-masted cranes equipped with block and tackle. Long stone architraves were sometimes reinforced with metal beams.

Structural walls were generally ashlar, whereas retaining walls needed to be polygonal or Lesbian (curve-jointed, sometimes with lead-strip interfacing). Massive city walls now became the norm to resist stone-throwing artillery, although ashlar, sometimes rubble-filled, persisted. Artillery towers punctuated city walls every 50–200 m as terrain allowed or required, and some city-walls enclosed significant agricultural land (as at Assos, Herakleia Latmos, and Messene). Such walls were 5–30 km long and are estimated to have consumed 200 man-days per meter to build. Forts with kilometer-circumference walls defended Attica and other extended territories.[8]

Archaic and classical hoplites had been armored and girded in bronze; soldiers of the Hellenistic phalanx were armored likewise, although corselets of glued linen, boiled leather, and even iron were available. The size of the phalanx and the use of elephants (deployed much like tanks in World War I) rendered cavalry relatively otiose. Armies had been one-third cavalry, but now decreased to one-sixth cavalry (Polyb. 5.79–84, 18.30), and cavalrymen began to bear shields, about three-fifths the diameter of those of the phalanx (100 cm diameter). Light-armed troops served as archers (with composite bows) and slingers. Assyrians deployed military incendiaries based on petroleum, to which Greeks now added pitch, quicklime, and sulfur, directing these ancestors of Byzantine Greek Fire against soldiers, siege engines, and ships.

Traditional siege engines – ladders, rams, and towers – now increased in size and complexity (Figure 23 from Biton, *fl.* 160), whereas the bow was magnified into the catapult. The 40 m tall *helepolis* built by Epimachos of Athens for Demetrios Poliorketes failed to take Rhodes, but succeeded at Salamis and became a model for later towers

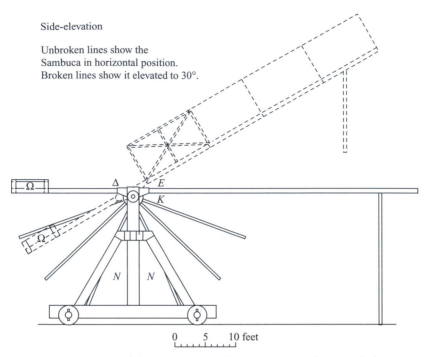

Side-elevation

Unbroken lines show the
Sambuca in horizontal position.
Broken lines show it elevated to 30°.

0   5   10 feet

FIGURE 23. Diagram of the *sambuca*, a Hellenistic siege machine made famous at the Roman siege of Syracuse, 213–211 B.C. [E. W. Marsden, *Greek and Roman Artillery. Technical Treatises* (Oxford, 1971) 93, fig. 4a; reprinted by permission of Oxford University Press].

(Diod. 20.48, 20.91; Philon *Belopoeica*; Biton *Belop.*). The earliest *katapaltes* was the *gastraphetes* ("belly-bow"), that is, a form of crossbow invented under Dionysios I in Syracuse in 399 (Diod. 14.41; Biton *Belop.*; Heron *Belop.*); for a generation this was improved in detail but not essence. A now-unknown engineer invented the torsion-spring catapult ca. 360 (the springs were twisting hair-bundles), and generals after Alexander deployed very large stone-throwing catapults (with ranges up to several hundred meters and shot up to 80 kg). Ktesibios invented bronze-spring and air-piston catapults as alternatives for hair-bundle springs (Philon *Belop.*). Around the same time, at Rhodes, one Dionysios of Alexandria designed a repeating arrow shooter (likened to the "Gatling gun"), driven by a link-chain running on polygonal gears (Philon *Belop.*) – seemingly inspired by the *halusis*. Artillery, both sited and as field pieces, was deployed selectively in the fourth century, but widely in the third and following centuries.

Ships plied the sea under sail, resorting to oars in calms or on attack. They were carvel-built (cp. *Odyssey* 5.246–251), had length-to-beam ratios of about 10:1 for warships and about 4:1 for cargo vessels (Moschion in Athenaios 5 [206–9]) and were fitted with stern-mounted steering oars. The *trieres* (trireme) ship of the line displaced up to 20 tons, whereas cargo vessels were in the 100–1,000-ton range. The *tetreres* (quadrireme), new in the late fifth century and the *penteres* that Dionysios I of Syracuse first commissioned (Diod. 14.42, 14.44) had extra men on one, then two, of the three banks of oars; Dionysios' son had advanced to the *hexeres* by ca. 360. The naval arms race instigated by Antigonos in 315 produced increasingly gigantic *poluereis*, with multiple men per oar. Kallixeinos of Rhodes describes the ultimate, a "40-banker" of ca. 220 (Athenaios 5 [203–4]); thereafter, shipyards reverted to the *hexeres* and the *dekeres*. Admirals decreasingly deployed these ships as rammers, preferring grappling and deck-mounted artillery.[9] The *lembos* and other lighters, with up to fifty oarsmen, impeded and harassed armadas of *poluereis* dreadnoughts. Warships were mostly square-rigged, whereas merchantmen now also had a foresail (*artemon*) and sometimes even a mizzen mast (*epidromos*, cp. Ath. 5 [208d-f], Plut. *Marcellus* 14.8), and some lighters now had fore-and-aft rigs. Sailors preferred running before the wind and reaching but did tack (*podiaion poieisthai*) a few points into the wind (ps.-Arist. *Mech.* 7 [851b6–14]; Nic. *Ther.* 268–270).

Technology is a social product that fosters society by providing means of common life and communication of goods and thoughts. The *polis* continued to be the locus of cultural life (see The City Beautiful in Chapter 8 in this volume). Gigantism was evident in prestige works like the Colossos of Rhodes, built by Chares of Lindos from bronze plates on a stone and iron armature, whose 30 m height was two-thirds that of the Statue of Liberty in New York. The lighthouse designed by Sostratos of Knidos on Pharos Island at Alexandria stood about 120 m tall and served to guide ships into harbor.

Transport between cities was primarily maritime, land transport being far costlier, because roads were mostly mere paths. Short tramways were grooved into stone (10 cm diameter by 20 cm wide), within which wagon wheels of about 140 cm gauge rolled at up to 10 km/hour: the sacred way near Eleusis and the *diolkos* at Corinth for portaging ships across the isthmus [Raepsaet (1993)]. The Seleukids constructed military highways on the Persian pattern (Diod. 19.57.5) because their land-locked empire was deficient in navigable waterways.

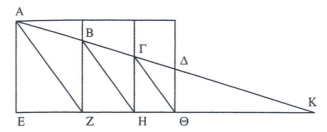

FIGURE 24. Diagram of Erastosthenes of Kyrene's duplication of the cube [G. L. Irby-Massie and P. T. Keyser, *Greek Science in the Hellenistic Era. A Sourcebook* (London & New York, 2002) 31, fig. 2.3; reprinted by permission of Routledge Press].

Most transport, especially the critical grain trade, was still by water. Cities around the Aegean imported grain from Sicily, Crimea, and the Ptolemaic realms, and in turn exported wine and oil; Athens continued to export pottery and honey, whereas Macedonia supplied lumber and pitch. Rhodes always and Corinth until 146 were important trade centers, whereas from 166 to 31 Delos was a great entrepôt. From about 100, the Ptolemaic fleet sailed the open-sea route between the Red Sea and India.

The products of technology provide luxury goods for leisure use, from spices for food and dyes for clothing, to materials for art, science, and book production. Traditional luxuries included murex-derived purple dye and silver from Athens, Macedonia, and Thrace, plus gold from Macedonia and Thrace. The Ptolemies now exploited Nubian gold (Agatharchides in Diod. 3.12–14), and India now supplied many botanicals for food and medicine. Exotic plants provided materials for perfumes. Book-rolls continued to be written on Egyptian papyrus (Thphr. *HP* 4.83.3–4, cp. Pliny 13.68–83), although the effort of the Pergamene kings to break the Ptolemaic monopoly by promoting parchment vastly increased book production. Andreas of Karystos (d. 216) and others developed new machines for setting bones and reducing dislocations.[10] Various texts document scientific apparatus, such as the anaphoric water clock of Ktesibios (Vitr. 9.8.8–10), the *dioptra* for sighting (Archimedes, Hipparchos, and esp. Heron *Dioptr.*), the hodometer probably invented by Archimedes (Vitr. 10.9), the root-extracting slide-rule of Eratosthenes (Figure 24), and the equatorial armillary for solstice determination (Hipparchos in Ptol. *Almagest* 3.1). A shipwreck has preserved a geared luni-solar calendar computer from about 82, capable of computing lunar eclipses.

CONCLUSION[11]

Technology supplied people with means to accomplish tasks they deemed worthwhile and provided sufficient leisure to support literate elites. Old ways of warfare and trade were profoundly altered by innovations; the fundamental technologies of water supply and flour production became more efficient. Machines of war and science demonstrated increasing understanding and control of natural forces. Scientists and physicians, members of the elite, continued to produce new theories and data about the natural world and the human body. Writers challenged the old syntheses on every front and produced enduring achievements in theory (mathematics and astronomy) and in practice (geography and botany) or even both in the case of medicine. The better-known accomplishments of the Roman and medieval eras depend on the work of often unknown or lost scientists and engineers of the Hellenistic era.

BIBLIOGRAPHICAL NOTE

The bibliography on science in antiquity consists primarily in general surveys, topical treatises, and author studies. Most surveys cover all of Greco-Roman antiquity. For a solid, general introduction to Greek science, see Rihll (1999), who surveys all of Greek science. For the relationship between science and society, see Lloyd (1983, 1991); Bowen (1991); and Tuplin and Rihll (2002) on the influence of sociological factors on mathematical study and the social context of ancient science. There exists no recent exposition on Hellenistic science since Lloyd (1973) that concentrates on philosophical and mathematical sciences. For selected Hellenistic sources in translation, see Irby-Massie & Keyser (2002).

Special studies are Cuomo (2001), who surveys Classical Greek to late Roman mathematics. Thomas (1968) offers accessible translations of Hellenistic mathematical treatises. For astronomy, Neugebauer (1975) is technical but essential. For astrology, Kidd (1997) provides text, translation, and valuable commentary on Aratos; Neugebauer and van Hoesen (1959) offer translations and commentary on Greek horoscopes; and Taub (2003) on meterology. For alchemy, see Keyser (1990).

Regarding Hellenistic medicine, von Staden (1989) is especially useful on Herophilos and other Hellenistic medical writers. For primary sources in translation up to Herophilos and Erasistratos, see Longrigg (1998). Von Staden (1989) translates all of Herophilos (and treats his school).

Landels (1978); White (1984); and Schneider (1992) offer useful surveys on ancient technology. For a generous selection of primary sources in translation, see Humphrey, Oleson, and Sherwood (1998). Drachmann (1963) explicates Heron's *Mechanika* and provides much data on other writers, whereas Marsden (1969–1971) remains indispensable for siege and artillery technology.

NOTES

1   All dates are B.C.E.
2   Wikander (2000) 352–4.
3   Habsieger, Kazarian, and Lando (1998), a reference we owe to Philip Thibodeau.
4   *Neura* refers both to nerves and to ligaments and tendons.
5   Arist. *PA* 1.5 [644b22–645a36]; Thphr. *Metaph.* 6 [8a19–20], *Lap.*, and *Ign.*; Poseidonios in Seneca *Ep.* 90.
6   Polyb. 8.5–7, 9.19–20, 10.43–47; Diod. 1.8.
7   Aisch. *Prometheus Bound* 442–506; Soph. *Ant.* 332–372; Hipp. *De vetere medicina* 3, Isokr. *Panegyricus* 32–33, 40.
8   For further discussion of fortifications, artillery, and military developments from the fourth century into the Hellenistic period, see Chapter 13 in this volume.
9   On ships and naval warfare in this period, see also Chapter 13 in this volume.
10 Drachmann (1963) 171–85.
11 We thank James R. Baron, Alan C. Bowen, Julie Laskaris, John H. Oakley, and Dagmar A. Riedel for critical readings and valuable suggestions.

13: HELLENISTIC MILITARY DEVELOPMENTS

Glenn R. Bugh

✑

To speak of military *developments* in the Hellenistic period is to assume that significant changes in warfare or technology justify a separate category called "Hellenistic." To a great degree, this assumption is false. In fact, the most significant developments in Greek warfare took place in the course of the fourth century.[1] To the world of Dionysios of Syracuse, Iphikrates of Athens, and Philip II and Alexander the Great of Macedonia belong the credit for revolutionizing warfare in the areas of mercenaries, infantry, the use of cavalry, and siege weapons. If we argue, with respect to warfare, that the Hellenistic world begins not at the death of Alexander the Great in 323,[2] but with the accession of his father Philip in 359, then we would be truer to the annunciation of a new age.[3] For the most part, the Greeks continued traditions existing in the Classical period but simply magnified them into what one scholar aptly described as "gigantism": large professional (mercenary) armies, greater specialization of arms and armor, terrifying machines of war, and huge ships.[4] War was still settled the "old-fashioned way" – by men fighting men on the battlefield, but it was no longer the exclusive province of the citizen army of the Classical polis.[5] Warfare in the Hellenistic period belonged primarily to the professionals and to the technical experts. And it was certainly the business of kings.[6]

MERCENARIES

In the Classical period, when faced with a military crisis, Greek city-states called out their able-bodied citizens [and resident aliens (metics) in Athens] over 18 years old to form ranks in a hoplite phalanx, a closely packed, serried formation of men each carrying a nonthrowing thrusting spear and armed (ideally) with a round shield (*hoplon*, from whence comes the name "hoplite"), helmet, greaves, and breastplate. They might also carry a short sword. Having chosen wide and level ground to maneuver masses of troops (which explains the number of important battles fought in the plains of Boiotia and Thessaly), they marched against their enemy, who was similarly equipped and arranged. This was hoplite warfare.[7] This style of warfare continued into the Hellenistic period, but in the course of the fourth century, it underwent a number of changes, primarily due to the reforms of Philip II of Macedonia.[8] These reforms would lead to a new kind of phalanx, termed the "Macedonian," and would eventually be adopted by most Hellenistic states (on this, see following discussion). The principle, however, remained the same: mass formations of armed men pushing against each other in the front ranks and thrusting with spears for a lethal blow.

In the course of the fourth century, there also occurred an increasing reliance on and recruitment (*xenologia*: Diod. 18.58.1; 19.57.5) of professional soldiers, mercenaries, called either *xenoi* (foreigners) or *misthophoroi* (men-for-pay).[9] The use of mercenaries was not a new phenomenon in the Greek world; in fact, as early as the Archaic period, Greeks had served as paid soldiers to Assyrian, Egyptian, and Persian royal employers, but these were in relatively small numbers and for a limited term of service. The large number of mercenaries that appeared at the end of the Peloponnesian War and into the fourth century seems to usher in a new age of military thinking. We might mention, for example, Xenophon's famous account (*Anabasis*) of 10,000 Greek soldiers in the ill-fated Persian expedition on behalf of the usurper Cyrus; the huge numbers of mercenaries[10] hired by Dionysios I of Syracuse to fight the Carthaginians for possession of Sicily and to advance his imperial ambitions (Diod. 14.41.4; 43.3); and the mercenaries of the Athenian general, Iphikrates in the early fourth century and those Athenian *condottieri* who followed his lead, Chabrias, Chares, and Apollodoros (Paus. 1.29.7).[11] Even the fourth century Spartan king, Agesilaos, sold his services twice as a mercenary captain.[12] In 372, Jason of Pherai created a huge army, supported by 6,000 mercenaries, to sustain his power in Thessaly.[13] The Phokian generals, Philomelos, Onomarchos, Phayllos, and Phalaikos seized Delphi and its famous oracle in the Third Sacred War (356–346) with the assistance of mercenaries and dared anyone to take it back.[14] Onomarchos and Phayllos became infamous [and impious for plundering Apollo's sanctuary and melting down gold and silver dedications for coin to pay the mercenaries (Diod. 16.56.5–6)] for offering high wages, one and half to two times the normal rate.[15] Philip II of Macedonia defeated the Phokians, liberated Delphi, and entered into southern Greek affairs with a shiny new Hellenic pedigree. Phalaikos, under the terms of a truce with Philip, was allowed to withdraw to the Peloponnese with his 8,000 mercenaries (Diod. 16.59.2–3).

Tainaron, on the southern tip of the Peloponnese, became famous in the late fourth century as a recruiting center and clearinghouse for mercenaries and their prospective employers. For example, during the Lamian War (323–322), the Athenian Leosthenes commanded up to 8,000 mercenaries recruited at Tainaron (Diod. 18.9.1–3); Aristodemos, general of Antigonos Monophthalmos, secured permission from the Spartans to recruit 8,000 *stratiotai* in 315 (Diod. 19.60.1); and in 303 Kleonymos, son of the Spartan king, Kleomenes II, enrolled 5,000 mercenaries in response to an appeal from Tarentum in southern Italy for military assistance against hostile Lucanians and Romans (Diod. 20.104.1–2).

In the wars of the Alexander's generals and throughout the third century, mercenaries were ubiquitous. Kings and cities sought out the services of mercenaries for their armies or garrisons.[16] The market lessons of Philomelos and Phayllos were not lost on the successors of Alexander the Great. In 318, Eumenes, locked in a fierce struggle with Antigonos Monophthalmos, sent his trusted friends throughout Asia Minor and the eastern Mediterranean as recruiting agents, offering top drachma (*axiologous misthous*) for soldiers.[17] According to Diodorus, the pay was so attractive that "many from the Greek cities" joined up. Then, as now, money speaks. When Antigonos and Demetrios Poliorketes invaded Egypt in 306, Ptolemy bribed their soldiers to defect in such numbers that it posed a threat to the entire expedition (Diod. 20.75.1–3).

If one reads selected passages from Isokrates (*Panegyricus* 115, 168) and Demosthenes (*First Philippic* 24), one might conclude that the arrival of the professional soldier in significant numbers led to the demise of citizen armies and the end of the Greek city-state.[18] Some Greeks did react negatively to these developments, but most of the evidence is situated within the context of Athenian rhetoric or comic stereotypes of New Comedy and its adaptors in the Roman world. I have argued elsewhere[19] that Menander's nuanced and often sympathetic portrait of mercenary captains in his comic plays bears little resemblance to the exaggerated, cartoon character of Pyrgopolynices in Plautus' *Miles Gloriosus*.

No one, not even Demosthenes, in the fourth century B.C. seriously questioned the military necessity of hiring professional soldiers to augment a city's own military forces. Aineias Taktikos, probably an Arkadian general from Stymphalos writing in the 350s (*How to Survive a Siege*), warns of the danger of maintaining more mercenaries than citizen troops because of security concerns (12.2–5), but he takes it as a given that professional soldiers have become a regular element in offensive and defensive military operations.[20] Both the risks and benefits were fully appreciated by Dionysios, tyrant of Syracuse, fifty years earlier. In 406, he won the tyranny by introducing great numbers of mercenaries into the city, inciting as much fear in the Syracusan population as did the enemy Carthaginians (Diod. 13.96.1–4). Yet, later in 396, having conquered the Carthaginian city of Motya with the services of these mercenaries, he faced a mutinous group of them and was forced to buy them off with grants of land once belonging to Leontinoi. He then proceeded to recruit other mercenaries to maintain his power (Diod. 14.78.1–3).

Athens manned its garrisons in part with mercenaries as early as the mid-fourth century and this practice continued into the Hellenistic period.[21] For example, *IG* ii² 379 (dated to 321/0 or 318) mentions a *strategos epi tous xenous* in charge of *to xenikon* and "may represent our earliest Attic inscription documenting a force of foreigners in service to Athens and the administrative apparatus to manage it."[22] In 319/18 the Athenians voted honors for a mercenary captain,[23] and an inscription dated to 298/7 records *xenoi* serving with Athenian citizens at the garrison at Sounion (*IG* ii² 1270). Foreign units (*tagmata*) even competed under their commanders, Homilos, Demeas, Isidoros, and Pyrrhos, in two events designated for *ethne* in the agonistic program of the Athenian Theseia in the second century.[24]

Inscriptions from Greek cities throughout the Hellenistic world document the presence of mercenaries in garrisons, either serving as the instruments of control by a king or maintained by the cities themselves.[25] One of the most informative (albeit problematic) documents detailing conditions of mercenary service is recorded in a treaty (dated 263–241) between Eumenes I of Pergamon and his mutinous mercenaries serving at Philetaireia and Attaleia.[26] The negotiated clauses of the inscription include access to low-cost grain and wine, guaranteed leave, back pay, guardianship of orphans, and duty-free rights to leave Pergamene territory. In this treaty, we have concrete proof of the ability of a self-representing group of mercenaries to leverage concessions from their employer or have him face the military consequences. Aineias Taktikos had warned of such dangers a hundred years before, as Dionysios of Syracuse experienced firsthand.

Groups of soldiers found their way into strategic military settlements, particularly in the territories of the Seleukids, and sometimes blended into the landscape through grants of citizenship. In Egypt, the early Ptolemies established Greek mercenaries on plots of land (*kleroi*) with the requirement that these "cleruchs" would serve in the army during times of war.[27] At other times, they farmed their lands. They were subject to taxation. Although legally owned by the king and reverting back to him on the death of the cleruch, by the end of the third century the allotment had become hereditary property. The Hellenistic kings needed manpower, and the mercenaries were ready and willing to fill this need.

Some Athenians were receptive to mercenary service and appear in the armies of the Successors between 315 and 301; for example, in 315, Ptolemy sent the Athenian Myrmidon to assist Asander, Macedonian satrap of Karia, in his struggles against Antigonos Monophthalmos (Diod. 19.62.2–5); in 312, Kassandros appointed the Athenian Lysandros as commander of Leukas (Diod. 19.88.5); in 308, "many Athenians" enlisted in the army of Ophellas (Ptolemy's governor of Cyrene) in his campaign against Carthage (Diod. 20.40.6); and Athenian citizens accompanied Demetrios Poliorketes to Cyprus in 307[28] and shared in his defeat at Ipsos in 301. Some of the captured Athenians chose to enlist in the army of the victor, Lysimachos, rather than return home when ransomed.[29]

"OF ARMS AND THE MEN..."

Infantry

As I mentioned earlier, in the Classical period, the style of warfare was dominated by the heavy-armed infantryman, the hoplite. The other arms, cavalry and light-armed troops (*psiloi*), along with ethnic specialists like Rhodian slingers or Cretan archers, were subordinate to the hoplite and the phalanx. The clash of hoplite armies decided the day. It is fair to say that heavy infantry was still the order of the day throughout most of the Hellenistic period, and the Hellenistic kings were keen to recruit sufficient numbers for their armies. The Macedonians, particularly Philip II, are credited with reforming the hoplite phalanx by a change in arms and armor.[30] Principally, this meant the introduction of a smaller, lighter shield and a much longer thrusting spear, the *sarissa*.

The *sarissa* came in different lengths at different times, from 15–18 ft at the time of Alexander to 21 ft in the second century (Polybios), and carried a small iron head and butt-spike. It was thus much longer than the traditional hoplite spear and required two hands to wield it. The ranks of soldiers were sixteen rows deep, the first five ranks able to project their *sarissai* beyond the front line. The rows from six to sixteen held their spears aloft and provided cover from enemy projectiles. The approaching Macedonian phalanx must have been a terrifying sight![31]

It has been suggested that Philip adopted and adapted a new military arm that was introduced into the Greek world in the late fifth and early fourth century, the peltast.[32] Of Thracian origin, the peltast could be classified as light infantry; he carried a small shield (*pelte*), wore little body armor, and carried two throwing javelins for fighting from a distance. He had proven his worth in the Amphipolis campaign in 422 (Thuc. 5.10.9), but an army of peltasts, under the command of the Athenian general Iphikrates, surprised the military experts by destroying a contingent of 600 Spartan hoplites near Corinth in 390 (Xen. *Hell.* 4.5.11–18). Twenty years later, Jason of Pherai had a very large contingent of peltasts in his army (Xen. *Hell.* 6.1.19). Philip II's Macedonian phalanx may then have constituted a body of "Iphikratean peltasts," although now equipped exclusively with a long thrusting spear.[33]

If the peltast inspired changes in Greek warfare in the fourth century, a uniquely Hellenistic innovation occurred approximately 100 years later. A new kind of infantryman appeared in Hellenistic armies, the *thureophoros*, named after the long oval shield he carried, the *thureos*. Scholars have suggested two origins for this kind of shield, both western: 1) the *scutum* used by Oscan peoples that Pyrrhos encountered during his campaigns in southern Italy in the 270s, and 2) the shield used by the Gauls during their invasions of Greece and Asia Minor at about the same time.[34] The *thureophoros* could fight at a distance with javelins or close in with his sword, *machaira*. This multitasking gave him greater versatility than the phalangite.[35] This type of shield was adopted by the Achaian and Boiotian Leagues during the early third century and is amply attested in gymnasiarchal victor lists on Samos (*IG* xii.6. 179–183) and in the athletic program of the Athenian festival of the Theseia in the mid-second century. The Attic inscriptions preserve the names of the victors for mock combat, the "*hoplomachia en thureoi (kai machaira)*," among various age classes of Athenian teenagers and ephebes.[36]

We close this section by mentioning briefly an elite infantry force, the *epilektoi*, that appears in inscriptions in the late fourth century and into the Hellenistic period.[37] They are attested in Athens, the Boiotian League, and the Achaian League.[38] One Attic inscription records a decree by a contingent of *epilektoi*, who volunteered for service with Demetrios Poliorketes around 303.[39] Affiliated by tribe and commanded by a tribal taxiarch, they appear to be an elite subset of the citizen hoplites, more highly trained, presumably, and serving as a quasi-permanent city militia, analogous perhaps to the ephebes. The Attic inscriptions are contemporaneous with the ephebic reforms reported in Aristotle's *Athenaion Politeia*. They represent an increase in military specialization and professionalism among the hoplite ranks in the late fourth century, perhaps rising to the skill level of the mercenaries. The fact that they issued decrees is a sign that they enjoyed a distinct civic self-identity. The military designation continues well into the Hellenistic period. The tribal competitions for the Athenian *epilektoi* (*euandria* [manliness] and *euhoplia* [good maintenance and use of arms] categories[40]) appear in the Theseia inscriptions of the mid-second century.[41]

Cavalry

In the Archaic and Classical periods, there were only three states that could claim to be genuine cavalry powers, Macedonia, Thessaly, and Boiotia, in great part because of the aristocratic nature of their societies and the availability of horse-breeding (*hippotrophia*) land. By the middle of the fifth century, democratic Athens had also created a respectable cavalry force of 1,000 men (with 200 horse archers) to match its imperial ambitions.[42] Other Greek states, including Sparta, relied on the strength of its hoplite armies or light-armed specialty troops. Sparta, in fact, did not feel the need to create a cavalry force until 424, seven years into the Peloponnesian War. The effectiveness, if not the necessity, of cavalry in support of infantry was not lost on contemporary observers, and this attitude spilled over into the struggles of the Greek city-states in the first half of the fourth century.[43] Xenophon, probably a member of the Athenian cavalry in his youth, wrote two military treatises, *The Cavalry Commander* and *On Horsemanship*, which emphasize the importance of careful maintenance and training of horse and rider. The goal was to create a more effective fighting force. It is well known that Philip II and, even more so, his son Alexander elevated the cavalry to high military importance, in both quality and quantity, greater than the Greek world had experienced and, to a certain degree, greater than the Macedonian kings who followed in the Hellenistic period. Alexander made his Campanion Cavalry a serious strike force, all the while continuing to emphasize the central role of the Macedonian phalanx. He also may have equipped some of his cavalry with a *sarissa*– similar to that held by the phalangites – and so identified as *sarissophoroi* wielding a thrusting lance of up to 15 ft.[44]

Prior to the Macedonian rise to power in the mid-fourth century, cavalry (with the exception of horse archers) was fairly uniform in appearance. Ideally, the horseman carried a javelin (or two) and sword, wore high boots, a Boiotian-style helmet, and a breastplate (*thorax*), and rode without the benefit of stirrups or a saddle.[45] Apparently, cavalrymen in the fourth century did not carry a shield; this piece of armor does not appear to have been adopted until the third century.[46]

In addition to the "regular" cavalry of the Classical period, there developed in the late fourth century and Hellenistic period variations of lighter and heavier cavalry. The heaviest cavalry were called *kataphrak-toi*, which meant literally "fully armored rider and horse." To maneuver with this extra weight required a bigger and more powerful horse than those common in the Greek world; the cataphracts should remind us a little of the knights of the Middle Ages (except the latter had the benefit of stirrups!). This type of cavalry was almost certainly borrowed from the eastern provinces of Alexander's empire, in the Iranian regions. The first Hellenistic king to incorporate cataphracts into his armies appears to have been the Seleukid Antiochos III at the end of the third century. There is no reference to them in his cavalry forces at the battle of Raphia in 217, but under the direct command of the son of Antiochos, they defeated the Aitolian cavalry of Ptolemy V at Panion in 200 (Polyb. 16.18.6–8). In 192, the envoy of Antiochos to T. Quinctius Flamininus could boast of them (Livy 35.48.3) and they figured prominently in Antiochos' army at the battle of Magnesia in 190/89 against the Romans (Livy 27.40.5, 11). In fact, numerically (3,000 on each flank) they represented the largest distinct cavalry contingent on the field. His defeat at the hands of the Romans apparently did not discourage their use in the armies of his successors. In the grand military procession at Daphne in Syria in 165, Antiochos IV Epiphanes included 1,500 cataphracts (Polyb. 30.25.9).

The cataphract will appear again in the armies of the Pontic king, Mithridates VI Eupator (120–63) as he attempted to expand his empire into Asia Minor and Greece in the early decades of the first century. This led to three wars with Rome. In fact, there may have been Pontic cataphracts stationed in Athens and the Peiraieus during the First Mithridatic War.[47] Later in the first century, the Roman general Lucullus faced Armenian cataphracts, and they will survive as a potent cavalry option in the east hundreds of years later. But one point is important to emphasize: They were absent from the armies of Classical Greece and were only embraced by the Seleukid and Pontic kings whose realms touched on eastern lands once part of Alexander's empire.

We now turn to two specialized troops of light cavalry, the *prodromoi* and the Tarentines. They appear for the first time in the fourth century and continue to be attested both in literature and inscriptions into the second century. The *prodromoi*, as the name implies, functioned as a light-armed mobile advance force, as skirmishers, scouts, couriers, and so forth. In his hippic treatise, *The Cavalry Commander*, written in the 360s, Xenophon advised the hipparch to equip his *prodromoi* well and to train them diligently in the use of the javelin. (1.25). These troops were included in the annual review of the Athenian cavalry by the Council of Five Hundred (*Ath.Pol.* 49.1). They are clearly citizens and must represent a special troop recruited outside of the regular cavalry. It has been plausibly suggested that these *prodromoi* were introduced to replace Athens' corps of 200 mounted archers, the *hippotoxotai*, deployed in the fifth and early fourth centuries.[48] A recently published inscription from the Athenian agora shows that, in later fourth century or early third, the *prodromoi* could act as a civic corporate entity, issuing a decree in honor of the two cavalry secretaries (*grammateis*).[49] In addition, references to *prodromoi* appear on lead cavalry tablets found in the Athenian agora and the Kerameikos (ancient cemetery) as late as the mid–third century.[50] This means that the Athenian *prodromoi* are attested during the period from ca. 360 to ca. 260, thereby bridging the Classical and Hellenistic periods.

We also hear of *prodromoi* serving in Alexander's army, but it is difficult to know whether there is any direct connection between the two other than the name. Alexander deployed four squadrons of *prodromoi* in his early campaigns.[51] Arrian reports on their various military activities: reconnaissance (3.7.7), leading the charge at Granikos (1.14.5–7), and participating in the major battles at Issos (2.9.2) and Gaugamela (3.12.3). They were an advanced strike force before the final battle with the Persian king (3.8.1–2) and pursued the king afterward (3.18.2, 3.20.1, 3.21.2). Apparently, they carried a *sarissa* and are referred to in our sources as *sarissophoroi*.[52] The use of this special weapon should distinguish them from the Athenian *prodromoi*, who were customarily equipped with the javelin (Xenophon).

The other light cavalry force in this period was known as the Tarentines. They threw the javelin at the enemy from a distance and were sometimes armed with a sword and a shield (Arrian *Tactica* 4.5–6).

They probably did originate in the southern Italian city of Tarentum, but by the Hellenistic period, the term had come to mean a particular type of cavalry or fighting style, regardless of the ethnic composition of the troop.[53] They figure prominently in the wars of the successors, emerging as a regular element in the armies of Antigonos Monophthalmos and his son Demetrios Poliorketes. In the decisive campaigns between Eumenes and Antigonos in 317–316, Antigonos fielded 2,200 of them "particularly skilled in ambuscade" (Diod. 19.29.2). Diodorus also mentions an advance guard of 100 Tarentines accompanying Antigonos' own body-guard of 300 horsemen (19.29.5). On the eve of the battle at Gabiene in 316, Antigonos sent his Median lancers (*longchophoroi*), 200 Tarentines, and all of his light infantry to intercept Eumenes' elephants before they linked up with his army,[54] and later during the battle, he dispatched the same Median cavalry and Tarentines to seize Eumenes' baggage train, with the goal of forcing Eumenes to withdraw (Diod. 19.42.2–3). In the Gaza campaign of 312, Demetrios was guarded by 100 Tarentines divided into three troops (Diod. 19.82.2). Sources attest the presence of Tarentine cavalry in the armies of Sparta, the Achaian League, Elis, and Antiochos III the Great at the end of the third century.[55]

Tarentines are also amply documented in Hellenistic Athens, first as mercenaries, later as a citizen cavalry corps. An inscription dated to the third century (*IG* ii² 2975) records a dedication by the *Tarantinoi* from the spoils of war (which enemy or war we cannot tell), and in his *Stratagems*, Polyainos 3.7.4 places Tarentine horsemen in Athens during the tyranny of Lachares (300–295). In 1994, a new inscription was uncovered in the Athenian agora that records a decree by a foreign mercenary troop of Tarentines in honor of the Athenian hipparchs and phylarchs in 281/0. Because we know from another inscription[56] that the canonical Athenian cavalry of 1,000 had fallen to 300 men at this same time, it is quite likely that the 500 cavalry sent by Athens to confront the invading Gauls at Thermopylai in 279 (Paus. 10.20.5) included this Tarentine mercenary force numbering 200.[57] By the middle of the second century, the Athenians had created a citizen cavalry force modeled on the Tarentines. *Tarantinoi* are mentioned in the festivals of the Theseia and the Pythais to Delphi, along with their commanders, the Tarantinarchs.[58] It is clear that this specialized force was distinct from the regular cavalry of Athens, whose numbers cannot be securely calculated in this period. The Athenians, by their own experience with mercenary Tarentines and the value attached to their services by other Hellenistic Greek states, must have concluded that they ought to establish their own citizen force of them. I have also suggested elsewhere that these mounted javelin men may have been intended to supersede the *prodromoi*, who had themselves replaced the *hippotoxotai* in the fourth century.[59] The tactical role of an advance strike force is shared by all three.

REALLY, REALLY BIG SHIPS

In the Classical period, particularly in the fifth century, the premier war-ship was the trireme. A long, sleek, light ship, it was rowed by 170 oars-men and staffed by 30 marines, archers, and sailors (with a helmsman) to make a total ship's crew of 200. It was equipped with a bronze ram on the prow to punch a hole in enemy ships or smash through their oars. There are still some questions about the interior arrangement, but most historians of ancient naval warfare believe that the "three" in triêrês refers to three banks of oars manned by one oarsman each and staggered one on top of the other.[60] In recent years, a full-scale replica of an ancient trireme has been constructed and put to trial tests in the Aegean Sea with crews of volunteer rowers. The top speed in these trials has been around nine knots. The *Olympias* now sits in dry dock in the Peiraieus harbor of Athens.

In the fourth century, Greeks began to experiment with larger, heavier ships.[61] Dionysios I of Syracuse is credited with having intro-duced a "four" and "five," that is, a quadrireme and quinquereme (Diod. 14.42.2–3). In the naval records of Athens, quadriremes appear as early as 330/29, quinqueremes not until 325/4.[62] In the *Athenaion Politeia* (46.1), Aristotle assumes the existence of both triremes and quadriremes, but there is no mention of quinqueremes at the Athenian naval facilities in the Peiraieus. On the eve of the Lamian War (323–322), the Athens voted for the preparation of 40 quadriremes and 200 triremes (Diod. 18.10.2; revised text).[63] At the battle of Salamis in Cyprus in 306, the Athenians contributed 30 quadriremes to Demetrios Poliorketes' forces. It is probable that the new "five" simply added two extra oarsmen to the three-bank (trireme) configuration, but that the "four" was reduced to two banks of oars manned by two rowers each, thus forty-four oars on each side.[64] In rapid succession at the end of the fourth century, naval architects began to build bigger and bigger ships, the largest one actually used in battle being a "ten." The greater size facilitated a larger comple-ment of fighting soldiers on the decks along with platforms for artillery (more on this follows). Boarding became as important as ramming, as the heavier warships relinquished speed and mobility for fighting and fire power. The trireme survived in the arsenal of Rhodes, a formidable Hellenistic naval power, and eventually formed the core of the imperial fleet of Rome.

The new look of naval warfare in the Hellenistic period can best be illustrated by one of our best-documented naval battles: at Salamis on Cyprus in 306 between Demetrios Poliorketes and Ptolemy I Soter.[65] Ptolemy had 140 (or 150) warships, the largest being quinqueremes, the smallest *quadriremes*. Demetrios, leaving ten of his quinqueremes to continue the siege of Salamis, sailed out to meet Ptolemy with a fleet mostly composed of quinqueremes, the largest of the rest including "sevens." In fact, his own flagship was a "seven." Having equipped his ships with bolt and stone-throwing artillery, Demetrios advanced rapidly on Ptolemy's lines, hurling arrows and stones as they came within range and then javelins and arrows as they drew closer. The rams then struck home. General melee ensued, men leaping aboard the other ships and engaged in hand-to-hand combat. By all accounts, Demetrios fought bravely on his flagship and drove back Ptolemy's lines. On the other wing, Ptolemy had defeated those opposing him with his heaviest ships, the quinqueremes, but the rest of his forces were in flight or destroyed. This great victory inspired Antigonos and Demetrios Poliorketes to proclaim themselves "kings." The rest of the Successors followed suit within the year.

Demetrios continued to up-size his ships. He had a "thirteen" in 301 (Plut. *Demetr.* 31.1; 32.2) and later "fifteens" and "sixteens" (Plut. *Demetr.* 20.4; 43.3–4). Plutarch characterized Demetrios' vessels as genuine warships (*Demetr.* 43.5), but the same cannot be said for the gargantuan ship of Ptolemy IV Philopator in the late third century – the "forty." Plutarch dismisses this ship for what it was, an expensive toy, intended purely as a cipher for royal power, not war (*Demetr.* 43.4). It is a perfect example of gigantism and self-indulgence, paradigmatic of the Hellenistic kings. Athenaios (5.203e–204d) tells us that it was 420 ft long, 57 ft wide, 72 ft high, and manned by 4,000 rowers, 400 sailors, and 2,850 soldiers. This amounts to over 7,000 men, far greater than the crew numbers for a modern aircraft carrier! As far as we know, it never saw military action.

A monster grain ship was built at about the same time in Syracuse. Again, Athenaios provides a detailed description (5.206d–209e). It was a "twenty" commissioned by Hieron II, tyrant of Syracuse, and built by the genius engineer, Archimedes (who had to invent a windlass to launch it). It required enough timber to build sixty quadriremes! The officers' cabin could hold fifteen couches, and like a modern cruise ship, it had a gymnasium, promenade, and a library. In spite of these (and other) creature comforts, it was still a warship, complete with eight towers (*pyrgoi*) for artillery and a parapet for a catapult (*lithobolos*) that could hurl a 180 lb stone or a bolt of 18 ft long! It had an effective range of 600 ft and was invented by Archimedes himself. The ship was also equipped with other clever and nasty machines of war attached to the masts. Appropriately, it was named "Syracusia." There was only one problem, however; it was too big to safely dock at harbors around the Mediterranean, so Hieron decided to offer it as a gift (along with grain) to Ptolemy (III) – and renamed it "Alexandris." It was pulled up on shore at Alexandria and presumably never moved again.

It is worth noting briefly that the term *cataphract* came to be applied to a covered warship, with decks and sidescreens to protect the rowers. This seems to be an inevitable development in the age of heavier ships, greater numbers of fighting men on board for close fighting, and artillery.[66] The astonishing variety of warships is a hallmark of the Hellenistic world; for example, the grand fleet of Ptolemy II Philadelphos included 2 "thirties," 1 "twenty," 4 "thirteens," 2 "twelves," 14 "elevens," 30 "nines," 37 "sevens," 5 "sixes," and 17 "fives" (Athenaios 5.203d). The number of *quadriremes* and lower were twice this amount. His struggles with the Macedonian king Antigonos Gonatas over control of the Aegean in the mid-third century and the maintenance of his far-flung thalassocracy in Asia Minor and the eastern Mediterranean demanded naval supremacy. His financial resources, as with the other Hellenistic kings, made it all possible. The Greek city-states simply could not compete at this level.

ELEPHANTS

Without much exaggeration, the only truly novel military arm in the armies of the Hellenistic world was the war elephant.[67] It did not appear in the armies of the Archaic or Classical Greek city-states. It belonged to the world of the Far East, to India (or later the continent of Africa), and it is not surprising that the most enthusiastic co-opters of this beast were the Seleukids, who had the most immediate access to them. Seleukos I Nikator kept 500 of them at Apameia (Strabo 16.2.10; C752). The Seleukids even put the symbol of the elephant on their coins. The association between elephants and the Seleukid kingdom even made its way into Roman comedy, when the braggart mercenary captain Pyrgopolynices, recruiting for a certain King Seleukos in Ephesos, boasts of his martial achievements by claiming to have defeated an elephant in India by striking it on the foreleg with his fist (*Miles Gloriosus* 24–30)!

The military use of elephants in Hellenistic warfare was confined to the period from the death of Alexander to the battle of Magnesia (190/89).[68] Alexander had first fought them in the army of Poros at the Hydaspes River in 326.[69] In the campaigns of Eumenes and Antigonos Monophthalmos in 317–316, both combatants fielded elephants,[70] and at Ipsos in 301, Seleukos' large elephant corps screened off Demetrios' cavalry, victorious over Seleukos' son, Antiochos, from returning from their pursuit in time to save his father.[71] This proved to be the decisive turning point of the battle.

In 280, at the battle of the Siris River in southern Italy, Pyrrhos chased off the Roman cavalry, their horses terrified by his twenty elephants.[72] A similar result is documented only five years later in Asia Minor. In 277, a large force of Gauls invaded the territories of the Seleukids. Antiochos I responded with a hastily organized army, including sixteen elephants, some peltasts, and light-armed troops, and met the Gauls at an unknown site in 275. Facing him were 20,000 Gallic cavalry, 80 scythed chariots, and 160 two-horse chariots. Deploying eight of his elephants in the center to deal with the chariots, he positioned the other eight on the wings to attack the cavalry. According to our principal account,[73] neither the Gauls nor their horses had seen an elephant, and terrified by the sight and sounds of the charging beasts, fell back in panic on their own infantry lines before they had even engaged. It was utter chaos, as chariots ripped apart their own troops with their cutting scythes. The elephants trampled those who could not flee. It became known as the "Elephant Victory." Antiochos decorated the war trophy with a carved elephant.

These two episodes demonstrate that elephants carried tremendous shock value when encountered for the first time, but they could also be neutralized by a well-disciplined and experienced army. Alexander the Great commanded such an army at the Hydaspes, and the Romans were not slow to adapt. At the final battle with Pyrrhos at Beneventum in 275, they pelted his elephants with javelins and drove them back into their own ranks. This sealed the victory and persuaded Pyrrhos of Epiros to seek adventures closer to home (Plut. *Pyrrhos* 25.2–5).

Polybios provides us with a vivid account of elephants in combat and the comparative fighting abilities of the Indian elephant versus the African (5.79–86.6). The Seleukid king, Antiochos III, invaded

Egypt and met the forces of Ptolemy IV Philopator at Raphia in 217.[74] Antiochos fielded 102 Indian elephants, and Ptolemy had 73 of African origin. Both kings initiated the battle with their elephants (5.84.1). Some of Ptolemy's elephants fought bravely against the much larger Indian elephants of Antiochos, head to head, tusk to tusk, pushing to force the opponent to give ground. Those who turned to flee were gored. Most of Ptolemy's elephants, however, could not stand the smell and trumpeting of the Indian elephants, nor their superior size and strength, and fled without engaging (5.84.2–7). This reaction threw them back on their own ranks in confusion. Polybios comments dismissively about the lack of fighting spirit of the African elephant, but considering the numerical superiority of Antiochos' elephant corps and their greater physical size, his comments seem unfair. In spite of the victory of Antiochos' elephants, he still lost the battle. Polybios reports that Antiochos lost five elephants, Ptolemy, sixteen; most of the rest were captured (5.86.6).[75] This battle has also become famous for Ptolemy's use of 20,000 native Egyptian troops, rather than Greeks or Macedonians, who were trained in Macedonian phalanx tactics (Polyb. 5.82.4). This marks a turning point in Ptolemaic history.

The last significant elephant force appearing in a Hellenistic army is at the battle of Magnesia-ad-Sipylum in 190/89 between Antiochos III and Rome.[76] Antiochos had a force of fifty-four elephants, the Romans, only sixteen. The Seleukid king also fielded scythed chariots and camels with Arab archers. It was an incredibly diverse and mixed ethnic force (characteristic of Hellenistic armies generally), outnumbering the Romans and their Pergamene allies, but still it failed to achieve victory. The Roman legions again showed their superiority over the Macedonian phalanx.[77] The elephants apparently played no critical role in the outcome in spite of their great size, head armor, and towers manned by a driver and four soldiers (37.40.4). In fact, Livy remarks that the Romans were accustomed to fighting elephants in their African wars, either by stepping aside and hurling their spears from the side, or by approaching perilously close they hamstrung them with their swords (37.42.5). The Romans had learned well since the Pyrrhic wars. Even in flight from the field, Antiochos' troops suffered from deadly and disorderly encounters with their own elephants, chariots, and camels (37.43.9; App. *Syriaca*. 35). Fifteen of his elephants were captured.

The mention of scythed chariots deserves a few words. There had been war chariots in Greece during the Mycenaean period, and they do appear as swift vehicles of transport to and from the battlefield in the Homeric epics. They were also used in processions and panhellenic contests for the elite in the Archaic and Classical periods, but as a weapon of war they did not survive the Bronze Age. They were well suited to the flat, open plains of Egypt and the Near East, but not to the rocky and mountainous terrain that typifies most of Greece. In the end, the high cost of maintenance made them showy symbols of centralized royal authority, not of city-states. Present in the Persian armies that faced Alexander, the war chariot was embraced by Seleukos I (Plut. *Demetr.* 48.2) and by his successors into the second century. We have already encountered them in the army of the Gauls in 275, and they were still being deployed by Mithridates VI of Pontos in the first century. The second century Panathenaia of Athens lists the "war chariot" as a festival event (*armati polemisterioi*), with King Eumenes II of Pergamon winning in 170/69, and two Athenians – both attested as cavalry commanders in the contemporary Theseia – in 166/5 and 162/1 respectively.[78]

Arguably, the war chariot ought to have been more effective on the battlefield, but Alexander had shown how to neutralize them at the battle of Gaugamela. It is perhaps telling that, at the battle of Magnesia, Antiochos had expected his chariots to create panic in the Roman lines, but just the opposite occurred. Eumenes forced the scythed chariots,[79] positioned in the front ranks of Antiochos' army, to flee by sending his cavalry, his swift Cretan archers, his light armed slingers, and his light infantry to attack the horses in open formations and shower them with missiles from all sides. Eumenes' mobile troops easily avoided the panicked and disorderly charges of the scythed chariots. They fell back on their own cataphracts. This action was the first step toward victory for the Romans. The panicked flight of the chariots incited the auxiliaries stationed next to them to flee, and this exposed the whole line, particularly the cataphracts, to the attack of the Roman cavalry (Livy 37.41.6–42.42.1–4).

MILITARY TECHNOLOGY

In terms of military technology, the fourth century must be viewed as revolutionary, and the many clever and deadly machines so closely identified with the Philip II, Alexander the Great, and Demetrios Poliorketes set the standard for the rest of the Hellenistic period. But they were not the first to recognize the practical value of siege machines and artillery. To Dionysios I of Syracuse goes the credit for the invention of the catapult (*katapeltikon*) in 399 (Diod. 14.42.1). Some have questioned this testimony, whereas others have accepted it at face value.[80] What is certain is that Dionysios built mighty machines of war to expel the Carthaginians from western Sicily. He was fully aware of the Carthage's deadly use of siege towers and battering rams against the Greek cities of Selinous, Akragas, and Gela in the years from 409 to 406.[81]

Dionysios was a quick student and only needed the right opportunity to try out his new bolt-shooting catapult and his own siege machines. In 397, he attacked the island fortress of Motya, the Carthaginian base of operations in western Sicily (Diod. 14.47.4–53.5). Dionysios' "engineers" (*architektones*) began the construction of a mole to the island, as Alexander the Great would do at the siege of Tyre in 332. When a Carthaginian relief fleet arrived, they were forced to withdraw under the missile onslaught of Dionysios' archers and slingers stationed on the ships and his land-based catapults. Diodorus comments that this weapon caused "great distress" (*megalen kataplexin*) because it was a new invention (*to protos eurethenai*, 14.50.4). Finally, his mole finished, Dionysios brought up war machines of every type, battering rams, and siege towers, six stories high, equipped with gangways to drop down on the houses. His arrow-throwing catapults – which did not seem to have been placed inside the siege towers as they would later be by Demetrios Poliorketes – kept the defenders off the walls (Diod. 14.51.1–7). Finally, the fortifications were breached, and the city fell. In the siege of the Greek city of Rhegion in 388, Dionysios constructed a great quantity of siege machines (*mechanemata*) and of such unbelievable size that they shook the walls (Diod. 14.108.3).

Having introduced the catapult and siege warfare on a massive scale, Dionysios' military thinking was apparently not readily adopted by the city-states of mainland Greece. Aineias Taktikos, writing in the 350s, confirms the use of large siege machines (*megala mechanemata*), now equipped with catapults (*katapaltai*, 32.8), but fails to suggest that the besieged city defend itself with its own artillery. Perhaps he assumed it. In any case, a technological breakthrough will occur at about this time – the introduction of the torsion catapult, perhaps by Philip II of Macedonia. The old catapult (*gastraphetes*) drew its power from a composite bow, whereas the new catapult used vertical torsion springs of corded human hair or sinew. When the bow was drawn back, the springs were twisted tighter and tighter. After the arrow was released, the springs returned to their former static position. The torsion catapult generated significantly greater striking force.[82]

Philip II of Macedonia is generally credited with having introduced the torsion catapult in the 340s, and even if this cannot be decisively proved, there is no question that he was committed to advanced military engineering, and this fascination was passed along to his son, Alexander, and to the Successors, notably, Demetrios Poliorketes, Pyrrhos, and Agathokles of Syracuse.[83] Military engineers now begin to be identified as individuals, Polyidos the Thessalian and his students Diades, who invented mobile siege towers (Vitruvius 10.13.3), Charias, Poseidonios, Epimachos of Athens, and Hegetor of Byzantion.[84] The sieges of Perinthos and Byzantion in 341/0[85] were a portent of things to come: Philip constructed 120 ft siege towers, taller than the city towers, rocked the walls with battering rams, and mined long stretches of the walls. He deployed a wide assortment of catapults (*oxybeleis*) and rained arrows down on the defenders on the battlements. Fortunately for the Perinthians, they were able to receive reinforcements of men, arrows, catapults (*katapeltas*) from Byzantion to counter Philip's siege weapons. Diodorus (16.74.5) tells us, however, that Philip had prepared a plentitude of arrows, siege machines (*mechanon poliorketikon plethos*), and other devices to carry on the siege. Perinthos could not be taken, however, and Philip initiated a second siege at Byzantion to cut off the supply route. In the end, the arrival of a coalition fleet led by Athens forced Philip to break off both sieges.

This military setback did not discourage Philip from developing his siege machinery, and the most obvious success story was his son's siege of Halikarnassos in 334 and of the Phoenician island fortress of Tyre in 332.[86] His mole, reminiscent of Dionysios' at Motya in 397, allowed him to deploy siege machinery by land, whereas his catapult-mounted ships attacked the walls of Tyre by sea. Here, as at Halikarnassos, a new type of catapult was deployed, a stone thrower (*petrobolos*). This allowed the besieger to breach the walls themselves or destroy buildings within the walls, not just chase off the defenders from the battlements. A catapult was constructed to accommodate a specific weight of stone ball, and preserved examples range from 4.4 kg to 65.5 kg. Examples of catapult balls have been found at Rhodes, Pergamon, Tel Dor, and Carthage.[87] The mother of all *petroi* weighed 78 kg (or over 170 lbs)! This megalithic monster belonged to Demetrios Poliorketes (Figure 25).

Aristotle, the teacher of Alexander and friend of the Macedonian court, recognized that a new age of warfare had arrived in the late fourth century. In his *Politics*, he comments that it is essential to possess the strongest fortifications to survive the new inventions in missiles (i.e., catapult bolts) and siege machines (*tas mechanas . . . pros tas poliorkias*, 7.10.6; 8). He cautions that, as attackers develop new machines of war, so must the city defenders. The Greek word repeatedly used in the text is a derivative of the verb *eurisko*, "to discover," or "to invent." It was

FIGURE 25. The three-talent stone projector of Demetrios Poliorketes [D. B. Campbell, *Greek and Roman Artillery 399 BC–AD 363* (Osprey, 2003) 27; courtesy of Brian Delf and www.ospreypublishing.com].

the ancient equivalent of the arms race. Certainly, he has Philip and Alexander in mind with these remarks.[88] In his narrative of the great siege of Rhodes, Diodorus would say the same things about Demetrios Poliorketes: "Demetrios deeply worried the Rhodians; not only by the size of his siege engines and the magnitude of his army, but also by the king's energy and ingenuity in sieges. For, being "mechanically inclined" [*eumechanos*] and devising many things beyond the art of master builders, he was called "Poliorketes"; for he displayed such superiority and force in his attacks that it seemed that no wall could withstand them" (20.92.1–2). Diodorus continues: "For it was in his time that greatest weapons [*bele*] were perfected and engines [*mechanai*] of all kinds far surpassing those that had existed among others; and this man launched the greatest ships after this siege, and after the death of his father" (20.92.5, Loeb trans.).

The military exploits of Demetrios for the years 307–303 amply justify this praise. During the campaign to liberate Athens from the control of Kassandros' agents in 307, Demetrios besieged his garrison on Munychia in the Peiraieus harbor. For two days, his catapults hurled arrows and stones at the troops defending the battlements and finally cleared the wall for a full-scale assault. Munychia quickly surrendered (Diod. 20.45.5–7).

We have already discussed Demetrios' great victory over Ptolemy's fleet off Salamis in Cyprus in 306 and his use of ship-borne catapults, but he also besieged the city by land with artillery, notably arrow-shooting and stone-throwing catapults of all types (*katapeltas oxybeleis kai lithobolous pantoious*) [Diod. 20.48.1]. The most famous siege machine was the *helepolis*, literally, "city-taker." It stood 135 ft high and was mounted on four large wheels. In each of its nine stories, Demetrios placed artillery: the largest stone-throwing catapults on the lower levels (capable of hurling a stone of over 170 lbs); in the middle levels, the largest arrow-shooting catapults; and in the upper stories, the lightest of the stone-throwing and arrow-shooting catapults. It required 200 men to operate these artillery pieces within the tower. He cleared the parapet walls with a barrage of stones and arrows. The defenders of Salamis gained a temporary reprieve by burning down the siege engines with fire arrows shot from the walls. Demetrios' naval victory, however, sealed its fate, and the city surrendered.

In 305, Demetrios began the great twelve-month siege of Rhodes.[89] In addition to a huge army, he had at his disposal a huge supply of armaments for the siege. He equipped the prows of his ships with arrow-shooting catapults (*oxybeleis*) [20.83.1], as he had done at Salamis the year before. He also refitted (armored?) the lightest of his ships with planks and port shutters, and put long-range arrow-shooting catapults on deck, along with some Cretan archers. Directing his attack at the harbor, Demetrios fastened together two cargo ships and built two tortoise-shaped sheds (*chelonas*) on their decks to house and protect his arrow-shooting and stone-throwing catapults. The Rhodians responded with artillery of their own and equipped cargo ships with a large number of arrow-shooting and stone-throwing catapults of all sizes (20.85.4). The contest for control of the harbor went on for eight days, Demetrios destroying the Rhodian artillery on the mole with his heavy stone-throwing catapults (Diod. 20.87.1), but finally he was forced to withdraw. After a week, Demetrios furiously attacked the Rhodian harbor fortifications again, this time with a combination of fire-arrows, stone-throwers, and arrow-shooters (20.88.1–3). The Rhodians counter-attacked with three of their best ships, ramming two catapult ships of Demetrios. The Rhodians were eventually able to retake the mole and open the harbor. Reinforcements and supplies then arrived from Ptolemy I and Knossos.

Demetrios shifted his siege operations to the land walls. He constructed another mobile *helepolis*, "a city-taker" siege tower, even grander than the one he had deployed at Salamis (Diod. 20.91.2–8). This monster was 120 ft high, weighed 360,000 lb, and was invented by the Athenian Epimachos (see also Chapter 12 in this volume). It was fitted with iron plates on three sides to counter the Rhodian catapults[90] and was punctuated with shuttered apertures for the artillery pieces. Mounted on eight huge solid wheels, it required 3,400 men to move it. It was the terrifying size of these siege engines that prompted Diodorus' attribution of "Poliorketes" to Demetrios (see previous discussion).

At this point in Diodorus' narrative, we learn that the Rhodians dispatched naval squadrons to attack Demetrios' ships and cut off his supply lines. One of these squadrons seized a convoy of cargo ships bringing materiel for Demetrios' siege machines and captured eleven "renowned engineers" (*technitai ton axiologon*) who were specialists in missiles and catapults (*katapeltas*, Diod. 20.93.5). This, too, is a sign of the times – military science and its practitioners were invaluable to warfare.[91] It is no accident that our fullest sources for military technology come from Hellenistic writers like Ktesibios of Alexandria (mid-third century), Biton (third century), Philon of Byzantion (ca. 200), the Roman Vitruvius (late first century), and in the Roman period, Heron of Alexandria (ca. 62 A.D.).[92] This continues a tradition of military manuals appearing in the fourth century (see previous discussion).

As for the *helepolis* at Rhodes, Demetrios filled his nine-story siege tower with heavy and light stone-throwing and arrow-shooting catapults (Diod. 20.95.2), as he had equipped his *helepolis* at Salamis (20.48.3, see previous discussion). With this siege machine, Demetrios was able to destroy the strongest of the towers (constructed of ashlar blocks) and shatter the curtain wall, effectively cutting off movement along the parapet. Heartened by the arrival of relief ships from Ptolemy, the Rhodians positioned all of their arrow-shooting and stone-throwing catapults on the wall to direct their artillery fire and fire arrows at the *helepolis* (20.96.3). Some of the iron plates broke loose, exposing the siege tower to fire, and Demetrios was forced to withdraw his machine to a safe distance. Diodorus records (20.97.1–2) that when Demetrios ordered his men to gather up the spent missiles on the battlefield, they recovered eight hundred fire arrows (*pyrophoroi*) of various sizes, and not less than 1,500 catapult arrows! We learn from Vitruvius that Diognetos, the military engineer of Rhodes, devised a plan to neutralize the *helepolis*: they flooded the approach to the walls during the night, and the tower became stuck in the mud the next day (10.16.7). The goal of a besieged city was always to keep the siege machines as far away from the city walls as possible; this could also be achieved by dry moats (or a series of them as at Epipolai on the heights above Syracuse), fire arrows, or counter artillery fire from the walls and towers. Eventually, Demetrios was forced to come to terms with the Rhodians.

One might expect that Demetrios' reputation suffered from his failure to take Rhodes, but his epithet, "Besieger," was secure. For example, in 303, one year later, Demetrios attacked Ptolemy's garrison at Sikyon, and the garrison withdrew to the acropolis. When Demetrios paused in bringing up his siege machines, the garrison "in panic" (*kataplagentes*) at the prospect of the coming assault, surrendered and sailed back to Egypt (Diod. 20.102.2). In the same year, Demetrios moved his war machines against the garrison on the heights of Acrocorinth. He intimidated them into surrendering by his deadly siege weapons and his reputation as a master of siege warfare (*eumechanos*) (Diod. 20.103.2). The Macedonian tradition of siege warfare continued on in the family of the Antigonids: In 217 Philip V campaigned against the city of Phthiotic Thebes in the region of Thessaly. In his train, Philip V assembled 150 arrow-shooting catapults and 25 stone-throwers (Polyb. 5.99.7).

After the siege of Rhodes, probably the most famous one was that of Syracuse in 213–211 by the Roman general Marcellus. The long-reigning ruler, Hieron II, had devoted much attention to the fortifications of the city. His chief military engineer was the famous Archimedes, a native son of Syracuse. Much of the sophisticated fortifications at Euryalos on the Epipolai plateau may have been his handiwork, although earlier phases under Agathokles and even Dionysios I are probably preserved.[93] It is generally accepted that as artillery became more and more powerful in the mid–fourth and third centuries, the defensive fortifications of Greek cities had to respond with equal sophistication and innovation.[94] These changes included larger and more massive towers, the replacing of great circuit walls with outworks and tall towers with artillery batteries, the indented trace, higher and thicker double-faced walls with solid rubble fill to resist heavy artillery and to support defensive catapults, and replacement of vulnerable crenellated parapets by a solid screen wall or covered *parados*. The massive five-pillar artillery bastion at Euryalos is one of the best-preserved examples, and some of the most elaborate (and appealing) city walls come from the late Classical and Hellenistic periods. F. E. Winter aptly observed, "It is easy to understand why the Hellenistic period as a whole affords no real parallels to the sensational achievements of Philip II and Alexander the Great. Long-developed techniques of attack and defense had simply played each other to a standstill."[95]

In the siege of Syracuse,[96] we learn of a number of siege innovations on both sides, for example, a full description of the *sambuca* (Figure 23)[97] deployed by the Romans to attack the sea walls (Polyb. 8.4.2–11). For the Syracusans, Archimedes directed the defenses with a series of clever devices: various-sized stone-throwers and arrow-shooters, heavier for long range, then lighter for closer action. He pierced the walls with loopholes and stationed archers and "scorpions" (*skorpidia*), small catapults, to shoot through them. Archimedes countered the *sambucae* with special cranes that swung over the walls and dropped heavy stones on top of them. Other pulley and crane devices lifted up the prows of the Roman ships with an iron claw and capsized them into the water (Polyb. 8.5–6.1–7). By land, Syracuse's arrow-shooting and stone-throwing catapults inflicted great damage on the Romans, the effect of Hieron II's money and Archimedes' genius.[98] The Romans now desisted from direct assault and invested Syracuse for eight months. The city fell only when an unguarded wall was scaled at night (Polyb. 8.37.2–11). Marcellus included catapults, *ballistas*, and other engines of war in his triumph (Livy 26.21.7).

For other Greek cities, we have epigraphical evidence of catapult use and training.[99] Athens appears to have had catapults as early as the mid-fourth century.[100] During the Lykurgan period in Athens (335–322), Aristotle (*AthPol.* 42.3) reports that the two-year ephebic program included training in hoplite combat, archery, the javelin, and the catapult (*katapalten*). Although the ephebic program was reduced to one year at the end of the fourth century B.C., these young men still continued to practice in the use of the catapult down to the end of the second century.[101] Inscriptions from 321/0, 318/7, and 306/5 record catapults or parts of them in the storerooms.[102] Still other inscriptions, spanning 200 years of the Hellenistic period, honor the artillery trainer, the *katapaltaphetes*, and at least in one case, we can trace the careers of several generations of Athenian artillery instructors from the same family, for example, Pedieus of Oia.[103] From the nearby island of Keos (Kea), an early third-century inscription[104] instructs the gymnasiarch to lead his ephebes out for practice in the javelin, archery, and the catapult three times a month, reminiscent of the training in Athenian *ephebeia*. A catapult and 300 arrows for the practice sessions are to be supplied by the Council and a competition with prizes organized. Finally, there are inscriptions from the *gymnasion* at Samos that record victor lists in arrow-shooting and stone-throwing catapults in the late third and second centuries.[105]

Continued support for ephebic training by Hellenistic cities tells us that citizen militias still functioned in a world of professional soldiers, mercenaries, and the great and diverse standing armies of the competing kings. Recent scholarship[106] has argued that the city-state and its institutions did not "decline" or disappear during the Hellenistic period; the polis lived on, still cherishing its autonomy and independence (see Chapter 3 in this volume). In this world of near-constant war, the independent Greek cities and the leagues maintained their military readiness, either for local and regional struggles or to leverage concessions from the kings. The *ephebeia* and the Hellenistic *gymnasion* continued to convert young men into soldiers.[107] The quasi-military festivals, like the Theseia or Panathenaia in second-century Athens, showcased and encouraged the military ethos of their citizens. And they hired mercenaries to man their garrisons and to augment their citizen forces, just as they had done in the past. In the end, the military developments of the Hellenistic period were extensions and expansions of the great age of military innovation in the fourth century. Gigantism and specialization were but stages in a process that defies sharp historical periodization.

"Graecia Capta Ferum ..."

In the end, it didn't make much difference what incredible war machines or specialized and diverse arms the Hellenistic kings deployed on the battlefield; the wars were still won by the Romans. By the middle of the second century, they had eliminated the Antigonid kingdom and emasculated the Seleukid kingdom. Ptolemaic Egypt was not absorbed into the Roman Empire until 30, but Egypt was a *de facto* dependency of Rome as early as 169. The question has always been, why didn't the Hellenistic kings do better against the Romans? Fortunately, we possess an acute analysis from Polybios who knew both systems firsthand. After the battle of Kynokephalai in 197, the preeminent Hellenistic Greek historian (see Chapter 6 in this volume) pauses in his narrative to compare the Roman legion to the Macedonian phalanx (18.28–32). His explanation has become commonplace: on clear and level ground, with no physical obstructions to break up the tight formation, the phalanx should be irresistible. But on uneven and obstructed terrain, the Roman legion was more flexible, could operate efficiently in smaller divisions (maniples), and its soldiers were more adaptable to the varying conditions. There are of course other factors,[108] but one can only wonder how Alexander the Great might have fared at the battle of Magnesia or Pydna. It has recently been argued[109] that the Hellenistic kings did try to respond to changing military realities by reforming their infantry more along Roman lines in the 160s, but it was obviously too little, too late. The Hellenistic world now belonged to Rome.

BIBLIOGRAPHICAL NOTE

For a concise and still useful introduction to military developments in the Hellenistic period, see Tarn (1930). The masterly two-volume study by Launey, *Recherches sur les armées hellénistiques* (1949–1950) has been reprinted and updated in its bibliography (1987). The five-volume series of studies by Pritchett (1971–1991) on Greek warfare has material relevant to the Hellenistic period. For more recent surveys on the subject, see the balanced essays by the French scholars, Lévêque (1968) and Préaux (1978), and the chapters by Garlan (1984) and Connolly (1984) in the *Cambridge Ancient History* series. Hamilton (1999); Shipley (2000); and Baker (2003) offer brief but informed discussions of select topics. The latest word on the subject, with helpful bibliography, is Chaniotis, *War in the Hellenistic World. A Social and Cultural History* (2005). As the title suggests, however, he has chosen to omit tactical and technical topics. Soon to be released is *The Cambridge History of Greek and Roman Warfare*, an anthology of original essays by international scholars on ancient military matters, including chapters by N. V. Sekunda and J. E. Landen on aspects of warfare in the Hellenistic period. I wish to express my gratitude to both for prepublication access to their manuscripts.

For mercenaries, see the standard work by Parke (1933), now supplemented by Marinovic (1988); McKechnie (1989); Baker (1999); and Trundle (2004) for the periods down to Alexander the Great. Only Griffith (1935); Launey (1949–1950); and Couvenhes (2004) focus exclusively on the Hellenistic period. For the Macedonian military system, see Adcock (1967); Snodgrass (1999); de Souza (2001); and Hatzopoulos (2001). The standard work on peltasts remains Best (1969). For cavalry developments, see Bugh (1988); Spence (1993); Worley

(1994); Gaebel (2002); and Corrigan (2004). Scullard (1974) remains basic for elephants in the Greek and Roman worlds.

For ships and naval warfare, see Casson (1991) and Morrison and Coates (1996), with earlier bibliography. For the special case of Rhodes, see Berthold (1984) and Gabrielsen (1997). On the topic of fortifications, consult Winter (1971); Garlan (1974); Lawrence (1979); Adam (1982); van de Maele & Fossey (1992); McNicoll (1986) and (1997); and Baker (2000). For the special case of Attic border forts and garrisons, see Ober (1985) and (1992); Munn (1993); Pouilloux (1954) and Petrakos (1999) [Rhamnous]; Couvenhes (2000); and Daly (2001). For siege machines and artillery, the standard works are Marsden (1969–1971) and Garlan (1974), the former providing a concise historical survey and texts and translations of the poliorcetic writers, Biton, Philon of Byzantion, and Heron of Alexandria; the latter, a text and French translation of Philon's *Poliorketika*. A translation of this work can also be found in Lawrence (1979). See Whitehead (1990) for translation and commentary of Aineias Taktikos. For the relevant chapters (Bk. 10, Chs 10–16) in Vitruvius' *Ten Books on Architecture*, see Rowland (1999) for translation, commentary, and illustrations. Very helpful for the general reader and richly illustrated are the two Osprey books by Campbell (2003a), and (2003b). Van Wees (2004) 138–45 provides a brief discussion, with useful illustrations, of siege warfare (see also on "mercenaries," pp. 71–6).

For the Hellenistic *ephebeia* in Athens, see Pélékidis (1962) and Burckhardt (2004); for Asia Minor, see Chankowski (2004). (A monograph on this topic is promised by the same author (Chankowski, in press)). For an important collection of papers on the Hellenistic gymnasion, see Kah and Scholz (2004), particularly Kah (2004) 47–90 and Hatzopoulos (2004) 91–6, for military training.

NOTES

1 Gaebel (2002) 283.
2 All dates in this chapter are B.C. unless specifically noted.
3 A case could be made that Dionysios I of Syracuse was the progenitor of the new age.
4 Préaux (1978) 329.
5 Ma (2000) has argued for the continued investment by Hellenistic *poleis* in maintaining their citizen militias.
6 See Austin (1986).
7 Snodgrass (1999).
8 Snodgrass (1999), Chapter 5.
9 Parke (1933); Baker (1999) 240–55; and now Trundle (2004).
10 Diod. 14.78.3 mentions 10,000 in 396 B.C.

11 See Pritchett (1971–1991), II (1974) 117–25.

12 See Cartledge (1987) 314–30.

13 Xen. *Hell.* 6.1.5; Parke (1933) 100–4.

14 Diod. 16.24.2; 25.1; 28.1; 32.4; 36.1; 37.2.

15 Diod. 16.25.1; 30.1; 36.1.

16 See Griffith (1935) and Couvenhes (2004). On citizen garrisons and their commanders in Asia Minor, see LaBarre (2004) 221–48.

17 Diod. 18.61.4–5; Plut. *Eumenes* 12. On the broader issue of mercenary payments in the Hellenistic period, see Krasilnikoff (1992) 23–36.

18 For a recent study of Athenian citizens as soldiers in the fourth century, see Burckhardt (1996).

19 Bugh (in press).

20 See 13.1–4; 18.8, 13, 22, 29; 23.11; 24.4; 28.5; 29.4.

21 See Daly (2001) and Petrakos (1999), vol. II, for garrison inscriptions from the Attic deme of Rhamnous.

22 Daly (2001) 270.

23 Woodhead (1997), no. 102.

24 *IG* ii² 956.13, I.53–55; 957.8, I.29–31; 958.11, I.50–52; 960.I.15–18; 961.I.15–18.

25 For summary and interpretation, see Chaniotis (2005) 88–93.

26 Text: *OGIS* 266; translations by Austin (1981) no. 196 and Bagnall and Derow (2004), no. 23. Discussion by Chaniotis (2005) 86–8.

27 For discussion, see also Chapters 2 and 5 in this volume.

28 Diod. 20.50.3. After Demetrios' victory at Salamis, he dedicated 1,200 suits of armor from the spoils to the Athenians (Plut. *Demetr.* 17.1).

29 *IG* ii² 657. For discussion, see Habicht (1997a) 78–81.

30 See Snodgrass (1999), Chapter 5; Le Bohec-Bouhet (1999) 257–75; and Sekunda (in press).

31 For an acute analysis after Philip's defeat at Kynoskephalai in 197, see Polyb. 18.29–33.

32 See Best (1969); Snodgrass (1999); and Sekunda (in press).

33 So Best (1969) 139–42 and Sekunda (in press).

34 Sekunda (in press).

35 Ma (2000) 354–57.

36 *IG* ii² 957.II.49–61; 958.II.69–70; 73–74. See Bugh (1992b) and Kah (2004) 62. On age classes in the Theseia, see Kennell (1999) 249–62.

37 Not to be confused with the elite 1,000-man cavalry contingent in the Seleukid army also referred to as *epilektoi* (Polyb. 30.25.8).

38 For bibliography, see Ma (2000) 344 and n. 38. He refers to them as "young elite troops." See also Launey (1949–1950) 1054.

39 *ISE.* I, no. 7. For other inscriptions referring to Athenian *epilektoi* in the late fourth century, see *IG* ii² 680 (*SEG* 33.144) (of the tribe Antiochis) 1209, and Woodhead (1997), no.105 (of the tribe Kekropis).

40 For translation of these terms, see Chaniotis (2005) 50.

41 *IG* ii² 956, 12–3; I.48–53; 957.I.26–28; 958, 10; I.44–49; 960.I.11–14; 961.9–14. For summary discussion of the Theseia, see Kah (2004) 75–7.

42 See Bugh (1988) 39–78.

43 Gaebel (2002) argues that the early fourth century is critical for the rise of cavalry in the Greek world.

44 For discussion and bibliography, see Corrigan (2004).

45 Xen. *On Horsemanship* 12. See Anderson (1961).

46 See Sekunda (in press). The best illustration of Macedonian cavalry carrying shields can be found on the trophy pillar relief at Delphi by L. Aemilius Paullus to commemorate his victory over Perseus, king of Macedonia, in 167 [see Kähler (1965), plates 16–19].

47 Bugh (1992a) 114–9.

48 Sekunda (1986) 54.

49 Bugh (1998) 83–90.

50 Bugh (1998) 88 for discussion and bibliography.

51 For discussion, see Worley (1994) 155–7.

52 Arrian 1.14.1, 6; 3.12.3; Curtius Rufus 4.15.13. See Corrigan (2004) for discussion.

53 For standard discussion, see Griffith (1935) 246–50.

54 Diod. 19.39.2–6. Antigonos' plan almost succeeded were it not for the expeditious arrival of Eumenes' relief column of 1,500 of his "strongest" (*kratistous*) cavalry and 3,000 light infantry.

55 Griffith (1935) 247. For example, Antiochos III had a force of Tarentine cavalry at the battles of Panion in 200 (Polyb. 16.18.7) and of Magnesia in 190/89 (Livy 37.40.13).

56 Threpsiades and Vanderpool (1963) 99–114 (=*SEG* 21.525; *ISE*. I, no.16)

57 For text and discussion, see Camp (1996) 252–8. For additional notes and clarifications to the text, see Parker (1997) 136 and Habicht (1997b) 121–4.

58 For epigraphical sources and discussion, see Bugh (1988) 197–8 and (1998) 88–9.

59 Bugh (1998) 89.

60 Morrison and Coates (1996).

61 For a learned discussion of types of Greek warships, see Morrison and Coates (1996) 255–77.

62 *IG* ii² 1627.275–278; ii² 1629.808–812.

63 Bosworth (2003b) 15 rejects Morrison and Coates' (1996) attempt to retain Diodorus' text reading of 40 triremes and 200 quadriremes.

64 Morrison and Coates (1996) 267–9.

65 Diod. 20.49–52; Plut. *Demetr.* 15–16. For modern account, see Morrison and Coates (1996) 22–30. Cf. the detailed account of the naval battle between Philip V of Macedonia and Attalos I of Pergamon near the island of Chios in 201/0 B.C. [Polyb. 16.2–7] and Morrison and Coates (1996) 78–85.

66 Morrison and Coates (1996) 369–70, on the effect of powerful catapults: "the need for what amounted to armoured decks could have been a significant factor in encouraging the development of heavier ships."

67 The standard treatments are Tarn (1930) 92–100 and Scullard (1974). See also Gaebel (2002) 295–9.

68 Tarn (1930) 92.

69 Holt (2003).

70 Antigonos had sixty-five (Diod. 19.27.1); Eumenes, 114 (Diod. 19.28.4, 40.4)

71 Plut. *Demetr.* 29.3–4. Diod. 20.113.4 specifies 480 elephants; Plut. *Demetr.* 28.3, only 400.

72 Plut. *Pyrrhos* 17. Cf. 21.7 where in the subsequent battle of Asculum, the Romans had to yield before the force of Pyrrhos' elephants no matter how valorous they

fought. In his *de Rerum Natura* 5.1302, Lucretius would call them *boves lucas turrito corpore* ("Lucanian cows with turrets").

73 Lucian, *Zeuxis* 8–11. Lucian was a second-century-A.D. sophist.

74 For succinct account, see Bar-Kochva (1976) 128–41.

75 Scullard (1974) 142 argues that the figures cannot be correct.

76 The principal sources are Livy 37.37–44 and Appian *Syriaca* 30–36, based on Polybios' lost account. For discussion, see Bar-Kochva (1976) 163–73.

77 See Polybios' (18.28–32) famous account of the strengths and weaknesses of each.

78 Tracy and Habicht (1991) 189, col. I.37–38; col. II.36–37; col. III.25–26. Eumenes enjoyed Athenian citizenship, being enrolled, appropriately, in the tribe Attalis. For the two Athenian horsemen, see Tracy and Habicht (1991) 206–7.

79 Livy 37.41.6–8 provides a vivid description of them.

80 Marsden (1969–1971), I accepts it; Campbell (2003a) 3–7 suggests that it applies only to the *gastraphetes* (belly-shooter), a one-man winched-pulled cross-bow-type weapon.

81 See Diod. 13.54.7, 55–57; 85.5.

82 For discussion, see Marsden (1969–1971), I and Campbell (2003a) 8–15.

83 For the Macedonian legacy in advanced artillery, see Marsden (1977) 211–23 and Keyser (1994) 27–59. For Agathokles' brutal siege at Utica, see Diod. 20.54.2–7.

84 For military engineers, see Garlan (1974) 207–11 and Winter (1971) 318: "Technical writers of later centuries themselves seem to have recognized the second half of the fourth century as the age of the greatest innovaters."

85 Diod. 16.74.2–77.3. See Marsden (1969–1971), I, 100–1.

86 Marsden (1969–1971), I, 102–3 and Keyser (1994) 40–50.

87 See Campbell (2003a) 15–22.

88 See Le Bohec-Bouhet (1999) 269–74.

89 For the principal ancient account, see Diod. 20.81–88, 20.91–100. For modern summaries, see Marsden (1969–1971), I, 105–8; Berthold (1984) 61–80; de Souza (1999) 43–6; Préaux (1978), vol. 1, 329–31: Winter (1971) 185–209, and on the Hellenistic fortifications of Rhodes: Winter (1992) 185–209.

90 Vitruvius (10.16.4) claims that it was reinforced with goatskins and rawhide to be able to withstand the impact of a 360 lb catapult ball!

91 Vitruvius recounts the story of the competition of the two architects, Diognetos and Kallias, for the position of military engineer for Rhodes (10.16.3–8)

92 For texts and translations of these writers, see Bibliographical Note.

93 Winter (1963) 363–87.

94 Garlan (1974); McNicoll (1986) 305–11 and (1997); Winter (1971); Lawrence (1979); Adam (1982); and Ober (1992) 147–69. For Attika, see Ober (1985) and Munn (1993).

95 Winter (1971) 331.

96 The ancient sources are Polybios, Livy, and Plutarch's biography of Marcellus (14.2–19). For summary, see Marsden (1969–1971), I, 108–9.

97 A pulley-operated covered assault bridge that drops down over the walls from specially modified and conjoined quinqueremes.

98 See Polyb. 8.7.1, 7; Livy 24.34.2, 13; Plut. *Mar.* 14.4, 9.

99 For a concise survey, see Launey (1949–1950) 830–34 and Marsden (1969–1971), I, 67–77.

100 *IG* ii² 1422, line 9, and 120, line 37 (redated to 353/2: *Hesperia* 7 (1938) 288.

101 For example, *IG* ii² 1006, line 65, dated to 123/2. However, we also learn from the same inscription that catapult training had lapsed for some years and that the ephebes repaired an old stone-throwing catapult. On the Attic *ephebeia* in the Hellenistic period, see Pélékidis (1962); Burckhardt (2004)193–206; and Tracy (2004) 207–10. For ephebic training in Asia Minor, see Chankowski (2004) 56–76.

102 *IG* ii² 1469; 1475; and 1487.

103 For sources and discussion, see Marsden (1969–1971), I, 71–3. Augmented by Tracy (1982)157–61.

104 *Syll.*³ 958.

105 *IG* XII.6.179–183.

106 Ma (2000) 337–76; Chankowski (2004); and Kah (2004) 47–90.

107 See Kennell (2003).

108 See Sekunda (in press).

109 Sekunda (2001).

14: GREEKS AND NON-GREEKS

Erich S. Gruen

⚮

W hatever else Greeks were, they were not barbarians – at least not by their own lights. After all, they spoke Greek. Others spoke in unintelligible tongues, thus sounding to Greek ears as so much "bar-bar-bar" (Strabo, 14.2.28). The term "barbarian" served to demarcate the Hellenic world from the non-Hellenic. It provided a useful device to establish (or construct) the distinctiveness of Greek values and character. When the term first came into fashion remains obscure. Its usage was rare indeed prior to the fifth century B.C.E. when the invasion of Persia galvanized the Greeks to develop a sharper sense of their own collective identity.[1] The initial connotation of "barbarian" may have been quite neutral and innocent, nothing more than "gobbledy-gook speaker." But in the fifth and fourth centuries, it began to carry a lot of extra baggage. It might suggest cultural or intellectual inferiority, lack of refinement, various insensibilities, brutality, chicanery, and a tendency to embrace despotism rather than the rule of law.[2]

It was certainly better to be a Greek than a barbarian. A famous saying, ascribed both to Thales and to Socrates, gave thanks to the gods for three things: "That I was born human not an animal, a man not a woman, and a Greek not a barbarian!" (Diog. Laert. 1.3). Whether either of those philosophers made such a statement we cannot know. But the ascription appears in a Hellenistic text, by the biographer Hermippos of Smyrna in the third century B.C.E. And it earned an echo in rabbinic writings – with, of course, a Jewish twist: a prayer of thanks to the Lord "who did not make me a slave, did not make me a woman, and did not make me a goy."

Climate alone produced essential differences between Europeans and Asians. Some Greeks, at least, had convinced themselves of the fact. That notion appears in a late fifth-century treatise, *Airs, Waters, Places*, attributed to Hippocrates. The uniformity of their seasons renders Asians soft and unwarlike, idle and prone to accept rule by despots; violent changes of climate make Europeans tougher, braver, self-reliant, and less inclined to submit to monarchs.[3] This idea gains sharper definition in Aristotle's *Politics*. He specifies the Greeks in particular as beneficiaries of the ideal geographical and climatic conditions. Other Europeans endure cold climates and may be hardy and tough, but they are stupid and incapable of governing themselves, let alone anyone else. Asians enjoy the warm weather and possess some intelligence, but they are enervated and lazy, readily enslaved by their rulers. Greeks hold the middle ground, both intelligent and spirited, thus, a free people capable of governing all mankind (1327b.23–24). Aristotle indeed may have practiced what he preached. A report has it that he advised his pupil Alexander the Great to be a leader for the Greeks but a master for the barbarians: Treat the former as friends and kinsmen, the latter as animals or plants (Plut. *Mor.* 329b). Alexander did not take the advice.

Climate, nature, and ethnicity were not necessarily determinative. Isokrates famously asserted that the name "Greeks" refers not to a race (*genos*) but to a mind-set (*dianoia*) and that the designation belongs to those who share our culture (*paideusis*) rather than our nature (*physis*) (*Panegyricus* 50). This implies that the Hellenic achievement was open to non-Greeks – but also that few would earn it. Isocrates, writing in support of a pan-Hellenic crusade against Persia, kept the distinction sharp.

The dichotomy, however, is much fuzzier than such statements, so often quoted, might suggest. One needs only to read Herodotos. To be sure, the word *barbaros* or a form thereof appears with great frequency in his text. But the vast majority of instances occur in the second half of his history when he treats the Persian war and the contrast between combatants in critical ways.[4] And this polarity barely, if at all, affects his ethnography. As is well known, Herodotos shows an even-handedness, indeed occasionally great admiration, for the traits, character, and accomplishments of non-Greek peoples, notably Egyptians, Persians, and Phoenicians, even Scythians, so much so that Plutarch later went so far as to label him a *philobarbaros* (*De Mal. Her.* 12). Of course, Plutarch here buys into the standard dichotomy. Herodotos, in fact, had a much more subtle and complex take on the interplay of Greeks and non-Greeks.[5] Plato also questioned the simplistic division of Greeks and barbarians, pointing out the multitudinous differences among the latter (*Politicus* 262d).

Greeks, as is clear, spoke with many voices. Even the great enemy of Hellas, the Persian regime, its rulers and its people, was viewed through diverse lenses. Xenophon wrote an encomiastic biography of Cyrus the Great, imaginary and fictitious, but all the more telling for that. The Persian monarch was selected as the image of the ideal ruler and the Persian empire as exemplary of admirable rule.[6] For most Greeks like Isokrates, Persia had become identified with luxury, servility, and decadence, an inviting target for attack (e.g., *Paneg.* 150–151). But Herakleides Pontikos, a pupil of Plato, writing on the eve of the Hellenistic age, pronounced the Persians and Medes as the noblest and bravest of barbarians: The enjoyment of pleasure is the mark of a liberal spirit (Athenaios, 12.512a–b). Alexander the Great had a mandate for conquest of the Persian empire. But, as is well known, the conqueror displayed a growing affinity for the institutions, practices, and values of the conquered. That may have irritated some of his Macedonian officers and troubled a few of his Greek advisers. But it was not wholly out of tune with Hellenic attitudes. The Alexandrian polymath Eratosthenes in the third century heaped praise on the king for that broad-minded attitude and for rejecting the crabbed advice of Aristotle. Eratosthenes took direct aim at those who would divide the world into Greeks and barbarians. If a division is to be made, men must be judged for their virtues and vices; there are plenty of admirable barbarians – take Indians and Arians, even Romans and Carthaginians – and plenty of bad Greeks (Strabo 1.4.9).

The polyphonic chorus predominates. How to interpret it? The idea that the Hellenistic age brought with it a wider tolerance for the outsider does not supply a satisfactory answer. As we have seen, diverse attitudes can be found – and not infrequently – in writers of the Classical era. Even the snide onomatopoetic explanation of the term *barbaros*, which was proffered by a Hellenistic writer (Strabo), need not be accurate for its origins. It looks like a direct borrowing from the Babylonian word *barbaru* that carries the meaning of "foreign," hence, perhaps not a Greek invention. Certainly others than Greeks employed it with a pejorative connotation. The Egyptians applied the designation to anyone who did not speak *their* language (Herod. 2.158). And the Greek/barbarian contrast still held in the Hellenistic period. Polybios employs it with regularity in regard to Gauls, Carthaginians, Spaniards, Parthians, and others – though rather more gingerly in regard to Romans.[7] Strabo can couple Greeks and Romans as distinct from rude barbarians, but he makes no secret of his firm conviction for Greek cultural superiority.[8] The increased contacts among peoples in the Hellenistic world of the Mediterranean bred greater familiarity but could still breed contempt. Non-Greek writers might compose their works in Greek – as did the Egyptian Manethon, the Babylonian Berossos, the Phoenician Sanchoniathon, the Jewish authors of the Septuagint, the Roman Fabius Pictor, and even king Artavasdes of Armenia. But Greeks did not employ the literary languages of the barbarian – to their cost.[9] So, the passage of time and the expansion of Hellas may not have marked quite so dramatic a change in the perception of the foreigner as we sometimes think. On this score, the conquests of Alexander were less than a watershed.

The prevailing impression is one of divergent and discordant, yet somehow interlocking and overlapping, constructs of Greeks and non-Greeks – from both sides. And the constructs respected no chronological boundaries. How best to approach this interplay of mutual perceptions? One avenue in particular will be pursued here: the examination of inventive fictions that crossed ethnic and cultural divides. A selective sample of such fictions can illuminate this highly complex process.

The Hellenic hero Perseus, slayer of the Gorgon and rescuer of Andromeda from the sea-monster, supplies a striking instance. Alexander the Great claimed him as an ancestor (Arrian, 3.3.2; Pliny, N.H., 15.46) and so did the Ptolemies.[10] Linkage with a celebrated mythological figure from the Greek past had obvious advantages for Hellenistic rulers. But much more than that. Perseus carried multiple connotations that commingled Hellas with Egypt and Persia.

The hero had Egyptian roots. He had been conceived by his mother Danae, an Argive princess, when Zeus penetrated her as a shower of gold (Apollodoros, 2.4.1). The royal house of Argos, in Greek legend, had strong migratory bonds with Egypt. A much earlier Argive princess Io, another conquest of the ever-inventive Zeus, had found her way to Egypt, either in the form of a white cow or as a kidnapped victim of the Phoenicians (Herod. 1.1.4–5). Her descendant Danaos later returned to Argos with his fifty daughters, the Danaids, in flight from the fifty sons of Aigyptos, the subject of Aeschylus' *Suppliants*, thus reviving their Argive lineage.[11] From that lineage stemmed Danae and then Perseus. The latter's adventures brought him to Libya, where he captured the head of the Gorgon, and then to the rescue of Andromeda, sometimes reckoned as a daughter of the Ethiopian royal house (Apollodoros, 2.4.3–5). More importantly, Perseus subsequently landed in Egypt itself, at the city of Chemmis, the site of his Egyptian heritage and the place where Egyptians still paid him homage through honorific festivals in Greek style at the time of Herodotos. The combination is noteworthy. Hellenic legends prompted the construct. But the Egyptians of Chemmis evidently found it valuable to appropriate the Greek hero for their own traditions.[12]

And not Egyptians alone. Perseus could do triple duty. A version of the Perseus/Andromeda tale has Andromeda as daughter of the Persian Cepheus. When Andromeda produced a son, Perseus named him Perses, left him in Persia (for Cepheus had no male heirs), and from him the Persians derived their name (Herod. 7.61; 1.125; Euripides, *apud* Apollodoros, 2.1.4). The origin of the story cannot be pinned down. As a Greek fable, it suggests the imposition of a Hellenic genealogy even on the most notorious enemy of Hellas. But it could as easily be a Persian initiative to incorporate Greek legend into their history.[13] The amalgamation had benefits either way. When the Persian king Xerxes prepared his invasion of Greece, he sent an envoy to Argos seeking its neutrality, and he gave as reason the kinship between Argives and Persians that stemmed from Perses, the issue of Perseus and Andromeda (Herod. 7.150–152). Herodotos himself does not vouch for the validity of the report. But it certainly circulated in his day. Both Argives and Persians were perfectly comfortable with it. And the idea that the house of Xerxes owed its origin to the shower of gold with which Zeus had impregnated Perseus' mother was accepted tradition in Athens (Aeschylus, *Persae*, 79–80).

The triple mixture is quite arresting. Hellenic tradition embraced Perseus, among other things tracing the Dorian kings back to that hero. At the same time, Greeks acknowledged that his mother Danae, from the royal house of Argos, had deeper roots in Egypt, thus making the Dorian chieftains ultimately Egyptians. No discomfort, it seems, troubled the purveyors of those genealogies. Some Persians, however, offered their own version. They were happy enough to accept Perseus as a forebear, but they questioned his Hellenic credentials. The hero, on their reckoning, was an Assyrian, who only later became Greek. But they had no hesitation in accepting the Hellenic tradition that the ancestors of Perseus' mother Danae were Egyptians.[14] This remarkable genealogical stew illuminates the ancient propensity to multiply and entangle lineages that cross ethnic boundaries. The juggling of Perseus allowed Persians to link parts of their heritage to Mesopotamia and to Egypt, as well as to Greece. Egyptians could erect a shrine to him, perhaps as incarnation of one of their own deities. And all the information reaches us through stories recycled by the Greeks. Alexander's claim on Perseus as a forefather would have deep resonance in Iranian as well as Hellenic lands. And the Ptolemies' linkage to Perseus carried meaning for both Greeks and Egyptians. The binary opposition of Greek and non-Greek seems altogether absent.

A multiplicity of legends linked the colossus of Rome to the world of the Greeks. The story that prevailed in the age of Augustus attached Roman origins to the greatest of Hellenic myths: the Trojan War. Troy's celebrated hero Aeneas, a son of Aphrodite, escaped the fall of his city, migrated to the west where his wanderings brought him to Italy, and spawned a lineage whose members ultimately founded Rome itself. The canonical version, however, had numerous predecessors. A bewildering variety of inventive concoctions circulated in the Hellenistic world, many of them claiming Greek migrants as responsible for peopling Latium and even founding Rome. In diverse tales, Achaian settlers gained the credit as often as, or more often than, Trojan refugees. Odysseus and his descendants played a prominent role, as wanderers *par excellence*. At least one strand of these bewildering traditions had Odysseus and Aeneas reach Italy together and collaborate in the founding of Rome.[15] The tales derive largely from Greek imagination. Their thrust, as is plain, was not to distance Hellas from the barbarian, but to embrace, incorporate, and appropriate him. As a form of Hellenic cultural imperialism, this causes no surprise. But there is more to it than that. The very overlap of Greek and Trojan genealogies shows that cultural amalgam rather than disjunction prevailed. Moreover, the Roman engagement in the adaptation and refashioning of these legends suggest interchange and reciprocity, not a one-way street.

The process can be illustrated by a particular but prominent element in the tradition: the affiliation of Rome with Arkadia. How far back this goes cannot be pinpointed. But a form of the story that took hold in the Hellenistic era set the connection many generations prior to the Trojan War itself. Romans derived, so it was alleged, from Aborigines, claimed by some as an autochthonous people, but identified by others as migrants from Arkadia in the central Peloponnesos. Dionysios of Halikarnassos, who advocates the latter version, cites sources as early as the fifth century in support. Whether the identification is theirs or Dionysios' own interpretation, the association suited the fancy of Greek writers, like Dionysios, who insisted on the Hellenic character of Rome (Dion. Hal. 1.10–13, 1.89.1–2). That notion goes back at least to the fourth century B.C.E. when Herakleides Pontikos declared Rome simply "a Greek city" (Plut. *Camillus* 22.2).

Aborigines as Arkadians in the most remote past, however, were too fuzzy and had less than impressive pedigrees. The Arkadian roots, therefore, gained further elaboration by summoning a more attractive figure, the hero Evander, son of Hermes by an Arkadian nymph. Those were impressive credentials. The tale that took shape had Evander lead a number of Arkadians to Italy where they planted a colony on an inviting hill near the Tiber, which they named Pallantion after their own home town – a site later adopted by the Romans as the Palatine (Dion. Hal. 1.31, 1.89.2; Strabo, 5.3.3). If further confirmation for the link were needed, the ubiquitous Herakles would provide it. Still another story brought Herakles, fresh from conquest in Spain, with a band of Greeks, including Arkadians, to a settlement on the Capitoline Hill in Rome. The great hero subsequently reinforced the Arkadian connection by marrying the daughter of Evander and generating offspring who would leave an Arkadian stamp on Rome (Dion. Hal. 1.34.1, 1.41–44). The legend finds echo in Polybios. He might pride himself on being a hard-headed, no-nonsense historian. But he also stemmed from Arkadia. It is hardly surprising that Polybios should find the legends of Evander at the origins of Rome irresistible. He endorsed the version that the Palatine took its name from Pallantion planted by Arkadians. But he has it named after young Pallas, son of Herakles, and grandson of Evander (Polyb. *apud* Dion. Hal. 1.32.1). The Hellenic features of Rome thus proliferated. Greek writers obviously found it satisfying to stress the Arkadian underpinnings of the western power.

And not Greeks alone. Roman intellectuals took up the tale with comparable relish. Fabius Pictor in the late third century not only recorded the arrival of Herakles in Italy but also credited Evander with bringing the alphabet, earlier taught to Greeks by Phoenicians, and thus giving double cultural authority to the Latin language (Fabius, fr. 1, Peter). Fabius, of course, wrote in Greek, a noted philhellene. But Cato the Elder himself, not normally identified with Hellenism, had no difficulty in taking a comparable line. He accepted the proposition that Aborigines in Italy from whom the Romans descended, were, in fact Greek (Dion. Hal. 1.11.1, 1.13.2). And he propagated, perhaps even expanded on, a tradition in which the Arkadians under Evander disseminated the Aiolic dialect among Italians, a tongue adopted by none other than Romulus himself (Cato, fr. 19, Peter; cf. fr. 56, Peter). The reciprocal playing with legends augmented the ties that intertwined Greeks with Romans.

The process became the more entangled when Aeneas and the Trojans were brought into the mix. Trojan origins for Rome had become increasingly orthodox doctrine, at least among Romans, by the late Hellenistic period. That need not, however, preclude the Hellenic ingredient. Inventive ingenuity would see to it. A tradition emerged that traced Aeneas' roots to Greece itself – indeed to Arkadia. The tale claimed Atlas as first king of Arkadia in the distant mists of antiquity, with a glorious lineage to follow that embraced Zeus himself and his Arkadian son Dardanos. On this story, Dardanos led out an Arkadian expedition, after floods had devastated his native land, to settle in the Troad. Hence, Aeneas, the quintessential Trojan, was in fact of Arkadian heritage (Dion. Hal. 60–61). Arkadian intellectuals welcomed and embellished the idea. Some had Aeneas settle in Arkadia after his departure from Troy and live out his days there. Others, however, combined the traditions and completed the circle: Aeneas, the Trojan of Arkadian heritage, moved from Troy to Arkadia, and then to Italy – where he bore a son named Romulus![16] The Troy-Arkadia-Rome line thus gained full expression. Greek writers obviously filled out the fictions. But eminent Romans happily entered into them. The great scholar Varro gave his endorsement to the tale of Aeneas' Arkadian origins (Servius, *Ad Aene.* 3.167, 7.207).

The whole matrix of legends underscores a complicated but interdependent process. Greek authors spun diverse stories that set Roman success in the context of Hellenic traditions. And Romans appropriated those traditions to spin them to their own purposes. This was no linear development but an intricate by-play in which the lines repeatedly crossed and turned back on themselves. The connections multiplied. And the Greek/non-Greek distinction dissolved.

A different permutation offers an unusually fascinating insight into the process: mutual perceptions of Greeks and Jews. In this double loop, Jews are constructed as Greek philosophers, whereas Greek philosophers emerge as dependent on Jewish lore. The idea of "otherness" is decidedly submerged.

A fragment of Theophrastos, pupil of Aristotle, characterizes Jews as "a nation of philosophers" who converse with one another about God, gaze at the stars and speculate about them, and summon the divinity through their prayers (Theophrastos in Porphyry, *De Abstinentia* II.26). Theophrastos plainly did not have solid testimony about the Jews.

To turn them into astrologers is plainly off the mark, as are some of his other comments regarding the sacrifice of live animals and even human sacrifice. Theophrastos evidently provided an *interpretatio Graeca*. Jewish monotheism may well have prompted it. For the Greeks, those who speculate about a solitary divinity must be philosophers by nature.[17] It is a fact of some note that this eminent thinker, not otherwise particularly enamored of Jews, about whom he was badly misinformed and whose sacrificial practices he contrasted with those of the Greeks, nevertheless reckoned them as a philosophic people. That categorization set them on a plane with other eastern nations to whom the Greeks imputed an "oriental wisdom" that generated respect.[18]

Theophrastos was not alone in this. A more remarkable narrative appears in the work of another Aristotelian pupil. Klearchos, from the Cyprian city of Soli, quoted his master (or rather put words into his mouth), describing a chance encounter in Asia Minor between Aristotle and an unnamed Jew from Coele-Syria. The man mightily impressed Aristotle. He tested the Greek philosopher's knowledge and that of his pupils and other scholars, and, as one who had lived in the company of many men of high cultivation (*paideia*), he imparted something more of his own. Aristotle discoursed in some detail about the Jew's marvelous steadfastness and restraint in his lifestyle. He observed indeed that this Jew was not only Greek in his language – but in his very soul (Klearchos in Jos. *Contra Apionem* (*CAp*) 180–182). The *interpretatio Graeca* is here imposed as well. For Klearchos, the skills of the cultivated Jew came from his long acquaintance with the learned men of Hellas. The ability to hold his own in philosophical dialogue exhibited the Hellenic soul.[19] But there is more to it than that. Klearchos cited Aristotle as identifying the Jewish people generally as descendants from the philosophers of India, men called Kalanoi by the Indians but Jews by the Syrians (Klearchos in Jos. *CAp.* 1.179). This complicates the heritage. Kalanoi, as such, do not exist; that is erroneous extrapolation from Kalanos, a celebrated Indian gymnosophist who sparred with Alexander the Great. But the association of Jews with Indian wise men is significant. Klearchos elsewhere claims that Indian gymnosophists descended from Persian *magoi*. And others conjectured that Jews themselves descended from *magoi* (Diog. Laert. I.9). These speculative fantasies, however remote from reality, carry meaning for the mentality of Greek intellectuals in the early Hellenistic period. Some of them, at least, reckoned Jews as a philosophic people, perhaps as the sect of philosophers among the Syrians, just as the *magoi* represented the philosophic elite of Persia

(Diog. Laert. 1.1). The combination of eastern wisdom and Hellenic *paideia* gave the Jew whom Aristotle purportedly encountered his special and admirable qualities.[20] This was no alien to be shunned.

The notion of Jews as philosophers certainly went beyond the school of Aristotle. The erudite Megasthenes served as envoy of Seleukos I at the court of the Indian ruler Chandragupta and lived in India for several years. He then composed, probably in the 290s, an extensive study of that land and its people, including the elevated caste of the Brahmans. A fragment of that work delivers the intriguing notice that everything that was said about nature by the ancients is also being said by those outside Greece who "philosophize," some of the views held by the Brahmans in India and some by the Jews in Syria (Megasthenes in Clem. Alex. *Stromata*, 1.15.72.5). Here again, Jews are juxtaposed to Indian wise men, although not as their descendants, and their opinions associated with those of Greek philosophers. The Hellenic writer makes the conjunction and suggests the priority of Hellenic ideas. But he is content to have them shared by the sages of the east.

Priority is a matter that Jews could be quite sensitive about. And they could also be quite clever about it. The Peripatetic school of Aristotle conceived of Jews as philosophers of eastern sagacity and Hellenic proclivity. One real Jewish philosopher, labeled indeed as a "Peripatetic," turned the conceptualization neatly on its head. Aristoboulos, writing probably in the mid-second century B.C.E. and possibly at the court of Ptolemy VI Philometor, produced a lengthy exegetical commentary on the Torah, perhaps in dialogue form, displaying his exposure to various Greek philosophical traditions.[21] Aristoboulos, however, had other things in mind than acknowledging debt to Hellenic predecessors. Indeed, he did the reverse. The Jewish intellectual took pains to show that the Hebrew Bible prompted some of the best of Greek philosophical thought! He claimed that the eminent Greek sage Pythagoras borrowed heavily from the books of Moses, framing his own precepts on the basis of Mosaic prescriptions (Aristoboulos in Euseb. *Praeparatio Evangelica (PE)*, 13.12.1). Socrates' fabled adherence to a "divine voice" simply followed in the path of Moses (Aristoboulos in Euseb. *PE*, 13.12.3–4). Plato, too, examined Mosaic law in meticulous detail before composing his own treatises (Aristoboulos in Euseb. *PE*, 13.12.1). Aristoboulos' inventiveness on this score extended even to Hellenistic writers. He quoted lines of the Stoic poet Aratos of Soli but substituted "God" for "Zeus," thereby to show that his paean to the pantheistic divinity reflected Jewish ideas (Aristoboulos in Euseb. *PE*, 3.12.6–7).

Aristoboulos went further still. He maintained that all philosophers concur in holding devotion to God as preeminent, a principle best enshrined in the law of the Torah (Aristoboulos in Euseb. *PE*, 13.12.8).

This breathtaking usurpation required some fancy footwork. How could Pythagoras, Socrates, or Plato have been acquainted with Mosaic precepts when they could not read Hebrew? Aristoboulos dodged the bullet with further inventiveness: He simply postulated the existence of Greek translations, at least of various parts of the Hebrew Bible, long before the composition of the Septuagint (Aristoboulos in Euseb. *PE*, 13.12.1). He had no qualms about compounding the fiction. It served the larger cause of making Moses responsible for the best in Greek philosophy.

The creative Aristoboulos heralded a long tradition of Jewish claims to the priority of their teachings and the indebtedness of Hellenic philosophers. The practice is reflected in the works of the great Jewish philosopher and exegete Philo of Alexandria. Philo traced the effects of Jewish learning back to Herakleitos: That early thinker took his cue from the teachings of Moses (Philo, *Legum Allegoria* 1.108; *Heres*, 214). As for the Platonic doctrine that the world is created but indestructible, Philo questions those who find its roots in Hesiod; it was there in the Pentateuch long before (Philo, *de Aeternitate Mundi* 17–19). Even Socrates' thoughts about God's fashioning of body parts that perform excretory functions drew on Moses (Philo, *Questions and Answers on Genesis*, 2.6)! And Hellenistic philosophy owes a comparable debt. Zeno's teaching that the wise must dominate the foolish comes straight from Isaac's command that Esau serve his brother Jacob (Philo, *Omnis Probus* 53–57). And the Stoic doctrine that the wise man alone is ruler and king is nothing more than a reference to Abraham in Genesis (Philo, *de Mutatione Nominum* 152; *de Somniis* 2.244).

The Jews insisted on their own precedence. But the repeated, even if fanciful, connections between biblical pronouncements and Hellenic ideas demonstrates the urge to associate Jewish learning with Greek philosophy. It provides the other side of the coin in which Greek intellectuals interpreted the erudition of Jews as an adaptation of Hellenic wisdom. This was not tension but reciprocity. The fact is strikingly illustrated by a Greek text that precedes chronologically any claim by Jews on the priority of the Bible to Greek philosophy. Hermippos of Smyrna, a biographer of Pythagoras, writing in the late third century B.C.E., reported that the great sage was said to have adapted many of the laws of the Jews for his own philosophy and that he, in fact, brought his teachings from the Jews to the Greeks (Hermippos in Jos. *CAp.* 1.165; Origen, *Contra Celsum* 1.15.334). This is arresting testimony. The acknowledgment of Jewish priority in philosophic wisdom comes from a Greek – perhaps before any Jew had thought up the idea. The two cultures are enmeshed rather than detached.

One final illustration brings the matter to full circle. Philo comments that the world contains multitudes of rich, eminent, and pleasure-seeking individuals, but very few who are wise, just, and virtuous. That latter small number, however, includes certain groups whom Philo specifies: the seven sages of Greece, the Persian *magoi,* the gymnosophists of India, and the Essenes among the Jews (Philo, *Omnis Probus,* 72–75). The Alexandrian Jew here echoes the constructs fashioned more than three centuries earlier by Greek thinkers like Megasthenes and Klearchos of Soli: the linkage of Hellenic philosophy to Jewish precepts and to eastern wisdom.

Contention over priority and precedence was common currency among Mediterranean peoples. Greeks had a passion for establishing their responsibility for the cultural contributions of other nations – and vice versa. That much is well known. Less well known is the fact that Greeks also had little difficulty in acknowledging the claims of others and building them into their own cultural personality.

The Phoenicians represent a revealing instance. Hellenic attitudes toward that people diverged and splintered. One can find numerous snide comments about Phoenicians as crafty merchants, profiteers, and deceitful characters, given to fraud and altogether untrustworthy.[22] Yet, popular legend, widely disseminated among Greeks, had it that Kadmos the Phoenician was founder of the great city of Thebes.[23] Some Greeks at least felt no qualms about associating their origins with the land of Lebanon. And Phoenicians themselves took the cue and exploited it. As a Hellenistic inscription from Sidon reveals, the city honored one of its own citizens for winning an athletic competition at the Nemean Games in Argos and exclaims that "Kadmeian Thebes" also rejoices in the victory of its mother city in Phoenicia.[24]

Cultural competition, however, offers an even more interesting angle. Philo of Byblos, a thoroughly Hellenized Phoenician writing in the early second century C.E., reflects it. Philo produced an erudite work on Phoenician history, culture, and religion, drawing on Sanchuniathon, a writer who allegedly lived before the Trojan War.

The material transmitted by Philo, however, almost certainly stems from Hellenistic speculation, wrapping itself in the name of Sanchuniathon to give the aura of distant antiquity.[25] Among other things, Philo made a point of asserting Phoenician priority in the invention and transmission of ancient tales regarding the origins of the gods and the universe. In particular, Philo preserves a Phoenician version of the Kronos legend that corresponds in part to the account in Hesiod's *Theogony*, but differs in most essentials – including the introduction of a Euhemeristic analysis that has the gods originate as men. And the learned Phoenician proceeds to assert that Hesiod and other Greek poets simply appropriated the tales from Phoenician writings and embellished, expanded, and bowdlerized them with gigantomachies, titanomachies, and castration fantasies of their own (Philo of Byblos in Euseb. *PE*, 1.10.40). Philo takes aim as well at Pherekydes, the sixth-century Greek writer on the birth of the gods and the cosmos. In Philo's view, Pherekydes, too, got his information from Phoenician sources (Philo of Byblos in Euseb. *PE*, 1.10.50). The whole Hellenic concept of cosmogony is thus derivative.

If there was a Greek response to these Phoenician claims, we don't have it. Hellenic writers preferred to cite Hesiod and let it go at that. What we do have, however, suggests that Greek intellectuals, or some of them at least, far from engaging in contentious rivalry with Phoenicia, could readily acknowledge Phoenician cultural precedence on certain fronts. A notable instance concerns the origins of atomic theory. Here, too, Phoenicians had claimed one of their own as its father, a certain Mochos, also identified as dating to a time prior to the Trojan war, whose works were subsequently translated (perhaps fabricated) by the Hellenistic Phoenician writer Laitos. Such a claim could be expected. What is more remarkable is the retailing of that construct by the eminent Greek historian, philosopher, and scientific thinker Poseidonios in the first century B.C.E. Poseidonios did not refute or dispute it. He took the testimony of "Mochos" seriously. Although some might credit Demokritos or Epicurus with first reckoning atoms as the basic units of matter, Poseidonios awarded that distinction to the Phoenician Mochos of Sidon (Poseidonios in Strabo, 16.2.24; Sext. Emp. *Adv. Mathematicos*, 9.359–364). The remarks of the learned Stoic philosopher open an important window on the mentality of the Hellenistic elite. Perhaps Poseidonios was taken in by the ascription of Laitos' Greek translation to a Phoenician thinker who preceded the Trojan war. But the willingness of the Hellenic intellectual to accept the priority of Near Eastern wisdom on a critical item of scientific theory counts for a lot. He preferred to embrace the association with Phoenician learning rather than to trump it.

A complicated relationship held between Greeks and Egyptians in Ptolemaic Egypt. The land had come under Greek authority after the arrival of Alexander the Great, whether as occupation or liberation – depending on one's perspective. Egyptians were sensitive about the matter. And the Ptolemies who ruled the nation had to address from the start the question of the legitimacy of a Greco-Macedonian ruling class in that land whose traditions long predated their own history. Both peoples struggled to work out the relationship to mutual satisfaction – or at least to represent it in a fashion that both would find palatable. That difficult and intricate process cannot be pursued here. But one absorbing tale allows entrance into the mental mechanism.

The so-called "Alexander Romance" constitutes a bewildering welter of folk tales, novelistic fiction, historical embellishments and distortions, and inventive concoctions, shaped and reshaped over a period of centuries. It survives in three main recensions, the earliest of which was composed around 300 C.E., but utilizing material that must go back to the early Hellenistic period.[26]

The opening portion of the text holds particular interest. The tale centers on Nectanebos II, the last Pharaoh of Egypt, ousted from power in 342 by a second Persian conquest of Egypt, driven to the south, and ending in obscurity. But he looms large in legend. The Persian dynasty that succeeded him did not last long, defeated and removed forever by the invasion of Alexander. The image or construct of the last Egyptian ruler took on particular importance in the decades after establishment of Ptolemaic authority. Egyptian national consciousness and the legitimacy of the new order were both at stake. In this milieu, the saga of Nectanebos in the Alexander Romance took shape.

A resumé of the narrative, or its relevant parts, is in order. The author introduces Nectanebos not only as the last Pharaoh but as a man especially skilled in the magical arts. Through reasoning power, he could bring all the elements of the universe to do his bidding. If war threatened, he did not bother with arms, weaponry, or military machines. He simply defeated enemies on land and sea with incantations, model ships and soldiers floated in a cauldron, and appeals to the god Ammon. This worked like a charm for a long time. But when one massive invasion took place, the cauldron delivered some alarming news: Egyptian gods were piloting the little wax boats of the enemy! Nectanebos got the message. He put on disguise, gathered what treasure he could stuff into his clothes, and fled the country. After wandering through a number of nations, he landed in Pella, seat of the Macedonian monarchy, the ruling capital of Philip II. There, the resourceful Nectanebos presented himself as an Egyptian seer and astrologer (*Alex. Rom.* 1.1–3.3).

The Egyptians themselves, bereft of their king after his mysterious vanishing act, sought guidance from the ancestor of the gods, who sent a reassuring oracle. The prediction affirmed that the monarch may have fled as an old man but would return to Egypt as a youth and subject the enemies of his countrymen. No one quite grasped the significance of the oracle at the time, but the Egyptians ordered it inscribed on Nectanebos' statue, hoping that some day it might be fulfilled (*Alex. Rom.* 1.3.4–6).

Nectanebos soon made quite a reputation in Macedon as an eminent seer, a reputation that reached the ears of the alluring queen Olympias, who summoned him to the palace. Her husband Philip was conveniently away at war – as was his wont. Nectanebos took full advantage, flattering the queen and boasting of his skills as dream interpreter, caster of horoscopes, and master of the magical arts. He then prophesied a future separation from Philip, who would marry another, but offered a far better compensation: Olympias would sleep with a god, none other than the Libyan ram-headed deity Ammon, with whom she would conceive a son, a future avenger of Philip's misdeeds. Nectanebos had hatched a dastardly erotic scheme. Alerting Olympias to the fact that she would first dream of intercourse with the god and would subsequently experience it, he exerted all his magical powers to induce precisely the right dream, thus persuading the queen of his prophetic gifts. Nectanebos now had Olympias where he wanted her. He forecast that the god would appear to her in the guise of a serpent, then in Ammon's own form, followed by that of Herakles and of Dionysos in turn, and finally (not surprisingly) taking the shape of Nectanebos himself. Olympias eagerly welcomed the prediction, proclaimed that if the forecast were fulfilled, she would announce him as father of the child and duly submitted herself to the mantic cloaked as multiple divinity. The queen rapidly became pregnant, her womb housing a child whom Nectanebos presciently prophesied to be invincible and dominant (*Alex. Rom.* 1.4–7).

There was, of course, still the problem of Philip. He returned to Macedon to discover a pregnant wife – whom he had obviously not impregnated. But Nectanebos' mantic powers managed to persuade the king that Olympias had been visited by a deity, no mere human adulterer. Philip was readily gulled. Olympias appropriately delivered a child amid lightning flashes, rolling thunder, and earthquakes. None could doubt that the father must have been divine. The boy, Alexander, who bore no resemblance to Philip or Olympias, had a great future in store (*Alex. Rom.*1. 8–12).

Young Alexander assimilated the martial prowess and fierce ambition of Philip, his early years consumed in rivalry with the king. Nectanebos continued to hang about the court, evidently enjoying the frequent absences of Philip. Alexander probed the prophetic powers of the seer and sought to benefit from his astrological knowledge. But in a stunning turnabout, the impetuous prince hurled Nectanebos against a rock, smashing his head, and exclaiming that he had no business investigating the mysteries of heaven when he could not command the earthly realm. The dying Nectanebos then revealed to Alexander that he was his own father, the consequence of his devious deception of Olympias. Alexander then felt both remorse and betrayal. He regretted the murder of his father but blamed him for never disclosing the deed until the end. Alexander informed his mother, and a proper burial followed (*Alex. Rom.* 1.13–15).

When the all-conquering Alexander eventually reached Egypt, the prognostications came to fruition. Priests and prophets hailed him as the new Pharaoh, his enthronement occurring in the ancient seat of Memphis. And Alexander noticed the statue of Nectanebos, with its inscription that forecast the return of the king, not as an elderly monarch but as a young man who would subdue the dreaded Persians. Alexander immediately embraced the statue, publicly proclaimed Nectanebos as his own father, and declared the fulfillment of the oracle (*Alex. Rom.* 1.34).

Such is the gist of the tale. How to interpret it? Egyptian conceptualization must lie at its core. The element of divine fatherhood for the ruler of the land holds a central place in the legend. This can hardly be anything but an allusion to the standard myth of Amon-Re as fathering the Pharaoh through a nocturnal visit to the queen in the guise of her husband.[27] Nectanebos' choice of divinity is hardly accidental. The attachment of this lofty lineage to Alexander brought the Macedonian king into line with Egyptian tradition, thus asserting a critical continuity between Pharaonic rule and Greco-Macedonian overlordship. The Egyptian element in this construct is fundamental.[28] In this fashion, the Egyptians could claim the accomplishments of Alexander for themselves. The overthrow of the Persian empire and the occupation of Egypt, therefore, came not at the hands of an alien conqueror but through the son of Pharaoh and under the aegis of Ammon. It would not be the first time that such a connection was concocted to camouflage the succumbing of Egypt to external power. A closely comparable story had assuaged the sensitivities of Egyptians after conquest of the land by the Persian king Cambyses in the sixth century. They transformed Cambyses into the son of Cyrus and an Egyptian princess, thus laying claim on the heritage of Cyrus the Great (Herod. 3.1–2). The parallel is nearly precise. This represents more than the ascription of divine sonship to Alexander. It constitutes Egyptian expropriation of the Macedonian achievement to their own purposes.

It would be a mistake to see this as "nationalist propaganda" with an anti-Macedonian bent.[29] The contrary holds. The thrust of the Egyptian construct was to subsume and transform the Hellenic overlord, not to reject or undermine him. Egyptian appropriation of celebrated Greek figures possessed a solid history. Reports had it that the most eminent of Greeks, like Orpheus, Homer, Pythagoras, Solon, and Plato, all gained their learning from visits to Egypt (Diod. 1.96–98). Alexander fit suitably in that company.

But that is not the whole story. This narrative had undergone more than one transmutation before attaining the form in which it has reached us. The Greek text has a strongly Greek flavor. A reworking at Hellenic hands needs to be taken into account. Sardonic and satirical elements inhere in the yarn. Of course, such elements were not foreign to Egyptian writings, even occasionally in mockery of their own rulers.[30] But an intriguing ambiguity, suggesting a give-and-take representation, characterizes the text, and accords it a special quality. Nectanebos appears as hero of the story, according Alexander an Egyptian lineage. Yet, the hero is flawed and suspect. Nectanebos is certainly no warrior (a stark contrast with Philip). He wins his battles with toy ships and necromancy. When a serious enemy appears on the horizon, he collects his goods, dons disguise, and flees for his life. His seduction of Olympias succeeds through trickery and skullduggery. Nor is Olympias a mere passive instrument in the fugitive Egyptian's lecherous scheme. She summoned him to the court in the first place. In a subtle touch, unnoticed by critics, the text hints that she knew precisely what was happening. When told that a succession of gods would arrive in her bedroom, Olympias responded to her would-be seducer by saying that, once a child was born, she would proclaim him the son of Nectanebos (*Alex. Rom.* 1.6.3–4). One might well wonder whether the queen was manipulating the situation to have her own back at Philip.

Nectanebos, in any case, hardly cuts an admirable figure. He comes to an early death in ridiculous fashion by being tossed on a jutting rock by the youthful Alexander. And it is noteworthy that Alexander, once he learns that Nectanebos is indeed his father, blames him for sealing his own fate by neglecting to mention that salient fact. Alexander takes full advantage of the situation when he encounters the inscribed oracle in Memphis, laying claim to Pharaonic heritage and accepting the forecast of conquering Persia as avenger of Egypt. But as the narrative makes clear, Alexander had inherited the qualities of Philip, not of Nectanebos.

The text, however, no more presents an anti-Egyptian message than an anti-Macedonian one. Olympias may have collaborated with or even engineered the scheme of Nectanebos. But the fugitive king managed to provide the Egyptian lineage that enabled his countrymen to associate themselves with the conqueror rather than the conquered. Alexander had eclipsed and even eliminated his flawed father. But he accepted the Egyptian connection and made it the rallying cry of his campaign against Persia.

How much of this narrative stems from Egyptian and how much from Greek reflection cannot be known. The date of composition remains elusive, and a quest for it is probably unhelpful. Nor does it much matter. In a text reworked many times, the strands naturally intertwine. And any specific date, even could it be known, would carry little meaning for the complex composition. One may presume that the narrative arose in the circumstances of Ptolemaic Egypt, in its initial form probably relatively early in the history of that regime. The Egyptians had reason to seek a reassuring accommodation to Hellenic rule. And the Ptolemies had reason to seek legitimacy in Egyptian eyes for their own usurpation. More than one constituency benefited from this elaborate tale. An aspect of high significance, however, needs emphasis. Neither Greeks nor Egyptians relegated the other to the status of barbarian.[31] On the contrary, each found cause for associating themselves with the achievements or traditions of the other.

Numerous comparable instances could be cited. The tangled tales carry a resounding message. Some were clearly concoctions by intellectuals, like the reports of Jews as philosophers and Greeks as students of the Bible, or the links of Rome to Arkadia, or the jumbled genealogy of Perseus. But most seeped into the public consciousness well beyond the level of the elite. Cults to Perseus in Egypt, the embrace of Greek/Trojan legends as part of Roman tradition, and the fanciful fable of Nectanebos reveal a resonance in various parts and among various peoples of the Hellenistic world. And they all betoken an openness to hybrid cultural identities in that world. The roots of Hellenic heroes could be found in Persia or Egypt, Arkadians appear at the origins of Rome, Greeks borrowed from the learning of Jews and Phoenicians, and Hellenistic rule in Alexandria stemmed from forebears with the mingled blood of Macedonian and Egyptian royalty. Fertile imaginations invented these fictions. But they expose a mentality that resisted the estrangement of the alien and preferred to blur the boundaries between Greek and non-Greek.

BIBLIOGRAPHICAL NOTE

The topics in this chapter range widely in expanse and chronology. No individual work encompasses all the themes touched on here. As a starting point on the subject, one can do no better than Momigliano's *Alien Wisdom: The Limits of Hellenization* (1979), a fundamental work with trenchant observations and insights. On the matter of Greeks and "barbarians" generally, Hartog (1988) and Hall (1989) have had perhaps the widest impact and influence. Other studies of value on that issue include Georges (1994); Tuplin (1999); Dubuisson (2001); and the collection of essays in Harrison (2002). The most sweeping examination of attitudes toward other ethnic groups in antiquity is Isaac (2004).

The mutual perceptions of Greeks and Egyptians have received important treatment recently by Vasunia (2001) and Stephens (2003). On the legends that linked Greeks and Romans, see Gruen (1992) and Erskine (2001). The cultural entanglements of Greeks and Jews are examined in Gruen (1998) and Collins (2000). A fine introduction to the Nectanebos story and the Alexander Romance may be found in Stoneman (1991).

NOTES

1 Hall (1989) 56–100; Hall (1997) 40–51; (2002) 172–89.
2 Cf. Tuplin (1999) 49–51.
3 *Airs, Waters, Places*, 12, 16, 23–24; see Thomas (2000) 86–98.
4 Lévy (1992) 194–6.
5 Hartog (1988), *passim*; Georges (1994) 167–206.
6 Hirsch (1985); Georges (1994) 228–41; Briant (2001).
7 Eckstein (1995) 119–25; Erskine (2000); Champion (2004).

8   Dueck (2000) 75–84.

9   Momigliano (1979) 7–21; Dubuisson (2001) 6–8.

10   Callimachus, fr. 655 (Pfeiffer); Isidorus, *Etym.* 17.7.7; see Pfeiffer (1949) 435.

11   Vasunia (2001) 40–58.

12   He was perhaps identified with Horus; see Lloyd (1976) 367–9; Stephens (2003) 25–6, 133.

13   Georges (1994) 66–71.

14   Herod. 6.54. A comparable but still more complex rendition by Hellanikos reports that the forebears of Andromeda were Chaldeans (Babylonians or Mesopotamians) who invaded Persia under her father Cepheus, the land subsequently colonized by Perses, son of Perseus and Andromeda; *FGrH*, ff 59–60. The two accounts, plainly different, nevertheless concur in seeing Persians as derived from a Mesopotamian people. These are not likely to be Greek inventions.

15   A summary of these legends, with bibliography, in Gruen (1992), 8–21.

16   Dion. Hal. 1.49.1–2; Strabo 13.1.53; Erskine (2001) 119–21.

17   Jaeger (1938) 131–4; Mélèze-Modrzejewski (1990) 107–8.

18   A more negative view of Theophrastos' attitude in Bar-Kochva (2000) 1–20.

19   Cf. Bar-Kochva (1997–1998) 10–4.

20   For various views on the tale told by Klearchos, see especially Lewy (1938) 205–35; Gutman (1963) 91–102; Bar-Kochva (1997–1998) 1–47.

21   On Aristoboulos, see especially Walter (1964); Holladay (1995). See also Gruen (1998) 246–51 and (2002) 221–3, with further bibliography.

22   Mazza (1988).

23   For example, Herod. 2.49, 5.57; Euripides, *Bacchae* 170–2; *Phoenissae* 5–6, 638–9; see Edwards (1979).

24   Moretti (1953) 41.

25   Baumgarten (1981), 48–51, 57; Attridge and Oden (1981), 3–9. This does not mean that the material itself may not represent authentic Near Eastern traditions that date back to the Bronze Age, as almost certainly they do; West (1966), 18–31.

26   For summaries of the complex strands of the "Alexander Romance" and its evolution, see recently Stoneman (1991) 8–17; Fraser (1996) 205–26.

27   Brunner (1964).

28   Cf. Lloyd (1982) 46–50; Huss (1994) 129–33; Stephens (2003) 67–73.

29   As do, for example, Lloyd (1982) 46–50; Huss (1994) 129–33.

30   Silverman (1995) 49–61; Stephens (2003) 71.

31   The people labeled as "barbarians" in the narrative are the enemies of Egypt, specified as including almost any people one could imagine in the east, ranging from Scythians to Euonimitai – but no Greeks; *Alex. Rom.* 1.2.2, 1.3.1.

15: RECENT TRENDS AND NEW DIRECTIONS

D. Graham J. Shipley[1]

✺

A PERIOD UNDERVALUED

In the last twenty years, there has been a quiet revolution in Hellenistic studies. To obtain reliable overviews of the period and its problems, English readers used to have to rely chiefly on large tomes or multivolume works, often decades old; specialist material was mainly in foreign-language scholarly journals. Now there is a wealth of new, high-quality yet accessible scholarship – not only in English – most noticeably in several multiauthored series.[2] There has been a veritable explosion of interest and published work.

History has probably never had so wide an audience as now, when our televisions invite us almost nightly to meet famous historical figures. Yet, the Hellenistic period has failed to secure a place in the popular imagination about the ancient world – unless one includes in it those twin peaks of popular culture, Alexander and Kleopatra, who pinion Hellenistic history at each end, leaving its 300-year core stretched to the point of invisibility and certainly untouched by video. Probably few television viewers realize that the most familiar version of the story of Jason and the Argonauts was written at this time. One is pleasantly astonished to find a battle between two Successors of Alexander being reenacted on network television and most entertainingly.[3] As an example of the negative impression the period still makes in some quarters, we may recall the famous eighteenth-century picture of Kleombrotos II of Sparta, held by the Tate Gallery in London. This admittedly rather formal work has excited the wrath of one critic, who thinks it so irrelevant to today's viewer that it should be sold and the proceeds used to buy new works.[4] It remains to be seen, therefore, whether the Hellenistic period can ever gain the affection of an English-speaking public in the way Classical Greece or the Roman Empire have. I know of only one recent, cheap, and authoritative paperback history of the period in English.[5] I doubt if even that standard work has sales comparable to the often desperately outdated surveys of Classical Greece that litter the backlists of some mainstream publishers.

Probably less scholarly work has been done on the Hellenistic period than on others; certainly, it is taught in fewer places. Why is this so?

There is an obvious and conventional answer, framed in terms of survival. There is no Hellenistic author, we are told, to compare with Homer, Herodotos, Thucydides, Aeschylus, and so on – the classical (or classic) canon. We also lack contemporary historical narratives for much of the period. But Polybios' Greek is not even as hard as that of Thucydides, and the absence of contemporary historians for the archaic period does not prevent shelves of books from being written about it. What, then, of Apollonios of Rhodes and Kallimachos? Poets of the age have sometimes been regarded as stylistically inferior to their fifth- and fourth-century forebears; but all that this really says is that the Classical period was the pioneer age and that later writers built on its foundations. By that measure, all the technical literature of the third and second centuries could never outweigh Plato and Aristotle. Archaic and Classical Greece resonate more strongly with modern readers. They are the eras to which we like to trace back so much that we admire in art, architecture, philosophy, and politics (though democracy was in truth much rarer then than later). Hellenistic Greece, by contrast, feels like second best, a diminution from earlier greatness: the *polis* no longer free, the pioneering discoveries and inventions long since made. This approach, it need hardly be said, does a great disservice to the post-Alexander age. Even the emphasis on incomplete survival of evidence embodies a misconception: The main extant classical works are just the tip of an iceberg.

Another problem is that "the" Hellenistic world is thought to be more complex, a collection of overlapping and interpenetrating worlds containing many cultures and economies.[6] It is easier to get a handle on the more restricted world of the sixth- and fifth-century Aegean, simpler to describe the bipolar world of Athens and Sparta – or so it is thought, for the Classical period in reality is just as complex. Perhaps simplistic stereotypes about earlier times are so ingrained in the general imagination, as most television programmes about Greek antiquity amply demonstrate, that redressing the balance involves a continual struggle with the "standard reading." The causes of this imbalance lie deep in the history and political culture of modern nation states, which project onto Classical Greece the values they wish to find there.

John Ferguson tried to rectify the balance by stressing the kinship between the Hellenistic period and our, or his, own times (in the 1960s) and drawing lessons for modern readers.[7] Other scholars do nothing to sharpen our appreciation when they paint a morose or lurid picture of life in third-century Greece, forgetting that democracy was more widespread, trade flourished, and towns enjoyed amenities they had never known.

WHY STUDY HELLENISTIC HISTORY?

One reason we study (or teach) history is that historical training, in any period, can help us to learn to be better thinkers in general. We encounter conflicts or gaps in the evidence that force us to choose between alternative interpretations and distinguish good arguments from bad. The experience of analysis gives us the tools to analyse the present-day world and our place in it[8] and even to make better-informed decisions about our own lives (even if we decide to retreat into pure scholarship). Perhaps the educationalists who advocate the development of transferable skills in humanities degrees are more right than they knew.

Why, then, study (or teach) one period rather than another? We must first be attracted by what we find there, for whatever accidental reason. Maybe we are attracted by dynastic scandal, pastoral poetry, baroque sculpture – or even (if we are feeling high-minded today) because the evidence raises issues of interpretation we want to map onto other ages, including our own. I do not mean we do, or should, study a period to discover its similarities with our own. That is no more critical than siding with the Athenians because they were democrats like us (though they weren't) and against the Spartans because they had serfs (should one dislike on principle all aristocrats in Russian literature?). "How much the inventors of democracy have contributed to human happiness! Let us identify with them." History should not be a beauty contest or a team sport, neither should it be a parade of the writer's preferences, though the temptation exists. As Joseph Conrad, that most humane author of empire, lamented a century ago: "As in political, so in literary action a man wins friends for himself mostly by the passion of his prejudices and by the consistent narrowness of his outlook."[9]

The purpose of *researching* history is to produce a better account of the past. One purpose of *studying* it is to explore key questions about how the world worked in a past time and learn how to respond critically to evidence. The exercise may sharpen our wits when we face the same questions in today's world, or have to stand up to our boss, or choose how to vote. All the more ludicrous, then, is the undervaluing of Polybios. The only worthy heir of Thucydides among surviving Greek authors, he built on the earlier writer's analytical technique, made it more systematic, and developed theories of causality and government that were influential for many centuries. The historian of the Roman takeover of Greece gives us the sharpest possible tools with which to deconstruct a world containing a single superpower and to make fundamental choices about compliance, collaboration, and resistance.[10]

It is extraordinary that the study of the Hellenistic period appears to need justification. To focus for a moment on origins and pick a few random examples: We have Theophrastos' pioneering work in natural science, the beginnings of pastoral poetry, and the invention of Epicurean, Stoic, and utopian philosophies. The advances in mathematics, astronomy, physics, and engineering that were made in this period still underlie modern science. It brought into being the first real scholarship and the Western world's first important libraries. Changes in polytheism and Judaism prepared the ground for Christianity. The art and architecture of the Hellenistic period were explicitly taken as models until the twentieth century. From the point of view of geographical dissemination, this was a more important period for Greek culture than any hitherto. It was the bridge between Greece and Rome, and its presence can still be felt. Some of the most spectacular monuments of Greece, western Asia, and Egypt date from these centuries. The cultural interaction set in place by Alexander and his successors, who grafted Hellenic culture onto the Near East – centuries before the Romans introduced "civilization" to western Europe – is one historical factor behind the problems of the Middle East today. Conversely, the impact of Near Eastern cultures on Greek lands, and ultimately the Roman empire, is a legacy that must not be minimized.

HISTORY AND HISTORIANS

This brings us to the sociology of research into the period. Why does the Hellenistic age seem to be theorized less, and to have benefited less from sociologically informed analysis, than earlier Greek periods?[11] In terms of academic structures, Hellenistic research seems more compartmentalized than for the Archaic and Classical periods, where scholars cross the boundaries between politics, art, archaeology, and literature and use a varied armoury of methods and approaches to produce a holistic picture. In contrast, Hellenistic science and philosophy are studied mainly by specialists in philosophy with little interest in social history or literature. Poets are analysed by specialists in poetry and are often given a rather perfunctory social and historical context. Epigraphists and papyrologists may feel that they have their work cut out dating texts and establishing what the words mean, and sometimes leave interpretation to others. Archaeologists and students of material culture, for this period, rarely theorize about the wider implications of their data.

There are, of course, exceptions to all those generalizations, particularly in the study of the Seleukid empire, where no scholar can afford to neglect any available evidence,[12] and in Ptolemaic studies, where a more holistic approach is now apparent.[13] As a historian, I observe that historians of other areas are hardly entitled to blame their more specialized colleagues unless they themselves have paused to consider how science, philosophy, art, or archaeology could enrich their accounts of political–military history and social change.[14] Many English-speaking historians still focus on the narrower kind of history. We have barely scratched the surface of gender relations in the Hellenistic period, for example.

Perhaps the change will occur by evolution. The history of Archaic and Classical Greece went through a similar preparatory stage of working out chronology and political history, particularly during the glut of new epigraphic and papyrological discoveries in the late nineteenth and early twentieth centuries. The scholarly austerity of the middle of the last century (in the English-speaking world, at least) was followed by a radicalizing period when a post–World War II generation of classicists stepped outside their subdisciplines and took a hard look at each others' methods. This may have been prompted in turn by changes in the teaching of classics, particularly in North America. Because the Hellenistic period was taught in few universities until the 1990s but is now catching on, we may be about to see a new generation who cross methodological boundaries more easily.

A BALANCE-SHEET OF ISSUES AND PROBLEMS

As part of an answer to the questions, "How can we make this period popular?" and "How can this period be theorized?" one may offer a few thoughts prompted by comparison between the Classical and Hellenistic periods.

The economy has always been prominent in the study of the period because of the sheer quantity of evidence, particularly from Egypt. It has been apparent for over a century, for example, that long-distance trade was an important aspect of the coordination of eastern Mediterranean societies. One area where the analysis leaves room for development is the interface of economy and individual. In the study of Greece in earlier times, much energy is devoted to debating the economic motives of citizens, farmers, and colonists – even whether an economy and economic motives existed at all. If this debate had taken full account of the Hellenistic period, it would scarcely have been possible for anyone to maintain the view that the Archaic or Classical Greek economy was minimal in scale and status-led in its modalities. Now that it is generally agreed that neither the minimalist nor the modernist take on ancient economies is satisfactory, we can move forward with new and interesting questions. Everything suggests that the economy developed rapidly in the Hellenistic period and that more calories were shifted further and more often in the network of "flows."[15] The purposes behind coinage, and the patterns of its circulation, are the focus of important new work.[16] We can use archaeology to explore changes in farming strategies and the distribution of landed property. Historians have begun to look beyond Rostovtzeff in different ways,[17] and this area of research seems, if anything, a more fertile territory for theoretical innovation and debate than the economies of the Classical period.

The period raises similar issues of politics and leadership to those raised by the fifth and fourth centuries B.C. Polybios, because he covers a longer period in more detail, gives us much more filling in our sandwich than Thucydides, if we wish to engage with issues of hegemony and imperial ideology. The international responsibilities of states, and the way they govern their affairs, are problematized in detail, for example by the triangle of Sparta, the Achaian League, and Rome, no less sharply than by the fifth-century Athenian empire.

Citizenship, society, and justice are subjects of endless debate surrounding Classical Athens. What was the ideology of citizenship, and what were the practicalities of involvement in the *polis*? What were citizens' aspirations, and how did *polis* values find public expression, for example, through rhetoric? Lacking oratorical sources for much of the Hellenistic period, we rely on retrospective accounts and civic documents. Recent analysis of the language of civic inscriptions from Asia Minor[18] shows that we could go further in this direction, reframing *polis* membership in a context of more fluid interaction between citizens and a more cosmopolitan, more mobile world.

In terms of ethnic definition and interethnic relations, it is true that the period has no literary equivalent of the classical Persian wars or the rise of antibarbarian sentiment.[19] But the Ptolemaic and Seleukid empires raise many problems about how groups coexisted or were assimilated, questions that extend beyond the lifetime of those empires well into the Roman period. The use of Greek and non-Greek documents alongside one another has much to contribute here.

Classical historians and archaeologists frequently collaborate to elucidate the interaction between public and private, for example, in the spheres of art and space. Here, too, the study of the Hellenistic world seems barely to have scratched the surface. The representation of hegemonic power, such as the Classical Greek world witnessed in imperial Athens, is no less sharply problematized through the urban foundations of the post-Alexander dynasties or by their architectural benefactions (or impositions) in older *poleis*.

A vast amount of study has been devoted to unpicking gender relations in Archaic and Classical Greece. Such work occasionally casts a glance towards the Hellenistic period,[20] but often without contextualizing the evidence in a new sociopolitical setting. There are excellent studies of royal women's strategies[21] and of women in civic life,[22] but only a limited amount of work has been done on the representation of gender in sculpture, pottery, drama, or law, such as we find in the study of earlier periods. The first steps have, however, been taken in using archaeological assemblages to approach changes in gender relations.[23]

Research into Hellenistic literature, as indicated earlier, is often a self-contained specialism. This contrasts strikingly with the study of Archaic and Classical Greece, where specialists in literature are not afraid to engage with burning questions about society, representation, and politics. The separation of subdisciplines may reflect that view that many of the literary producers of the third and second centuries were indeed more insulated from politics, more self-regarding. Some certainly were under the sway of royal patrons, but there had always been such patrons (one thinks of Euripides and Plato). Was literature now to a lesser extent a forum for the public exploration of issues, as it preeminently was in Classical Athens? Was it less expressive of local culture, less connected to issues that concerned citizens of particular *poleis*? This is not always so. New Comedy was a vehicle for exploring the concerns of ordinary folk, as has recently been argued for Menander;[24] the popularity of his work among the papyri of Egypt attests to interest in his work at all levels of Greek society there.[25] Further rigorous analysis may give opportunities to ground literature in society more thoroughly, and to clarify the extent to which changes in literature reflected wider changes in social discourse and practice.

ARCHAEOLOGY

Enormous amounts have been written about the architecture and sculpture of the period. We now understand pretty well how these genres developed and what their purposes were.[26] Historians must acknowledge, however, that archaeology is not just a font of new pottery, sculpture, and inscriptions! Taking "archaeology" in a wider sense, there is an urgent need for archaeologists and historians to assimilate material culture, to problematize its reading, and to work out methodological principles for approaching real societies through it, as has been done extensively for the Classical period.

Much has been done, nonetheless, to elucidate the chronology and styles of Hellenistic pottery, particularly from excavations by the Greek Archaeological Service and Archaeological Society of Athens, as well as by foreign schools working on sites across the eastern Mediterranean.[27] Following the advances in the understanding of Greek town planning in the mid-twentieth century, further progress is beginning to be made in the analysis of domestic space,[28] particularly from the point of view of gender,[29] decoration,[30] and material assemblages.[31] Even in these areas, however, Hellenistic archaeology is undertheorized, still catching up with Classical – no doubt because fewer researchers work in this period.

Above all, there is a need for a synthetic survey of urban archaeology (see Chapter 3 in this volume). It suffers from the relatively small number of settlements for which detailed plans and chronologies exist, particularly in Greece. Excavation has become almost prohibitively expensive, if not impossible, in the stressed conditions of the Middle East and Mesopotamia. Even where it is possible, it is understandably hedged around with increasing regulations. It is particularly unfortunate, therefore, that some earlier excavators paid scant attention to Hellenistic remains. In less troubled areas, such as Greece, more could still be done through the study of standing remains, such as fortifications.

Survey archaeology, a relatively new source of data, has not yet yielded conclusive answers to questions about rural settlement and town–country relations,[32] but engagement with the data sharpens our ability to theorize about land use. Although the numbers and sizes of artefact scatters cannot tell us who owned a site or lived there, the combination of survey data with conclusions drawn from historical evidence of social relations, from analogies with modern land use, from geological or geomorphological data, and from *a priori* reasoning can force us to identify the most plausible explanation of the observed patterns of artefact distribution. Some studies, for example, contextualize survey data within an argument that rural dependency between free inhabitants played a greater part in Greek life than has generally been acknowledged.[33]

Regionalism has been an important area of investigation in many academic fields, including the history of many periods, archaeological theory, and modern political studies. So far, in Hellenistic studies, it has been an implicit rather than explicit tool of analysis. This is understandable when the culture regions of Greece seem so well defined and durable, but we must remember that they are, and were, constructs. Nevertheless, important regional studies are emerging, though based on historical data rather than archaeology. More problematized and archaeologically informed studies are to be hoped for, which will engage with up-to-date assessments of social and economic change.

On a related front, ecological history and appraisals of the environment have put down roots, so to speak, in parallel with field survey projects and interaction with the study of the *longue durée*.[34] It remains to be seen how much influence the recent theories of microenvironments and microecologies, which purport to break down the boundary between town and country, will eventually have.[35]

HISTORICAL REASSESSMENTS

Some of the most interesting tasks facing us today reflect a need to build on recent insights gained in specialist studies and reapply them to other parts of the Hellenistic field. We need, for example, to follow through the implications of new observations about the scope and overall character of the period.[36] To what extent is it meaningful to posit a historical caesura at 323, or 262, or at any date? The recent "discovery" that democracy endured down to at least the first century B.C. (Chapter 3) needs to be taken on board in all study of Hellenistic communities. Did Athenian democracy make a quantum leap at any given moment? Did the *polis* undergo more rapid transformation at one juncture rather than others? Recent work on the power relationships and ideological expression of Seleukid rule over Greek cities invites us to apply the same insights to other parts of the Hellenistic world.[37] Programmatic statements on economies need to be translated into active research.[38] Compendious investigation into the nature of the *polis* down to ca. 300 B.C. opens the door to a radical rethink of cities in the post-Alexander world.[39] That, in turn, should motivate regional studies of the internal dynamics of *poleis* within their landscapes, of supra-*polis* associations,[40] and – a topical subject in Europe, this – of federalism, which has received surprisingly little scrutiny in the past generation.

The impact of major political changes on Old Greece needs to be examined; the Greek peninsula, though the subject of numerous detailed studies, has tended to get left behind in the study of the wider Hellenistic world. Methodologies of explaining ethnic and other forms of identity, which have been developed mainly for other periods,[41] need to be rethought and reapplied to the more complex circumstances of the third to first centuries. The remarks made earlier about approaching social relations and gender through material culture apply here too. Recent work on the social "consumption" of literature and the extent to which literature (including technical and scientific literature) did or did not engage with questions of wider relevance need to be brought into play. Above all, historians need to be aware of material culture and its implications for society.

CONCLUSION

We are still working out answers to so many, and such large, questions about the Hellenistic period that a coherent overview seems attainable only by presenting the reader with a large amount of detail to bring out regional and chronological nuances.[42] The sheer length of many recent surveys of the period confirms that much that is fundamental remains unclear. Even to make a persuasive new interpretation of one aspect, one ideally needs to set it in the context of many other investigations. So few interpretations and explanations are as yet the subject of a settled consensus that I readily concur with the editor of this volume, in his original prospectus, that "we have only scratched the surface of the period."[43]

NOTES

1   I am grateful to Glenn R. Bugh and Colin Adams for constructive criticisms of earlier drafts. They bear no responsibility for the final outcome.

2   Esp. the series "Hellenistic Culture and Society" (42 vols. to date; Berkeley, 1987–) and "Studies in Hellenistic Civilization" (9 vols., Aarhus, 1990–9). Among mainly non-English series, note the engaging "Hellenismestudier" (11 vols., in Danish; Aarhus, 1989–95) and the more technical "Studia Hellenistica" (38 vols., various languages including English; Leuven, 1942–), and "Studi ellenistici" (ed. B. Virgilio; 14 vols. to date, in Italian; Pisa, 1984–).

3   E.g. Rhaphia, in *Time Commanders* (BBC-2, October 23, 2003).

4   I hope my old friend Iain Pears will understand if I take a different view. See Cartledge and Spawforth (2002) 268, citing a U.K. national newspaper of October 15, 2000 (in fact, the *Sunday Telegraph*). The painting is Benjamin West's *Kleombrotos Ordered Into Banishment by Leonidas II, King of Sparta* (1770).

5   Walbank (1992).

6   Cf. Archibald et al. (2001).

7   Ferguson (1973).

8   Cf. generally Morley (2000); Rhodes (2003). For an insightful account of the study of history, see Arnold (2000).

9   Conrad (1998) 15.

10   I am grateful to Peter Derow for his clarification of this point in a lecture at Wadham College, Oxford, on April 3, 2004.

11   Though cf. the works of Walbank, and Hopkins (1978).

12   See the synthetic work such as (to name just one example) Sherwin-White and Kuhrt (1993).

13   See, for example, Thompson (1988); see Chapter 5 in this volume.

14   Shipley (2000), esp. ch. 5, 7, and 9, attempts to integrate society and culture.

15   A term adopted from Davies (1998).

16   For example, Aperghis (2001); Meadows (2001).

17   See, especially, Davies (2001).

18   Ma (1999).

19   See, for example, Hall (1989).

20   Pomeroy (1984) is a detailed study.

21   See, for example, Carney (1988); Carney (1991).

22   For example, van Bremen (1996); also van Bremen (2003) on the family.

23   For example, Houby-Nielsen (1996); Houby-Nielsen (1997); Houby-Nielsen (1998); Rotroff, this volume, Chapter 7.

24   Salmenkivi (1997); Rosivach (2001).

25   van Minnen (1994).

26   See, for example, Pollitt (1986); Hughes Fowler (1989); Ridgway (1990–2002); Stewart (1993a).

27   A sign of the rich data, barely exploited as yet, is the outstanding series from the periodic (1989, 1990, 1994, 1997, 2000, 2004) "Scientific Meeting on Hellenistic Pottery" (*Epistimonikí Synándisi gia tin Ellinistikí Keramikí*), containing hundreds of papers dealing mostly with excavated assemblages.

28   For example, Ling (1984).

29   Nevett (1995); Nevett (1999).

30   Westgate (2000).
31   Ault and Nevett (1999).
32   Alcock and Cherry (2003); Osborne (2004).
33   Shipley (2001–2002); Shipley (2002a), (2002b).
34   See Shipley and Salmon (1996).
35   Horden and Purcell (2000).
36   For example, Bichler (1983); more controversially, Dreyer (1999) [cf. Shipley (2004)].
37   Ma (1999).
38   Davies (2001).
39   See, for example, the various volumes from the Copenhagen Polis Centre (CPC) project directed by M. H. Hansen. Central ideas: Hansen (1998); Hansen (2000b); Hansen (2003). CPC gazetteer: Hansen and Nielsen (2004).
40   For example, Nielsen (2002) on subregionalism within classical Arkadia.
41   Especially Hall (2001) and Nielsen (1999). See also Malkin and Raaflaub, eds. (2001).
42   Consider, for example, the level of detail in Davies (1984); Green (1990); Shipley (2000); Davies (2001); Erskine (2003).
43   Glenn Bugh, personal communication, 2002.

HELLENISTIC DYNASTIES

MACEDONIAN KINGS

360/59–336	Philip II
336–323	Alexander III (the Great)
323–317	Philip III Arrhidaios
323–310	Alexander IV (son of Alexander III)
317–316	Olympias
316–297	Kassandros
297–294	Three sons of Kassandros
294–288	Demetrios I Poliorketes
288–285	Pyrrhos of Epiros
288–281	Lysimachos
281–279	Ptolemaios Keraunos (son of Ptolemy I)
ca. 277–239	Antigonos II Gonatas (son of Demetrios I)
239–229	Demetrios II
229–221	Antigonos III Doson
221–179	Philip V
179–168	Perseus

THE PTOLEMIES

305–283	Ptolemy I Soter
285–246	Ptolemy II Philadelphos
246–221	Ptolemy III Euergetes
221–204	Ptolemy IV Philopator
204–180	Ptolemy V Epiphanes
180–145	Ptolemy VI Philometor
170–163	Ptolemy VIII Euergetes II Physkon
170–164, 163–116	Kleopatra II
145	Ptolemy VII Neos Philopator

145–116	Ptolemy VIII (restored)
139–101	Kleopatra III
116–107	Ptolemy IX Soter II Lathyros
107–88	Ptolemy X Alexander I
101–88	Kleopatra Berenike
88–81	Ptolemy IX (restored)
80	Kleopatra Berenike
80	Ptolemy XI Alexander II
80–58	Ptolemy XII Neos Dionysos Auletes
58–55	Berenike IV
56–55	Archelaos (husband of Berenike IV)
55–51	Ptolemy XII (restored)
51–30	Kleopatra VII Philopator (the famous one)
47–44	Ptolemy XIV (brother of Kleopatra)

THE SELEUKIDS

305–281	Seleukos I Nikator
281–261	Antiochos I Soter
261–246	Antiochos II Theos
246–226/5	Seleukos II Kallinikos
226/5–223	Seleukos III Soter
223–187	Antiochos III (the Great)
187–175	Seleukos IV Philopator
175–164	Antiochos IV Epiphanes
164–162	Antiochos V Eupator
162–150	Demetrios I Soter
150–145	Alexander Balas
145–140	Demetrios II Nikator
145–142 or 139/8	Antiochos VI Epiphanes
139/8–129	Antiochos VII Sidetes
126/5–123	Kleopatra Thea
126/5–96	Antiochos VIII Grypos
126	Seleukos V
114/3–95	Antiochos IX Philopator
95	Seleukos VI
95	Antiochos X Eusebes Philopator
95–88	Demetrios III Philopator Soter
95	Antiochos XI Epiphanes Philadelphos
95–84/3	Philip I (twin of Antiochos XI)

87	Antiochos XII Dionysos
84/3	Philip II
69–63	Antiochos XIII Philadelphos

T H E   A T T A L I D S

283–263	Philetairos (not king)
263–241	Eumenes I (not king; nephew of Philetairos)
241–197	Attalos I Soter (Eumenes I's cousin, adopted)
197–159/8	Eumenes II Soter
159/8–139/8	Attalos II
139/8–133	Attalos III (kingdom to Rome)
133–129	Aristonikos (Eumenes III)

G R E C O - B A C T R I A N   A N D   I N D O - G R E E K   K I N G S
(D A T E S   A P P R O X I M A T E)

256–248	Diodotos I
248–235	Diodotos II
235–200	Euthydemos I
200–190	Euthydemos II
200–185	Demetrios I
195–185	Antimachos I
185–180	Pantaleon
185–175	Demetrios II
180–165	Agathokles
171–155	Eukratides I
165–130	Menandros

. . . and many others attested principally by coins to end of first century B.C.

WORKS CITED

Acosta-Hughes, A. (2002) *Polyeideia: The Iambi of Callimachus and the Archaic Iambic Tradition*. Berkeley & Los Angeles.

Adam, J.-P. (1982) *L'architecture militaire grecque*. Paris.

Adams, W. (1979) 'On the argument from ceramics to history', *Current Anthropology* 20: 727–44.

Adcock, F. E. (1967) *The Greek and Macedonian Art of War*. Berkeley.

Ager, S. L. (1996) *Interstate Arbitrations in the Greek World, 337–90 BC*. Berkeley, Los Angeles, & London.

Ajootian, A. (1997) 'The only happy couple', in C. Lyons & A. O. Kozlowski-Ostrow, eds., *Naked Truths*, 220–42. London & New York.

Alcock, S. E. (1993) *Graecia Capta: The Landscapes of Roman Greece*. Cambridge, New York & Melbourne.

———— (1994) 'Breaking up the Hellenistic world: survey and society', in I. Morris, ed., *Classical Greece: Ancient Histories and Modern Archaeologies*, 171–90. Cambridge.

———— (2002) *Archaeologies of the Greek Past: Landscape, Monuments, and Memories*. Cambridge.

Alcock, S. E. & J. F. Cherry, eds. (2003) *Side by Side Survey: Comparative Regional Studies in the Mediterranean World*. Oxford.

Aleshire, S. B. (1989) *The Athenian Asklepieion: The People, their Dedications, and the Inventories*. Amsterdam.

Algra, K., J. Mansfeld & M. Schofield, eds. (1999) *The Cambridge History of Hellenistic Philosophy*. Cambridge.

Allen, G., and L. D. Caskey (1911) 'The East Stoa in the Asclepeium at Athens.' *AJA* 15: 32–43.

Allen, R. E. (1983) *The Attalid Kingdom: A Constitutional History*. Oxford.

Aloñso-Nuñez, J. M. (1990) 'The emergence of universal historiography from the 4th to the 2nd centuries B.C.,' in Verdin et al., 173–92.

———— (2002) *The Idea of Universal History in Greece. From Herodotos to the Age of Augustus*. Amsterdam.

Alsop, J. (1982) *The Rare Art Traditions. A History of Art Collecting and Its Linked Phenomena*. Princeton.

Anderson, J. K. (1961) *Ancient Greek Horsemanship*. Berkeley.

Andreae, B. (2001) *Skulptur des Hellenismus*. Munich.

Andreau, J., P. Briant & R. Descat, eds. (1997) *Économie antique. Prix et formation des prix dans les économies antiques. Entretiens d'Archéologie et d'Histoire – Saint Bertrand de Comminges 3*. St Bertrand de Comminges.

Andronikos, M. (1984) *Vergina: The Royal Tombs*. Athens.

Annas, J. E. (1992) *Hellenistic Philosophy of Mind*. Berkeley.

———— (1993) *The Morality of Happiness*. New York & Oxford.

Anson, E. M. (2004) *Eumenes of Cardia: A Greek Among Macedonians*. Leiden & Boston.

Aperghis, M. (2001) 'Population – production – taxation – coinage: a model for the Seleukid economy', in Archibald et al. (2001) 69–102.

———— (2004) *The Seleukid Royal Economy. The Finances and Financial Administration of the Seleukid Empire*. Cambridge.

Archibald, Z. H., J. K. Davies, V. Gabrielsen & G. J. Oliver, eds. (2001) *Hellenistic Economies*. London & New York.

Archibald, Z. H., J. K. Davies & V. Gabrielsen, eds. (in press) *Making, Moving and Managing. The New World of Ancient Economies, 323–31 BC*. Oxford.

Ariel, D. T. (1990) *Imported Stamped Amphora Handles, Coins, Worked Bone and Ivory, and Glass*. Jerusalem.

Arnold, J. H. (2000) *History: A Very Short Introduction*. Oxford & New York.

Asheri, D. (1969) *Leggi greche sul problema dei debiti*. Pisa.

Ashton, R. H. J. (2001) 'The coinage of Rhodes, 408–c. 190 BC', in Meadows & Shipton, 79–115.

Astin, A. E. (1978) *Cato the Censor*. Oxford.

Attridge, H. & R. Oden (1981) *Philo of Byblos: The Phoenician History*. Washington, DC.

Ault, B. A. & L. C. Nevett (1999) 'Digging houses: archaeologies of classical and hellenistic Greek domestic assemblages', in P. M. Allison, ed., *The Archaeology of Household Activities*, 43–56. London & New York.

Austin, C. & G. Bastianini, eds. (2002) *Posidippi Pellaei quae supersunt omnia*. Milan.

Austin, M. M. (1981) *The Hellenistic World from Alexander to the Roman Conquest: A Selection of Ancient Sources in Translation*. Cambridge.

———— (1986) 'Hellenistic kings, war, and the economy', *CQ* 36: 450–66.

———— (in press) *The Hellenistic World from Alexander to the Roman Conquest: A Selection of Ancient Sources in Translation*, 2nd edn. Cambridge.

Avram, A. (1996) *Les timbres amphoriques: 1. Thasos*. Paris.

Badian, E. (1958) 'Alexander the Great and the unity of mankind', *Historia* 7: 425–44.

———— (1960) 'The death of Parmenio', *TAPA* 91: 324–38.

———— (1961) 'Harpalus', *JHS* 81: 16–43.

———— (1967) 'A king's notebooks', *HSCP* 72:183–204.

———— (1981) 'The deification of Alexander the Great', in Dell & Borza, 27–71.

———— (1988) 'Two postscripts on the marriage of Phila and Balacrus', *ZPE* 72: 116–18.

———— (1994a) 'Agis III: revisions and reflections', in Worthington (1994a) 258–92.

———— (1994b) 'Herodotus on Alexander I of Macedon: a study in some subtle silences', in Hornblower, ed., (1994) 107–30.

———— (2000) 'Conspiracies', in Bosworth & Baynham, 50–95.

———— (2002) 'Plutarch's unconfessed skill. The biographer as a critical historian', in T. Hantos, ed., *Laurea internationalis. Festschrift für Jochen Bleicken zum 75. Geburtstag*, 26–44. Stuttgart.

Bagnall, R. S. (1976) *The Administration of the Ptolemaic Possessions outside Egypt*. Leiden.

———— (1984) 'The origins of Ptolemaic cleruchs', *BASP* 21: 7–20.

Bagnall, R. S. & P. Derow, eds. (2004) *The Hellenistic Period: Historical Sources in Translation*, 2nd edn. Oxford.

Bagnall, R. S. & B. W. Frier (1994) *The Demography of Roman Egypt*. Cambridge.

Baker, P. (1999) 'Les mercenaires', in Prost, ed., (1999) 240–55.

—— (2000) "Coûts des garnisons et fortifications dans les cités à l'époque hellénistique," in Andreau et al., 177–96.

—— (2003) 'Warfare', in Erskine, (2003) 373–88.

Bakhuizen, S. C., ed. (1992) *A Greek City of the Fourth Century BC*. Rome.

Ballasteros-Pastor, L. (2003) 'Le discours du Scythe à Alexandre le Grand (Quinte-Curce 7.8.12–30)', *RhM* 146: 23–37.

Bandelli, G. (1999) 'Roma e l'Adriatico nel III secolo a.C.', in L. Braccesi, ed., *La Dalmazia e l'altra sponda. Problemi di archaiologhia adriatica*, 175–193. Florence.

Barbantani, S. (2001) *FATIS NIKHFOROS. Frammenti di elegia encomiastica nell'età delle guerre galatiche*. Milan.

Barchiesi, A. (1997) *The Poet and the Prince*. Berkeley & Los Angeles.

Bar-Kochva, B. (1976) *The Seleucid Army. Organization and Tactics in the Greek Campaigns*. Cambridge.

—— (1997–1998) 'Aristotle, the learned Jew, and the Indian Kalanoi', *Tarbiz*, 67: 435–81 (in Hebrew).

—— (2000) 'The first description of the Jews in Greek literature: Jewish sacrifice rituals and the anthropological theory of Theophrastus', in J. Schwartz, *Jerusalem and Eretz Israel*, vol. I, 43–69. Tel Aviv (in Hebrew).

Barton, T. (1994) *Ancient Astrology*. London.

Baslez, M.-F. (1996) 'Place et rôle des associations dans la cité d'Athènes au IVème siècle', in Carlier, ed., 281–92.

Bass, G. F., ed. (1972) *A History of Seafaring Based on Underwater Archaeology*. London.

Bats, M. (1988) *Vaisselle et alimentation à Olbia de Provence (v. 350–v. 50 av. J.-C.): modèles culturels et catégories céramiques*. Paris.

Baumgarten, A. (1981) *The Phoenician History of Philo of Byblos*. Leiden.

Baynham, E. J. (1998) *Alexander the Great. The Unique History of Quintus Curtius*. Ann Arbor, MI.

—— (2003) 'The ancient evidence for Alexander the Great', in Roisman, 3–29.

Beard, M. & J. Henderson (2001) *Classical Art: From Greece to Rome*. Oxford.

Becker, L. C. (1998) *A New Stoicism*. Princeton.

Beltinger, A. R. (1963) *Essays on the Coinage of Alexander the Great*. New York.

Berggren, J. L. & A. Jones (1991) *Euclid's Phaenomena*. New York.

Bergmann, B. & C. Kondoleon, eds. (1999) *The Art of Ancient Spectacle*. Washington, DC.

Berktold, P., J. Schmidt & C. Wacker, eds. (1996) *Akarnanien: eine Landschaft im antiken Griechenland*. Würzburg.

Berlin, A. & K. W. Slane (1997) *Tel Anafa II: The Hellenistic and Roman Pottery*. Ann Arbor, MI.

Bernard, P. (1967) 'Aï Khanum on the Oxus: a hellenistic city in central Asia', *Proceedings of the British Academy* 53: 71–95.

—— (1978) 'Campagne de fouilles 1976–1977 à Ai-Khanoum,' *CRAI*: 421–63.

Berthold, R. M. (1984) *Rhodes in the Hellenistic Age*. Ithaca & London.

Bertrand, J.-M. (1990) 'Formes de discours politiques: décrets des cités grecques et correspondance des rois hellénistiques', in C. Nicolet, ed., *Du pouvoir dans l'antiquité: mots et réalités*, 101–15. Paris & Geneva.

Besques, S. (1971) *Catalogue raisonné des figurines et reliefs en terre-cuite grecs, étrusques et romains III: Époques hellénistiques et romaine. Grèce et Asie Mineure.* Paris.

Best, J. G. P. (1969) *Thracian Peltasts and Their Influence on Greek Warfare.* Groningen.

Bevan, E. R. (1902) *The House of Seleucus,* 2 vols. London.

———— (1927) *The House of Ptolemy: A History of Egypt Under the Ptolemaic Dynasty.* London (repr. Chicago 1968, 1989).

Bianchi Bandinelli, R., ed. (1977) *Storia e civiltà dei Greci, 7–8: La società ellenistica: economia, diritto, religione.* Milano.

Bichler, R. (1983) *'Hellenismus': Geschichte und Problematik eines Epochenbegriffs.* Darmstadt.

Bieber, M. (1961) *The Sculpture of the Hellenistic Age.* New York.

Bienkowski, P. & A. R. Millard (2000) *Dictionary of the Ancient Near East.* London.

Bilde, P. G. (1993) 'Mouldmade bowls, centres and peripheries in the Hellenistic world', in Bilde, P., T. Engberg-Pedersen, L. Hannestad, J. Zahle & K. Randsborg, eds. *Centre and Periphery in the Hellenistic World,* 192–209. Aarhus, 1993.

Bilde, P. G., T. Engberg-Pedersen, L. Hannestad & J. Zahle, eds. (1991) *Rhodos i hellenistisk tid.* Aarhus.

Billows, R. A. (1990) *Antigonos the One-Eyed and the Creation of the Hellenistic State.* Berkeley.

———— (1995) *Kings and Colonists.* Leiden.

Bing, P. (1988) *The Well-Read Muse.* Göttingen.

Bingen, J. (1997) '*I. Philae* I 4, un moment d'un règne, d'un temple et d'un culte', in *Akten des 21. Internationalen Papyrologenkongresses = Archiv Beiheft 3.* I, 88–97. Berlin.

Blackwell, C. W. (1999) *In the Absence of Alexander. Harpalus and the Failure of Macedonian Authority.* New York.

Blum, R. (1991) *Kallimachos. The Alexandrian Library and the Origins of Bibliography.* Madison.

Blundell, S. (1995) *Women in Ancient Greece.* New York & Oxford.

Boardman, J. (1994) *The Diffusion of Classical Art in Antiquity.* Princeton.

Bogaert, R. (1968) *Banques et banquiers dans les cités grecques.* Leiden.

Bopearachchi, O., and P. Flandrin (2005) *Le Portrait d'Alexandre le Grand. Histoire d'une découverte pour l'humanité.* Monaco.

Bosworth, A. B. (1980a) 'Alexander and the Iranians', *JHS* 100: 1–21.

———— (1980b) *A Historical Commentary on Arrian's History of Alexander, vol. 1. Commentary on Books I–III.* Oxford.

———— (1988a) *Conquest and Empire. The Reign of Alexander the Great.* Cambridge.

———— (1988b) *From Arrian to Alexander. Studies in Historical Interpretation.* Oxford.

———— (1994) 'A new Macedonian prince', *CQ* 44: 57–65.

———— (1995) *A Historical Commentary on Arrian's History of Alexander, vol. II, Commentary on Books IV–V.* Oxford.

———— (1996) *Alexander and the East. The Tragedy of Triumph.* Oxford.

———— (2000) 'Introduction', in Bosworth & Baynham (2000) 1–22.

———— (2002) *The Legacy of Alexander. Politics, Warfare, and Propaganda under the Successors.* Oxford.

———— (2003a) 'Plus ça change . . . Ancient Historians and their Sources', *CA* 22: 167–98.

———— (2003b) 'Why did Athens lose the Lamian War', in Palagia & Tracy, eds. (2003) 14–22.

Bosworth, A. B. & E. J. Baynham, eds. (2000) *Alexander the Great in Fact and Fiction.* Oxford.

Bowen, A. C., ed. (1991) *Science and Philosophy in Classical Greece.* London.

Bresson, A. (in press), 'Coinage and money supply in the Hellenistic age', in Archibald et al. (in press).

Briant, P. (1982) *Rois, tributs et paysans.* Paris.

———— (1996) *Histoire de l'Empire Perse. De Cyrus à Alexandre.* Paris.

———— (2001) 'History and ideology: the Greeks and "Persian decadence"', in Harrison (2002) 193–210.

———— (2002) *From Cyrus to Alexander. A History of the Persian Empire.* Trans. P. T. Daniels. Winona Lake, IN.

Brice, W. C., ed. (1978) *The Environmental History of the Near and Middle East since the Last Ice Age.* New York.

Bringmann, K. (2001) 'Grain, timber and money. Hellenistic kings, finance, buildings and foundations in Greek cities', in Archibald et al. (2001) 205–14.

Brosius, M. (1996) *Women in Ancient Persia (559–331 BC).* Oxford.

———— (2003) 'Alexander and the Persians', in Roisman, 169–93.

Brown, T. S. (1958) *Timaeus of Tauromenium.* Berkeley & Los Angeles.

Bruneau, P. (1970), *Recherches sur les cultes de Délos à l'époque hellénistique et à l'époque impériale.* Paris.

Bruneau, P. & J. Ducat (1965) *Guide de Délos,* 2nd edn. Paris.

Bruneau, P., C. Vatin & U. Bezerra (1970) *L'îlot de la Maison des comédiens* (Exploration archéologique de Délos XXVII). Paris.

Brunner, H. (1964) *Die Geburt des Gottkönigs, Ägyptologische Abhandlungen,* 10. Wiesbaden.

Brunschwig, J. (1999) 'The beginnings of Hellenistic epistemology', in Algra et al., 229–59.

Brunschwig, J. & D. Sedley (2003) 'Hellenistic philosophy', in Sedley (2003) 151–83.

Bugh, G. R. (1988) *The Horsemen of Athens.* Princeton.

———— (1992a) 'Athenion and Aristion of Athens', *Phoenix* 46: 108–23.

———— (1992b) 'The Theseia in late Hellenistic Athens', *ZPE* 83: 20–37.

———— (1998) 'Cavalry inscriptions from the Athenian agora', *Hesperia* 67: 1–10.

———— (in press) 'Menander's mercenaries', in N. Sekunda, ed. (in press). *Proceedings of the First International Conference on Hellenistic Warfare,* Torun, Poland, October 2003.

Bulloch, A. W., E. S. Gruen, A. A. Long & A. Stewart, eds. (1993) *Images and Ideologies. Self-definition in the Hellenistic World.* Berkeley.

Buraselis, K. (1988) Review of Högemann (1985), *GGA* 240: 224–45.

———— (2003) 'Considerations on symmachia and sympoliteia in the hellenistic period', in Buraselis & Zoumboulakis, eds. (2003) 39–50.

Buraselis, K. & K. Zoumboulakis, eds. (2003) *The Idea of European Community in History,* vol. II, *Aspects of Connecting Poleis and Ethne in Ancient Greece.* Athens.

Burckhardt, L. A. (1996) *Bürger und Soldaten. Aspekte der politischen und militärischen Rolle athenischer Bürger im Kriegswesen des 4.Jahrhunderts v. Chr.* Stuttgart.

———— (2004) 'Die attische Ephebie in hellenistischer Zeit', in Kah & Scholz, 193–206.

Burford Cooper, A. (1977–8) 'The family farm in ancient Greece', *CJ* 73: 162–175.

———— (1993) *Land and Labor in the Greek World.* Baltimore & London.

Burkert, W. (1993) 'Concordia discors: the literary and the archaeological evidence on the sanctuary of Samothrace', in N. Marinatos & R. Hägg, eds. *Greek Sanctuaries: New Approaches*, 178–191. London.

Burstein, S. M. (1985) *The Hellenistic Age From the Battle of Ipsos to the Death of Kleopatra VII* (Translated Documents of Greece and Rome, 3). Cambridge.

Burton, J. (1995) *Theocritus's Urban Mimes*. Berkeley & Los Angeles.

Bussi, S. (2002) 'Mariages endogames en Égypte hellénistique et romaine', *Revue historique de droit français et étranger* 80: 1–22.

Cahill, N. (2002) *Household and City Organization at Olynthus*. New Haven & London.

Calder, W. M. (1996) 'The Seuthopolis inscription', in Wallace & Harris, 167–78.

Cambiano, G. (1999) 'Philosophy, science and medicine', in Algra et al., 585–613.

Cameron, A. (1995) *Callimachus and His Critics*. Princeton.

Camp, J. (1996) 'Excavations in the Athenian Agora 1994 and 1995', *Hesperia* 65: 252–8.

———— (2000) 'Walls and the polis', in P. Flensted-Jensen et al., eds., *Polis and Politics: Studies in Ancient Greek History*, 41–57. Copenhagen.

———— (2003a) *Greek and Roman Artillery 399 BC–AD 363*. Oxford (Osprey).

———— (2003b) *Greek and Roman Siege Machinery 399 BC–AD 363*. Oxford (Osprey).

Canfora, L. (1990) 'Le but de l'historiographie selon Diodore', in Verdin et al. (1990) 313–22.

Carlier, P., ed. (1996) *Le IVe siècle av. J.-C.: approches historiographiques*. Nancy & Paris.

Carney, E. D. (1988) 'Eponymous women: royal women and city names', *Ancient History Bulletin* 2: 134–42.

———— (1991) '"What's in a name?" The emergence of a title for royal women in the hellenistic period', in S. B. Pomeroy, ed., *Women's History and Ancient History*, 154–72. Chapel Hill & London.

———— (2000) *Women and Monarchy in Macedonia*. Norman, OK.

Cartledge, P. (1987) *Agesilaos and the Crisis of Sparta*. Baltimore, MD.

Cartledge, P., P. Garnsey & E. S. Gruen, eds. (1997) *Hellenistic Constructs. Essays in Culture, History, and Historiography*. Berkeley & Los Angeles.

Cartledge, P. A., E. E. Cohen & L. Foxhall, eds. (2002) *Money, Labour, and Land. Approaches to the Economies of Ancient Greece*. London & New York.

Cartledge, P. A. & A. Spawforth (2002) *Hellenistic and Roman Sparta: A Tale of Two Cities*, 2nd edn. London & New York.

Cary, M. (1951) *A History of the Greek World 323–146 B.C.*, 2nd edn. London.

Casson, L. (1971) *Ships and Seamanship in the Ancient World*. Princeton.

———— (1991) *The Ancient Mariners. Sea Farers and Sea Fighters of the Mediterranean in Ancient Times*, 2nd edn. Princeton.

———— (2001) *Libraries in the Ancient World*. New Haven.

Cébeillac-Gervasoni, M. & L. Lamoine, eds. (2003) *Les élites et leurs facettes. Les élites locales dans le monde hellénistique et romain* (Collection de l'école française de Rome 309; Collection Erga 3). Rome & Clermont.

Chamonard, J. (1922) *Le quartier du théatre* (Exploration archéologique de Délos VIII). Paris.

Chamoux, F. (2003) *Hellenistic Civilization*. Oxford.

Champion, C. (2004) *Cultural Politics in Polybius' Histories*. Berkeley.

Chaniotis, A., ed. (1999a) *From Minoan Farmers to Roman Traders. Sidelights on the Economy of Ancient Crete*. Stuttgart.

————— (1999b) 'Milking the mountains: economic activities on the Cretan uplands in the Classical and Hellenistic period', in Chaniotis (1999a) 181–220.

————— (2002) 'Foreign soldiers – native girls? Constructing and crossing boundaries in Hellenistic cities with foreign garrisons', in A. Chaniotis & P. Ducrey, eds., *Army and Power in the Ancient World*, 99–113. Stuttgart.

————— (2005) *War in the Hellenistic World. A Social and Cultural History*. Malden, MA, Oxford & Australia.

Chankowski, A. S. (1993) 'Date et circonstances de l'institution de l'éphébie à Érétrie', *Dialogues d'histoire ancienne* 19: 17–44.

————— (2004) "L'entraînement militaire des éphèbes dans les cités grecques d'Asie Mineure à l'époque hellénistique: nécessité pratique ou tradition atrophiée?" in Couvenhes & Fernoux, 55–76.

————— (in press) *L'éphébie hellénistique: étude d'une institution civique dans les cités grecques des îles de la Mer Égée et de l'Asie Mineure (IVe–Ier siècles avant J. C.)*. Paris.

Chevallier, R. (1991) *L'artiste, le collectioneur, et le faussaire: pour une sociologie de l'art romaine*. Paris.

Clarke, K. (1999) *Between Geography and History. Hellenistic Construction of the Roman World*. Oxford.

Clarysse, W. (1998) 'Ethnic diversity and dialect among the Greeks of Hellenistic Egypt' in A. M. F. W. Verhoogt & S. P. Vleeming, eds., *The Two Faces of Graeco-Roman Egypt*, 1–13. Boston.

Clarysse, W. & D. J. Thompson (in press) *Counting the People in Hellenistic Egypt*, 2 vols. Cambridge.

Clauss, J. J. (1993) *The Best of the Argonauts*. Berkeley & Los Angeles.

Clayton, P. A. (1996) 'The Pharos of Alexandria: the numismatic evidence', *Minerva* 7: 7–9.

————— (1998) 'Ancient Alexandria rediscovered', *Minerva* 9: 41–2.

Cohen, A. (1997) *The Alexander Mosaic: Stories of Victory and Defeat*. Cambridge & New York.

Cohen, B. (2000) *Not the Classical Ideal. Athens and the Construction of the Other in Greek Art*. Leiden.

Cohen, E. E. (1992) *Athenian Economy and Society. A Banking Perspective*. Princeton.

————— (2003) 'Progressive taxation and the fostering of maritime trade in classical Athens', in Lo Cascio, 17–32.

Cohen, G. M. (1978) *The Seleucid Colonies: Studies in Founding, Administration and Organization*. Wiesbaden.

————— (1995) *The Hellenistic Settlements in Europe, the Islands, and Asia Minor*. Berkeley, Los Angeles & London.

Cole, S. G. (1984) *Theoi Megaloi: The Cult of the Great Gods at Samothrace*. Leiden.

Cole, T. (1991) *The Origins of Rhetoric in Ancient Greece*. Baltimore & London.

Colledge, M. (1987) 'Greek and Non-Greek interaction in the art and architecture of the Hellenistic east', in Kuhrt & Sherwin-White, 134–62.

Collins, J. J. (2000) *Between Athens and Jerusalem*, 2nd edn. Grand Rapids, MI.

Connolly, P. (1984) 'Hellenistic warfare', in Ling, ed. (1984) 81–90.

Conrad, J. (1998) 'A personal record', in M. Kalnins, ed., *Joseph Conrad, A Personal Record; The Mirror of the Sea*, 3–127. London.

Cornell, T. J. (1995) *The Beginnings of Rome. Italy and Rome from the Bronze Age to the Punic Wars (c.1000–264 BC)*. London & New York.

Corrigan, D. M. (2004) *Riders on High: An Interdisciplinary Study of the Macedonian Cavalry of Alexander the Great*, unpublished doctoral dissertation, University of Texas, Austin.

Coulton, J. J. (1976) *The Architectural Development of the Greek Stoa*. Oxford.

Couvenhes, J.-C. (2000) *Les garnisons de l'Attique du IVe s. au Ier s. av. J.-C. par les inscriptions*. Université Paris IV-Sorbonne.

———— (2004) 'Les cités grecques d'Asie Mineure et le mercenariat à l'époque hellénistique', in Couvenhes & Fernoux, 77–113.

Couvenhes, J.-C. & H.-L. Fernoux (2004) *Les Cités grecques et la guerre en Asie Mineure à l'époque hellénistique* [Actes de la Journée d'Études de Lyon, 10 October 2003]. Presses Universitaires François-Rabelais.

Cox, C. A. (2002) 'Crossing boundaries through marriage in Menander's Dyskolos', *CQ* 52: 391–394.

Cuomo, S. (2001) *Ancient Mathematics*. London.

Daly, K. (2001) *Citizens, Soldiers, and Citizen-Soldiers in the Attic Garrisons in the Fourth to the Second Centuries BCE*, unpublished doctoral dissertation, Harvard.

Daszewski, W. (1985) *Corpus of Mosaics from Egypt*, vol. I *Hellenistic and Early Roman Period*. Mainz.

Davidson, G. R. (1952) *The Minor Objects* (Corinth XII). Princeton.

Davies, J. K. (1984) 'Cultural, social and economic features of the hellenistic world', in Walbank et al. (1984) 257–320.

———— (1998) 'Ancient economies: models and muddles', in Parkins & Smith, 225–56.

———— (2001) 'Hellenistic economies in the post-Finley era', in Archibald et al. (2001) 11–62.

———— (in press) 'The economic consequences of Hellenistic palaces', in Archibald et al. (in press).

Debidour, M. (1986) "En classant les timbres Thasiens," in J.-Y. Empereur and Y. Garlan, eds., *Recherches sur les amphores grecques* (*BCH* Supplément 13), 311–34. Paris.

De Callataÿ, F. (1995) 'Calculating ancient coin production: seeking a balance', *NC* 155: 289–311.

———— (in press) 'A quantitative survey of Hellenistic coinages: recent achievements', in Archibald et al. (in press).

Deetz, J. (1967) *Invitation to Archaeology*. Garden City, NY.

———— (1996) *In Small Things Forgotten: An Archaeology of Early American Life*. New York.

de Grummond, N. & B. S. Ridgway, eds. (2000) *From Pergamon to Sperlonga*. Berkeley & Los Angeles.

Dell, H. & E. N. Borza, eds. (1981) *Ancient Macedonian Studies in Honour of Charles F. Edson*. Thessaloniki.

Delorme, J. (1960) *Gymnasion*. Paris.

Descat, R. (2003) 'Qu'est-ce que l'économie royale?', in Prost (2003) 149–68.

de Souza, P. (1999) *Piracy in the Graeco-Roman World*. Cambridge.

———— (2001) 'Hellenistic and Macedonian Warfare 400–200,' in C. Messenger, ed. *The Reader's Guide to Military History*. London.

Dettori, E. (2000) *Filita grammatico. Testimonianze e frammenti*. Rome.

Dignas, B. (2002) *Economy of the Sacred in Hellenistic and Roman Asia Minor*. Oxford.

Drachmann, A. G. (1963) *The Mechanical Technology of Greek and Roman Antiquity*. Copenhagen.

Dreyer, B. (1999) *Untersuchungen zur Geschichte des spätklassischen Athen: 322–ca.230 v. Chr.* Stuttgart.

Dreyfus, R. & E. Schraudolph, eds. (1996–1997) *Pergamon: The Telephos Frieze from the Great Altar*, 2 vols. San Francisco & Austin, TX.

Droysen, G. (1910) *Johann Gustav Droysen. Erste Teil. Bis zum Beginn der Frankfürter Tätigkeit.* Leipzig & Berlin.

Droysen, J. G. (1931) *Geschichte Alexanders des Grossen.* Leipzig.

———— (1952) *Geschichte des Hellenismus. Erster Teil. Geschichte Alexanders des Grossen.* Basel.

Dubuisson, M. (2001) 'Barbares et barbarie dans le monde gréco-romain: du concept au slogan,' *AC* 70: 1–16.

Dueck, D. (2000) *Strabo of Amasia.* London.

Dunbabin, K. (1998) 'Ut Graeco more Giberetur: Greeks and Romans on the dining couch,' in I. Nielsen & H. S. Nielsen, eds., *Meals in a Social Context*, 81–101. Aarhus.

———— (1999) *Mosaics of the Greek and Roman World.* Cambridge.

Eckstein, A. (1995) *Moral Vision in the Histories of Polybius.* Berkeley.

———— (1997) '*Physis* and *nomos*: Polybius, the Romans, and Cato the Elder', in Cartledge et al. (1997) 175–98.

Edwards, G. R. (1975) *Corinthian Hellenistic Pottery* (Corinth VII, iii). Princeton.

Edwards, R. (1979) *Kadmos the Phoenician.* Amsterdam.

Eilers, C. (2002) *Roman Patrons of Greek Cities.* Oxford.

Ellis, W. M. (1994) *Ptolemy of Egypt.* London & New York.

Empereur, J.-Y. (1982) 'Les anse d'amphores timbrées et les amphores: aspects quantitatifs', *BCH* 106: 219–233.

Empereur, J.-Y. & A. Hesnard. (1987) 'Les amphores hellénistiques,' in *Céramiques hellénistiques et romaines*, vol. II, 7–71. Paris.

Empereur, J.-Y. (1995) 'Alexandrie, Égypte', in 'Rapports sur les travaux menés en collaboration avec l'École Française en 1994', *BCH* 119.2: 743–60.

———— (1996a) 'Alexandria: the underwater site near Qaitbay fort', *Egyptian Archaeology* 8: 7–10.

———— (1996b) 'Alexandrie, Égypte', in 'Travaux menés en collaboration avec l'École Française en 1995', *BCH* 120.2: 959–70.

———— (1996c) 'The discovery of the Pharos of Alexandria', *Minerva* 7: 5–6.

———— (1996d) 'Raising statues and blocks from the sea at Alexandria', *Egyptian Archaeology* 9: 19–22.

———— (1997) 'Alexandrie, Égypte', in 'Travaux menés en collaboration avec l'École Française en 1996', *BCH* 121.2: 831–47.

———— (1998a) *Alexandria Rediscovered.* London.

———— (1998b) 'Alexandrie, Égypte', in 'Travaux menés en collaboration avec l'École Française en 1997', *BCH* 122.2: 611–38.

———— (1999a) 'Alexandria: the necropolis', *Egyptian Archaeology* 15: 26–8.

———— (1999b) 'Alexandrie, Égypte', in 'Travaux menés en collaboration avec l'École Française en 1998', *BCH* 123.2: 545–68.

———— (1999c) 'Diving on a sunken city', *Archaeology* 52: 36–43.

———— (2000a) 'Alexandrie: fondation royale et désenclavement du monde', in C. Nicolet et al., eds., *Mégapoles méditerranéennes: géographie urbaine retrospective*, 228–44. Paris.

———— (2000b) 'Alexandrie, Égypte', in 'Travaux menés en collaboration avec l'École Française en 1999', *BCH* 124.2: 595–619.

———— (2001) 'Alexandrie, Égypte', in 'Travaux menés en collaboration avec l'École Française en 2000', *BCH* 125.2: 679–700.

———— (2002) 'Alexandrie, Égypte', in 'Travaux menés en collaboration avec l'École Française en 2001', *BCH* 126.2: 615–26.

Empereur, J.-Y., A. Hesse, & O. Picard (1994) 'Alexandrie (Égypte) 1992–1993', in 'Rapport sur les travaux menés en collaboration avec l'École Française en 1993', *BCH* 118.2: 503–19.

Errington, R. M. (1969) *Philopoemen*. Oxford.

———— (1990) *A History of Macedonia*. Berkeley.

Erskine, A. (2000) 'Polybios and barbarian Rome', *Mediterraneo Antico*, 3: 165–182.

———— (2001) *Troy between Greece and Rome*. Oxford.

———— ed. (2003) *A Companion to the Hellenistic World*. Oxford, Melbourne, & Berlin.

Étienne, R. & M. Piérart (1975) 'Un décret du koinon des Hellènes à Platées en l'honneur de Glaucon, fils d'Étéoclès, d'Athènes', *BCH* 99: 51–75.

Fantuzzi, M. (2005) 'Posidippus at Court: The Contribution of the Hippika of the P.Mil.Vogl. VIII 309 to the Ideology of Ptolemaic Kingship', in K. Gutzwiller, ed. (2005) 249–68.

Fantuzzi, M. & R. Hunter (2002) *Muse e Modelli*. Rome & Bari.

———— (2005) *Tradition and Innovation in Hellenistic Poetry*. Cambridge.

Faraguna, M. (1992) *Atene nell'età di Alessandro*. Roma.

Farrington, B. (1967) *The Faith of Epicurus*. London.

Ferguson, J. (1973) *The Heritage of Hellenism*. London.

Figueira, T. J. (1993) 'Notes on hellenistic Aigina', in T. J. Figueira, ed., *Excursions in Epichoric History: Aiginetan Essays*, 377–98. Lanham, MD.

Finkielsztejn, G. (1995) 'Chronologie basse des timbres amphoriques rhodiens et evaluation des exportations d'amphores', in T. Fischer-Hansen, ed., *Ancient Sicily*, 279–296. Copenhagen.

———— (2001) *Chronologie détaillée et révisée des éponymes amphoriques rhodiens, de 270 à 108 av. J.-C. environ: Premier bilan*. Oxford.

Flower, M. A. (1994) *Theopompus of Chios. History and Rhetoric in the Fourth Century BC*. Oxford.

Foraboschi, D. (1998) 'Economia reale e riflessione teorica', in Settis, 665–80.

Forbes, H. (1996) 'The uses of the uncultivated landscape in modern Greece: a pointer to the value of the wilderness in antiquity?' in Shipley & Salmon, 68–97.

Fowler, B. H. (1989) *The Hellenistic Aesthetic*. Madison.

Fox, M. (1993) 'History and rhetoric in Dionysius of Halicarnassus', *JRS* 83: 31–47.

Foxhall, L. (2002) 'Access to resources in classical Greece. The egalitarianism of the polis in practice', in Cartledge et al. (2002) 209–220.

Foxhall, L. & H. A. Forbes (1982) 'Sitometreia: the role of grain as a staple food in classical antiquity', *Chiron* 12: 41–89.

Fraser, P. M. (1972) *Ptolemaic Alexandria*, 3 vols. Oxford.

———— (1996) *Cities of Alexander the Great*. Oxford.

Frederiksen, R. (2002) 'The Greek theatre: a typical building in the urban centre of the polis?' in T. H. Nielsen, ed., *Even More Studies in the Ancient Greek Polis*, 65–124. Stuttgart.

Fredricksmeyer, E. (2003) 'Alexander's Religion and Divinity', in Roisman, 253–78.

Frösén J., ed. (1997) *Early Hellenistic Athens: Symptoms of a Change*. Helsinki.

Fuchs, M. (1999) *In hoc etiam genere Graeciae nihil cedamus: Studien zur Romanisierung der spräthellenistischen Kunst im 1. Jh. v. Chr.* Mainz.

Gabbert, J. (1997) *Antigonos II Gonatas: A Political Biography*. London & New York.

Gabrielsen, V. (1997) *The Naval Aristocracy of Hellenistic Rhodes*. Aarhus.

———— (2001) 'The Rhodian associations and economic activity', in Archibald et al. (2001) 215–44.

———— (2003) "Piracy and the slave-trade", in Erskine (2003) 389–404.

———— (in press) 'Banking and credit operations in the Hellenistic world', in Archibald et al. (in press).

Gabrielsen, V., P. Bilde, P. Troels-Engberg, L. Hannestad & J. Zahle (1999) *Hellenistic Rhodes: Politics, Culture, and Society*. Aarhus & Oakville, CT.

Gaebel, R. E. (2002) *Cavalry Operations in the Ancient Greek World*. Norman, OK.

Gallant, T. W. (1991) *Risk and Survival in Ancient Greece*. Stanford.

Gardin, J.-C. (1980) 'L'archéologie du paysage bactrien', *CRAI*: 480–501.

———— (1990) 'La céramique hellénistique en Asie Centrale. Problemes d'interpretation', in *Akten des XIII. Internationalen Kongresses für klassische Archäologie: Berlin 1988*, 187–193. Mainz.

Garlan, Y. (1974) *Recherches de poliorcétique grecque*. Paris.

Garlan, Y. (1984) 'War and siegecraft', in Walbank et al. (1984) 353–62.

———— (2000) *Amphores et timbres amphoriques grecs: Entre érudition et idéologie*. Paris.

Garland, R. S. J. (2001) *The Piraeus: From the Fifth to the First Century BC*, 2nd edn. London.

Garnsey, P. D. A. & C. R. Whittaker, eds. (1983) *Trade and Famine in Classical Antiquity*. Cambridge.

———— (1988) *Famine and Food Supply in the Graeco-Roman World. Responses to Risk and Crisis*. Cambridge.

Gauthier, P. (1972) Review of Vatin (1970), *REG* 85: 208–213.

———— (1985) *Les cités grecques et leurs bienfaiteurs (BCH Supplément XII)*. Paris.

———— (1990) 'Quorum et participation civique dans les démocraties grecques', *Cahiers Glotz*, 1: 73–99.

———— (1993) 'Les cités hellénistiques', in M. H. Hansen (1993) 211–31.

Gehrke, H.-J. (1986) *Jenseits von Athen und Sparta: das dritte Griechenland und seine Staatenwelt*. München.

Geller, M. J. & H. Maehler, eds. (1995) *Legal Documents of the Hellenistic World*. London.

Georges, P. (1994) *Barbarian Asia and the Greek Experience*. Baltimore, MD.

Giangrande, G. (1970) 'Hellenistic poetry and Homer', *AC* 39: 46–77.

Gibbons, D. (2001) 'Shipwrecks and Hellenistic Trade', in Archibald et al. (2001) 273–312.

Ginouvès, R., ed. (1994) *Macedonia: from Philip II to the Roman Conquest*. Princeton.

Glucker, J. (1998) 'Theophrastus, the academy, and the Athenian philosophical atmosphere', in J. M. van Ophuijsen & M. van Raalte, eds., *Theophrastus: Reappraising the Sources*, 299–316. Brunswick, NJ.

Goddio, F., A. Bernand & E. Bernand (1998) 'L'épigraphie sous-marine dans le port oriental d'Alexandrie', *ZPE* 121: 131–43.

Golden, M. (1990) *Children and Childhood in Classical Athens*. Baltimore & London.

Goldhill, S. (2002) *The Invention of Prose*. Oxford.

Gomme, A. W. (1937) 'The end of the city–state', in A. W. Gomme, *Essays in Greek History and Literature*, 204–48. Oxford.

Goody, J. (1976) *Production and Reproduction: A Comparative Study of the Domestic Domain*. Cambridge.

Grace, V. R. (1949) 'Standard pottery containers of the ancient Greek world', in *Commemorative Studies in Honor of Theodore Leslie Shear*, 175–89. Baltimore, MD.

———— (1956) 'The Canaanite Jar', in S. S. Weinburg, ed., *The Aegean and the Near East: Studies Presented to Hetty Goldman on the Occasion of her Seventy-Fifth Birthday*, 80–109. Locust Valley, NY.

———— (1979) *Amphoras and the Ancient Wine Trade*. Princeton.

———— (1985) 'The Middle Stoa dated by amphora stamps', *Hesperia* 54: 1–54.

Grace, V. R. & M. Savvatianou-Petropoulakou (1970) 'Les timbres amphoriques grecs', in Bruneau et al. (1970) 277–382.

Graf, F. (1985) *Nordionische Kulte*. Rome.

Grainger, J. D. (1990) *Seleukos Nikator: Constructing a Hellenistic Kingdom*. London & New York.

———— (1999) *The League of the Aitolians*. Leiden.

Green, P. (1990) *Alexander to Actium: The Historical Evolution of the Hellenistic Age*. Berkeley & Los Angeles.

———— (1991) *Alexander of Macedon 356–323 BC. A Historical Biography*. Berkeley.

———— (1997) *The Argonautika by Apollonios Rhodios*. Berkeley & Los Angeles.

Griffin, A. (1982) *Sikyon*. Oxford.

Griffin, M. (1989) 'Philosophy, politics and politicians at Rome', in M. Griffin & J. Barnes, eds., *Philosophia Togata*, 1–37. Oxford.

Griffith, G. T. (1935) *Mercenaries of the Hellenistic World*. Cambridge, UK.

———— (1966) *Alexander the Great. The Main Problems*. Cambridge, UK.

Grimm, G. (1998) *Alexandrien: Die erste Königstadt der hellenistischen Welt*. Mainz am Rhein.

Grove, A. T. & O. Rackham (2001) *The Nature of Mediterranean Europe. An Ecological History*. New Haven & London.

Gruen, E. (1992) *Culture and National Identity in Republican Rome*. Ithaca, NY.

———— (1998) *Heritage and Hellenism: The Reinvention of Jewish Tradition*. Berkeley.

———— (2002) *Diaspora: Jews amidst Greeks and Romans*. Cambridge, MA.

Gutman, Y. (1963) *The Beginnings of Jewish-Hellenistic Literature*, 2 vols. Jerusalem.

Gutzwiller, K. (1991) *Theocritus's Pastoral Analogies. Transformation of a Genre*. Madison, WI.

———— (1996) 'Theocritean Poetry Books' in M. A. Harder, R. F. Regtuit & G. C. Wakker, eds., *Hellenistica Groningana 2: Theocritus*, 119–48. Groningen.

———— (1998) *Poetic Garlands: Hellenistic Epigrams in Context*. Berkeley & Los Angeles.

———— (2005) ed. *The New Posidippus. A Hellenistic Poetry Book*. Oxford.

Habicht, C. (1970) *Gottmenschentum und griechische Städte*, 2nd edn. Munich.

———— (1990) 'Athens and the Attalids in the Second Century B.C.', *Hesperia* 59: 561–77.

———— (1994) 'Hellenistic Athens and her philosophers' in C. Habicht, *Athen in hellenistischer Zeit*, 231–47. Munich.

———— (1996) 'Athens, Samos, and Alexander the Great', *Transactions of the American Philosophical Society* 140.3: 397–403.

———— (1997a) *Athens from Alexander to Antony*. Cambridge, MA.

———— (1997b) 'Ein neues Zeugnis der athenischen Kavallerie', *ZPE* 115: 121–4.

Habsieger, L., M. Kazarian & S. Lando (1998) 'On the second number of Plutarch', *Amer. Math. Monthly* 105: 446.

Hägg, T. (1983) *The Novel in Antiquity*. Berkeley & Los Angeles.

Hall, E. (1989) *Inventing the Barbarian: Greek Self-definition through Tragedy*. Oxford.

Hall, J. M. (1997) *Ethnic Identity in Greek Antiquity*. Cambridge.

———— (2001) 'Contested ethnicities: perceptions of Macedonia within evolving definitions of Greek identity', in I. Malkin, ed., *Ancient Perceptions of Greek Ethnicity*, 159–86/5. Cambridge, MA & London.

———— (2002) *Hellenicity: Between Ethnicity and Culture*. Chicago.

Halliwell, S. (2002) *The Aesthetics of Mimesis*. Princeton.

Hamilton, C. D. (1999) 'The Hellenistic World', in Raaflaub & Rosenstein, 163–91.

Hamilton, J. R. (1968) *Plutarch Alexander. A Commentary*. Oxford.

Hamma, K., ed. (1996) *Alexandria and Alexandrianism*. Malibu, CA.

Hammond, N. G. L. (1989) *Alexander the Great. King, Commander and Statesman*, 2nd edn. Bristol.

———— (1990) 'Royal pages, personal pages and boys trained in the Macedonian manner during the period of the Temenid monarchy', *Historia* 39: 261–90.

Hammond, N. G. L. & G. T. Griffith (1979) *A History of Macedonia,* vol. II 550-336 B.C. Oxford.

Hanfmann, G. M. A. (1983) *Sardis from Prehistoric to Roman Times*. Cambridge, MA.

Hannestad, L. (1983) *The Hellenistic Pottery from Failaka*. Aarhus.

Hansen, E. V. (1947) *The Attalids of Pergamum*. Ithaca, NY.

Hansen, M. H. (1993) *The Ancient Greek City-State*. Copenhagen.

———— (1995a) 'The "autonomous city-state": ancient fact or modern fiction?' in Hansen & Raaflaub (1995) 21–43.

———— (1995b) 'Kome: a study in how the Greeks designated and classified settlements which were not poleis', in Hansen & Raaflaub (1995) 45–81.

———— (1997a) 'The Copenhagen inventory of poleis and the lex Hafniensis de civitate', in L. G. Mitchell & P. J. Rhodes, eds., *The Development of the Polis in Archaic Greece*, 9–23. London & New York.

———— (1997b) 'A typology of dependent poleis', in T. H. Nielsen, ed., *Yet More Studies in the Ancient Greek Polis*, 29–37. Stuttgart.

———— (1998) *Polis and City-State: An Ancient Concept and its Modern Equivalent*. Copenhagen.

———— (1999) *The Athenian Democracy in the Age of Demosthenes: Structure, Principles, and Ideology*, 2nd edn. London.

———— ed. (2000a) *A Comparative Study of Thirty City-State Cultures: An Investigation Conducted by the Copenhagen Polis Centre*. Copenhagen.

———— (2000b) 'The Hellenic polis', in M. H. Hansen (2000a) 141–87.

———— ed. (2002) *A Comparative Study of Six City-state Cultures: An Investigation Conducted by the Copenhagen Polis Centre*. Copenhagen.

———— (2003) '95 theses about the Greek polis in the archaic and classical periods: a report on the results obtained by the Copenhagen Polis Centre in the period 1993–2003', *Historia* 52: 257–82.

———— (2004) 'The concept of the consumption city applied to the Greek polis', in T. H. Nielsen, ed., *Once Again: Studies in the Ancient Greek Polis*, 9–47. Copenhagen.

Hansen, M. H., L. Bjerstrup, T. H. Nielsen, L. Rubinstein & T. Vestergaard (1990) 'The demography of the Attic demes: the evidence of the sepulchral inscriptions', *Analecta Romana Instituti Danici* 19: 25–44.

Hansen, M. H. & T. Fischer-Hansen (1994) 'Monumental political architecture in archaic and classical Greek poleis: evidence and historical significance', in D. Whitehead ed., *From Political Architecture to Stephanus Byzantius: Sources for the Ancient Greek Polis*, 23–90. Stuttgart.

Hansen, M. H. & T. H. Nielsen, eds. (2004) *An Inventory of Poleis c.650–c.323 BC*. Oxford.

Hansen, M. H. & K. Raaflaub, eds. (1995) *Studies in the Ancient Greek Polis*. Stuttgart.

Harrison, T., ed. (2002) *Greeks and Barbarians*. Edinburgh.

Hartog, F. (1988) *The Mirror of Herodotus*. Berkeley.

Harvey, A. E. (1955) 'The classification of Greek lyric poetry', *CQ* 5: 157–75.

Harward, J. (1982) *Greek Domestic Sculpture and the Origins of Private Art Patronage*, unpublished doctoral dissertation, Harvard.

Hatzidakis, P. I. (1997) 'Building south of the Hieron of Promachonos. A *taberna vinaria* on Delos', in *Praktika* of the 4th Scientific Conference on Hellenistic Pottery, May 1994, 291–307. Athens (in Greek).

Hatzopoulos, M. B. (2001) *L'organisation de l'armée Macédonienne sous les Antigonides. Problèmes anciens et documents nouveaux*. Athens.

––––––– (2004) "La formation militaire dans les gymnases hellénistiques," in Kah & Scholz, 91–96.

Heckel, W. (1977) 'The conspiracy against Philotas', *Phoenix* 31: 9–21.

––––––– (1987) 'A grandson of Antipater at Delos', *ZPE* 70: 161–2.

––––––– (1992) *The Marshals of Alexander's Empire*. London.

––––––– (2002) *The Wars of Alexander the Great 336–323 BC*. Oxford.

Heichelheim, F. M. (1930) *Wirtschaftliche Schwankungen der Zeit von Alexander bis Augustus*. Reprint, 1979. New York.

Hellenkemper-Salies, G., ed. (1994) *Das Wrack: Die antike Schiffsfund von Mahdia*. Köln.

Hellmann, M.-C. (1992) *Recherches sur le vocabulaire de l'architecture grecque, d'après les inscriptions de Délos*. Paris.

Helly, B. (1973) *Gonnoi*, 2 vols. Amsterdam.

Herman, G. (1997) 'The court society of the Hellenistic age', in Cartledge et al. (1997) 199–224.

Higgins, R. A. (1967) *Greek Terracottas*. London.

––––––– (1980) *Greek and Roman Jewellery*, 2nd ed. London.

––––––– (1986) *Tanagra and the Figurines*. Princeton.

Himmelmann, N. (1983) *Alexandria und der Realismus in der griechischen Kunst*. Tübingen.

Hirsch, S. (1985) *The Friendship of the Barbarians*. Hanover, NH.

Hoepfner, W., ed. (1999) *Geschichte des Wohnens I, 5000 v. Chr.-500 n. Chr. Vorgeschichte, Frühgeschichte, Antike*. Stuttgart.

––––––– ed. (2002) *Antike Bibliotheken*. Mainz.

Hoepfner, W. & G. Brands, eds. (1996) *Basileia: Die Paläste der hellenistischen Könige*. Mainz.

Hoepfner, W. & E.-L. Schwandner (1994) *Haus und Stadt im klassischen Griechenland*, 2nd edn. München.

Högemann, P. (1985) *Alexander der Große und Arabien*. Munich.

Hölbl, G. (2001) *A History of the Ptolemaic Empire*. London & New York.

Hoff, M. C. (1997) 'Laceratae Athenae: Sulla's siege of Athens in 87/6 B.C. and its aftermath', in Hoff & Rotroff (1997) 33–51.

Hoff, M. C. & S. I. Rotroff, eds. (1997) *The Romanization of Athens*. Oxford.

Holladay, C. (1995) *Fragments from Hellenistic Jewish Authors: Vol. III: Aristobulus*. Atlanta, GA.

Holleaux, M. (1942) *Études d'épigraphie et d'histoire grecques. III. Lagides et Séleucides*. Paris.

———— (1942a) 'Ceux qui sont dans le baggage', in Holleaux (1942) 15–26.

———— (1942b) 'Inscriptions de Séleucie-de-Piérie', in Holleaux (1942) 199–254.

Hollis, A. (1990) *Callimachus: Hecale*. Oxford.

Holt, F. L. (1988) *Alexander the Great and Bactria. The Formation of a Greek Frontier*. Leiden.

———— (1999) *Thundering Zeus: The Making of Hellenistic Bactria*. Berkeley.

———— (2003) *Alexander the Great and the Mystery of the Elephant Medallions*. Berkeley.

Honigman, S. (2003a) 'Noms sémitiques à Edfou et Thèbes', *BASP* 40.1/4: 63–118.

———— (2003b) 'Politeumata and ethnicity in Ptolemaic and Roman Egypt', *AncSoc* 33: 61–102.

Hopkins, K. (1978) 'Between slavery and freedom: on freeing slaves at Delphi', in K. Hopkins, *Conquerors and Slaves*, 133–71. Cambridge.

Horden, P. & N. Purcell (2000) *The Corrupting Sea: A Study of Mediterranean History*. Oxford & Malden, MA.

Hornblower, J. (1981) *Hieronymus of Cardia*. Oxford.

Hornblower, S. ed. (1994) *Greek Historiography*. Oxford.

Horrocks, G. (1997) *Greek: A History of the Language and its Speakers*. London & New York.

Houby-Nielsen, S. (1996) 'Revival of archaic funerary practices in the hellenistic and Roman Kerameikos', *PDIA* 2: 129–46.

———— (1997) 'Grave gifts, women, and conventional values in hellenistic Athens', in P. Bilde et al., eds., *Conventional Values of the Hellenistic Greeks*, 220–62, pls. 8–14. Aarhus.

———— (1998) 'Revival of archaic funerary practices in the hellenistic and Roman Kerameikos', *PDIA* 2: 129–46.

Hughes Fowler, B., ed. (1989) *The Hellenistic Aesthetic*. Bristol.

Humphrey, J. W., J. Oleson & A. Sherwood. (1998) *Greek and Roman Technology: A Sourcebook*. London.

Humphreys, S. C. (1980) 'Family tombs and tomb cult in ancient Athens: tradition or traditionalism?' *JHS* 100: 96–126.

Hunter, R. (1993a) *The Argonautica of Apollonius Rhodius: Literary Studies*. Cambridge.

———— (1993b) 'The presentation of Herodas' mimiamboi', *Antichthon* 27: 31–44.

———— (1996) *Theocritus and the Archaeology of Greek Poetry*. Cambridge.

Huss, W. (1994) *Der makedonische König und die ägyptischen Priester*. Wiesbaden.

Hutchinson, G. (1988) *Hellenistic Poetry*. Oxford.

Inwood, B., ed. (2003) *Cambridge Companion to the Stoics*. Cambridge.

Irby-Massie, G. L. & P. T. Keyser (2002) *Greek Science of the Hellenistic Era: A Sourcebook*. London.

Irwin, T. (1989) *Classical Thought*. Oxford.

Isaac, B. (2004) *The Invention of Racism in Classical Antiquity*. Princeton.

Jaeger, W. (1938) 'Greeks and Jews', *Journal of Religion* 18: 127–43.

Jaschinski, S. (1981) *Alexander und Griechenland unter dem Eindruck der Flucht des Harpalos*. Bonn.

Jones, C. P. (1999) 'The union of Latmos and Pidasa', *EA* 31: 1–7.

Jones, N. F. (1987) *Public Organization in Ancient Greece: A Documentary Study*. Philadelphia, PA.

────── (1999) *The Associations of Classical Athens*. New York.

Kah, D. (2004) "Militärische Ausbildung im hellenistischen Gymnasion," in Kah & Scholz, 47–90.

Kah, D. and P. Scholz, eds. (2004) *Das hellenistiche Gymnasion*. Berlin.

Kähler, H. (1965) *Der Fries vom Reiterdenkmal des Aemilius Paullus in Delphi*. Berlin.

Kebric, R. B. (1977) *In the Shadow of Macedon: Duris of Samos*. Wiesbaden.

Kennedy, G. A. (1994) *A New History of Classical Rhetoric*. Princeton.

Kennell, N. (1999) "Age categories and chronology in the Hellenistic Theseia," *Phoenix* 53: 249–62.

────── (2003) "The later Greek ephebate. A philosophical school for the *jeunesse dorée*?" Unpublished APA paper, New Orleans.

Kent, J. H. (1948) 'The temple estates of Delos, Rheneia, and Mykonos', *Hesperia* 17:243–338.

Kern, P. B. (1999) *Ancient Siege Warfare*. Bloomington, IN.

Keyser, P. T. (1990) 'Alchemy in the ancient world', *ICS* 15: 353–78.

────── (1994) 'The use of artillery by Philip II and Alexander the Great', *AncW* 25: 27–59.

Kidd, D., ed. (1997) *Aratus. Phaenomena*. Cambridge.

Kiderlen, M. (1995) *Megale Oikia. Untersuchungen zur Entwicklung aufwendiger griechischer Stadthausarchitiktur von der Früharchaik bis ins 3 Jh. v.Chr.*, 2 vols. Hürth.

Kienast, H. J. (1997) 'The tower of the winds in Athens: Hellenistic or Roman?' in Hoff & Rotroff (1997) 53–65.

Kitchen, K. A. (2001) "Economics in ancient Arabia: from Alexander to the Augustans', in Archibald et al. (2001) 157–73.

Klein, W. (1921) *Vom antiken Rokoko*. Vienna.

Kloppenborg, J. & S. Wilson, eds. (1996) *Voluntary Associations in the Graeco-Roman World*. London.

Kourinou, E. (2000) *Sparta. Contribution to its Monumental Topography*. Athens (in Greek).

Kralli, I. (1999–2000) 'Athens and her leading citizens in the early Hellenistic period (338–261 B.C.): the evidence of the decrees awarding the highest honors', *Archaiognosia* 10: 133–62.

Krasilnikoff, J. A. (1992) 'Aegean mercenaries in the fourth to second centuries B.C. A study in payment, plunder, and logistics of ancient Greek armies', *C&M* 43: 23–36.

Kreeb, M. (1984) 'Studien zur figürlichen Ausstattung delischer Privathaüser', *BCH* 108: 317–43.

Krevans, N. (1993) 'Fighting against Antimachus: the *Lyde* and the *Aetia* Reconsidered' in M. A. Harder, R. F. Regtuit, & G. C. Wacker, eds., *Hellenistica Groningana1: Callimachus*, 149–60. Groningen.

Kroll, J. H. (1993) *The Greek Coins* (The Athenian Agora XXVI). Princeton.

Kroll, W. (1924) *Studien zum Verständnis der römischen Literatur*. Stuttgart.

Kuhrt, A. & S. M. Sherwin-White, eds. (1987) *Hellenism in the East. The Interaction of Greek and Non-Greek Civilizations from Syria to Central Asia after Alexander*. London.

Kurtz, D. & J. Boardman (1971) *Greek Burial Customs*. London.

Kutbay, B. L. (1998) *Palaces and Large Residences of the Hellenistic Age.* Lampeter, UK.

La'da, C. A. (1996) *Ethnic Designations in Hellenistic Egypt,* unpublished doctoral dissertation, University of Cambridge.

——— (2002) *Foreign Ethnics in Hellenistic Egypt.* Leuven.

Labarre, G. (1996) *Les Cités de Lesbos: époques hellénistique et impériale.* Paris.

——— (2004) 'Phrourarques et phrouroi des cités grecques d'Asie Mineure à l'époque hellénistique' in Couvenhes & Fernoux (2004) 221–48.

Landels, J. G. (1978) *Engineering in the Ancient World.* Berkeley.

Landucci Gattinoni, F. (2003) *L'arte del potere: vita e opera di Cassandro di Macedonia.* Stuttgart.

Lane Fox, R. (1973) *Alexander the Great.* London.

——— (1996) 'Text and image: Alexander the Great, coins and elephants', *BICS* 41: 87–108.

Lapatin, K. D. S. (2001) *Chryselephantine Statuary in the Ancient Mediterranean World.* Oxford.

Larsen, J. A. O. (1968) *Greek Federal States: Their Institutions and History.* Oxford.

Larsen, J. A. O. & P. J. Rhodes (1996) 'Isopoliteia', in *OCD³*, 771.

Laubscher, H. P. (1982) *Fischer und Landleute.* Mainz.

Launey, M. (1949–1950) *Recherches sur les armées hellénistiques,* 2 vols. Paris (updated repr. 1987).

Lauter, H. (1986) *Die Architektur des Hellenismus.* Darmstadt.

Lawall, M. (in press) 'Amphoras and hellenistic economics. addressing the (over)-emphasis on stamped amphora handles', in Archibald et al. (in press).

——— (2004) 'Nothing to do with Mendaian Amphoras? Athenaeus 11.784c', in R. B Egan & J. Joyal, eds., *Daimonopylai. Essays in Classics and the Classical Tradition Presented to Edmund G. Berry.* Winnipeg.

Lawrence, A. W. (1996) *Greek Architecture,* 5th edn. New Haven & London.

——— (1979) *Greek Aims in Fortification.* Oxford.

Le Bohec-Bouhet, S. (1999) 'Les techniques de la guerre au IVe s.', in Prost, ed. (1999) 257–75.

Lefkowitz, M. (1981) *The Lives of the Greek Poets.* London.

Leiwo, M. (1997) 'Religion, or other reasons? Private associations in Athens', in Frösén, 103–17.

Lenger, M.-Th. (1990) *Corpus des ordonnances des Ptolémées.* Bruxelles.

Lerner, J. D. (1999) *The Impact of Seleucid Decline: the Foundation of Arsacid Parthia and Graeco-Bactria.* Stuttgart.

Lévêque, P. (1957) *Pyrrhos.* Paris.

——— (1968) 'La guerre à l'époque hellénistique', in Vernant, ed., 261–87.

Lévy, E. (1992) 'Hérodote *philobarbaros* ou la vision du barbare chez Hérodote', in R. Lonis, ed., *L'Etranger dans le monde grec,* vol. II, 193–244. Nancy.

Lewis, D. M. (1962) 'The chronology of the Athenian new style coinage', *NC⁷* 2: 275–300.

——— (1997) *Selected Papers in Greek and Near Eastern History.* Cambridge.

Lewis, M. (2000) 'The hellenistic period', in Wikander, 631–648.

Lewis, N. (1986) *Greeks in Ptolemaic Egypt. Case Studies in the Social History of the Hellenistic World.* Oxford.

Lewy, H. (1938) 'Aristotle and the Jewish Sage according to Clearchus of Soli', *Harvard Theological Review* 31: 205–35.

Lightfoot, J. (2002) 'Nothing to do with the technitai of Dionysus?' in P. Easterling & E. Hall, eds., *Greek and Roman Actors: Aspects of an Ancient Profession*, 209–24. Cambridge.

Ling, R., ed. (1984) *The Cambridge Ancient History*, Plates to Vol. II, Part 1: *The Hellenistic World to the Coming of the Romans*. New edition. Cambridge.

_____ (1991) *Roman Painting*. Cambridge & New York.

_____ (1998) *Ancient Mosaics*. Princeton.

Lissarrague, F. (1990) *The Aesthetics of the Greek Banquet: Images of Wine and Ritual*. Princeton.

Lloyd, A. B. (1976) *Herodotus, Book II: Commentary, 1–98*. Leiden.

_____ (1982) 'Nationalist propaganda in Ptolemaic Egypt', *Historia* 31: 33–55.

Lloyd, G. E. R. (1973) *Greek Science after Aristotle*. New York.

_____ (1983) *Science, Folklore, and Ideology*. Cambridge.

_____ (1991) *Methods and Problems in Greek Science*. Cambridge.

Lo Cascio, E., ed. (2003) *Credito e moneta nel mondo Romano*. Bari.

Long, A. A. (1986) *Hellenistic Philosophy*, 2nd edn. London.

_____ (1996) *Stoic Studies*. Cambridge.

Long, A. A. & D. N. Sedley (1987) *The Hellenistic Philosophers*. Cambridge.

Longrigg, J. (1988) 'Anatomy in Alexandria', *BJHS* 21: 455–88.

_____ (1998) *Greek Medicine from the Heroic to the Hellenistic Age*. London.

Lonis, R. (1996) 'Poliorcétique et *stasis* dans la première moitié du IVe siècle av. J.-C.', in Carlier, 241–57.

Lubar, S. & W. D. Kingery (1993) *History from Things: Essays on Material Culture*. Washington, DC.

Lund, H. S. (1992) *Lysimachus: A Study in Early Hellenistic Kingship*. London & New York.

Ma, J. (1999) *Antiochos III and the Cities of Western Asia Minor*. Oxford.

_____ (2000) "Fighting *poleis* of the hellenistic world," in van Wees, 337–76.

_____ (2003) 'Dans les pas d'Antiochos III: l'Asie Mineure entre pouvoir et discours', in Prost (2003), 243–59.

Malkin, I. & K. Raaflaub, eds. (2001) *Ancient Perceptions of Greek Ethnicity*. Cambridge, MA and London.

Manning, J. (2003) *Land and Power in Ptolemaic Egypt. The Structure of Land Tenure*. Cambridge.

Marasco, G. (1986) 'Interessi commerciali e fattori politici nella condotta romana in Illiria (230–219 A.C.)', *SCO* 36: 35–112.

_____ (1988) *Economia, commerci e politica del Mediterraneo fra il III e il II secolo a.C.* Firenze.

Marcadé, J. (1969) *Au Musée de Délos. Étude sur la sculpture hellénistique en ronde-bosse découverte dans l'île*. Paris.

Marincola, J. M. (1997) *Authority and Tradition in Classical Historiography*. Cambridge.

_____ (2001) *Greek Historians*. Oxford.

Marinovic, L. P. (1988) *Le mercenariat grec au IVe s. avant notre ère et la crise de la polis*. Paris.

Markoe, G., ed. (2003) *Petra Rediscovered: Lost City of the Nabateans*, New York.

Marrou, H.-I. (1948) *Histoire de l'éducation dans l'antiquité I. Le monde grec*. Paris.

Marsden, E. W. (1969–1971) *Greek and Roman Artillery*, 2 vols. Oxford.

—— (1977) 'Macedonian military machinery and its designers under Philip and Alexander', *Archaia Macedonia* 2: 211–23.

Martin, R. (1974) *L'Urbanisme dans la Grèce antique*, 2nd edn. Paris.

Mastromarco, G. (1984) *The Public of Herondas*. Amsterdam.

Mates, B. (1961) *Stoic Logic*, 2nd edn. Berkeley.

Matthews, V. J. (1996) *Antimachus of Colophon*. Leiden.

Mattusch, C. C. (1997) *The Victorious Youth*. Malibu.

Mazza, F. (1988) 'The Phoenicians as seen by the ancient world', in S. Moscati, ed., *The Phoenicians*, 548–67. New York.

McCredie, J. R. (1966) *Fortified Military Camps in Attica*. Princeton.

—— (1994) 'A Samothracian enigma', *Hesperia* 43: 454–459.

McInerney, J. (1999) *The Folds of Parnassos: Land and Ethnicity in Ancient Phokis*. Austin, TX.

McKechnie, P. R. (1989) *Outsiders in the Greek Cities in the Fourth Century B.C.* London.

McKenzie, J. M. (1990) *The Architecture of Petra*. Oxford.

—— (2003) 'Glimpsing Alexandria from archaeological evidence', *Journal of Roman Archaeology* 16: 35–63.

McNicoll, A. W. (1986) 'Developments in techniques of siegecraft and fortifications in the Greek world ca. 400–100 B.C.', in P. Leriche & H. Tréziny, eds., *La fortification dans l'histoire du monde grec*, 305–11. Paris.

—— (1997) *Hellenistic Fortifications from the Aegean to the Euphrates*. Oxford.

Meadows, A. (2001) 'Money, freedom, and empire in the hellenistic world', in Meadows & Shipton, 53–63.

Meadows, A. & K. Shipton, eds. (2001) *Money and its Uses in the Ancient Greek World*. Cambridge.

Melaerts, H. & L. Mooren (2002) *Le rôle et le statut de la femme en Égypte hellénistique, romaine et byzantine*. Leuven.

Mélèze-Modrzejewski, J. (1990) 'L'image du Juif dans le pensée grecque vers 300 avant notre ère', in A. Kasher, *Greece and Rome in Eretz Israel*, 105–18. Jerusalem.

—— (1999) 'Le droit hellénistique et la famille grecque', in C. Bontems, ed., *Nonagesimo anno: mélanges en hommage à Jean Gaudemet*, 261–80. Paris.

Merkelbach, R. & J. Stauber (1998) *Steinepigramme aus dem griechischen Osten*, vol. I. Stuttgart & Leipzig.

Meyboom, P. G. P. (1995) *The Nile Mosaic of Palestrina: Early Evidence of Egyptian Religion in Italy*. Leiden & New York.

Migeotte, L. (1984) *L'emprunt publique dans les cités grecques. Receuil des documents et analyse critique*. Quebec & Paris.

Mikalson, J. D. (1998) *Religion in Hellenistic Athens*. Berkeley.

—— (2005) *Ancient Greek Religion*. Blackwell.

Miller, M. C. (1997) *Athens and Persia in the Fifth Century BC. A Study in Cultural Receptivity*. Cambridge.

Miller, S. G. (1995) 'Architecture as evidence for the identity of the early polis', in Hansen & Raaflaub (1995) 201–44.

—— (2001) *The Early Hellenistic Stadium* (Excavations at Nemea II). Berkeley & Los Angeles.

Millett, P. (1989) 'Patronage and its avoidance in classical Athens', in Wallace-Hadrill, 15–47.

Milns, R. D. (1976) 'The army of Alexander the Great', *Entretiens Hardt* 22: 87–136.

Moles. J. L. (1995) 'The Cynics and Politics', in A. Laks & M. Schofield, eds., *Justice and Generosity*, 129–58. Cambridge.

——— (1996) 'Cynic cosmopolitanism', in R. B. Banham & M.-O. Goulet-Cazé, eds., *The Cynics*, 105–20. Berkeley.

Mollard-Besques, S. (1963) *Catalogue raisonné des figurines et reliefs en terre-cuite grecs, étrusques et romains*, vol. II *Myrina*. Paris.

Momigliano, A. (1955) 'Per il centenario dell' 'Alessandro Magno' di J. G. Droysen', in A. Momigliano, *Contributo alla storia degli studi classici.*, 263–73. Rome.

——— (1971) *The Development of Greek Biography*. Cambridge, MA.

——— (1977) *Essays in Ancient and Modern Historiography*. Oxford.

——— (1979) *Alien Wisdom: The Limits of Hellenization*. Cambridge.

——— (1990) *The Classical Foundations of Modern Historiography*. Berkeley, Los Angeles, & Oxford.

Mooren, L. (1975) *The Aulic Titulature in Ptolemaic Egypt: Introduction and Prosopography*. Brussels.

——— (1977) *La hiérarchie de cour ptolémaïque. Contribution à l'étude des institutions et des classes dirigeantes à l'époque hellénistique*. Leuven.

Moreno, P. (1994) *Scultura Ellenistica*. Rome.

Moretti, L. (1953) *Iscrizione agonistiche greche*. Rome.

——— (1967, 1976) *Iscrizioni storiche ellenistiche*. 2 vols. Firenze.

Mørkholm, O. (1991) *Early Hellenistic Coinage: From the Accession of Alexander to the Peace of Apamea (336–188 B.C.)*. Cambridge & New York.

Morley, N. (2000) *Ancient History: Key Themes and Approaches*. London & New York.

Morrison, J. S. & J. F. Coates (1996) *Greek and Roman Oared Warships*. Oxford.

Müller, K. (1965) *Geographi Graeci minores*, 2 vols. Paris. Hildesheim: Olms repr. of 1855–1861 ed.

Munn, M. (1993) *The Defense of Attica. The Dema Wall and the Boiotian War of 378–375 B.C.* Berkeley.

Murray, O., ed. (1990) *Sympotica: A Symposium on the Symposion*. Oxford.

Neugebauer, O. (1975) *History of Ancient Mathematical Astronomy*. Berlin.

Neugebauer, O. & H. B. van Hosen (1959) *Greek Horoscopes*. Philadelphia.

Nevett, L. C. (1995) 'The organisation of space in classical and hellenistic houses from mainland Greece and the western colonies', in N. Spencer, ed., *Time, Tradition and Society in Greek Archaeology: Bridging the 'Great Divide'*, 89–108. London & New York.

——— (1999) *House and Society in the Ancient Greek World*. Cambridge.

——— (2002) 'Continuity and change in Greek households under Roman rule: the role of women in the domestic context', in E. N. Ostenfeld, ed., *Greek Romans and Roman Greeks*, 81–100. Aarhus.

Nicolet, C. (2000) 'Fragments pour une géographie urbaine comparée: à propos d'Alexandrie', in Nicolet et al., eds., 245–52.

Nicolet, C., R. Ilbert & J.-C. Depaule, eds. (2000) *Mégapoles méditerranéennes: géographie urbaine rétrospective*. Paris.

Nielsen, I. (1994) *Hellenistic Palaces: Tradition and Renewal*. Aarhus.

——— ed. (2001) *The Royal Palace Institution in the First Millennium B.C.* Aarhus.

Nielsen, T. H. (1999) 'The concept of Arkadia: the people, their land, and their organisation', in T. Nielsen, ed., *Defining Ancient Arkadia*, 16–79. Copenhagen.

——— (2002) *Arkadia and its Poleis in the Archaic and Classical Periods*. Göttingen.

Nilsson, M. P. (1961) *Geschichte der griechischen Religion*, 2 vols, 2nd edn. Munich.

Nisetich, F. (2001) *The Poems of Callimachus.* Oxford.

Nouhaud, M. (1982) *L'utilisation de l'histoire par les orateurs attiques.* Paris.

Nussbaum, M. C. (1994) *The Therapy of Desire: Theory and Practice in Hellenistic Ethics.* Princeton.

Ober, J. (1985) *Fortress Attica. Defense of the Athenian Land Frontier, 404–322.* Leiden.

———— (1992) 'Towards a typology of Greek artillery towers: the first and second generations (c. 375–275 B.C.)', in van de Maele & Fossey, 147–69.

Ogden, D. (1996) *Greek Bastardy in the Classical and the Hellenistic Periods.* Oxford.

———— (1999) *Polygamy, Prostitutes and Death: the Hellenistic Dynasties.* London.

———— ed. (2002) *The Hellenistic World. New Perspectives.* London.

Ogden, J. (1982) *Jewellery of the Ancient World.* New York.

Oleson, J. P. (2000) 'Irrigation', in Wikander, 183–215.

Oliver, G. (2001) 'Regions and micro-regions: grain for Rhamnous', in Archibald et al. (2001) 137–55.

Olshausen, E. (1974) *Prosopographie der hellenistische Königsgesandten*, vol. I. Louvain.

Olson, S. D. (1991) 'Firewood and charcoal in classical Athens', *Hesperia* 60: 411–20.

Olson, S. D. & A. Sens (1999) *Matro of Pitane and the Tradition of Epic Parody in the Fourth Century BCE.* Atlanta, GA.

Onians, J. (1979) *Art and Thought in the Hellenistic Age. The Greek World View, 350–50 B.C.* London.

Orlandos, A. K. & I. N. Travlos (1986) *Lexikon of Ancient Architectural Terms.* Athens. (in Greek).

Osborne, M. J. (1981–1983) *Naturalization in Athens*, 4 vols. Brussels.

Osborne, R. (2004) 'Greek archaeology: a survey of recent work', *AJA* 108: 87–102.

Osborne, R. & P. J. Rhodes (2003) *Greek Historical Inscriptions, 404–323 BC.* Oxford & New York.

Owens, E. J. (1991) *The City in the Greek and Roman World.* London & New York.

Palagia, O. & S. V. Tracy, eds. (2003) *The Macedonians in Athens 322–229 B.C.* Oxford.

Panagopoulou, K. (2001) 'The Antigonids: patterns of a royal economy', in Archibald et al. (2001) 313–64.

Parke, H. W. (1933) *Greek Mercenary Soldiers from the Earliest Times to the Battle of Ipsus.* Oxford.

Parker, A. J. (1992) *Ancient Shipwrecks of the Mediterranean and the Roman Provinces.* Oxford.

Parker, R. (1996) *Athenian Religion: A History.* Oxford.

———— (1997) "Full rations for the Tarantinoi in Athens: a note on the new decree," *ZPE* 115: 136.

Parkin, T. G. (1992) *Demography and Roman Society.* Baltimore, MD & London.

Parkins, H. & C. J. Smith, eds. (1998) *Trade, Traders, and the Ancient City.* London & New York.

Patterson, C. B. (1998) *The Family in Greek History.* Cambridge, MA & London.

Pearson, L. (1960) *The Lost Histories of Alexander the Great.* New York.

———— (1986) 'The speeches in Timaeus' history', *AJP* 107: 350–68.

Pélékidis, C. (1962) *Histoire de l'éphébie attique.* Paris.

Pelling, C. B. R. (2000) *Literary Texts and the Greek Historian.* London.

Perlman, P. (2000) *City and Sanctuary in Ancient Greece: The Theorodokia in the Peloponnese.* Göttingen.

Perrin-Saminadayar, É. (2003) 'Des élites intellectuelles à Athènes à l'époque hellénistique? Non, des notables', in Cébeillac-Gervasoni & Lamoine, 383–400.

Pestman, P. W. (1961) *Marriage and Matrimonial Property in Ancient Egypt: A Contribution to Establishing the Legal Position of Women.* Leiden.

Petrakos, V. C. (1999) *The Deme of Rhamnous,* 2 vols. Athens (in Greek).

Pfeiffer, R. (1949) *Callimachus,* vol. I. Oxford.

———— (1968) *A History of Classical Scholarship from the Beginnings to the End of the Hellenistic Age.* Oxford.

Pfister, R., ed. (1951) *Die Reisebilder des Herakleides.* Wien.

Pfrommer, M. (1990) *Untersuchungen zur Chronologie früh- und hochhellenistischen Goldschmucks.* Tübingen.

———— (1998) *Untersuchungen zur Chronologie und Komposition des Alexandermosaiks auf antiquarischer Grundlage.* Mainz am Rhein.

Pfuhl, E. & H. Möbius (1977–1979) *Die ostgriechishen Grabreliefs,* 2 vols. Mainz am Rhein.

Picard, C. (1921) *Exploration archéologique de Délos,* vol. IV *L'Établissement des Poseidoniastes de Bérytos.* Paris.

Plantzos, D. (1996a) 'Hellenistic cameos: Problems of Classification and Chronology', *BICS* 41: 115–31.

———— (1996b) 'Ptolemaic cameos of the 2nd and 1st centuries B.C.', *Oxford Journal of Archaeology* 15: 39–61.

———— (1999) *Hellenistic Engraved Gems.* Oxford.

Poddighe, E. (2002) *Nel segno di Antipatro. L'eclissi della democrazia ateniese dal 323/2 al 319/8 a.C.* Rome.

Pollitt, J. J. (1974) *The Ancient View of Greek Art: Criticism, History, and Terminology.* New Haven, CT.

———— (1986) *Art in the Hellenistic Age.* Cambridge.

Pomeroy, S. B. (1984) *Women in Hellenistic Egypt: From Alexander to Cleopatra.* New York.

———— (1993) 'Infanticide in Hellenistic Greece', in A. Cameron & A. Kuhrt, eds., *Images of Women in Antiquity,* 207–222. London.

———— (1994) 'Family history in Ptolemaic Egypt', in A. Bülow-Jacobsen, ed., *Proceedings of the 20th International Congress of Papyrologists,* 593–97. Copenhagen.

———— (1996) 'Families in Ptolemaic Egypt: continuity, change, and coercion', in R. W. Wallace & E. M. Harris, eds., *Transitions to Empire. Essays in Greco-Roman History, 360–146 BC, in Honor of E. Badian,* 241–53. Norman, OK.

———— (1997) *Families in Classical and Hellenistic Greece: Representations and Realities.* Oxford.

Porten, B. & A. Yardeni (1999) *Textbook of Aramaic Documents from Ancient Egypt,* 4 vols. Winona Lake, IN.

Potts, D. T. (1990) *The Arabian Gulf in Antiquity,* 2 vols. Oxford.

Pouilloux, J. (1954) *La forteresse de Rhamnonte.* Paris.

Préaux, Cl. (1939) *L'économie royale des Lagides.* Bruxelles.

———— (1978) *Le monde hellénistique: la Grèce et l' orient de la morte d' Alexandre à la conquête romaine de la Grèce (323–146 av. J.-C.),* 2 vols. Paris.

Pritchett, W. K. (1971–1991) *The Greek State at War,* 5 vols. Berkeley.

Prost, F., ed. (1999) *Armées et sociétés de la Grèce classique.* Paris.

———— ed. (2003) *L'orient méditerranéen de la mort d'Alexandre aux campagnes de Pompée. Cités et royaumes à l'époque hellénistique.* Toulouse.

Raaflaub, K. & N. Rosenstein, eds. (1999) *War and Society in the Ancient and Medieval Worlds.* Cambridge, MA & London.

Radt, W. (1999) *Pergamon: Geschichte und Bauten einer antiken Metropole.* Darmstadt.

Raepsaet, G. (1993) 'Le diolkos de l'Isthme à Corinthe: son trace, son fonctionnement,' *BCH* 117: 233–56.

Rathje W. & C. Murphy (1992) *Rubbish!: The Archaeology of Garbage.* New York.

Rauh, N. (1998) *The Sacred Bonds of Commerce. Religion, Economy, Trade and Society at Hellenistic and Roman Delos.* Amsterdam.

Rawson, E. (1985) *Intellectual Life in the Late Roman Republic.* London.

Reeder, E. D., ed. (1988) *Hellenistic Art in the Walters Art Gallery.* Baltimore.

Reger, G. (1994) *Regionalism and Change in the Economy of Independent Delos: 314–167 BC.* Berkeley, Los Angeles, & Oxford.

———— (2003) 'The economy', in Erskine (2003) 331–53.

Reinders, H. R. (1988) *New Halos: A Hellenistic Town in Thessalia, Greece.* Utrecht.

Rhodes, P. J. (1997) with D. M. Lewis, *The Decrees of the Greek States.* Oxford.

———— (2003) *Ancient Democracy and Modern Ideology.* London.

Rice, E. E. (1983) *The Grand Procession of Ptolemy Philadelphus.* Oxford.

Ridgway, B. S. (1999) *Prayers in Stone. Greek Architectural Sculpture ca. 600–100 B.C.E.* Berkeley & Los Angeles.

———— (1990–2002) *Hellenistic Sculpture,* 3 vols. Madison.

Rigsby, K. J. (1996) *Asylia: Territorial Inviolability in the Hellenistic World.* Berkeley, Los Angeles & London.

Rihll, T. E. (1999) *Greek Science.* Oxford.

Robert, L. (1968) 'De Delphes à l'Oxus. Inscriptions grecques nouvelles de la Bactriane', *CRAI*: 416–57, 510–51.

Robert, L. & J. Robert (1989) *Claros,* vol. I. Paris.

Robinson, C. A. (1953) *The History of Alexander the Great,* vol. I. Providence, RI.

Roisman, J., ed. (2003) *Brill's Companion to Alexander the Great.* Leiden.

Rood, T. (in press) in C. J. Tuplin, ed., (in press) *The World of Xenophon (Historia Einzelschriften* xxx). Munich.

Rosenmeyer, T. (1969) *The Green Cabinet: Theocritus and the European Pastoral Lyric.* Berkeley & Los Angeles.

Rosivach, V. J. (2001) 'Class matters in the Dyskolos of Menander', *CQ* 51: 127–34.

Rostovetzeff, M. I. (1953) *The Social and Economic History of the Hellenistic World,* 3 vols. Oxford.

Rotroff, S. I. (1982) *Hellenistic Pottery: Athenian and Imported Moldmade Bowls* (The Athenian Agora XXII). Princeton.

———— (1982) 'Silver, glass, and clay evidence for the dating of Hellenistic luxury tableware', *Hesperia* 51: 329–37.

———— (1984) 'Spool Saltcellars in the Athenian Agora', *Hesperia* 53: 343–54.

———— (1996) *The Missing Krater and the Hellenistic Symposium: Drinking in the Age of Alexander the Great.* Christchurch, NZ.

———— (1997a) 'From Greek to Roman in Athenian ceramics', in Hoff & Rotroff (1997) 97–116.

———— (1997b) 'The Greeks and the other in the age of Alexander', in J. E. Coleman & C. A. Walz, eds, *Greeks and Barbarians,* 221–35. Bethesda, MD.

—— (1997c) *Hellenistic Pottery: Athenian and Imported Wheelmade Table Ware and Related Material* (The Athenian Agora XXIX). Princeton.

—— (2001) 'Pottery as Historical Artifact: Hellenistic Athens', *AJA* 105: 269 (abstract).

—— (2005) *Hellenistic Pottery: The Plain Wares* (The Athenian Agora XXXIII). Princeton.

Rotroff, S. I. & A. Oliver, Jr. (in press) *Hellenistic Pottery*. Cambridge, MA.

Rouveret, A. (1989) *Histoire et imaginaire de la peinture ancienne (Ve siècle av. J.-C. – 1er siècle ap. J.-C.* Paris & Rome.

Rowland, I. D., trans (1999) *Vitruvius. Ten Books on Architecture*. Cambridge.

Rowlandson, J., ed. (1998) *Women and Society in Greek and Roman Egypt: A Source Book.* Cambridge.

Sachs, A. & H. Hunger (1988, 1989, 1996) *Astronomical Diaries and Related Texts from Babylonia. Diaries from 652 BC to 61 BC.*, 3 vols. Vienna.

Sacks, K. (1981) *Polybius on the Writing of History*. Berkeley & Los Angeles.

Sallares, R. (1991) *The Ecology of the Ancient Greek World*. London.

Saller, R. P. (1994) *Patriarchy, Property and Death in the Roman Family*. Cambridge.

—— (2001) 'The family and society', in J. Bodel, ed., *Epigraphic Evidence. Ancient History from Inscriptions*, 95–117. London & New York.

Salles, J.-F. (1987) 'The Arab–Persian gulf under the Seleucids', in Kuhrt & Sherwin–White, 75–109.

Salmenkivi, E. (1997) 'Family life in the comedies of Menander', in Frösén, 183–94.

Sartre, M. (1995) *L'Asie Mineure et l'Anatolie d'Alexandre à Dioclétien (IVe s. av. J.-C.-IIIᵉ s. ap. J.-C.)*. Paris.

—— (2001) *D'Alexandre à Zénobie. Histoire du Levant antique, IVᵉ siècle av. J.-C.-IIIe siècle ap. J.-C.* Paris.

Savalli, I. (1985) 'I neocittadini nelle città ellenistiche. Note sulla concessione e l'acquisizione della *politeia*', *Historia* 34: 387–431.

Savalli-Lestrade, I. (1998) *Les philoi royaux dans l'Asie hellénistique*. Geneva.

—— (2003) 'Remarques sur les élites dans les *poleis* hellénistiques', in Cébeillac-Gervasoni & Lamoine, 51–64.

Schäfer, J. (1968) *Hellenistische Keramik aus Pergamon*. Berlin.

Schaeffer, J. S., N. H. Ramage & C. H. Greenewalt (1997) *The Corinthian, Attic, and Lakonian Pottery from Sardis*. Cambridge, MA.

Scheidel, W. (1995) 'Incest revisited: three notes on the demography of sibling marriage in Roman Egypt', *BASP* 32: 143–55.

—— (1996a) 'Brother-sister and parent-child marriage outside royal families in ancient Egypt and Iran: a challenge to the sociobiological view of incest avoidance', *Ethology and Sociobiology* 17: 319–40.

—— (1996b) *Measuring Sex, Age and Death in the Roman Empire. Explorations in Ancient Demography*. Ann Arbor.

—— (1997) 'Brother-sister marriage in Roman Egypt', *Journal of Biosocial Science* 29: 361–71.

Schneider, C. (1967–1969) *Kulturgeschichte des Hellenismus*, 2 vols. Munich.

Schneider, H. (1992) *Einführung in die antike Technikgeschichte*. Darmstadt.

Schober, L. (1981) *Untersuchungen zur Geschichte Babyloniens und der Oberen Satrapien von 323–303 v.Chr.* Frankfurt.

Schofield, M. (1999) 'Academic epistemology', in Algra et al., 323–51.

Scholten, J. B. (1997) *The Politics of Plunder: Aitolians and their Koinon in the Early Hellenistic Era, 279–217 BC*. Berkeley, Los Angeles, & London.

Schuler, C. (1998) *Ländliche Siedlungen und Gemeinden im hellenistischen und römischen Kleinasien*. München.

Schultz, P. (in press) 'Leochares' Portraits for the Philippeion at Olympia', in Schultz & von den Hoff. (in press).

Schultz, P. & R. von den Hoff, eds. (in press) *New Directions in Early Hellenistic Portraiture*. Cambridge.

Schuster, A. M. H. (1997) 'Alexandria harbor finds', *Archaeology* 50: 18.

———— (1999) 'Mapping Alexandria's royal quarters', *Archaeology* 52: 44–6.

Scullard, H. H. (1974) *The Elephant in the Greek and Roman World*. Ithaca, NY.

Sedley, D. (1998) *Lucretius and the Transformation of Greek Wisdom*. Cambridge.

———— ed. (2003) *The Cambridge Companion to Greek and Roman Philosophy*. Cambridge.

Sekunda, N. (1984) *The Army of Alexander the Great*. London.

———— (2001) *Hellenistic Infantry Reform in the 160's BC*. Poland.

———— (in press). 'Military Forces in the Hellenistic World and the Roman Republic', in *Cambridge History of Greek and Roman Warfare*. Cambridge.

———— ed. (in press) *Proceedings of the First International Conference on Hellenistic Warfare*, held at Torun, Poland, October 2003.

Selden, D. L. (1998) 'Alibis', *CA* 17: 289–412.

Sens, A. (2003) 'Doricisms in the new and old Posidippus' in B. Acosta-Hughes, E. Kosmetatou, & M. Baumbach, eds., *Labored in Papyrus Leaves: Perspectives on an Epigram Collection Attributed to Posidippus (P.Mil.Vogl.)*, 65–83. Cambridge, MA.

Settis, S., ed. (1998) *I Greci. Storia cultura arte società*, vol. 2: *Una storia greca* III: *Trasformazioni*. Torino.

Sharples, R. W. (1996) *Stoics, Epicureans and Sceptics*. London.

Sherk, R. K. (1984) *Rome and the Greek East to the death of Augustus* (Translated Documents of Greece & Rome, 4). Cambridge.

Sherwin-White, S. M. (1978) *Ancient Cos: An Historical Study from the Dorian Settlement to the Imperial Period*. Göttingen.

Sherwin-White, S. & A. Kuhrt (1993) *From Samarkhand to Sardis: A New Approach to the Seleucid Empire*. Berkeley.

Shipley, G. (1987) *A History of Samos 800–188 BC*. Oxford.

———— (2000) *The Greek World after Alexander, 323–30 BC*. London.

———— (2001–2002) 'Social changes in Sparta and Laconia in the Hellenistic period,' in the *6th Peloponnesian Congress*, ii. 433–45. Greek trans. E. Boutsika & E. Panagopoulou.

———— (2002a) 'Hidden landscapes: Greek field survey data and hellenistic history', in Ogden, (2002) 177–98.

———— (2002b) 'Rural landscape change in hellenistic Greece', in K. Ascani, V. Gabrielsen, K. Kvist & A. Rasmussen, eds., *Ancient History Matters: Studies Presented to Jens Erik Skydsgaard on his 70th Birthday*, 39–45. Rome.

———— (2004) review of B. Dreyer, *Untersuchungen zur Geschichte des spätklassischen Athen*, in *CR* 54.1: 159–60.

Shipley, G. & J. Salmon, eds. (1996) *Human Landscapes in Classical Antiquity: Environment and Culture*. London & New York.

Silverman, D. (1995) 'The Nature of Egyptian Kingship', in D. O'Connor & D. Silverman, eds., *Ancient Egyptian Kingship*, 49–94. Leiden.

Smith, R. R. R. (1991) *Hellenistic Sculpture*. London & New York.

Snodgrass, A. M. (1999) *Arms and Armor of the Greeks*. Baltimore, MD.

Sorabji, R. (2000) *Emotion and Peace of Mind: from Stoic Agitation to Christian Temptation*. Oxford.

Spence, I. G. (1993) *The Cavalry of Classical Greece*. Oxford.

Stähli A. (1999) *Die Verweigerung der Lüste. Erotische Gruppen in der antiken Plastik*. Frankfurt am Main.

Steele, J. (1992) *Hellenistic Architecture in Asia Minor*. London.

Stephens, S. (2003) *Seeing Double: Intercultural Poetics in Ptolemaic Alexandria*. Berkeley & Los Angeles.

Stephens, S. & J. J. Winkler (1995) *Ancient Greek Novels: the Fragments, Introduction, Text, Translation and Commentary*. Princeton.

Stewart, A. (1990) *Greek Sculpture: An Exploration*, 2 vols. New Haven & London.

———— (1993a) *Faces of Power: Alexander's Image and Hellenistic Politics*. Berkeley & Los Angeles.

———— (1993b) 'Narration and allusion in the Hellenistic baroque', in P. J. Holliday, ed., *Narrative and Event in Ancient Art*, 130–74. Cambridge.

———— (1996) *Art, Desire, and the Body in Ancient Greece*. Cambridge.

———— (2003) 'The Portraiture of Alexander', in Roisman, 31–66.

———— (2004) *Attalos, Athens, and the Akropolis. The Pergamene "Little Barbarians" and their Roman and Renaissance Legacy*. Cambridge.

———— (2005a, in press) 'Alexander, Philitas, and the *skeletos*: Poseidippos and truth in early Hellenistic portraiture', in Schultz & von den Hoff (in press).

———— (2005b) 'Poseidippos and the truth in sculpture,' in Gutzwiller, ed., (2005) 183–205.

———— (in press) 'Baroque classics: the Tragic Muse and the *Exemplum*', in J. Porter, ed, *Classical Pasts: The Classical Traditions of Greco-Roman Antiquity*. Cambridge.

Stewart, A. & S. R. Martin (2003) 'New discoveries at Tel Dor, Israel', *Hesperia* 72: 121–45.

Stewart, Z. (1977) 'La religione', in Bianchi Bandinelli, ed., *Storia e civiltà dei Greci*, vol. VIII, 503–616. Milan.

Stillwell, R., ed. (1976) *The Princeton Encyclopedia of Classical Sites*. Princeton.

Stoneman, R. (1991) *The Greek Alexander Romance*. London.

Strong, D. (1966) *Greek and Roman Gold and Silver Plate*. London.

Tarán, S. L. (1979) *The Art of Variation in the Greek Epigram*. Leiden.

Tarn, W. W. (1930) *Hellenistic Military and Naval Developments*. Cambridge.

———— (1948) *Alexander the Great*, 2 vols. Cambridge.

———— (1969) *Antigonos Gonatas*. Oxford (reprint of 1913 edition).

Tarn, W. W. & G. T. Griffith (1952) *Hellenistic Civilization*, 3rd edn. London.

Tarrant, H. (1985) *Scepticism or Platonism*. Cambridge.

Taub, L. (2003) *Ancient Metrology*. London.

Thapar, R. (1997) *Asoka and the Decline of the Mauryas*, 2nd edn. Delhi & Oxford.

Themelis, P. (1996) 'Damophon', in O. Palagia & J. J. Pollitt, eds., *Personal Styles in Greek Sculpture*, 154–85. Cambridge.

Thériault, G. (1996) *Le Culte d'Homonoia dans les cités grecques*. Lyon.

Thomas, I. (1968) *Greek Mathematical Works: From Aristarchus to Pappus*, vol. II. Cambridge, MA.

Thomas, R. (2000) *Herodotus in Context*. Cambridge.

Thompson, D. J. (1988) *Memphis under the Ptolemies*. Princeton.

——— (2001) 'Hellenistic Hellenes: the case of Ptolemaic Egypt', in I. Malkin, ed., *Ancient Perceptions of Greek Ethnicity*, 301–22. Cambridge, MA & London.

——— (2002) 'Families in early Ptolemaic Egypt', in Ogden (2002) 137–56.

——— (2003) 'The Ptolemies and Egypt', in Erskine (2003) 105–20.

Thompson, H. A. (1937) 'Buildings on the west side of the Agora', *Hesperia* 6: 1–226.

Thompson, M. (1961) *The New Style Silver Coinage of Athens*, 2 vols. New York.

Threpsiades, J. & E. Vanderpool (1963) 'Pros tois Hermais', *Deltion* 18: 99–114.

Tölle–Kastenbein, R. (1974) *Das Kastro Tigani: die Bauten und Funde griechischer, römischer und byzantinischer Zeit*. Bonn.

Tomlinson, R. A. (1972) *Argos and the Argolid: From the End of the Bronze Age to the Roman Occupation*. London.

——— (1976) *Greek Sanctuaries*. London.

——— (1995) 'The town plan of hellenistic Alexandria', in *Alessandria e il mondo ellenistico-romano: primo centenario del Museo Greco-Romano*, 236–40. Rome.

Tracy, S. V. (1982) in *Studies in Attic Epigraphy, History, and Topography Presented to Eugene Vanderpool (Hesperia Supplement XIX)*, 159–61. Princeton.

——— (2004) 'Reflections on the Athenian Ephebeia in the Hellenistic Age', in Kah & Scholz, 207–10.

Tracy, S. V. & Ch. Habicht (1991) 'New and Old Panathenaic Victory Lists', *Hesperia* 60: 187–236.

Travlos, J. (1971) *A Pictorial Dictionary of Ancient Athens*. London.

Tronson, A. (1984) 'Satyrus the peripatetic and the marriages of Philip II', *JHS* 104: 116–26.

Trundle, M. (2004) *Greek Mercenaries*. London.

Tuplin, C. (1999) 'Greek racism? Observations on the character and limits of Greek ethnic prejudice', in G. R. Tsetskhladze, *Ancient Greeks, West and East*, 47–75. Leiden.

Tuplin, C. & T. E. Rihll (2002) *Science and Mathematics in Ancient Greek Culture*. Oxford.

Turner, E. (1984) 'Ptolemaic Egypt', in Walbank et al. (1984) 118–174.

Uhlenbrock, J. P., ed. (1990) *The Coroplast's Art: Greek Terracottas of the Hellenistic World*. New York.

Ussher, S. (1999) *Greek Oratory. Tradition and Originality*. Oxford.

van Bremen, R. (1996) *The Limits of Participation: Women and Civic Life in the Greek East in the Hellenistic and Roman Periods*. Amsterdam.

——— (2003) 'Family structures', in Erskine (2003) 313–30.

van de Maele, S. & J. M. Fossey, eds. (1992) *Fortificationes Antiquae*. Amsterdam.

van der Spek, R. J. (1987) 'The Babylonian city', in Kuhrt & Sherwin-White, 57–74.

——— (1995) 'Land ownership in Babylonian cuneiform documents,' in Geller & Maehler, 173–245.

——— (2000) 'The effect of war on the prices of barley and agricultural land in hellenistic Babylonia', in Andreau et al., 293–313.

——— (2001) 'The theatre of Babylon in cuneiform', in W. H. van Soldt, ed., *Studies Presented to Klaas R. Veenhof on the Occasion of his Sixty-Fifth Birthday*, 445–56. Leiden.

Vandorpe, K. (2002) 'Apollonia, a businesswoman in a multicultural society (Pathyris, 2nd–1st centuries BC)', in Melaerts & Mooren, 325–36.

van Minnen, P. (1994) 'House-to-house enquiries: an interdisciplinary approach to Roman Karanis', *ZPE* 100: 227–51.

van Wees, H. (2004) *Greek Warfare. Myths and Realities*. London.

Vasunia, P. (2001) *The Gift of the Nile: Hellenizing Egypt from Aeschylus to Alexander*. Berkeley.

Vatin, Cl. (1970) *Recherches sur le mariage et la condition de la femme mariée à l'époque hellénistique*. Paris.

Verdin, H., G. Schepens & E. De Keyser, eds. (1990) *Purposes of History. Studies in Greek Historiography from the 4th to the 2nd Centuries B.C.* Louvain.

Vérilhac, A.-M. & C. Vial (1998) *Le mariage grec*. Athens & Paris.

Verity, A. & R. Hunter (2002) *Theocritus: Idylls*. Oxford.

Vernant, J.-P., ed. (1968) *Problèmes de la guerre en Grèce ancienne*. Paris.

Veyne, P. (1990) *Bread and Circuses. Historical Sociology and Political Pluralism*. London.

Vita–Finzi, C. (1969) *The Mediterranean Valleys*. Cambridge.

von den Hoff, R. & P. Schultz, eds. (in press) *Early Hellenistic Portraiture: Image, Style, Context*. Cambridge.

von Hesberg, H. (1998) 'Riti e produzione artistica delle corti ellenistiche', in Settis, 177–214.

von Reden, S. (2001) 'The politics of monetization in third-century BC Egypt', in Meadows & Shipton, 65–76.

von Staden, H. (1989) *Herophilus*. Cambridge.

Voutiras, E. (1990) 'ΗΦΑΙΣΤΙΩΝ ΗΡΩΣ' *Egnatia* 2: 123–73.

Walbank, F. W. (1957–1979) *A Historical Commentary on Polybius*, 3 vols. Oxford.

———— (1972) *Polybius*. Berkeley, Los Angeles & London.

———— (1979) 'Appendix: the Achaean assemblies', in Walbank (1957–1979), vol. III, 406–14.

———— (1984) 'Macedonia and Greece', in Walbank et al. (1984) 221–56.

———— (1985) *Selected Papers. Studies in Greek and Roman History and Historiography*. Cambridge.

———— (1992) *The Hellenistic World*. London.

———— (2002) *Polybius, Rome and the Hellenistic World. Essays and Reflections*. Cambridge.

Walbank, F. W., A. E. Astin, M. W. Frederiksen & R. M. Ogilvie, eds. (1984) *The Cambridge Ancient History*, vol. VII.1: *The Hellenistic World,* 2nd edn. Cambridge.

Walker, S. & P. Higgs, eds. (2001) *Cleopatra of Egypt: From History to Myth*. London.

Walter, H. (1976) *Das Heraion von Samos: Ursprung und Wandel eines griechischen Heiligtums*. München.

Walter, N. (1964) *Der Thoraausleger Aristobulos*. Berlin.

Warren, J. (2004) *Facing Death: Epicurus and his Critics*. Oxford.

Webster, T. B. L. (1964) *Hellenistic Poetry and Art*. London.

Welles, C. B. (1934) *Royal Correspondence in the Hellenistic Period*. New Haven.

West, M. L. (1966) *Hesiod: Theogony*. Oxford.

———— (1982) *Greek Metre*. Oxford.

Westgate, R. (2000) '*Pavimenta atque emblemata vermiculata*: Regional Styles in Hellenistic Mosaic and the First Mosaics at Pompeii', *AJA* 104: 255–75.

Westgate, R. C. (2000) 'Space and decoration in hellenistic houses', *ABSA* 95: 391–426.

Whitbread, I. K. (1995) *Greek Transport Amphorae: A Petrological and Archaeological Study*. Athens.

Whitby, M. (1998) 'The grain trade of Athens in the fourth century BC', in Parkins & Smith, 102–128.

White, K. D. (1984) *Greek and Roman Technology*. London.

Whitehead, D. (1986) *The Demes of Attica 508/7–ca. 250 BC: A Political and Social Study.* Princeton.

———— (1990) *Aineias the Tactician. How to Survive under Siege.* Oxford.

———— (2000) *Hypereides: The Forensic Speeches.* Oxford.

Wiedemann, T. (1990) 'Rhetoric in Polybius', in Verdin et al., 289–300.

Wiemer, H.-U. (2002) *Krieg, Handel und Piraterie: Untersuchungen zur Geschichte des hellenistischen Rhodos.* Berlin.

Wikander, Ö., ed. (2000) *Handbook of Ancient Water Technology.* Leiden.

Wilcken, U. (1967) *Alexander the Great.* New York.

Will, E. (1979–1982) *Histoire politique du monde hellénistique: 323–30 av. J.-C.* 2 vols., 2nd edn. Nancy.

Williams, B. (1993) *Shame and Necessity.* Berkeley.

Williams, D., ed. (1998) *The Art of the Greek Goldsmith.* London.

Wilson, A. (2000) 'Land drainage', in Wikander, 303–17.

Wimmel, W. (1960) *Kallimachos in Rom: Die Nachfolge seines apologetischen Dichtens in der Augusteerzeit.* Wiesbaden.

Winter, F. E. (1963) 'The Chronology of the Euryalos Fortress,' *AJA* 63: 363–87.

———— (1971) *Greek Fortifications.* Toronto.

———— (1992) 'Philon of Byzantion and the Hellenistic Fortifications of Rhodos', in van de Maele & Fossey, 185–209.

Wolff, H. J. (1939) *Written and Unwritten Marriages in Hellenistic and Post-classical Roman Law.* Haverford, PA.

Woodhead, A. G. (1997) *The Athenian Agora, Vol. XVI: Inscriptions: The Decrees.* Princeton.

Woodman, A. H. (1988) *Rhetoric in Classical Historiography.* London & Sydney.

Wooten, C. (1973) 'The ambassador's speech: a particularly hellenistic genre', *Quarterly Journal of Speech* 59: 209–12.

Worley, L. J. (1994) *Hippeis. The Cavalry of Ancient Greece.* Colorado.

Worthington, I. (1992) *A Historical Commentary on Dinarchus. Rhetoric and Conspiracy in Later Fourth-Century Athens.* Ann Arbor, MI.

———— (1994a) 'The Harpalus Affair and the Greek Response to Macedonian Hegemony', in I. Worthington, (1994b) 307–30. Oxford.

———— ed. (1994b) *Ventures into Greek History.* Oxford.

Wörrle, M. (2003) 'Inschriften von Herackleia am Latmos III. Der Synoikismos der Latmioi mit den Pidaseis,' *Chiron* 33: 121–43.

Wycherley, R. E. (1962) *How the Greeks Built Cities*, 2nd edn. London & New York.

———— (1978) *The Stones of Athens.* Princeton.

Yegül, F. (1992) *Baths and Bathing in Classical Antiquity.* Cambridge.

Zanker, G. (2004) *Modes of Viewing in Hellenistic Poetry and Art.* Madison, WI.

Zanker, P. (1993) 'The Hellenistic grave stelai from Smyrna: identity and self-image in the polis', in Bulloch et al., 212–230.

———— (1995) *The Mask of Socrates: The Image of the Intellectual in Antiquity.* Berkeley & Los Angeles.

Zarins, J. (1992) 'Camel' in D. N. Freedman, G. A. Herion, D. F. Graf & J. D. Pleins, eds., *Anchor Bible Dictionary*, vol. I, 824–26. New York.

INDEX

Academy. *See* Plato
Achaemenids, 12, 16, 80, 97, 148
Achaian League, 37, 52, 63, 64, 96,
    118–119, 121, 125, 270, 271, 274, 320;
    Achaia, 122
Acragas (Sicily), 281
Acrocorinth, 37, 286
Actium, battle of (31 BC), 141
Aegae (Macedonia), 32, 45
L. Aemilius Paullus, 118–119, 292
Agathe Tyche ('Good Fortune'), 212–213
Agathokles, son of Lysimachos, 34, 50
Agathokles of Syracuse, 282, 286, 293
Agesilaos, Spartan king, 266
Ai Khanum (Afghanistan), 5, 17, 18, 47,
    55, 91, 147
Aineias Taktikos, 268, 281
Ainesidemos, Sceptic philosopher, 226,
    237
Aitolian League, 21, 37, 63–64, 96;
    cavalry of, 272
Aitolians, 21, 29
alchemy, 247–248
Alexander III (the Great) 2, 9–23
    (Chapter 1 *passim*), 50, 287, 296, 303,
    311, 315; in the *Alexander Romance*, 310,
    312; in 'Alexander Mosaic', 173; city
    foundations, 16, e.g., Alexandria
    Eschate, 17, 26; sarcophagus of, 41,
    65. Scattered references *passim*.
Alexander IV (posthumous son of
    Alexander the Great), 30, 50; executed
    by Kassandros, 31–32
Alexander Aitolus, 190–191
Alexander of Epiros, 50

Alexander Romance, 308–312, 313. *See also*
    Alexander III
Alexandria, 39, 41–42, 55, 64–66, 82, 84,
    85, 88, 99, 101, 102, 108, 115, 161,
    180, 181, 187, 200, 210; amphora
    handles at, 142, 143; baroque
    architecture in, 171; cameo
    invented at, 179; Library of, 1, 167,
    188, 189, 190, 191, 209, 241–242;
    medicine in, 250–251, 252; Museum
    of, 41, 82, 167, 188, 190, 225, 241,
    248; plan of, 163; Ptolemaieia festival
    celebrated at, 65, 161, 214; religious
    heterogeneity, 208, 210, 217, 221;
    Sarapeion at, 165, 170. *See also*
    Sarapis
Alexandris (formerly *Syracusia*), 277
Alkmaion of Kroton, Pythagorean
    philosopher, 249
Amastris, 26
Ammon Ra (Re), 46, 308, 309, 310–311
Ammonios, son of Dionysios of Athens,
    140
Amphipolis, 38, 270
Amyntas III of Macedonia, 19, 27, 50
Anaxagoras, philosopher, 250
Andreas of Karystos, 262
andron, 145–146, 152
Androtion, historian of Athens, 128
Antigonos I Monophthalmos ('the
    One-Eyed'), 11, 12, 14, 22, 29, 30, 50,
    81, 261, 267; *Antigonis*, new tribe of
    Athens, 32, 100; cult worship of, 20,
    36–48, 214; 'freedom of the Greeks',
    62, 213–214; Ipsos, battle of, 121;